Father Mathew, Temperance and Irish Identity

To my parents

Father Mathew, Temperance and Irish Identity

PAUL A. TOWNEND

IRISH ACADEMIC PRESS
DUBLIN • PORTLAND, OR

First published in 2002 by
IRISH ACADEMIC PRESS
44, Northumberland Road, Dublin 4, Ireland

and in the United States of America by
IRISH ACADEMIC PRESS
c/o ISBS, 5824 N.E. Hassalo Street, Portland
Oregon 97213-3644

Website: www.iap.ie

British Library Cataloguing in Publication Data

Townend, Paul A.
Father Mathew, temperance and irish identity
1. Mathew, Theobald, 1790–1856 2. Cork Total Abstinence Society 3. Temperance – Ireland – Cork (County) – Societies, etc. 4. Temperance – Ireland – Cork (County) – History – 19th century 5. Cork (Ireland: County) – History – 19th century
I. Title
362.2'92'524'094195'0903

ISBN 0-7165-2737-5

Library of Congress Cataloging-in-Publication Data

A catalog record of this book is
available from the Library of Congress.

Typeset in 10.5 pt on 12.5 pt Palatino by Vitaset, Paddock Wood, Kent
Printed by
MPG Books Ltd., Bodmin, Cornwall

Contents

List of Figures and Tables

Preface

This project, which had its beginnings in my dissertation work at the University of Chicago, has long been in development, and my list of debts is a humbling one. Assistance has come from many quarters, but I am singularly obliged for the insights and encouragement of my very dear mentor Emmet Larkin. Indeed, I think it is only fair to say that without him this book could not have been written. Grateful as I am for his attention to this particular project, I am still more appreciative of the model of professionalism he has always provided.

I am also very much obliged to Stephen Pincus, Andrew Greeley, Charles Gray, Lloyd Rudolph, and Lawrence J. McCaffrey for reading all or part of my developing argument, and for providing invaluable guidance and direction. I am also grateful to many of my former graduate student colleagues who learned more about Father Mathew and Irish history than they ever expected to, even while their attentions improved my writing and research. I should particularly like to mention Michele O'Neil, Devin Pendas, Sean Gilsdorf, Stephanie Whitlock, and Jennifer Heuer. I owe an obvious historiographical debt to Elizabeth Malcolm, Colm Kerrigan, John Quinn, and George Bretherton, whose own work on Father Mathew and Temperance has stimulated my thinking and added so much to my own understanding of this important subject. The advice of my readers and Linda Longmore at Irish Academic Press have also been invaluable, and I have also benefited a great deal from the kind attentions of Jonathan Manley at Irish Academic Press.

This project has been supported in one way or another by a number of organizations and institutions, including the Andrew W. Mellon Foundation and the University of Chicago. I am very much indebted to my colleagues associated with the American Conference on Irish Studies, who have been willing to listen to more than their share of these ideas in half-baked form. I appreciate the access I have been granted to various archival collections, including the British Newspaper Library at Collindale, the Royal Irish Academy, the National Library of Ireland, the Irish National Archives, the diocesan archives of Cashel and

Dublin, the Cork Archives Institute, the Religious Society of Friends Historical Library in Dublin, the libraries of Trinity College and St Patrick's College, Maynooth, and of course the Capuchin Provincial Archives in Church Street (custodians of the Mathew Papers) for their cooperation and hospitality.

Personally, I have been upheld and maintained by many individuals and communities while this project percolated. Most practically, Sherry Gutman and the University of Chicago House System did their best to make sure I had a roof over my head while I wrote. Arthur and then Theo were spurs to much activity, while Virginia, for her part, merely made all else possible by her love, her support, and her patience.

If the setting of pen to paper remains an act of supreme arrogance, the listing of the debts incurred in the production of a project of this nature is sure to remind the author of the collaborative nature of the enterprise. I of course remain responsible for any errors of commission and omission that this text may yet contain.

Introduction: The Temperance Crusade in Ireland, 1838–1848

Father Theobald Mathew's Temperance crusade was the single most extraordinary social movement that occurred in pre-famine Ireland. Indeed, it must rank among the more unique and under-examined mass mobilisations of men and women in modern European history. This is evidenced not only by the enormous number of people involved in the Temperance campaign and its revolutionary impact on Irish popular culture, but also by the sweeping effects of the movement on both the social fabric and the evolving national consciousness. Over its first five years, beginning in 1838, the Capuchin friar's 'Cork Total Abstinence Society' (or CTAS) enrolled somewhere between three and five million Irish men, women and children (at least half the population), each of whom renounced the use of alcohol for life. Father Mathew's missionary career as a preacher of Temperance and distributor of 'the pledge' flourished at hundreds of mass meetings throughout Ireland and among the Irish diaspora communities in parts of Scotland, England and, later, America. He became, with Daniel O'Connell, internationally-known and the most widely admired Irishman of his day.

THE HISTORIOGRAPHY OF THE CORK TOTAL ABSTINENCE SOCIETY

The CTAS has received almost no serious historical attention before this last decade. There were a number of more or less hagiographical biographies of Father Mathew, all of which were published before 1948, including the journalist/politician John Francis Maguire's entertaining but inaccurate account of the career of his close friend, *Father Mathew* (1863). Other significant efforts included that of Mathew's grand nephew, Frank Mathew, who authored a thought-provoking if little-noted 'life and times' of his famous relative in 1890. Two more full-length biographies appeared in the 1940s, in part the products of the dedicated researches of two clerics interested in having Mathew promoted to the status of a saint. Frank Rogers published the interesting but ultimately unsatisfying *Father Theobald Mathew* in 1943, while Mathew's fellow Capuchin, Father Augustine, produced his meticulously researched *Footprints of Father Mathew* in 1947. None of these authors was a professional historian, and none of them sought to produce a definitive study of the Cork Total Abstinence Society. Because of their focus on the complex, engaging and fascinating personality of Father Mathew, the movement he led was inevitably held in the wings, and the role of the Capuchin in what was actually a complex popular crusade assumed increasingly mythic proportions.

The CTAS as a social movement fared little better at the hands of the historical profession. It is difficult to escape the conclusion that the campaign, a vital piece of Irish social history, was overlooked by a historiography devoted to other kinds of subjects, particularly the examination of the parallel development of both constitutional and violent resistance to British rule in Ireland. The strange story of the quixotic Capuchin had something of the appearance of a passing popular enthusiasm, an ultimately insignificant, and even embarrassing, lost cause. To the extent the CTAS was noted at all, it was primarily as an extension of Daniel O'Connell's Repeal campaign of the early 1840s.[1] The consequences of this neglect are most evident in the dismissive passing references to the movement that can be found in most general histories of Ireland, such as R.F. Forster's *Modern Ireland* (1988).

H.F. Kearney's brief article in 1979, 'Father Mathew, Apostle of Modernization?', encouraged historians to take a closer look at Mathew and his organisation, and in the years that followed, beginning with Elizabeth Malcolm's important work which culminated in *Ireland Sober, Ireland Free: Drink and Temperance in 19th Century Ireland* (1986), the challenge was to some degree taken up. Malcolm's book is both careful and thought-provoking, although her interest in developing a narrative that traces the history of temperance in Ireland over the entire nineteenth century obscures much of what was unique about Father Mathew's crusade. Two American historians focused more closely on Mathew's Temperance movement. George Bretherton completed his Columbia doctoral thesis on Temperance in Ireland from 1829 to 1847, with a significant focus on Mathew, in 1978, and has continued to investigate Father Mathew in subsequent years.[2] More recently, John Quinn completed a Notre Dame University dissertation on Father Mathew and Irish Temperance in 1992, and has published articles since then which focus on Mathew's relationship to his Church and his tour of America.[3] There is much useful information and insight in the work of Bretherton and Quinn, but neither has yet succeeded in producing a definitive study of Mathew's movement. In 1992, Colm Kerrigan, in *Father Mathew and the Irish Temperance Movement, 1838–1849*, attempted to provide the field of Irish history with what it so clearly lacked – a close, professional study of Mathew and the CTAS, and a measured appreciation of the movement's place in Irish history. Kerrigan's book, although well-researched and useful, is too brief and leaves too many questions unanswered, although it does represent the most substantial published effort to date to explain the nature of the Temperance crusade.

To a greater or lesser extent, a collective shortcoming that all this later professional work shares with the earlier biographies of Mathew has been the tendency to lose the movement in its leader. Mathew's character and position in the CTAS are by no means irrelevant to an understanding of that organisation, but to focus on the heroic figure whose statues still dot the Irish landscape, from O'Connell Street in Dublin to Thomastown in Tipperary and Patrick's Bridge in Cork, is to misunderstand the nature of the CTAS. The most striking feature of the Temperance movement as it developed in Ireland was the bottom-up, popular and patriotic nature of the CTAS as a social movement. The response of millions of Irish men and women to the coherent message that a wide range of Temperance activists, including but not limited to Father Mathew, brought to them cannot, and should not, be attributed in its entirety to the charisma and talent of one man. Any satisfying explanation for the CTAS's success ultimately depends on a careful appreciation of the complex appeal of the movement's leadership, message and vision to the Irish people in their millions, because it was the combination of that call and the popular response to it that made the Temperance movement such a remarkable phenomenon.

THE RISE OF THE CORK TOTAL ABSTINENCE SOCIETY

Among Irish Catholics, Temperance was a marginal cause when Theobald Mathew, a popular Cork priest, agreed to become the President of the small Cork Total Abstinence Society in 1838. The rapid expansion of the CTAS that followed took place in three major stages. During the first, which lasted from April 1838 until late November 1839, the movement grew dramatically but locally, from a few dozen members to more than 50,000. The personable and charming Father Mathew was recruited and cajoled into endorsing the movement by local activists in Cork, largely because he was uniquely positioned to enhance Temperance's image and gain local converts. Mathew came from a distinguished Irish patrician family, and was well-known as an eminently respectable gentleman.[4] At the same time, his unaffected empathy for the poor, his tireless ministry to Cork's underprivileged, and his practical charitable exploits marked him out as a priest with considerable popular credibility.[5] During this initial period of growth, Mathew presided over meetings that were generally led by other men. The CTAS adopted an intensely evangelistic outlook, drew upon Temperance advocates from Dublin and England, despatched missionaries to surrounding towns, and developed open and efficient membership practices designed to encourage mass enrolment. All of the CTAS's advocates made direct appeals to Irish patriotism, and clearly hoped and expected that the movement would come to embrace all of the Irish people.

The second period was one of regional expansion, and began in late November and early December 1839, when Father Mathew visited Waterford and Limerick, where he dispensed the Temperance pledge to unexpected and unprecedented crowds, supposed to have numbered in the high tens if not hundreds of thousands, and continued into March of 1840. These meetings established Mathew as the unquestioned leader of the CTAS, and inaugurated a remarkable period of missionary activity on behalf of Temperance that was to last for the next several years. Wherever Temperance meetings were held in southwest and south-central Ireland, Father Mathew was met by enormous crowds, and administered the pledge to countless 'batches' of hundreds and even thousands of people. This overwhelming enthusiasm was the most striking aspect of the CTAS's rise after 1838. By the spring of 1840, enthusiasm for Temperance was general throughout Ireland, and Father Mathew was styled as the great 'Apostle of Temperance' when he was not being described as a second coming of Saint Patrick.

During the third and longest stage of expansion, which lasted from late March 1840, until the end of 1842, the CTAS developed into a national movement with millions of followers all over Ireland outside North East Ulster. Father Mathew's visit to Dublin in March 1840 succeeded in raising the movement's visibility still further, and enhancing its limited appeal to the Irish middle and upper classes. After Father Mathew was invited to administer the pledge at Ireland's national seminary, St Patrick's College at Maynooth, invitations to visit parishes all over Ireland poured into Cork. Mathew's circuit expanded, and Temperance societies began to thrive in practically every town in Ireland. The CTAS's message resonated, the people embraced the movement, and the organisation succeeded on a scale that was as unprecedented as it was astounding. By 1843, every indication was that at least half of the adult population of Ireland had 'taken the pledge', while public drunkenness had virtually disappeared in many areas.

THE CORK TOTAL ABSTINENCE SOCIETY TRIUMPHANT

Father Mathew's status as a folk hero was more a consequence than a cause of the CTAS's success. The incredible size and enthusiasm of the crowds that gathered wherever the 'Great Apostle of Temperance' held his frequent meetings attested as much to the compelling appeal and need for his organisation's message as to the personal charisma of Father Mathew. Father Mathew played a larger role in articulating and spreading Temperance's gospel than he did in shaping it. The CTAS offered a powerful and effective ideology that was conveyed in a variety of media by a number of messengers. Taking the camp-meeting enthusiasm and the rhetoric of self-improvement that were already hallmarks of Temperance efforts, the CTAS crafted a distinctly Irish crusade, laden with pietistic and patriotic features.[6] Time and time again, Mathew and his allies promised the Irish people that Temperance would make them 'a blank slate', a new creation capable of rising above their present abject state of sectarianism, poverty and national humiliation and entering into a promised land of cooperation, prosperity and self-respect.[7] If Temperance as a transatlantic movement was, as some have argued, a symptom of rapidly evolving middle-class sensibilities or, more elaborately, of the inexorable development of modes of social control in industrialised, modern, state-centred cultures, it was also, particularly in its Irish context, an enormously popular movement that exhorted the masses to assist in the creation of a new kind of society.[8] In effect, it insisted that they become mobilised.

The response to that demand could be found all over Ireland. The country underwent dramatic change as pubs, shebeens and whiskey punch were abandoned for coffee houses, reading-rooms and tea. Across most of Ireland, public life became marked by the fiercely determined Temperance ethic. Hundreds of enthusiastic local societies erected temperance halls, and sponsored bands, parades, teetotaller dances and banquets, life insurance and even emigration societies. While the CTAS was popularly understood to provide for the material and moral improvement of the individual, this spectacular and collective dimension of Irish Temperance was viewed by most participants as an indispensable feature of the cause. Irish people were quite conscious of the fact that their new habits flew in the face of longstanding stereotypes and caricatures, and delighted in their

Temperance processions, mass meetings and other public occasions which celebrated sobriety and order. Much of the CTAS's appeal was located in the belief that popular Temperance displays confuted those outside of Ireland (particularly in England) who revelled in and exploited the 'degraded' state of the Irish nation and its people.

THE DECLINE OF THE CORK TOTAL ABSTINENCE SOCIETY

The CTAS's moral revolution was never consolidated. By 1843–44 it was becoming increasingly evident that the Temperance cause was a troubled one. Despite its boundless popularity, the remarkable success of the CTAS masked at least three serious problems. In the first place, the movement failed to attract sufficient support from the middle and particularly the upper classes in Ireland. This failure offered no serious impediment to the crusade's expansion in terms of numbers, but it certainly made institutionalising the movement, through the establishment and support of flourishing local societies, more difficult than it might otherwise have been.

Secondly, and more seriously, the CTAS failed to obtain the full endorsement of the Catholic Church for its activities and organisation. This failure was critical, because local Temperance societies absolutely depended on the assistance and good offices of local clergy. Although Mathew was popular with an overwhelming majority of the Catholic population, he and his movement were never actively supported by much more than a third of Irish priests and bishops. There were many reasons for the reluctance, suspicion, indifference and even outright opposition with which the majority of the clergy greeted the CTAS's crusade. Mathew was personally distrusted by many clergymen, if not for his political agnosticism, theological liberalism or ecumenical tendencies, then for his gentlemanly airs, his informal clerical education or his status as a friar. Temperance as practiced by the CTAS, moreover, brought up a number of uncomfortable theological and pastoral issues which seemed to many in the Church to be, in the long run, more likely to endanger the souls of the faithful than to bring about their salvation. Finally, the controversial nature of Mathew's movement (and of Mathew himself) produced a host of powerful enemies in the Irish Church just at a time when that Church was already riven with divisive controversies over its role in Irish society. Ironically, the movement that Mathew hoped would unite all Irishmen itself fell victim in the end to divisions in the Irish Church.

Thirdly, the CTAS was also a victim of its own success. The

widespread embrace of the movement's transformative, patriotic and communitarian rhetoric led many to expect immediate and dramatic social and political change. Because the movement's leaders offered no coherent vision of what would happen once general sobriety had been established in Ireland, the CTAS's social revolution was vulnerable to political co-option, and that is precisely what Daniel O'Connell succeeded in doing with his Repeal movement. Because O'Connell was so successful in marrying, in the popular mind, the moral transformation of Ireland with the achievement of her national legislative independence, the leadership of the Temperance movement fragmented, the momentum of the CTAS stalled, and the moral authority of the Temperance cause soon became fatally entangled in the winning of Repeal. The consequences were ultimately devastating to the Temperance movement as Father Mathew had tried to define and direct it.

The breakdown of the movement after 1843 was manifested in widespread pledge breaking, a rise in alcohol production, and, most importantly, the collapse of the network of local behaviour, practices and sanctions that had been so important in sustaining the cause in its early years. Theobald Mathew's finances, meanwhile, were in awful disarray, and public efforts to relieve his debts were curiously unsuccessful. 'Backsliding' became an increasing problem, and in that sense the way in which the movement collapsed bears a tragic witness to the popular, bottom-up nature of the movement's initial accomplishments. Temperance's retreat was rapid and general, despite the best efforts of Mathew and his loyal supporters to slow the process. By 1845, the CTAS was in terminal decline. By the time the Famine of 1846–49 devastated Ireland, the movement's ranks were broken and a retreat was already well underway.

THE CORK TOTAL ABSTINENCE SOCIETY'S PLACE IN IRISH HISTORY

An evaluation of the significance of the CTAS's 'moral revolution' is a subject best left to the conclusion of this book. Suffice it to say here that the examination of the movement that follows provides invaluable insight into the political and social dynamics of an important period of Irish history. Because of the enormous scale of the movement, its dramatic impact on all aspects of public life, and the sheer volume of contemporary interest the cause and its millions of adherents received from participants, observers and opponents, there is no more fruitful starting point for enhancing the understanding of Irish culture, society and politics in the 1830s and 1840s.

On these grounds alone CTAS deserves close scrutiny, but there are also dimensions of the crusade which ought to peak the interest, not only of historians of nineteenth-century Ireland, and of Temperance, but also of those who are more generally concerned with popular culture, the trajectories of radical and popular social movements, and, perhaps most directly, the origins and development of national identity in colonial circumstances.[9] One of the most striking aspects of the Temperance crusade as it evolved was the place that patriotism, national historical sensibilities, and a kind of cultural nationalism played in enhancing and even structuring the movement's appeal. The Temperance movement was much more than a vehicle for the development of nationalist thought in Ireland, of course, but no understanding of the CTAS would be complete without a considered appreciation of this fact. In the same way no satisfactory attempt to come to terms with the significance of the crusade can neglect to consider its implications. One of the principal goals of this book, then, is to relate Father Mathew's singular success as the 'Apostle of Temperance' to more widely relevant questions about his movement's contribution to the ongoing construction and imagining of collective identity and nationalism in pre-famine Ireland.

CHAPTER ONE

A Moral Revolution

The expansion of the Cork Total Abstinence Society (CTAS), from a local association with a few dozen members in April 1838 to a regional mass movement with tens and then hundreds of thousands of adherents, and, finally, a national crusade with several million some four years later, was a remarkable accomplishment, and bears careful examination. Those who have studied the Temperance movement have given much weight in their explanations of its initial success to the unanticipated reaction of the superstitious Irish peasantry to the mystique and personal charisma of the society's President, Father Theobald Mathew.[1] In fact, the rise of the CTAS was both a more calculated, and a more complex phenomena than such an explanation allows.

BACKGROUND: TEMPERANCE AND DRINKING IN IRELAND BEFORE THE CORK TOTAL ABSTINENCE SOCIETY[2]

Any understanding of the magnitude of the change wrought by the CTAS must begin by appreciating the dominant place of drinking in pre-famine Irish culture. Whether or not Irish alcohol consumption was particularly high by prevailing European standards is an open, and probably unanswerable question, largely because the very significant amount of illegal distillation in Ireland rendered government statistics on the subject virtually useless for comparative purposes.[3] Still, anecdotal evidence on the widespread use and abuse of alcohol in early nineteenth century Ireland is legion. Certainly the stereotype of the drunken Irishman was well in place. In 1805, Thomas Newenham could already observe that 'much has been said on the subject of the drunkenness of the Irish' in particular, their unfortunate 'irresistible partiality to whiskey'.[4] Father Mathew echoed Newenham when in 1842 he lamented, in a letter to an ecclesiastical colleague, that 'whiskey, whiskey, punch, punch, was the darling drink in every circle, and brought death into every dwelling'.[5] In fact, Mathew and other Irish

Temperance activists made frequent references to the Irish reputation for heavy drinking, and according to most observers the problem was an endemic and growing one in the early decades of the nineteenth century. Precise figures for the consumption of legal whisky (Ireland's intoxicant of choice) in the years before Father Mathew's crusade are available, and in themselves indicate a staggering rate of alcohol consumption (see Table 1.1, below). Additionally, as the accompanying population and per-capita consumption statistics demonstrate, through the 1830s legal whiskey consumption was increasing faster than the population, at least until 1836.

Table 1.1: Proof-gallons* charged with duty in Ireland, 1831–1838, with population and per capita consumption.**

YEAR	GALLONS	POPULATION	PER CAPITA CONSUMPTION
1831	8,710,672	7,767,401	1.12
1832	8,657,755	(7,829,634)	1.11
1833	8,168,596	(7,891,867)	1.04
1834	9,708,415	7,954,100	1.22
1835	11,381,228	(7,985,675)	1.43
1836	12,248,772	(8,017,250)	1.53
1837	11,235,635	(8,048,825)	1.40
1838	12,296,842	(8,080,400)	1.52

*A proof-gallon is an alcohol constant (57.10 per cent alcohol by volume).

** Spirit production figures from *Parliamentary Papers*, H.C. 1852–53 (547) XCIX. Population figure for 1831 from Fitzpatrick and Vaughn, *Irish Historical Abstract* (Dublin: RIC, 1978), for 1834, *First Report of the Commissioners of Public Instruction, Ireland* (London: HMSO, 1835), p. 74. Figures in parentheses are estimated based on 1831, 1834, and 1841 official figures.

'Drinking', historian Susanna Barrows points out, 'more than most other leisure activities, derives its meaning from its social context and setting.'[6] The contexts and settings for drinking in Ireland in 1838 were predominantly public. Drinking while working was the norm for many, particularly in urban areas, just as it was in other parts of Britain and in the United States. Elaborate 'fine' and 'treating' systems were in widespread use in crafts and trades, which ritualised alcohol consumption. Wages were typically paid at public houses, with the purchase of at least one round of drinks expected. In both rural and urban areas in Ireland prodigious drinking at patterns, fairs, wakes, weddings, christenings and stations was a long-established custom.[7] Generally speaking, most Irish people drank together and in considerable numbers, using great volumes of alcohol to mark a wide variety of occasions. For this reason, drinking's antithesis, Temperance, radically set its face, not merely against private habit, but also against a very public and practically universal way of life.

Temperance as an organised reform movement was barely two decades old in the later 1830s, but it was already proving to be popular and remarkably adaptable. From its American beginnings, when the development of numerous local organisations in Massachusetts and Connecticut culminated in the formal establishment in 1825 of the American Temperance Society, Temperance had spread rapidly, not only to Britain, but also throughout Europe, particularly northern Germany and Scandinavia.[8] As indicated by its geographical pedigree, Temperance was primarily advocated and advanced by Protestant Evangelicals, and Ireland was no exception.[9] The formal Temperance movement in Ireland began in 1829 with the establishment of a number of societies across Ireland, including the Presbyterian minister John Edgar's Ulster Temperance Society in Belfast, the independent minister George Carr's New Ross Temperance Society, and the Dublin organisation of the Quaker physician Joshua Harvey. Up until 1838, the Irish Temperance movement was predominantly, although by no means exclusively, urban, middle class and Protestant.[10]

Through the 1830s, small Temperance societies slowly spread across the country, but their progress was impeded by internal disputes about the virtues of total abstinence versus moderation, culminating by the end of the 1830s in the rancorous but general triumph of total abstainers.[11] Meanwhile, the increasing sectarian divisions that Irish society was so plagued by ensured that very few of these organisations involved either the Catholic clergy or the influential laity, which severely limited their popular appeal.[12] James Doyle, the Catholic Bishop of Kildare and Leighlin, was the most significant Catholic voice raised in support of these early Protestant Temperance efforts, but he surely spoke for many when, in 1829, he told one activist that the cause had but 'small moral influence' in Ireland because it was advocated by 'Gentlemen' (he might have added 'Protestants') who preached 'a temperance they themselves do not always practice' to a people 'who have not before experienced their friendship and protection'.[13] Doyle further doubted 'that such societies in this country at this time, with our present laws and social government, can be productive of any great, or extensive, or permanent good'. His ambivalence on the subject of organised Temperance was typical even of those many Catholics who also appreciated the damage that excessive drinking was doing in Irish society. John Francis Maguire's later assertion that, until 1838,

Temperance was regarded by nearly all Irish Catholics as 'a form of social eccentricity bordering very nearly on madness' represented only a slight exaggeration.[14]

The relative lack of progress made by other Temperance societies in Ireland renders the expansion of the 'South Branch' of the CTAS established in Cork city by Father Mathew in April 1838 all the more remarkable. During the some 18 months between that date and November 1839, over 60,000 Irish men and women took the organisation's pledge of total abstinence. Over the course of this period of strong but uneven expansion, the CTAS not only assumed most of the characteristics of the regional and national crusade it was to become, but its proponents also adopted and began to proclaim an intensely missionary Temperance gospel. An examination of the leadership, structures and pattern of growth of the CTAS during this period reveals a great deal about the nature of the movement's initial appeal to the Irish people.

LEADERSHIP

Prior to Theobald Mathew's assumption of the presidency of the CTAS, the leadership of the beleaguered Temperance cause in Cork had been a Protestant preserve. The principal advocates of total abstinence in Cork before March 1838 were Nicholas Dunscombe, the Church of Ireland rector of Saint Peter's, Richard Dowden, a Unitarian merchant, and William Martin, an elderly Quaker shopkeeper of imposing physical presence, who was active in many reform causes. Dunscombe's church and Martin's shop were the main meeting places for Cork's modest Temperance society in its early days. Martin was the founder and leader, and it was he who recruited Father Mathew. Mathew had, as most historians of the movement have noted, a long-term personal acquaintance with Martin, a result of their mutual commitment to aiding the poor of Cork. It was that acquaintance that led Martin, apparently over a period of years, to, as Father Mathew later put it, 'press and urge and at length force me' to agree to lead a 'South Branch' of the Cork society.[15]

Martin was not alone in his attempts to 'press and urge' the popular friar. James McKenna and John O'Connell, two active Catholic members of Dunscombe's society, were also instrumental in persuading Mathew finally to accept Martin's invitation.[16] By 1838, lay Catholics were beginning to play an increasingly important part in Cork's Temperance society. At that time, the most influential and important of these was perhaps McKenna. John Francis Maguire noted the prominence of Frank Walsh, a barrister and a 'local celebrity, one of the best popular orators of the day'.[17] Maguire also might have included himself, soon to become the editor of the CTAS's newspaper, and Thomas Lyons, soon to become the first Catholic Lord Mayor of Cork under the reformed corporation, as important and enthusiastic early Catholic Temperance activists.[18] Relatively little attention has been paid to the role played by these early propagandists in shaping as well as reflecting popular understanding of the Temperance movement's objectives. A fuller appreciation of their influence over the movement's early development, however, requires an examination of the limited nature of Mathew's own initial involvement in the cause.

Sometime early in March 1838, McKenna and O'Connell led a deputation of Catholic members from the St Peter's society to call on Father Mathew. 'He was a young priest', O'Connell recalled, 'well-liked, and very popular amongst the working classes.' They probably knew Mathew had just recently 'promised against all sorts of liquors for twelve months', according to a delighted correspondent of Richard Dowden's.[19] After a second meeting the following week, which was also attended by Martin and was mainly concerned with explaining the practical side of organising and running a Temperance society, Mathew promised to consider joining the movement. He asked for a month to weigh the decision.

Clearly, what McKenna, O'Connell and others were seeking was credible Catholic clerical leadership that would gain a hearing for what John Francis Maguire called 'The doctrine of total abstinence'. Maguire described the frustration of early Temperance activists in a pamphlet he published in 1838 designed to encourage Cork's Catholic population to take the pledge:

> A few years since, the doctrine of total abstinence was scouted at as the day dream of some enthusiastic visionary, who proposed an impossibility for adoption. It was looked on as a wild scheme that could never be reduced to practise, unless, perhaps, through the devotion of some few fanatics, who would cling to it with a desperation equal to its impracticability. Even the most intelligent men of our city thought that they could discover beneath the surface an undercurrent of a dangerous tendency and character – that under the pretence of teaching the people to be temperate, those teachers were endeavouring to undermine them from their religious faith, and wean them from the creed of their fathers.[20]

Not only did Temperance seem to be a fanatical, fringe cause to many, but in Cork, as in many other parts of Ireland, brewers, distillers, publicans and spirit-grocers composed a substantial part of the respectable Catholic middle class.[21] They were large contributors to charity and church-building, two activities Father Mathew was much engaged in. Father Mathew's own brother, for example, was a distiller, and, throughout Ireland, the term 'water-drinker' inspired suspicion, if not outright scorn.

Perhaps most importantly, as Maguire's observations indicated, proselytising was often associated with Temperance efforts in Ireland. There is evidence that several other Catholic priests in Cork were recruited to aid the CTAS about this same time, doubtless in an attempt to counter this devastating criticism of the movement. This was not unusual in the late 1830s, as several priests in various parts of the country began to take up the cause in earnest.[22] In addition to Father O'Sullivan, John O'Connell also mentioned Francis Mahoney, who lectured in Cork on behalf of Temperance before Father Mathew joined the movement, while Richard Dowden in his correspondence praises a Father Browne who also took the pledge for a year early in 1838.[23] The *Cork Standard* reported a Temperance meeting at St Nicholas on 5 April, where an announcement was made that no fewer than three priests (unnamed, but undoubtedly including Mathew) would each be joining the Cork society and conducting Temperance meetings in their schoolrooms, as Mathew in fact began to do the following week.[24]

Mathew's willingness to consider joining the movement represented a coup of the first order of magnitude. Mathew's popularity and credibility extended to all social circles in the city, a legacy of his distinguished family background and his reputation as a devoted, practical and civic-minded priest. As his initial hesitation indicated, Father Mathew was a reluctant convert to Temperance, for reasons which were easy enough to understand. In 1838, Mathew was a man with many causes and many commitments. He was heavily involved in local affairs, and was the Provincial of the Irish Capuchins. In addition to ordinary pastoral duties at the Capuchin friary in Blackamoor Lane, Father Mathew had established schools for boys and girls. His efforts on behalf of Cork's poor were well-known. He conducted a local Josephian Society, which extended aid and comfort to hundreds of poor families in the area. He also owned a burial ground often used for pauper's funerals, and was engaged in building his own new church on Charlotte's Quay, an enterprise that was proving to be time-consuming, litigious and very expensive.[25]

Although Mathew was not known to be a formal advocate of total abstinence, Cork's Temperance activists knew that few better understood the damage that drunkenness was doing to the Irish poor.[26] Mathew's many charitable undertakings and his daily contact with the poor in the area around the Capuchin house and friary had made the social consequences of rampant intemperance apparent to him. As he later informed Tobias Kirby, the vice-rector of the Irish College in Rome, in 1842,

> no one living in Italy can conceive the ruin and desolation, temporal and eternal, occasioned here by alcoholic drinks. Thousands every year are hurried out of the world in a state of drunkenness, and are consequently lost forever.[27]

'Twelve millions of money were expended every year in this country on whiskey and porter', he explained to Kirby a short time later, 'which has made us the most wretched people on the face of the earth.'[28] These comments by Mathew indicate that he struggled mightily with his conscience in the late 1830s on the question of drink, and that his decision to join the Temperance movement arose out of a deep concern about the effects of drunkenness on the Irish people.

If Mathew's conscience convinced him that something needed to be done, McKenna, O'Connell and other local activists eventually persuaded him that teetotalism offered the only real solution to the problem. As Mathew later explained to a meeting in Cork in 1841, 'drunkenness was the Great Leviathan of the waters – the Beast of the Apocalypse mentioned in scripture'.[29] He had been, he insisted, 'originally induced by this – he trusted under the direction of God – to enter into the cause, for God had been grievously offended by crimes arising from drunkenness'. O'Connell and McKenna's initial visit to him had stemmed in part from an incident involving a proselytising effort by a visiting clergyman. Mathew's decision to become involved in the cause, therefore, arose from his concern for the spiritual well-being of Catholic members of existing Temperance societies.

On 10 April 1838, Father Mathew, at a meeting in his school rooms in Blackamoor Lane, spoke to a small audience and signed his name in a roll book as president of the newly established 'Sullivan's Quay' or 'South Branch' of the Cork Total Abstinence Association, with James McKenna as the branch secretary. Some 25 years later, Maguire published Mathew's brief remarks on the occasion.[30] Mathew began his address by alluding to 'personal considerations' which he needed to 'cast aside', a reference, no doubt, to the potential social consequences of his new-found fanatical inclinations. 'I have often been asked to do what I am about to do this night', Mathew claimed, adding that after reflection he now felt compelled, as 'a minister of the Gospel', to join the cause for the sake of 'the humbler classes', who were 'naturally most exposed' to the temptations of drink. 'I much fear', he warned his new associates, 'that your kind partiality has made you overlook my many defects, and attribute to me merits which I am very far from possessing.' Still, Mathew resolved, 'if one poor soul could be rescued from destruction by what we are now attempting, it would be giving glory to God, and well worth all the trouble we could take'.

Reaction to Father Mathew's conversion, proclaimed throughout Cork the following day, was incredulous. According to McKenna, 'for one person who gave credit to Father Mathew heading the society, hundreds, nay, thousands, laughed, sneered, disbelieved, and said it was all falsehood, and humbug'.[31] Maguire confirmed this, noting that many 'ridiculed the notion of his joining with the "fanatics"'.[32] Despite these criticisms, one certain effect of his association with the cause was renewed interest in the society among Catholics, no matter how surprising they may have found his initial involvement. Father Mathew's considerable reputation for practical benevolence led many to reevaluate Temperance.

Mathew's mythic status as the great charismatic Temperance crusader of pre-famine Ireland, however, was not derived from the early part he played in the CTAS. During his initial involvement with the movement Mathew did not embrace total abstinence with the enthusiasm he would later demonstrate, nor did he immediately move into a position of active leadership. Beyond lending a certain degree of credibility and credit, and providing a place to meet, Mathew played a passive and often an absentee part in early CTAS meetings. Although he must have attended occasionally, Mathew was not mentioned in most accounts of CTAS meetings prior to November 1839. Maguire observed that 'at first, Father Mathew did not speak at any length, and preferred the speaking should fall to the share of others'.[33] In fact Mathew did not attend the second meeting of his organisation, leaving it to Michael Reardon, one of his Capuchin confrères, to preside, and if he did attend the third, he said little or nothing.[34] Mathew was nowhere to be found in the next press notice of the society which appeared in early June, when the CTAS held two large meetings.[35] Mathew was toasted *in absentia* at the societies' first large tea party the following January, because, as Richard Dowden explained, he 'did not like the public bustle of such a meeting', and again at a temperate Saint Patrick's gathering a few months later.[36] Mathew's initial role was primarily to receive and bless postulants, first at occasional meetings and later as they began to appear at his Cove Street residence. In the first year and a half of the Cork society's existence, therefore, Mathew's position as president of the CTAS, while symbolically very important, was in practical terms a passive and a ceremonial one. His nominal subordinates determined and articulated the goals and objectives of the CTAS, and also undertook the organising, advertising and evangelising that produced the Temperance movement's initial singular success.

Mathew's involvement did allow younger Catholics who were already associated with the movement in Cork to move into positions of leadership. In their president's absence, the lay Temperance activists defined the movement, and they did so in terms that were intensely missionary. Interest in expanding membership was by no means unusual in Temperance societies of the day, but the Cork organisation appears to have been particularly aggressive and determined in its efforts. The CTAS's early rules and propaganda were clearly designed to encourage the spread of the society beyond Cork city. John O'Connell maintained that even before Mathew's involvement the society despatched speakers to various towns near Cork in an attempt to establish branch organisations throughout the area.[37] Contemporary newspaper accounts support his recollection.[38] The CTAS also imported Temperance celebrities in an attempt to make converts, including John Hockings, Temperance's most celebrated English evangelist, who spoke to Mathew's society in June 1838, and John Smith, Dublin's 'King of the Teetotallers', who appeared the following October.[39]

What was most striking, however, was the prophetic, zealous and emotional tone of both the local meetings in Cork and the movement's advertising. During 1838 and much of 1839, proceedings were reported principally in the journals of the Temperance movement, but also occasionally in the Cork papers. At the centre of most of this activity was James McKenna. As the CTAS's organiser, and Father Mathew's travelling assistant, McKenna was much more involved than Mathew in the movement's initial growth. He spoke at most of the early meetings that there is a record of, corresponded with all the Irish Temperance newspapers on the cause's progress in Cork, and promoted upcoming meetings by printing and distributing posters and handbills.[40] By his own account, McKenna was zealous in his efforts on the cause's behalf. The day after Father Mathew declared for Temperance, for example, 'large posters were provided by James McKenna', who 'got them posted through the city, on these posters the Very Reverend Mr Mathew's name as President of the Society was publicly announced signed James McKenna, Secretary'.[41] It is not surprising that Maguire noted printing expenses for the cause averaged £8–10 per week, a very large, but 'indispensable outlay'.[42]

Little is known about McKenna. His own writings reveal nothing about his background, although he apparently had been a soldier.[43] Maguire noted only that he was 'commonly called Kenna' and that he 'had known the two sides' of the Temperance question 'from personal experience'. McKenna's prose reveals the passionate conviction of a Temperance zealot. Maguire observed that his compelling speeches 'frequently partook of the character of rhapsodies, rather startling to the ear of the critic, but to which the evident sincerity of the speaker imparted a genuine ring'.[44] Even after Father Mathew established his pattern of charity sermon preaching in late 1839, McKenna often preceded him on the speaker's platform.[45] McKenna's early vision, as articulated in his speeches and letters to newspapers, concentrated on two related themes – the powerful example set by the number of converts attracted (whether the number concerned was a few hundred or tens of thousands) and the urgent need for the movement to become national and to embrace the entire Irish people. The audacity of this simple message, particularly in the movement's earliest days, was remarkable, but McKenna's bold and prophetic call was clearly inspirational to many.

McKenna's obsession with numbers manifested itself from the very beginning. An advertisement which appeared in the *Cork Standard* on 11 July 1838, signed by McKenna, claimed 1,115 members for Mathew's society, with 381 having joined since the first of the month. In bold, capital letters it noted that 'ONE HUNDRED AND FOURTEEN signed at one meeting this week'.[46] Advertising in major newspapers was at that time an unusual approach for a Temperance society, but little more than a week later McKenna repeated the tactic. The *Cork Standard* printed a public notice of thanks to Mr Conway and Mrs O'Connor for the use of the Cork Horse Bazaar by the movement, and proclaimed that the number of converts now exceeded 1,500.[47] McKenna took to carrying the society's rapidly expanding roll book with him on visits to branch societies and produced it at meetings, including at Dunmanway in August 1838, where he proudly brandished the list of 3,000 members. At another meeting in Cork the following October, McKenna 'held up in his hand the great roll, containing the names of the [6,500] members', and proclaiming, 'behold, the unfurled flag of freedom'.[48]

The numbers pledged became an even more important part of the movement's appeal as the CTAS grew. At a large tea party in Cork on 21 January 1839, for example, 'a banner floated over the head of the chair with the words "9,000 Members" on it', a fact that was emphasised in the first words spoken by the chairman of the meeting, Richard Dowden.[49] In his emotional toast to Father Mathew that followed, McKenna vowed that this considerable expansion was only beginning, reminding the nearly 800 present that 'small and insignificant streams originate noble and majestic rivers; such was the commencement and such may the progress be, of the great abstinence principle'.[50] In McKenna's report to the *Dublin Weekly Herald* two months later, he announced that 10,500 had already enrolled, and added that he fully expected there would be at least another 30,000 by the year's end.[51]

The second significant theme of McKenna's letters and speeches was an aggressive and forceful appeal to Irish patriotism, amounting to an urgent call for the collective regeneration of the Irish people from a state of national degradation by the adoption of total abstinence. The movement's first newspaper advertisement in the *Cork Standard* of July 1838 had made a particular appeal to all 'patriotic' Irishmen to join the new Temperance organisation.[52] In a letter to the *Philanthropist and National Temperance Advertiser* the following August, after noting the numbers enrolled, McKenna concluded by insisting that intemperance was 'the greatest foe that ever a nation was faced with'.[53] Less than two months later, he was more specific and even prophetic, in yet another progress report in the *PNTA*:

> The brand of intemperance that degrades the character of Irishmen, and proclaimed a nation's bondage will soon, with the divine aid, be obliterated from the pages of history and the foul stain be blotted out in the glorious struggle for the moral liberty of Ireland's sons and daughters.[54]

McKenna's most dramatic appeal to patriotism and 'moral liberty', however, took place at the Cork society's first large public tea party in January 1839. The event was clearly an attempt to raise the organisation's profile, and McKenna's speech, the centrepiece of the evening, was reported in all the prominent Cork papers, and was thus widely circulated. McKenna began by solemnly informing the audience that they were 'assembled in the great cause of Ireland's regeneration'.[55] Ireland in the past had been like a 'prison ship', McKenna explained, but now Temperance, 'this growing element in our society' was formed of Mathew's 'free men – men freed by [Mathew's] own hand – from worse than iron chains, and shown by him how they can rise up and walk'. McKenna concluded with a poem, apparently of his own composition:

> Sound the trumpet o'er Erin's fairy land,
> See, Temperance triumphs, she comes with her band;
> The temperance badge see her patriots wearing,
> We come with the laurels of victory won –
> Intemperance we've conquered, our trophies we're bearing,
> Come Temperance brothers, in triumph march on!

By the following March, McKenna was discussing the CTAS in ever more strident patriotic, collective terms. The employment generated by new industries 'erected on the ruins' of distilleries, he told the *Dublin Weekly Herald*, would 'give our native land prosperity, peace and happiness, and form a new era in the history of Ireland'.[56] Drink kept the nation 'in degrading bondage', but this new generation of Temperance reformers would be forever 'enshrined in the hearts of the people of Ireland; we hope that a glorious future is in reserve for our country'. Indeed, 'the time is fast coming when she will no longer be held up to scorn and degraded among the nations of the earth'. Intemperance, he maintained, was 'once a powerful, but now a declining enemy'. 'The friends of Ireland', he concluded, 'will see her triumphant over every obstacle by which her enemies endeavour to arrest her moral happiness and freedom.' Precisely who those enemies were was not made clear, but McKenna did criticise distillers, landlords and a 'mercenary government' that had 'so far forgotten its duties as to pander to the vices of the people'. By May, he had reduced the CTAS's manifesto to a single sentence: 'The good man who pledges breaks the fetters of moral slavery, and delivers a nation from self-degrading thraldom.'[57]

The real significance of McKenna's views was that they were indicative of a widely held and often-invoked understanding of the CTAS's cause. In the summer of 1838, for example, the budding journalist John Francis Maguire had published an interesting pamphlet dedicated to Father Mathew, describing the cause's success in Cork.[58] One of the CTAS's earliest propaganda pieces, written in a simple style designed to explain Temperance to the sceptical working man, it revealed that the cause was already being cast in a collective, national and political mould. As with McKenna, the real evil of drink for Maguire was that the Irish people were 'degraded by it as low as it is possible'.[59] While in tone much of the work was typical of pre-Mathewite Temperance efforts, emphasising its benefits for 'the working classes' and extolling 'the real comforts they may attain by ceasing to indulge', drink was also characterised as 'truly the greatest curse of our unfortunate country'. Drunkenness was 'that which has kept her far behind her sister – England, in refinement and development'. Maguire, even in these early days, writing on behalf of a movement that numbered, according to the pamphlet, some 5,000, insisted that Temperance was inherently political, 'the true legislator for the poor and humble man'.[60] The CTAS's branch societies in Cork, 'spread all over the city', were, in effect, schools to give men 'sense and intelligence' while 'their meetings are those of order and respectability, for every man who frequents them is convinced that he has an interest – a stake in the question – the stake of his own temporal – aye, and eternal – welfare'.[61] Temperance, which 'outstrips in its march the slow progress of all political reform, and at one fell swoop … removes the abuses of centuries', was the popular beginning of the end of an unresponsive and failed political system.

No explanation of the singular early development of the CTAS can afford to ignore, for example, the testimony of men like John Bowes, a Cork nailer, who, encouraged by John Francis Maguire, converted to teetotalism in August 1838. Bowes did not emphasise, in writing to the *Dublin Weekly Herald* the following year, his improved physical and moral condition.[62] Rather, he declared intemperance, in its Irish context, to be a form of slavery. Mathew's society would, 'in a very short time', Bowes prophesied, 'banish from our native country the bitter cup of intemperance and make Ireland what she ought to be – "Great, glorious, and free"'. If Mathew gave the CTAS greater credibility, as well as a president known for practical charity and benevolence, it was his lieutenants who suggested to Bowes and many like him what membership in the society meant – both for members as individuals, and for Ireland as a nation.

STRUCTURES

As the CTAS grew in 1838–39, its structure also became more elaborate. From an early date, those who took the pledge were aware that they were enlisting in an organisation, with rules, meetings and a leadership structure. In August 1838, a progress report appeared in the *Philanthropist and National Temperance Advertiser*, indicating that Mathew's society had established a number of branches within the city, and held three meetings a week.[63] New members underwent a short probationary period, and there was also a 'visiting committee' of 40, charged with verifying and ensuring the fidelity of new members. A few weeks later, John Francis Maguire described 'societies spread over our city'.[64] One of these, located in the North parish, was said to be under the patronage of John Murphy, the Bishop of Cork.[65]

By March 1839, McKenna claimed seven parish-based societies within Cork city, sub-divided into districts, each with its own reading and meeting rooms and a visiting committee.[66] This structure was part of a still larger body, as William Martin explained to the Irish Temperance Union's first annual convention in Dublin in May, which he attended as the CTAS's appointed delegate.[67] Martin described three main branches of the society – Saint Peter's, led by Dunscombe, Prince

Street, led by Dowden, and Mathew's South Branch. Each branch had its own reading rooms and separate meetings. While Mathew's organisation was clearly thriving, with its own branch organisations and weekly two-hour meetings, the Prince and St Peter's branches met only monthly, with 'occasional conversations'. Martin also described a one-month probationary period, at the end of which new members received a Temperance card and began subscribing (if they could) one penny per week to the reading room.

CTAS members, in addition to taking an oral pledge and entering their names on the membership role, also received cards, medals, printed advice and a set of the society's rules. The pledge itself was a standard one, usual with slight variations, to societies all over Europe and the United States. It stated simply, 'I promise to abstain from all intoxicating drinks, except used medicinally, and by the order of a medical man, and to discountenance the cause and practice of intemperance'. During the course of the crusade, this language underwent some modifications and additions, such as the removal of the medical exception and the addition of an explicit sacramental exception.

John Hockings's visit to Cork in June 1838, noted above, actually had critical long-term consequences for the movement. Hockings, one of a handful of Temperance's full-time travelling advocates, was usually paid an honorarium by local organisers, but he also profited by the sale of medals, which were becoming popular tokens of fidelity and identity in many societies throughout the United Kingdom.[68] His example, Maguire recalled, 'was followed, on his own account, by James McKenna'.[69] Father Mathew later related how McKenna, desperate to meet the printing and advertising expenses of the fledgling movement and to save its leader from rapidly mounting debt, 'earnestly requested permission to sell the medals' which had initially been given away.[70] After some consideration, Mathew agreed. In succeeding years, Mathew was to expend much of his personal capital, moral and financial, in a never-entirely-successful effort to disprove accusations that his mission was little more than a scheme to profit by a traffic in pewter medals, sold at one shilling each.

The CTAS's medals were important because they served as reminders of the pledge, and also as miniature Temperance catechisms for the many illiterates who took the pledge. Mathew's medals were large, approximately 45 millimetres across, and inscribed with familiar religious symbolism (see Figure 1). Most were made of pewter, although some silver and gold medals were also available for particularly distinguished members. On one side, a well-dressed man, carrying a banner, 'prosperity', and woman, 'domestic comfort', stood next to a

Figure 1.1: Medal of the Cork Total Abstinence Society (by courtesy of Spencer Radnich)

lamb, surmounted by a cross and an angel. This scene was overlaid by the Latin phrase, '*IN HOC SIGNO VINCES*'.[71] The reverse side had the words of the pledge within a shining cross, together with Mathew's name and the society's foundation date.

In addition to medals, early converts were also given a numbered pledge card with a graphic representation on one side of a temperate family enjoying domestic felicity, all well-dressed, sitting by the fireside reading, surrounded by doves, cornucopia, and savings banks, contrasted with a family enduring intemperate discord on the other, with the husband threatening his wife and child with a hammer, surrounded by vultures and serpent-entwined whiskey bottles. To the many illiterates who pledged, the card and medal were of particular significance, but the newly-enrolled also received Temperance handouts or broadsheets, as well as a copy of the societies' rules for regulating meetings and reading rooms.[72] Precisely what information the earliest broadsheets and pamphlets given to new converts contained is unknown, but it was almost certainly Temperance propaganda in its most graphic form. Maguire noted, of William Martin, that for years he 'had been accustomed to decorate his shop window with flaring placards and startling pictures, which silently though forcibly advocated his darling cause'.[73] Martin received 'whatever came from the temperance printing presses', and was particularly fond of 'striking' propaganda; 'it was impossible that the colours could be laid on too thick for William's satisfaction'.[74] Doubtless Martin and others in Cork had a large reserve of older Temperance literature which they rapidly distributed, but several pamphlets were produced locally as well, including John Francis Maguire's *The Doctrine of Total Abstinence Justified*.[75] A one-page handbill entitled *Advice to a Member of the Total Abstinence Society* was, by October 1839, already 'widely circulated by the Rev. Mr Mathew' to teetotallers upon their taking the pledge in Cork, and was probably typical of the societies' earliest publicity efforts.[76] The handbill struck a messianic tone. In addition to urging converts to avoid 'the tavern and the porter-house – they are fatal both to their victims and their keepers', new members were advised to 'unite' with other members of the society in their own communities by 'show[ing] them your card and medal', and to 'promote the blessed cause of total abstinence' together.

The rules, simple and straightforward, were probably based on those of Martin's society. An early version specifically aimed at regulating Temperance meeting rooms survives, and the same rules were printed in November 1839 by the *Dublin Evening Press*. This version assumes the organisation already had many separate branches which had established meeting places, and was probably drawn up sometime early in

1839, no doubt adapted from the South Branch's original regulations. They are worth quoting in their entirety, both for the insight they provide into the workings of the early movement, and because of their evident modular character.

1) No one admitted to these rooms but a subscriber.
2) No one admitted to be a subscriber to these rooms but faithful members of the above-mentioned society.
3) The committee rooms are to be closed during divine services on Sunday.
4) No resolution of this committee to be considered valid, until approved by the Rev. President.
5) Five members to constitute a meeting, who are to move one of the persons present to the chair, who is to preside for the preservation of order.
6) No agent from Temperance or other societies to be permitted to speak or interfere, unless recommended by the Very Rev. President or the clergyman of the parish.
7) No religious or political controversies to be allowed, on any account.
8) No tracts to be received by the committee, until they have been read and approved by the Rev. President, or the clergyman of the parish.
9) No public processions of the Total Abstinence Society without the approbation of the clergymen of the district.
10) No person even suspected of being a member of any association, or of being bound by combination oaths, to be allowed to become a subscriber of this room, without having fully cleared himself of the accusation before a clergyman of the parish.
11) That a committee be appointed in every parish to visit, once a week, the members of the Total Abstinence Society and report their conduct at the general meeting of the committee.
12) That, for the accommodation of the poor, the subscription be as low as possible, so that no teetotaller shall be excluded from the room, on account of poverty. (Signed, T. Mathew, President.)[77]

The rules shed some light on the early structures and priorities of the developing movement. Mathew clearly envisioned the clergy cooperating with, and leading, local societies – which would themselves conduct regular, ordered meetings. Rules 3, 4, 5 and 9 make Mathew's concern with maintaining as much clerical control as possible over the public behaviour of the teetotallers as a body evident. Rules 1,

2, 6, 8 and 11 gave the society's president full responsibility for governing the formation of teetotallers. Rules 7 and 10 reveal Mathew's determination to prevent his society from becoming a front for political activity, legal or illegal. Rule 12 was of particular importance. Because Mathew hoped to keep the CTAS as inclusive and broad-based as possible, he prevented any dues structure which would no doubt have ensured that the organisation would become just another club for the upwardly-mobile working class, as many other Temperance societies in Ireland and Britain already had.

NUMBERS

The organisational development of the CTAS was matched by a remarkable upsurge in membership. The movement's growth was astonishing. The table below (Table 1.2), based primarily on contemporary newspaper accounts, indicates just how rapidly the CTAS expanded during its first year and a half of existence.

Table 1.2: CTAS membership growth, April 1838–November 1839

DATE	17/4/38	24/4/38	1/7/38	11/7/38	23/7/38	14/8/38	8/9/38	19/10/38	21/1/39
MEMBERS	73	122	734	1,115	1,500	3,000	4,100	6,500	9,000
SOURCE	*PNTA*	*PNTA*	*CS*	*CS*	*CS*	*CS*	*ITLG*	*PNTA*	*SR*
	25/4/38	25/4/38	11/7/38	11/7/38	23/7/38	27/8/38	8/9/38	27/10/38	26/1/39

DATE	11/3/39	4/5/39	8/6/39	3/8/39	14/9/39	2/10/39	19/10/39	14/11/39
MEMBERS	10,500	11,000	12,000	21,000	42,219	43,000	52,707	66,364
SOURCE	*DWH*	*DWH*	*SR*	*DWH*	*SR*	*SR*	*DWH*	*DEP*
	30/3/39	4/5/39	8/6/39	3/8/39	21/9/39	5/10/39	19/10/39	28/11/39

These figures appear to be reliable, since they come from several sources which were consistent with each other, and were occasionally confirmed by other sources.[78] Initially, the roll book was used scrupulously to record new members, and these figures should in any case be preferred to McKenna's wholly unreliable later exaggerations.

The movement grew steadily if unevenly during the nearly 85 weeks from 10 April 1838 to 14 November 1839. It is helpful to distinguish three periods of growth during this year and a half (see Table 1.3). An initial period, from the CTAS's establishment in April 1838, until the middle of the following October, marked by an ever-increasing number of weekly postulants, was succeeded by a time of a declining rate of expansion, from that date until the following spring. The final period of local growth, during which the CTAS grew sixfold, lasted from early

May 1839 until Father Mathew began his formal missionary career at the end of November, and was marked by an upsurge in membership that accelerated as time went on.

Table 1.3: Three periods of early CTAS growth

Period	First Date	Members	Second Date	Members	No. of Weeks	No. Added	Avg Weekly Growth
1	17/4/38	73	19/10/38	6,500	26	6,427	243
2	19/10/38	6,500	4/5/39	11,000	30	4,500	150
3	4/5/39	11,000	14/11/39	66,360	29	55,360	1,909

The earliest growth (period 1) of the CTAS has often been exaggerated, a tendency that began with the crusade's first substantial history, the unpublished work of James McKenna. In it, McKenna claimed that 57 signed the pledge with Mathew on 8 April and that the new society had 330 members after its second meeting a week later, and nearly 1,000 before a month had passed.[79] As he was secretary of the CTAS, and presumably in possession of the roll book when he was writing around 1843, McKenna's information ought to be credible, but in fact he was frequently careless with numbers, and other contemporary evidence indicates the growth was a good deal slower.

Early in May, for example, a W.A. Caldwell wrote to the Dublin-based *Philanthropist and National Temperance Advertiser*, enthusiastically describing the societies' third weekly meeting, attended, he claimed, by over 1,000 interested spectators.[80] William Martin spoke, as did a Rev. H.H. Campbell, a J. Kenagh, and Caldwell himself. Although 'considerable annoyance was given by a drunken man' (not an uncommon feature of Temperance meetings), Caldwell claimed that 29 signed the pledge book that evening, which, when added to the 73 who had pledged at the first two meetings and 20 others who had pledged between meetings, gave the society a strength, as of 24 April, of 122. Caldwell's contemporary account should be preferred to McKenna's, who probably recalled the unprecedented attendance at the second and third meetings as distinguished from the relatively small numbers pledged.

For this period, new members were local. Much of the initial upsurge in membership must have been a consequence of Mathew's own extensive personal connections, which were naturally most significant in Cork, especially among the poor whom he had served so devotedly for some 20 years. Particularly obliged were those whose family members had been interred at little or no cost in his cemetery, those who had been consoled or nursed by him during the cholera epidemic of 1832, those who had benefited by his open-handed generosity, and those who had been assisted by his active army of charitable Josephians. Only somewhat less obliged were the 'better sort' among the working classes, who had in many cases been educated at his school or who had themselves served as Josephians.

This considerable influence of Father Mathew among the poor contributed to the early class composition of the CTAS. While the first meeting was 'drawn from the middle walk of life with here and there an artisan or labourer looking ill at ease in the cramped dignity of his Sunday clothes', the movement rapidly became plebeian, even by the working-class standards of previous temperance societies.[81] The third meeting's working-class attendance of more than 1,000, including the disruptive drunk, indicates the trend.[82] In July, when the schoolrooms would no longer suffice, the society obtained the free use of The Horse Bazaar, a decidedly *déclassé* cavernous pavilion with a capacity of 4,000 near Father Mathew's residence in Cove Street in the poorer section of the city.[83] In August, McKenna, evangelising in Dunmanway, claimed that most of the 3,000 members were 'tradesmen and labourers', many 'most anxious that the employers of Cork should consider the propriety of entering into a resolution that foremen should not be permitted to engage in the publican's business'.[84] Later that month, McKenna described a society composed, for the greater part, of 'the most intelligent and respectable tradesmen of Cork'.[85] A more neutral source, the *Southern Reporter*, in its first report of a Temperance meeting, described a 21 January tea party as a raucous overflowing gathering of some 1,000 of the lower orders, lured by 20 singers, tea, bread and a 6d admission charge.[86]

From October 1838, however, until the following May, the number of members joining per week went into steady decline, from 243 per week in the earlier period to about 150 per week (see Table 1.3, period 2). Furthermore, the rate of decline became more pronounced over time, indicating that something more than a mere seasonal variation was at work. In the nearly two months from 11 March until 4 May, only some 500 members joined, or less than 70 per week. This probably reflects the fact that most of those in Cork who were willing to pledge had done so, while people from the countryside were not coming in to take the pledge in significant numbers. The crusade had not yet stagnated by any means, but it had obviously plateaued.

The slower rate of growth, however, from October 1838 to May 1839, did not continue. McKenna was pleasantly surprised early in May when 100 people arrived in the course of one day to take the pledge. Most, if not all, were country people. In a letter he immediately dashed off to the Temperance paper the *Dublin Weekly Herald*, he marvelled that so many 'persons come 60–80 miles from Cork without any other business but enrolling themselves in this society'.[87] McKenna anticipated a steady summer increase of '2–300' weekly, and credited the improving weather for the sudden influx. Whatever the cause, the dam had certainly broken. The numbers enrolled weekly during this third period (see Table 1.3, period 3) were well beyond even McKenna's greatest expectations, and expanded at an ever-increasing rate. By 3 August, some 10,000 new members had joined, an average of more than 725 per week, doubling or tripling McKenna's initial estimates, while from 3 August to 14 November, 45,360 joined at the astounding rate of 3,024 new members per week.

This third period of growth represents a crucial turning point for the cause, and helps to set Mathew's society apart from its predecessors and all other contemporary Catholic societies. From May 1839 onward, most of those who took the pledge must have come from outside Cork city. These converts, Temperance pilgrims with little or no sense of personal obligation or respect for Father Mathew, returned to their own communities marked out by their cards and medals, as well as their refusal to participate in traditional patterns of behaviour. Urged on by the words of the pledge itself, as well as by the handbills, rules and advice they received in Cork, they formed (or in some cases revitalised) numerous vigorous societies that now began to appear throughout Munster.[88] Through word of mouth and power of example, they elevated the CTAS into a missionary body with many branches outside Cork. This critical late summer and early autumn departure for the CTAS transformed Temperance from a successful local movement into an emerging regional phenomena.

As Elizabeth Malcolm has pointed out, this membership explosion requires an explanation. She suggests that a superstitious peasantry, disturbed by the 'severe and widespread failure of the potato crop which occurred during this period', poured into Cork city on a kind of religious pilgrimage, determined to secure medals and the blessing of a renowned holy man 'to ward off such disasters in the future, if not to bring good fortune in the immediate struggle for survival'.[89] Secondarily, labourers, cottiers and small farmers were attempting to appease employers and landlords, anxious for sober workers and tenants.[90]

Neither of these explanations is completely satisfactory. As Colm Kerrigan has noted, there was nothing in contemporary sources that linked popular superstitions about Temperance to concerns about staple crop shortages.[91] The relationship between 'superstition' and the Temperance crusade was in fact a very complex one, and will be examined in detail in the next chapter. At present, it is worth noting that Tables 1.2 and 1.3 make it clear that the CTAS's membership upsurge began in May, at the end of planting season, independent of the partial potato crop failure that occurred later in 1839. That potato crop failure, furthermore, while severe in Connaught and parts of the midlands, was less evident in southern Munster, the areas where Mathew's converts were coming from.[92] The fact that staple food shortages were characteristic of a period of very rapid expansion for the CTAS (August–October 1839), therefore, hardly provides a satisfactory explanation. Whatever motives, superstitious or not, were at work in increasing interest in Temperance over the course of 1839, only after the harvest, in the midst of fair weather, were many agricultural labourers likely to have the funds to finance trips to Cork, and the obligatory 'farewell to whiskey' benders that were such a noticeable characteristic of the movement in its early days. In this sense, the exponential expansion of the autumn of 1839 represented a natural enough seasonal acceleration of a dramatic upsurge in interest that had begun several months earlier.

In regard to the involvement of employers and landlords in encouraging those beholden to them to take the pledge, there were undoubtedly some of both who did so, especially later in 1839. Large business concerns – victuallers in Limerick and Waterford, mines in Tipperary – were active in some cases, as were masters of small numbers of servants, and some, like Paddy, diarist Elizabeth Smith's gardener, took the pledge at least in part to appease employers.[93] In Cork, by the autumn of 1839, furthermore, men and women charged with public drunkenness were, as a matter of course, told by magistrates to take Mathew's pledge, and some may have avoided a fine or imprisonment in this way.[94] In Limerick and Waterford, as has already been noticed, an array of civic and religious authorities heartily endorsed the movement, even to the point of extending pecuniary assistance to those travelling to Cork to take it. Priests who became zealous in the cause were also in a position to encourage conversions among their parishioners, and some no doubt did so.

While some employers and landlords encouraged workers and servants to take the pledge, however, others actively discouraged it because they were convinced that drink maintained health and strength, especially for those who laboured under difficult conditions.[95] Others resisted Temperance because they disliked disruptions and divisions among workers, or because they were interested in the public houses where wages were paid out, or because they realised tenants often paid rent with the proceeds of illicit distillation.[96] Some, like Lord Lorton, who tried to keep his tenants from pledging when Father Mathew came to Boyle, Co. Roscommon in September 1840, appeared to consider the movement a time-consuming distraction.[97] And if the clergy in many places encouraged the growth of the CTAS, they were just as likely in others to do the opposite. Irish tenants and workers, furthermore, were notoriously resistant to such paternalistic encouragement, and it is difficult to imagine why long-criticised drinking customs would suddenly become particularly susceptible to pressure from above. Temperance reformers in Ireland prior to 1838, after all, had made much of the peculiar stubbornness of the great mass of the Irish people in this regard. Few early observers of the Temperance cause, even hostile ones, accused Mathew's followers of calculated opportunism. Pressure from above to pledge, while it did occur, was sporadic at best, a fact that Mathew and other advocates of the cause complained about repeatedly. The conclusion of a reporter from *Tait's Edinburgh Magazine*, in Ireland in early 1840 when charged with explaining the movement's expansion (that 'in comparatively few instances was any persuasion attempted by superiors, either lay or clerical') seems credible.[98]

A more satisfactory explanation for this sudden upsurge in membership is likely to be found in an appreciation of the peculiar characteristics of the CTAS – the society's leadership and organisation, and the nature of its appeal to the Irish people. Other factors – Mathew's reputation, financial resources and credit allowed travel, printing and medal production on a wholesale scale – played a very significant role as well. Still, it is unwise to ignore the attractive power of the movement's own message and organisation in favour of some more elaborate or subjective explanation. The CTAS actively reached out into the surrounding countryside – by bringing Temperance celebrities to Cork, by holding large public gatherings, by despatching representatives to neighbouring towns, and, most importantly, by encouraging converts to band together and 'discountenance the causes and practice of intemperance'. It marked out its members with graphic medals and cards, and, as will be examined later, a complex network of collective behaviour including frequent meetings, parades, processions and tea parties. James McKenna publicised these gatherings on a grand scale, blanketing Cork with posters and buying advertising space in local papers.

The combination of advertising, increasing press coverage, oral testimony, and the powerful example of converted Temperance pilgrims within local communities, was extremely effective in raising the movement's profile and broadening its appeal. Mathew's society grew as rapidly as it did largely because expansion was aggressively pursued by McKenna, Maguire and others with remarkable ambition, skill, innovation and energy, as part and parcel of their own (and Mathew's) understanding of the nature and destiny of this new organisation. As other Temperance societies in Ireland in the late 1830s (some of them led by charismatic priests) did, the CTAS's leaders preached improvement in the material and spiritual circumstances of the individual. Unlike others, however, practically from its inception the CTAS leadership also convincingly and consistently communicated a coherent and ambitious emotional grand design, promising a new era of national redemption and regeneration from a state of collective degradation.[99] The CTAS, with its expansionist ideology, modular rules, branch societies, cards, medals, and a minimal initiation process, as well as its popular leader, preached more than individual reformation; it proposed a powerful collective moral revolution on a massive scale, and urged the entire nation as such to join in affecting it.

By mid-November 1839, more than 66,000 names were entered into the society's great book. The organisation was already marked by a proliferation of branch societies in Cork and throughout Munster. Temperance in Cork had evolved into a system, complete with literature, rules for new local societies to follow, and inexpensive and widely-recognised tokens of membership, all designed to accommodate the efficient initiation of new members. Hundreds of country people arrived daily in Cork 'with no other business' than to take the pledge. Pledging was promoted by McKenna, Maguire and its other impassioned advocates in patriotic, prophetic and inclusive terms as the answer to all ills, national and particular, while the scale of the movement's accomplishments had become an ever-more convincing component of the CTAS's appeal. What no one could have realised or anticipated, however, was that the Irish people would soon respond in their aggregate numbers in a way that would swiftly transform this very successful local Temperance movement into a regional crusade.

CHAPTER TWO

The Movement Explodes

By late 1839, with local success ensured by a flood of converts, the CTAS seemed destined to continue to expand. The first part of this chapter examines the details of how that expansion occurred, moving Temperance to the very centre of the national stage. The second part engages the principle question raised by the first, that is, why did so many seek to pledge? While the previous chapter demonstrated the early aggressive ideology of the CTAS, and suggested that the society was particularly dedicated to, and organised for, the spreading of Temperance, there is a great deal that remains to be discovered about the nature of popular enthusiasm for the cause.

PART I: 'A MORAL AND GLORIOUS REVOLUTION'

By the autumn of 1839 it was becoming apparent that the Temperance movement begun in Cork 18 months earlier was entering into a new stage of development, one marked by unparalleled popular enthusiasm for the crusade and its leader throughout the southwest of Ireland. The first indication of this enthusiasm, besides the remarkable upsurge in the number of postulants arriving in Cork to take the pledge, occurred when Father Mathew attracted spontaneous crowds while making two family visits – one to his brother's residence at Castlelake near Cashel in Co. Tipperary in August of 1839; and the other to his boyhood home at Thomastown in the same county a month later.[1]

These visits certainly alerted Mathew and his supporters to the growing enthusiasm for Temperance that existed in the people of Munster. Apparently the scale of the CTAS's success in Cork was widely known, while Mathew's reputation for 'curing' drunkenness was already becoming legend. Despite this early evidence that more converts could be gained if he would visit the countryside, Mathew still appeared reluctant to reduce his entire ministry to the promotion of Temperance.[2] His position as Provincial of his order had just been renewed for a third time, and according to a visiting clerical colleague, Mathew did not permit his Temperance work to interfere with 'the performance of sacerdotal or charitable engagements, which seemed to have no end throughout the whole day'.[3] Maguire also claimed that for as long as it was possible Mathew 'was as much a priest as ever', and kept 'the same early hours, the same attendance in the confessional, the same attention to his clerical duties, the same activity and punctuality in whatever he had to perform'.[4]

Eventually, however, it became clear that something unprecedented was taking place. As the late summer turned into autumn, thousands of pilgrims continued every week to take the pledge at 'all hours of the day and evening – even to ten or eleven o'clock at night – "batches" of ten, twenty, or even thirty', crowding into Mathew's small parlour in Cove Street, 'converted into a reception room'.[5] It was only, Maguire asserted, as his successes became unmistakable that Mathew himself began to catch 'the contagion of the movement', despite 'former apprehensions as to the difficulties he would have to encounter, and the risk of failure in his undertaking'.[6] He became 'as confident and fearless as the most responsible member of his already vast society'. It was during these weeks that Mathew's conversion to the Temperance cause became more evident and enthusiastic. The release of his considerable store of talent and energy in service of the cause was to be crucial in transforming the movement.

At the heart of the membership surge that so inspired Mathew was clearly the example and activity of the many new and rejuvenated local societies, which were themselves a consequence of the expansionist ideology of the CTAS. In August, for example, the *Galway Patriot* described a local Temperance society, complete with a visiting committee and officers, composed of 450 members (some of them once 'notorious tipplers') who had taken the pledge in Cork from Father Mathew.[7] The cumulative impression of enthusiasm and activity these organisations afforded was striking, all the more so when so much improvement became evident in those of whom so little was expected. As John N. Barron, a constable at Ennistymon, reported, with some surprise, 'the greatest drunkards have now become the most industrious and well-conducted'.[8] In most communities it was in fact these notorious drinkers who pledged first, and the example was not lost on others.[9] In another account of the same phenomenon, a magazine reporter investigating the rise of the movement described the case of Denis McCarthy, a boatman in Killarney, who had gone to Cork 'with six others of the greatest drinkers in the neighbourhood', all of whom returned, sober, and involved themselves in Temperance activities.[10]

John Brian, a bell-hanger from Killarney, explained to the reporter that he had 'drank from love of whiskey', and described the local reaction to his conversion:

> When his neighbours heard of his going, they shook their heads and said – 'If Brian gives up drinking, we'll think something of Father Mathew's new system. He'll never get back from Cork without getting drunk.' When he came back sober, they said, 'He'll never hold out a fortnight.' At the end of the fortnight, they gave him six weeks, and, seeing him still sober, they went themselves.

The role of Temperance societies will be examined in greater detail in a subsequent chapter, but it is important to note here that they often organised demonstrations and parades to attract attention and win converts. In Clonmel, in November 1839, John Power, a curate at Saints Peter and Paul, led 400 Temperance society members in procession to evening prayer.[11] The *Southern Reporter, Dublin Evening Post* and *Waterford Chronicle* all reported on a Temperance funeral in the same town that attracted 5,000, while similar occasions at Limerick, Mitchelstown, Tipperary, Donaskeigh and Cove drew muchcomment.[12] A 'Temperance wedding' at Clonmel drew the attention of the *Tipperary Free Press* in October, and prompted the further observation that '200 walked through the town yesterday on their way to Cork'.[13] The same month the Tullamore, Co. Kerry society held a well-attended 'Tea Festival', where they exhibited graphic transparencies:

> the last was a drunkard's coat of arms, representing on the right a woman with a child on one arm and a bottle in the other hand, pouring its contents down her throat while her wretched, naked appearance, dishevelled hair, and care-worn countenance truly depicted a drunkard's state. On the left was a plate with a bare bone, a pawn-brokers sign, the goal and gallows, thus frightfully representing the evils and misery, and too frequently the awful ends that follow the constant use of ardent spirits.[14]

It is obvious, moreover, that the celebrations of many other societies must have gone unreported in the popular press. As the editor of the *Dublin Weekly Herald* observed, Temperance had to overcome the weight of both interest and prejudice to attract attention. In October the Temperance weekly noted in an editorial that it was only the 'unprecedented' accomplishments of Father Mathew that had 'awakened the dormant energies of the press', while a month later another editorial ('Why is the Press Silent?') pointed out that public houses took in many papers and claimed that distillers were directly involved in the publication of others.[15]

Still, the scale of the CTAS's success in Cork, as well as the intense activity of rejuvenated local societies, gradually began to produce a wealth of free publicity. As the *Tipperary Free Press* proclaimed on 2 October, the wave of Temperance enthusiasm 'has now riveted the attention of every class in the community', including Irish journalists.[16] By the autumn of 1839, the public behaviour of Temperance societies and expanding press coverage of the same spread enthusiasm for Temperance's progress. A new sort of editorial began appearing in many non-Temperance papers, describing in at least neutral if not glowing terms the operation of Temperance societies and their potential social benefits.[17]

As the crusade expanded, editorialists became even more enthusiastic. In September 1839, the *Dublin Evening Post* initially observed, with some surprise, that 'it would appear that the Rev. Mr Mathew has managed to make more converts in Ireland than all the societies have yet been able to accomplish'. A month later, the *Post*'s editor, F.W. Conway, concluded that 'a great moral reformation is now underway in the South of Ireland, the importance of which, as regards the improvement of the state of society, the habits and conditions of the population, and ultimately the prosperity of the country, it would be impossible to overestimate'.[18] In September, the *Southern Reporter* announced the membership figures for the CTAS, and made the astounding (and quite untrue) assertion that no member had yet broken the pledge.[19] In October, the *Tipperary Free Press* described a 'moral and glorious revolution which every man who loves his kind and his country, must delight to contemplate', a movement which 'advances with wondrous rapidity, and bids fair, ere long to spread its blessed influence all over our land'.[20] A few days later, the *Southern Reporter* also proclaimed the 'moral and glorious' nature of the Temperance 'revolution', a description of the movement that soon became common currency.[21]

Given all this enthusiasm, it is not surprising that Mathew began to receive invitations from local societies to administer the pledge. On 24 October, for example, he was urged by a Temperance society in Wexford to 'extend [his] labours' to Ireland's "remotest corners" by visiting that town.[22] He refused not only this request, but also another the following month from a society in Belfast, because with 500 joining on the day his response was written and 4,000 pledging weekly, Mathew explained, it was 'utterly impossible for me to leave Cork at present for more than a day or two, and even during that time the poor people, who come here from all parts of the kingdom to take the pledge, would suffer great inconvenience'.[23]

Two episcopal requests, however, proved to be special cases, as they both came from neighbouring dioceses where the bishops were enthusiastic supporters of the Temperance work of Father Mathew. On 4 November he was invited by Nicholas Foran, the Bishop of Waterford, to visit that city.[24] Some time earlier, Mathew had also agreed to a visit to Limerick at the end of November, at the request of its bishop John Ryan, to preach a charity sermon on behalf of the Sexton Street Female Poor School, conducted by the Presentation sisters.[25] When this sermon had been originally arranged, it did not include any plans to administer the pledge. Once it became clear, however, that Ryan expected him to pledge new members to his society while at Limerick, Mathew then agreed to visit Waterford early in December, to advance the cause of Temperance by administering the pledge.[26]

Even before the CTAS had been launched, Limerick had an active Temperance society.[27] One of the first Temperance reading rooms and coffee houses in Ireland had been established there in April 1838.[28] As in other places, a branch of the CTAS, the St Mary's society, with hundreds of active members, many of whom had gone to Cork to take the pledge from Mathew, soon eclipsed older organisations, both in numbers and in activity.[29] Hundreds had taken the pledge from John Clarke, a curate in Bishop Ryan's mensal parish, St John's, but pilgrimages to Father Mathew in Cork were preferred.[30] A fund had been established by a few wealthy individuals and employers to defer expenses for those going to Cork to take the pledge.[31]

In the weeks leading up to the visit, Temperance enthusiasm in Limerick was brought to the boiling point. A letter to Mathew from Limerick's mayor, G. Fitzgerald, had been circulated widely.[32] Fitzgerald, who wrote to thank Mathew for sending him a Temperance pamphlet, endorsed the crusade in glowing terms, and acknowledged that Mathew's 'unparalleled exertions in the cause of temperance' had been, 'under God, crowned with the most single success, and, I believe, in no place more than Limerick'.[33] There, Fitzgerald had also noticed a marked decrease in deaths, half of which, he claimed, 'were caused, whether directly or indirectly, by intoxicating liquors'. He concluded by forecasting a 'moral regeneration' that was 'really most astonishing'.

Even while this letter was circulating, Limerick was the site of one of the more remarkable Temperance demonstrations yet seen in Ireland. The occasion was the funeral on 6 October of 'a carpenter by the name of Regan, who died in the fever hospital'.[34]

> Seventy five members [of the temperance society] and six clergymen, with scarves and hat-bands, preceded the hearse, which was followed by

> nearly 800 teetotallers, each with his medal exhibited. A great number of respectable persons joined the procession through the principle streets of the city. The moral effect of such interesting proceedings on the minds of those not already connected with this society must be very considerable.

In such an atmosphere, Mathew's visit was all the more eagerly awaited. By the end of October, the newspapers began advertising the visit, and preparations were made for a very elaborate welcome.[35] The week before his arrival, the enthusiasm was causing Father Mathew, whose 'intention [was] to make my visit … as private as circumstances will allow', anxiety.[36] In a letter to one of the organisers, John Nolan, a curate in St Mary's parish, Mathew was concerned about 'the Limerick papers announcing the intention of the members of the Total Abstinence Society to invite me to a Temperance tea party, and to certify in other ways their gratitude for the benefits conferred on them by their admission into our society'. Such 'public compliments', he warned, were 'most repugnant of my feelings'. Mathew did promise to visit the CTAS's committee rooms.

Mathew followed this letter with another one a day or so later to James Raleigh, a curate in Bishop Ryan's second mensal parish, St Michael's. Father Mathew promised to 'be at the disposal of His Lordship, Dr Ryan', all day on the Monday following his Sunday charity sermon.[37] Again, Mathew asked his 'dear friend' to 'exert yourself to save me from temperance parties, addresses, processions, etc. At any risk, I am resolved not to make a spectacle of myself.' All of this was very much in keeping with Mathew's modest understanding of his own role in the Temperance system as practised in Cork. He still had little desire to be the centre of Temperance attention.

Mathew's letters were duly published in the days prior to his visit, but they did little to dampen popular enthusiasm. On the eve of his arrival, a reporter observed that 'many persons who never contemplated such a change, whose habits of life, in the opinion of their neighbours, required no such change, carried away by the feelings of enthusiasm which are now so general, have resolved to join the order of temperance'.[38] The initial expectation seems to have been that on the Monday after his charity sermon, Father Mathew would reaffirm or pledge for the first time a few thousand members of Limerick's Temperance societies. To this end, James McKenna was sent on ahead on Friday, 29 November, with 2,000 medals and cards.[39] He discovered, on his arrival, that over 3,000 had already signed a register indicating their resolve to take the pledge at Mathew's hands.

Whatever suspicions McKenna and Mathew had that they had

underestimated the scale of the event began to assume a sharper focus over the course of Friday night and Saturday morning, as the hundreds streaming into the city from the surrounding country as far away as Galway and Mayo became thousands, then tens of thousands.[40] Limerick's population of 48,000 multiplied several times over, and accommodation and public order became serious problems.[41] What transpired between Mathew's arrival on the afternoon of Saturday, 30 November and his departure the following Tuesday evening he later described as 'glorious, but awful'.[42] Amidst scenes of chaos and confusion that occasioned much property damage, several injuries, and probably at least one death, Mathew (who eventually had to be provided with a mounted military escort) administered the pledge for hours on end to 'batches' of postulants, with only the briefest of pauses for food and sleep. By repetition of the pledge, he lost his voice, and any hope of distributing medals and cards or adding names of new members to the rolls of the CTAS had to be abandoned. By the time he left Limerick, it was universally believed that somewhere between 120,000 and 200,000 Irish men, women and children had taken the pledge at his hands.[43]

The details of these four days have been treated ably by other historians.[44] What must be emphasised here is that Limerick was a crucial turning point for Mathew's movement, and that it inaugurated an entirely new phase in the CTAS's development. First and foremost, the events at Limerick were unprecedented and afforded a spectacle of the very highest order of magnitude. There had been many large gatherings of people in Ireland in previous years – at anti-tithe demonstrations, for example, and in conjunction with the earlier campaign for Catholic Emancipation – but none could rival what transpired when Mathew visited Limerick.[45] The evidence indicates that, regardless of their previous opinions about Temperance, the Irish people were stunned by the enormity of the event. An account by the *Limerick Standard* – a Tory paper, and no supporter of Mathew's views on Temperance – is worth quoting at length, because it serves to convey some of the bewilderment that witnesses experienced:

> The entire previous day and night, and all day yesterday, thousands upon thousands of the country people were flocking into town from all parts of the country, some having come a distance of one hundred miles for the purpose. The various thoroughfares were literally covered with people, and the steamers plying on the Shannon brought up each trip human cargoes, varying in numbers from five hundred to one thousand. The holds of the vessels were literally crammed ... it was really frightening to see the rolling of the vessels as they approached the quay. The

> crowd at the chapel was immense, and in vain did the police oppose the progress of the ignorant multitude – they were struck over and over again amidst cries of 'kill the rascals' – 'Strike them down', and ultimately the mob had it all its own way. But, if the crowd and confusion were great on Sunday, it was infinitely more so yesterday, as reinforcements were hourly pouring in on all sides ... during the entire day the spacious streets of our city seemed completely covered with human beings running to and fro, many of them in a beastly state of intoxication, after drinking their 'farewell' to whiskey and blindly rushing to take the Temperance Pledge. We have witnessed many scenes of uproar and confusion, and seen large bodies of people together, but such a scene as the city presented yesterday, we have never witnessed.[46]

After such scenes, the CTAS could no longer be regarded as a curious obsession confined to Cork and its environs and pursued by a few thousand fanatics. The crowds at Limerick had transformed it into an inescapable regional phenomenon.

This new mass public dimension of the Temperance movement had the practical effect of rendering its potential self-evident. If, as has been shown, some of the CTAS's early activists had envisioned and promoted a Temperance movement destined to embrace all of Ireland, Limerick demonstrated for all to see that the vision might soon become reality. Indeed, given the events of those few days, it seemed destined to do so. If the Limerick meeting drew 150,000 to the ranks, what might a few visits to other parts of the country accomplish? What would happen when Mathew visited Waterford? What if he should accept invitations certain to be made by bishops in other parts of the country? How many might pledge in Clonmel, Kilkenny, Wexford and Dublin itself?

Finally, Mathew's own position within the movement of necessity underwent a transformation. If his role in the cause had grown in the weeks before Limerick, those four days were Father Mathew's particular triumph. His succession to active, practically exclusive leadership was a sudden event, the unplanned consequence of popular enthusiasm, and one that was to have a profound effect on the Temperance movement. Up to this point the dignified Father Mathew had presided over the movement, not led it. He had always been the nominal head of the organisations and structures, but his personal enthusiasm for the cause had been mounting for some time. Now he had now become convinced that God was vitally interested in its greatest possible success. He was certain, he informed a Quaker acquaintance the week after Limerick, that 'Providence' had 'blessed the Society', and hoped that 'the extension of temperance societies will be realized'.[47] 'Truly', Mathew added, 'the aspect of things seems to tend to the universal triumph of the good cause and I hope that the day will come when the drunkard will be regarded as an object of abhorrence and contempt by all classes of society.' Temperance was well on its way to becoming Mathew's consuming passion, or as he would later express it, 'my whole heart is engaged in this one tremendous object'.[48] The events at Limerick established him in his new role as the actual as well as the titular leader of the crusade.

Mathew's visit a week later, on 10 December, to Waterford confirmed the success of the movement and its leader by demonstrating that what had happened in Limerick was no aberration. Like John Ryan in Limerick, Nicholas Foran, the Bishop of Waterford, was an enthusiastic supporter of the cause, and, as in Limerick, there were particularly active local societies, which had recently sponsored notable public demonstrations. Mathew attempted to downplay the enthusiasm directed towards his person by slipping into the city a day early, but the attempts to contain the crowds and their excitement were just as futile as they had been in Limerick, despite a much more carefully choreographed visit.[49] Once again a lengthy quote from a contemporary newspaper account goes a long way towards recapturing the incredible excitement generated by Mathew's visit to Waterford:

> Never in the course of our lives did we witness anything comparable to the enthusiasm of the people … It is impossible for pen to do it justice, and beyond the reach of imagination to conceive anything its parallel. To those at a distance the details we have endeavoured to collect and embody may appear exaggerated and the work more of fancy than of fact; but we can only assert that we pledge ourselves to the literal accuracy of every circumstance we furnish … an intense feeling appears to have taken hold of the popular mind – a feeling widely spread and deeply rooted – planted, we verily believe, in a religious soil, and promising to bring forth the fruits of joy and happiness … But even the sceptic has learned that a great – an unexpected movement has at length set in, and he scarcely doubts, from what he has seen, that it will stop before it embraces the entire of the land … It was a truly glorious sight, and one which can never be effaced from the memory of those who witnessed it. As each batch rose up after repeating the words of the pledge, brightness glowed in their countenances – such expressions as 'Thank God, we are happy now' – 'Heaven bless you, Father Mathew', issued from the lips of the regenerated … Ballad singers chanting temperance songs, and songs in praise of Father Mathew, are heard in every street. Heretofore none other then baccnalian [sic] songs were heard from the lips of these vocalists. Parties are driving a profitable trade by hawking certain statistics with respect to the progress of the cause … The cheers of the people are loud and universal; they press upon him from every side, and bow down in homage before him. Though the cavalry and police are

> exerting themselves to keep the crowds from approaching, and impeding his way, they find it impossible. The people are impetuous, and [are] with difficulty restrained from bearing him upon their shoulders ... Popular enthusiasm has never, we believe, been carried to such an inconceivable degree.[50]

Although pains were taken by some incredulous observers to keep an accurate count, as at Limerick, the numbers pledged could only be estimated. The *Waterford Mirror* reported that some 80,000 had pledged, and a figure somewhere between 70,000 and 90,000 appears to be reasonable.[51] In just over a week, therefore, Father Mathew had enlarged his already considerable society by a factor of about five, and, even on a conservative estimate, the CTAS now had well over a quarter-million members.

The response in Limerick and Waterford inspired Mathew to accept further invitations to expand his missionary work. Before he left Waterford, Mathew had informed Bishop Foran that he planned to visit nearby Wexford shortly, and he promised the people of Clonmel that he would visit there within a week.[52] 'Invitations', as one of his biographers explained, 'were pouring from every side.'[53] Later that month he was granted free travel on Peter Purcell's system of coaches, and made steady use of the privilege.[54] From December 1839 until the end of March 1840, Mathew gave at least 25 missions in 24 towns (Clonmel received two visits) in the nine southwestern counties of Ireland, as indicated on Map 1 in the Map Appendix, all at the request of the local parish priest and Temperance society, each with the approval of a local bishop.[55] Mathew therefore averaged nearly two towns a week for the 13-week span, a blistering pace that meant that after Christmas he was seldom in Cork for more than a day or two at a time. Each of these meetings attracted thousands if not tens of thousands of new recruits, and it was not unusual for a crowd to assemble at those towns where the horses were changed and for hundreds to take the pledge then and there.[56] As the *Waterford Chronicle* pointed out, after his successful visit to Galway in March, where some 60,000 to 80,000 pledged, the Temperance movement had converted much of the southwest of the country, and the enthusiasm was, if anything, still growing. 'His reception here has fully borne out the glowing and almost incredible description of his progress through the Southern portions of this kingdom, with which the public has been so familiar during the last six months.'[57] By early April, the CTAS claimed some two million members, which was clearly an exaggeration.[58] Still, the actual numbers pledged were enormous, almost certainly a million and perhaps many more.

PART II: 'A UNIVERSAL CONSPIRACY'

> *What are the causes – what the motives – how can so many be got to abandon so prevailing a propensity? Is it political? Is it religious, Jesuitical, revolutionary, or what is it?*
>
> – *The Pilot*, March 1840.

One of the keys to appreciating how significant a change in the social landscape Temperance had effected is to realise how difficult a time astonished observers in late 1839 and early 1840 had in explaining what was universally acknowledged to be a moral revolution. In general, however, it can be said that emerging characterisations of the Temperance movement fell into one of four by no means necessarily mutually exclusive major categories, providing providential, rational, conspiratorial and superstitious explanations for the success of the CTAS. Despite the movement's ecumenical roots and its explicit rejection of politics as such, however, these categories of explanation ultimately fed into broader, pre-existing public debates. The degree to which the new phenomena of mass Temperance quickly became involved in contemporary sectarian and political divisions bears depressing witness to the primacy of those divisions in pre-Famine Irish society.

Those who adhered to a providential characterisation of Temperance's rise maintained quite simply that the extraordinary enthusiasm was inexplicable; that it must in fact be the direct result of divine intervention on a scale seldom seen in human history. Mathew's letter of 9 December quoted above indicates that he was of this opinion, and many agreed with him, including Nicholas Foran, Waterford's Bishop, who told teetotallers at a meeting held in the wake of Mathew's visit that the movement's success was 'the work of Divine Providence'.[59] The *Southern Reporter*'s editor termed the 'truly blessed revolution' a 'miraculous project', while the editor of the *Tipperary Free Press* felt that it was 'impossible to overestimate the importance of this great moral movement, by which, as by a spell, the leading ill of an entire people is cast off'.[60] The sentiments of the press were echoed in popular ballads and poems.[61]

A second characterisation – rationalism – was often combined with providentialism and drew heavily on the movement's own propaganda. Its proponents insisted that the Irish people were reacting rationally to the CTAS's call to reject their most serious social problem, and that postulants recognised the many potential benefits to the individual of sobriety. The massive scale of the response was the result of a widely-shared sense of Ireland's degraded status, and a common appreciation of the central role alcohol played in perpetuating that degradation. Popular enthusiasm for the cause, therefore, was ultimately based on the rising tide of public opinion, itself founded on a growing sense that Temperance could transform the nation by establishing what James McKenna and John Francis Maguire had termed 'moral liberty'. In such a spirit the *Cork Standard* lauded 'feelings of enthusiasm which are now so general', the *Waterford Chronicle* noted that 'a change, an inconceivable change has come over the spirit of the people', while the *Dublin Weekly Herald* explained that there was 'something more than excitement in the present movement; something more than the confidence which the people place in the potency of Mr Mathew'.[62]

Proponents of a rational view of the movement insisted that the cause's true nature, despite the enthusiasm which surrounded the CTAS, was plainly evident. As 'a miner' from Kill explained to the *Waterford Chronicle*, 'the movement was not so hot or so quick as many imagine'.[63] 'When the present opportunity was offered and supported by their own ministers', the miner argued, 'it was gladly seized as a rescue from a vice which men were already tired.' The editor of the *Waterford Chronicle* also insisted that most of the people knew exactly what they were doing when they took the pledge, pointing out that 'no thinking, rational man can be so stultified as not to have perceived that a very large portion, also, of the squalid poverty of our countrymen has been owing to the demoralising and soul-destroying propensity for ardent spirits'.[64]

Those who insisted on the cause's fundamental rationality often emphasised Temperance's patriotic dimension. The *Southern Reporter*'s editor decided that Temperance would, 'we confidently trust, be among the most efficient agents in effecting the moral and social regeneration of our country'.[65] 'The New Christmas Ballad', noted above, echoed the sentiment, and described the new Irishmen, 'all brothers'. 'And with the cash that made us brutes,/We'll found mechanic's institutes … Plenty and piety,/Peace and sobriety,/Flourish as long as from drink we abstain.' The anonymous author of the poem did not hesitate to make clear the collective nature of the new movement: 'From north to south, from east to west,/We'll conquer all the land./For Ireland, old Ireland, this is the happy day!'

The conspiratorial and superstitious characterisations of the rise of the CTAS were less sympathetic than those of providentialism and rationalism, and found their most vehement expression in the Tory press. Those who upheld the conspiratorial explanation, which was deeply rooted in Protestant/English fears, were quite hostile to the cause. The *Carlow Sentinal*'s editor, for example, warned that

> Thousands we know have flocked to the standard of Priest Mathew. This fact not only should excite suspicion, but jealousy when we remember that the people flocked in crowds to the chapels in the County of Wexford, and pledged themselves to abstain from the consumption of ardent spirits, just before the rebellion burst forth on the country – breathing blood and slaughter on every side.[66]

A still more anxious editorial in the *Limerick Standard* the same month insisted that 'we are *openly menaced with rebellion in Ireland*'.[67]

> It is in aid of such an event that the Mathewite reform, as it is called, is so much lauded by the Irish priesthood and the Popish press, and it is in aid of such an event that the Roman Catholics who take the pledge are ordered to the confessional *as they now are*, and thus it is, that the whole system of teetotal reform and organisation is found a powerful engine in aid of that plot, we have no manner of doubt.

By January, the *London Times* was quoting the *Dublin Gazette*'s condemnation 'in plain language' of the cause as 'a universal conspiracy' involving the 'multitudes', only 'temporarily against a flagrant evil'.[68] The movement was 'capable, at an hour's notice', the *Gazette* warned, of 'applying its enrolment and ensignery to any purpose, now mysterious and known but to a few, to which that few might deem it right to direct the energies of this conscription'. Nor was this paranoid argument the preserve of a few. By early 1840, the idea that, whatever Mathew's intentions, his campaign served as a 'powerful engine' in the service of some approaching Irish rebellion was quite widespread.[69]

A final, more condescending if sometimes less hostile explanation for the rise of the CTAS maintained that Mathew's success was a consequence of the intensely superstitious, passionate and irrational nature of the Irish peasantry. The vague accusation that the movement thrived in a climate of 'superstition' was commonplace. As early as July 1839, for example, the *Nenagh Guardian* scornfully noticed the work of 'Priest Mathew', and related a story about his alleged 'magical power'.[70] The most strident and persistent charges of superstitious motivations, of course, came from those Protestant quarters that regarded Catholicism in general, and Irish Catholics in particular, as prone to irrational behaviour. Irish Catholics, many believed, were so deeply steeped in superstition that it was impossible to imagine any form of popular collective behaviour occurring in Ireland that was *not* rooted in an irrational appreciation of the supernatural, and, quite probably, the diabolical.

This attitude was intensified after Limerick and Waterford. The size and turmoil of these meetings reinforced a variety of stereotypes, and led the *Kerry Post*, for example, to brand Limerick a 'deeply disgusting affair' that provided clear evidence of the unseemly 'influence' of priestcraft.[71] The *Waterford Mail*, was particularly disturbed by the spectacle of 'a mortal hailed as a deity, before whom thousands fell prostrate in adoration', and could 'conceive no terms of reprobation sufficiently strong' to describe the event.[72] In the very same spirit, the *Standard* approvingly reprinted an editorial from the *Carlow Sentinel*, which warned that the movement's success 'does not emanate from any desire founded on pure religion to abstain from vice, but from motivations of superstitious reverence to the supposed miraculous powers possessed by the Cork Priest'.[73] 'The poor people', the *Sentinel* charged, 'steeped and saturated with bigotry, are now falling away from drunkenness and into the opposite extreme of gross superstition; for surely in the darkest age of Popery, the votaries of priest-craft could not believe a more soul-destroying doctrine than this; that pieces of medal, purchased in Birmingham by the gross, can perform miracles in Ireland, when passing through the hands of a sinful creature like Priest Mathew.' By July, the editor of the *Mayo Constitution* was simply reflecting a common Protestant opinion when he termed Father Mathew's visit to Castlebar 'a great day for superstition'.[74]

Each of these explanations of Temperance's earliest dramatic successes intensified as the movement prospered during 1840 and after. In many ways, however, fundamental divisions – between those who viewed the CTAS as a blessing from God, or a harbinger of bloodshed and rebellion; between those who saw the campaign either as a demonstration of the underlying common sense of the Irish people, or as a species of the worst sort of superstitious ignorance – had been firmly established. The political implications of the movement quickly came to revolve around Daniel O'Connell's Repeal campaign, and will be explored at length in subsequent chapters. The reason vs. superstition debate, however, is worth examining at this point in greater detail, as it leads directly to the central question raised by the crusade's important early achievements – why did so many pledge so quickly?

To begin with, it is important to acknowledge the very real limitations of any explanation that relies on the superstitious character of the peasantry. That position, a favourite of some critics of the movement, has been partly endorsed by contemporary scholarly observers.[75] Leaving aside the subjective and pejorative nature of the term, there are evidentiary and theoretical problems with locating the motivation to pledge in superstition. It is certainly correct to point out that a wealth of evidence associates aspects of 'superstition', or folk belief, with the

Temperance movement, and establishes those beliefs as being widespread by late 1839 throughout the southwest of Ireland. In particular, Father Mathew was widely supposed to have the power to work miraculous cures. This was, however, a fairly commonplace, even a stock attribute among certain Irish priests.[76] If this belief alone was sufficient to explain the CTAS's appeal there would have been many successful mass movements led by priests in pre-Famine Ireland. In fact, it would have been odd, given the enormous success of the movement, if Mathew had not been invested with them by some of the people. Such powers were often markers, rather than conveyors, of respect and authority. While it was likely that this notion contributed to the widespread conviction that Mathew's pledge was particularly effective and carried with it a kind of blessing, it is by no means clear that Mathew's 'magical' properties were a cause rather than a consequence of his success, particularly since there is no mention of such a belief among the earliest accounts of pledging in Cork, nor is there any indication that such beliefs about Mathew preceded his involvement with Temperance.[77] Other superstitions centred on pledge-breaking, which was often associated with a wide range of divinely ordained punishments.[78] Men and women who disregarded so powerful an obligation were widely believed to subject themselves to much supernatural misfortune, up to and often including death, as a consequence.

Besides these two core beliefs – in Mathew's magical powers, and in the eager anticipation of divine wrath and retributive justice for pledge-breakers – which might be termed superstitions, there also appears to have been a less commonplace belief that the Temperance medal acted as a kind of talisman or charm. It does need to be noted that, although much was made of superstitions about Temperance medals, according to Mathew and others, many who took the pledge never bothered to obtain them, or did so only to appease employers.[79]

The Constabulary Circulars of March 1840 specifically addressed the role of superstition in the growth and practice of Temperance. The results of the circulars are interesting, if far from conclusive. Police were asked if 'taking the pledge appear to be associated with superstitious feelings in many instances; – such as the expectation of immediate manifestations of Divine judgement, in the event of violating it, etc.'[80] The varied responses may have been prejudiced by the leading and confusing nature of the question – some respondents simply answered 'yes', while others focused only on the question's second part. Overall, however, of 69 responses, nearly two-thirds (45) agreed that superstition played some role in the movement. Of these, more than two-thirds (27) confined their comments to popular fears about divine punishment for pledge breakers – Constable W. Coffey, for instance, reported from county Galway that people believed that 'calamity befalls breakers', while B. Clinch observed 'it is the general impression among the people that the violation of the pledge will expose the violator to the anger of heaven'.

Of the 18 remaining responses which acknowledged superstitious behaviour, nine condemned the movement briefly and in general terms for being superstitious, while only nine directly maintained that the decision to pledge was in itself sometimes or often involved with superstition. Several respondents associated the movement's superstitious character with its sectarian composition. John Binoon in Portuma, Co. Galway, for example, believed that the pledge was associated with 'religious and superstitious feelings in almost every instance', while sub-inspector W. Booth felt that the best indicator of the movement's superstitious nature was that masses were said for the society and its members. Some thought superstition was 'diminishing' or evident only in 'several instances' or 'only among the very lowest orders' and 'the very ignorant', while for others it was a factor 'in a great many instances' or 'almost always'.

Eighteen other respondents did not answer the question, although from other comments, at least half of those viewed the pledge as a rational and considered act. A half-dozen explicitly denied that superstition was a significant characteristic of the movement at all. Captain Leyne, based in Nenagh, Co. Tipperary, insisted, typically, that 'the people appear to be fully sensible of the incalculable advantages to be derived from the alteration in their condition, as deeply affecting their social and moral interests'. This range of responses may reflect local differences, or the varying dispositions or investigative abilities of constables, but, given that many of the observers were Protestants, they are more likely the product of the kinds of sectarian biases and prejudices that make the whole question of superstition so perilous to the historian in the first place.

While the question and the responses to it in the circulars are too subjective to provide much more than anecdotal evidence, they make it clear that Mathew's contemporaries were vitally interested in the allegedly superstitious nature of the crusade. A glance at the Irish papers of the day, moreover, confirms that there was intense interest. Charges of superstition sparked some very vigorous defences of the crusade which argued for the essentially rational nature of the movement. An early example appeared in the *Southern Reporter* on 23 November 1839, in response to a report, quoted in full, from 'a London Tory journal' under the heading 'Wretched Superstition', which related that 'a priest in the South of Ireland has been lately inducing thousands of misguided papists in that country to flock to him, telling them that he can cure them from the love of whiskey; he gives his dupes a little piece of wood, or medal, over which he performs some mumming tricks, and for which he charges an exorbitant price, and the poor creatures depart with a firm conviction that the "relic" has the power of preserving them from the vice of drunkenness.'[81] This was held up as a 'ludicrous, and at the same time lamentable' example of 'the effect of the superstition and ignorance of the Popish peasantry'. The *Southern Reporter*'s outraged editor denied that pledging was a manifestation of superstition, charging that 'it would better suit the purposes of the people's enemies that they should remain slaves to this debasing foible'. 'A sober people', the editor remarked, 'have more leisure – more penetration – and more inclination to turn their attention to political subjects, from which their enemies would willingly shut them out.'

Others who argued that Temperance was rooted in rationality attributed the success of Mathew to his credibility in the Catholic community, a credibility founded on his practical charity. In December 1839, for example, the *Waterford Chronicle* quoted a Dublin barrister named Moore as asserting, at a Temperance meeting, 'in reply to the base wretches who talk so glibly about superstition', that 'one of the chief reasons of Mr Mathew's influence over the people was his well-known character for public and private benevolence – he was beloved as one of the most charitable men in Cork'.[82] Moore's explanation was a common one. James Bermingham's history of the movement, for example, published in the spring of 1840, also explained the movement's initial appeal in much the same way.[83]

Informed critics such as constable A.B. Hill in Dunmore, Co. Kilkenny acknowledged that Mathew did little or nothing to encourage popular superstitions. 'The deportment of the Rev. Mr Mathew', Hill reported to his superiors, 'did not create or encourage such [superstitions]. His was the mild demeanour of a clergyman giving individually his blessing to thousands and to a people who would not quit the ground without it.'[84] The very public and heated nature of the controversy nevertheless eventually prompted a response from Mathew. In September 1840, he engaged in a public exchange of letters with a Protestant clergyman in Claremorris. In a dignified reply to criticisms of the nature of his movement, Mathew denied that the act of pledging provided an example of mass hysteria, delusion, or collective superstition.[85] What superstitions existed in connection with the cause were 'as dust in the balance' of Temperance's manifest rational blessings. 'If I could prevent them without impeding the glorious cause', Mathew explained, of the superstitions which had sprung up in connection with his success, 'they would not have been permitted.' Mathew's position was the official view of the CTAS. John Francis Maguire, editorialising in the first number of the movement's organ, the *Cork Total Abstainer*, flatly rejected superstitious explanations for the movement's growth. 'As far as the city of Cork is concerned', he declared, 'we utterly deny the justice of the charge [of superstitious motivation to pledge]. To be sure there may be – as in other cases – a very few and singular exceptions.'[86]

Some conceded still less ground. John Kenyon, the curate of Silvermines in Co. Tipperary and a vocal participant in the superstition/rationality debate, admitted that most Catholics considered Mathew to be a holy man, and that many thought they saw the hand of God in the movement. Undoubtedly, he reasoned, this influenced many in their decision to join the society. Kenyon remained convinced, however, that the 'calumny of superstition' was little more than an expression of bigotry:

> Superstition, then, I would remark, in the mouths of certain Protestants, applies to almost every rite of our holy religion, and implies every insult thereto ... To expect a cure through Father Mathew is no more superstitious then to expect it through the sacrament of extreme unction. This letter, I know, will be called superstitious by Protestants; but so will baptism by some Quakers; so will prayer itself by liberals of the thorough temper. Catholics cannot help all this. Persons may no doubt be guilty of superstition in receiving the pledge and expecting a cure from Father Mathew, but they might also be guilty of the same crime in receiving the adorable Eucharist from his hands.[87]

All of this vociferous contemporary debate on the subject reveals much about perceptions of the CTAS as Catholic, but very little about the actual part that superstition played in the movement's initial success. That 'superstition', in the sense of the pre-Famine Irish peasantry's well-known (and perhaps overly-appreciated) concern with the supernatural, attached itself to the crusade is an undeniable but an ultimately uninformative observation. Superstition has its own logic, and needs to be understood on its own terms. The particular superstitions that were most frequently associated with the Temperance movement centred around the general notion that God endorsed the cause, as well as healings, the punishment of backsliders, and, less frequently, the supernatural properties of Temperance medals. None of these beliefs, however widely held they may have been, provides a satisfying explanation for the scale of the movement's initial success. Mathew was doubtless invested by some with the power to 'cure' drunkenness, but that did not compel people to visit him seeking such a cure, or convince the masses that drinking was, for whatever reason, wrong at all times and in all places. If the people merely sought blessings or marks of divine approval, there were a wealth of other, more reliable, less onerous and novel avenues for obtaining them, including holy wells, pilgrimages and fasting. None of the evidence from the movement's earliest meetings and almost none of its extant propaganda made even the most veiled appeal to these, or any other superstitions.[88] The fact that there was a great deal of evidence of popular beliefs associated with the breaking of the pledge but far fewer connected with the taking of it is significant. The pledge itself, and the decision to pledge in particular, was not generally associated with specific 'superstitious' practices. Even those who regarded the movement with disdain or suspicion, for example, seldom asserted that there were specific superstitions that led people to pledge out of fear or a desire for good luck. The underlying question – why the movement became suddenly so attractive to so many who knew so little about Temperance and Father Mathew prior to 1839 – remains.

Putting aside for the moment the interested gloss placed on pledging by advocates and critics of the cause, it is important to acknowledge that an atomised reconstruction of the motivation for pledging of the hundreds of thousands who had done so by December 1839, or the millions of Mathew's disciples who pledged shortly after, would of course be quite impossible. Even in those few cases where some of the relevant facts are known, there is simply too much speculation involved. What are we to make, for example, of the behaviour of George Carr, the parish priest of New Ross, who made two trips to Waterford during Mathew's first visit there, each time with many hundreds of parishioners in tow?[89] Was Carr currying favour with Nicholas Foran, his teetotal bishop? Attempting to control popular enthusiasm? Following what he perceived to be Divine direction? Did he cajole, threaten or inspire his parishioners, or was he swept along by them? And what of the wistful middle-aged man, apparently 'a fervent votary of the Jolly God' observed at an early meeting, who, after draining a glass of whiskey, was supposed to have said "Farewell, whiskey, my darling; we part now for ever. God be with you." 'The ejaculation', a reporter further informed us, 'was echoed with enthusiasm by his companions, and, having drained out the last drop, they went en-masse to the place of general rendez-vous.'[90] And when the crippled, the blind and the lame jostled Mathew in Waterford and other places, took the pledge and begged Mathew's touch or blessing, should the historian assume that did they do so only in the 'superstitious' expectation of a miraculous deliverance from their obvious afflictions?

With this in mind, it is still worthwhile to assemble some of the anecdotal accounts from the movement's early days in order to attempt to understand what was leading Irish men and women to take the pledge in such numbers. As the last chapter noted, some who pledged were compelled or encouraged to do so by employers, landlords and clergy. In this regard, however, pressure from family, friends and community quickly became far more important. Some of the best moments in Maguire's biography of Mathew, for example, are entertaining descriptions of reluctant postulants. Maguire spent time in Mathew's parlour assisting in the enrolment of early members, and his description of 'Patsy', a 'big, brawny fellow, with rough voice, bloodshot eyes, and tattered clothes' is a composite.[91] Maguire refers to him as 'one of a class', brought to Mathew by their 'poor wives and mothers endeavouring to soothe and keep them under control':

> But just as Patsy was about effecting his escape, and swearing that 'he would never be the one of his name to demane himself by taking their dirty pledge', he was certain to be arrested by Father Mathew himself … Catching Patsy with a grasp stronger than the one from which he had escaped, Father Mathew would say, in a cheerful voice to Patsy, as if that gentleman had come of his own free will to implore the pledge at his own hands – 'Welcome! Welcome, my dear, delighted to see you. Glad you are come to me. You are doing a good day's work for yourself and your family. You will have God's blessing on your head. Poverty is no crime, my dear child, it is sin alone that lowers us in the eyes of God. Kneel down, my dear (a strong pressure on Patsy's shoulder, under which Patsy reluctantly sinks to his knees) and repeat the words of the pledge after me …' What could poor Patsy do but yield, as that magnetic hand rested affectionately on his tangled locks? And so Patsy's name was added to the long muster roll of the pledged.

While there are other accounts of families bringing barely repentant hard-drinking relatives to Father Mathew, much of the influence brought to bear on individuals to pledge was more broadly communal. This was notably the case after Limerick and Waterford, when mass meetings created the context in which most took the pledge, but there was a communal character to the movement from its earliest days in Cork, and even from the beginning most appear to have pledged in the company of family and friends. The emerging critical mass of teetotallers ensured that at least in some places those who chose not to pledge risked much more than the loss of the good offices of their social superiors, or, in the case of the 'superstitious', a run of bad luck – they risked rejection at the hands of their friends and neighbours. Sometimes such social pressure could be cruel, as an encounter related at a Waterford Temperance meeting by Father Mathew revealed.[92] Near Bundoran, in Co. Donegal, a young girl had stopped his coach. 'O

Father Mathew', she was supposed to have related tearfully, 'I will lose my life if you don't give me the pledge – How is that, my child – I am the only one on the bog, she replied, that has not taken it, and all the neighbours are telling me I am stealing turf.' In places like Dungarvan, where many if not all of the fishermen took the pledge, it was equally difficult to remain unpledged.[93] And if pressure from co-workers could be a spur to pledge, imagine the anxiety of unpledged women at Carrick-on-Suir, when, in a burst of enthusiasm after the Waterford meeting, hundreds of 'the young men who have joined the ranks of the temperance society' resolved to choose only 'for their partners of life females of their own society – complete tee-totallers'.[94] Some of the constabulary reports support this picture of widespread social pressure to pledge. Constables were asked about the state of relations between the pledged and the unpledged in their localities, and many reported 'a strong feeling manifested, on the part of those who have accepted it, towards those who have declined it; they sometimes refuse to work with them'.[95] As Temperance became widely adopted, many, no doubt, feared being left behind by their communities, which, at the end of the day, was all the security that most of the peasantry had in this world.

It has already been argued, however, despite these examples of the many ways that reluctant men and women were strongly encouraged to join the ranks of the temperate, that most who pledged did so willingly, even eagerly, sometimes in the face of pressure not to. The communal zeal of converts during these months of initial expansion for the CTAS still reveals a great deal about the nature of Temperance as a popular movement. Indeed, the cause's most striking feature was the enthusiasm, emotion and eagerness with which most of the people embraced it. Reluctant pledgers were the exception, not the rule. The people attended Temperance meetings as they attended a fair, and with the exception of the administration of the pledge itself, there was nothing solemn about the occasion, particularly not in these early days when 'farewells to whiskey' were indulged in with vigour. The accounts presented of Limerick and Waterford bear out this point. Many walked nearly 100 miles to attend the gatherings, although the Waterford meeting took place in a steady rain. James Bermingham's description of Mathew's visit to Borrisokane, of which he was the parish priest, in the spring of 1840 reinforces the uninhibited enthusiasm that marked Mathew's early visits:

> Mr Mathew arrived late at night, and unexpectedly. Only a few had been aware of his arrival; and in the morning when I waited on him, the postulants were but thinly scattered ... fame, however, was busy trumpeting the rev. gentleman's visit to our neighbourhood ... each moment Mr Mathew was on the point of moving away; but each moment

> brought numbers from the surrounding parishes, who having heard that the rev. Gentleman had been in Borrisokane, threw aside their various implements of industry, and hurried to enlist themselves under the standard of temperance … fatigued and breathless, men, women and children rushed forward indiscriminately to take the pledge.[96]

Several contemporary sources note that Temperance, before and during this second phase of rapid expansion, had caught the popular imagination. The mobbing of Mathew on visits to his family in August and September 1839 were a reflection of the positive light that Temperance had come to be seen in. A miner, writing in the *Cork Standard* in November 1839, captured the mood perfectly in his description of the joyous expedition of a group of fellow-workers to take the pledge, and finished his letter by proclaiming 'What a great reformation is this! Grand in its manner, for it is instantaneous – grand in its extent – spreading to thousands – yes, and it will be to millions; grand in its effect – changing from vice to virtue – giving happiness to families – peace – yes, and it will Liberty to the Country. God prosper the cause.'[97] James Haughton, a Dublin social reformer and a friend of Mathew's, summed up the situation when he recalled, 'it was the people who gathered round [Mathew] and threw themselves heart and soul into the movement'.[98]

Temperance had become effectively linked to a variety of other ideas about Ireland's past and future, which added immensely to its appeal. It was talked about everywhere, as W. Jones, a constable stationed in Dunmanway, Co. Cork, was informed by a friend in the country early in 1840: 'The chief topic of conversation recently has been the benefits, and the progress of temperance.'[99] This enthusiastic spirit, when combined with the electric atmosphere of enormous crowds, music and processions that marked the first hugely successful mass meetings, inspired many to pledge. To quote the *Limerick Chronicle*, on the eve of Mathew's arrival in that city, 'many persons who never contemplated such a change, whose habits of life, in the opinion of their neighbours, required no such change, carried away by the feelings of enthusiasm which are now so general, have resolved to join the order of temperance'.[100] By March 1840, the spread of Temperance through much of the southwest of Ireland had been sudden, dramatic and largely unanticipated. Mathew, who had consistently underestimated the appeal of his campaign, was growing in confidence.[101] Over the coming months, the CTAS was to come into its own as a national movement, as Mathew's missions spread to Dublin, much of the north and west of Ireland, and indeed throughout every part of the country he was able to visit.

CHAPTER THREE

Temperance Triumphant: A Moral Revolution Achieved

For all its speed, the tremendous initial progress of the CTAS had not been entirely even. If the Temperance movement was to sustain its expansion and achieve its own oft-proclaimed objective of regenerating a degraded Ireland, the organisation needed not only broad popular appeal across the entire country, but also strong support from the more influential classes of Irish society. Mathew and his lieutenants did all they could to gain that support from the clergy of all denominations as well as the aristocracy and the upper classes. Their efforts were particularly aggressive during and immediately following Father Mathew's first visit to Dublin in March 1840. While its success in winning over these important groups in the community was only partial, the degree to which the CTAS managed to transform Irish society in the short run was nothing short of astounding. Mathew's missionary labours extended to every corner of Ireland. By the end of 1840, and for the next several years, Irish public life was marked by a vigorous, enthusiastic and pervasive Temperance ethic. That ethic, like the early expansion of the movement, was built upon popular, rather than elite, foundations. The moral revolution had triumphed.

By March 1840, Father Mathew and the CTAS had come a long way towards realising the complete transformation of Irish society that they had begun so quixotically some two years earlier. To the surprise and amazement of all observers, a nearly universally temperate and thoroughly regenerated Ireland now seemed a genuine possibility. In those parts of the country that Mathew had visited, the change was widely recognised. By mid-March, when Saint Patrick's Day, which had come to be marked by much heavy drinking, passed off quietly and soberly across the south, it only confirmed that a revolution had occurred. As one newspaper editor pointed out:

> Saint Patrick's Day has come and gone. It came laden with promise to the

> confiding – with doubt, nay, with the certainty it would be sullied, to others – but the Rubicon has been passed, and Irishmen have shown what they will they can do – and that in the inflexible adherence to duty and principle they have no superiors in any part of the globe. Our accounts from every part of the South are of a character the most cheering.[1]

The same newspaper also reported that 'it is now an ordinary prayer, in conversation, to hope that "God may prosper the good cause"'.[2] The *Connaught Journal*, for its part, was no less amazed by near universal sobriety in that province:

> It may be questioned whether the annals of profane history can furnish anything like a parallel to the mighty moral revolution which for some time past has been under the guiding hand of the emancipator the Very Rev. T. Mathew, who has been (And not undeservedly) styled the great Apostle of Temperance – how strange to the philosopher! How gratifying to the patriot! And how sublimely beautiful to the philanthropist! – appears the great contrast between the moral condition of Ireland a few months ago and her condition at present.[3]

Set against the Temperance crusade's already considerable accomplishments, and even greater promise, however, were at least two significant barriers to its continued progress. In the first place, Mathew's crusade depended on the support of the local clergy, particularly given that the CTAS's own widely-promulgated rules placed them at the head of parish-based branch societies. Not only was the active and enthusiastic leadership of the parish clergy essential, therefore, for the organisation of effective local societies, but the continued geographical expansion of the crusade also depended on the willingness of Catholic clergy and bishops to invite Mathew to their parishes and dioceses, because Mathew was absolutely opposed to unsanctioned visits. The evolving relationship between Mathew's crusade and his Church was complex and will be examined in detail later, but it must be noted here that while a substantial portion of the clergy had welcomed the crusade, many with a great deal of enthusiasm, support for Temperance was by no means the norm among the clergy in early 1840, and even qualified endorsement was absent in many quarters. In order to continue its expansion, and to sustain local societies, the movement needed to imbue more of the clergy with the excitement already affecting the laity.

In the second place, the movement needed to enhance its limited appeal, to date, among Ireland's upper classes. The argument has been made in previous chapters that the CTAS was characterised by a strong determination to convert all Irish men and women, regardless of class or creed, as a consequence of its leadership's ideology and sense of mission. The hesitancy of many outside of the lower classes to enlist in the crusade was a cause for much concern within the CTAS. James Haughton, the Dublin Quaker Temperance advocate and a close associate of Father Mathew, diagnosed the problem in February 1840, in the midst of the initial enthusiasm for the cause, when he noted that 'the poor are willing to listen to our advice, and are joining our association with alacrity', but 'the rich keep aloof'. 'What', wondered Haughton, 'is the cause of this? Are they so enslaved to their drinking customs, that they cannot give them up for the benefit of their fellow-men?'[4] As the upper orders in pre-famine Ireland were disproportionately Protestant, to some extent this difficulty must be understood as a natural reflection of pre-existing sectarian cleavages. Mathew's first mission to Limerick had, in keeping with his ecumenical reputation and the CTAS's Protestant roots, managed to attract several hundred Protestant postulants, an encouraging sign.[5] Immediately afterwards, however, Mathew's crusade was branded by much of the Protestant press as a prime example of superstitious 'popish priestcraft', and Protestants seldom pledged thereafter, as at Waterford, where only two were known to have done so.[6] An ugly sectarian controversy over a Protestant rector's refusal to allow Mathew the use of the Rock of Cashel for a meeting there in February 1840 contributed to the problem, and the movement never became popular with Protestants.[7] The evidence makes it clear, however, that Catholics above a certain rank also held back from the crusade in its early months.

Along with its sectarian dimension, the CTAS's class problem had two other important aspects. The first of these related to obtaining the approval and patronage of the aristocracy and the very wealthy, most of whom were Protestants. The second involved inducing the increasingly Catholic 'middle classes', consisting of professionals, larger tenant farmers, merchants, substantial shopkeepers, and well-to-do tradesmen, to assume active leadership roles in the burgeoning crusade. Haughton's contention that the crusade had not succeeded in enlisting either Protestant or Catholic upper-class support was borne out by the Constabulary Reports, which provide a revealing glimpse of the class structure of the movement as it stood in March 1840. Constables were asked to report how many men above the working class had taken the pledge. The responses naturally reflected varying degrees of sensitivity about class on the part of the constabulary, but of the 60 extant replies, 50 describe a movement dominated by the poorer classes. Ten respondents thought the cause had succeeded to some degree in enlisting all levels of society, at least among Catholics, and in a few places, there did appear to be a great deal of involvement in the movement by 'gentlemen' and the well-to-do. At Tralee, for example, constable G. Rich reported that, while most who pledged were 'servants and the lower orders', the resident gentry 'of all parties' had endorsed the movement. At Cahir in Co. Tipperary, meanwhile, 'a great number of both men and women above working class' had pledged, according to constable Louis Anderson, an observation that was echoed at Newport and Nenagh in the same county, as well as at Enniscorthy, Co. Wexford and Listowel in Kerry, and in both Limerick and Waterford cities.

Most of the constabulary, however, viewed things differently. They described a movement disproportionately composed of labourers, servants and tradesmen, leavened with some proportion of shopkeepers and small farmers. Sub Inspector P. Morgan reported that in Roscrea, Co. Tipperary, none 'above the rank of shopkeepers and clerks' had pledged.[8] Similarly, a Captain Duff reported from Borrisokane, also in Tipperary, that those who pledged there were 'disproportionately from the lower class'. John McLeod, in Tipperary Town, thought that the pledged there were from 'the middle and the lower classes'. Labourers, clerks and servants not surprisingly comprised a disproportionate share of the CTAS's early adherents. These men and women stood to gain the most from the Temperance movement's promises of instant social respectability and improved material circumstances, and the constabulary reports certainly reveal their enthusiasm for the cause.

The presence of farmers and shopkeepers, who joined in numbers, if not always in proportion to their share of the population, and who constituted the practical elite of the CTAS, led many observers like McLeod to determine that Temperance had a broader appeal. The participation of the better class of farmers in particular was an important gauge of the long-term viability of the crusade, and some constables took careful note of their involvement.[9] Given the close contacts between shopkeepers and the farmers, tradesmen and labourers who patronised them, it is not surprising that this class should be more inclined to join so popular a movement. When they joined, shopkeepers seem to have done so in large numbers.[10]

While shopkeepers, and to a lesser extent comfortable tenant farmers, joined in some areas, it is important to note that in others, respondents described societies bereft of respectable membership. W.J. Tracy, RM, responded from Bruff, Co. Limerick, that Temperance there was a matter for 'the lower orders almost exclusively', by which he meant 'tradesmen, small farmers, labourers and servants of both sexes', while G. Fitzgerald, RM, reported that in Killenaule, Co. Tipperary the pledged were also 'almost exclusively working class men and women'.[11] In Kilkenny town, the few shopkeepers and 'respectable mechanics' who had pledged were anxious to return their medals, and Constable Thompson reported that 'this class of persons do not appear to feel any interest in the progress of temperance'.

The constabulary reports, therefore, do indicate that there was a widespread reluctance among certain classes to join the Temperance society. Doubtless some were suspicious of the crusade's air of enthusiastic extremism. To a large extent, however, this reluctance must be attributed to the fact that the CTAS, because it actively recruited among the nation at large and placed no financial or literacy barriers to membership, possessed a decidedly plebeian profile that discouraged many from participating. Judging from the CTAS's own appeals, there were widespread anxieties about the potential damage to the dignity of individuals caused by the rituals associated with public pledging; fears that those who pledged would be perceived to have been drunkards; and concern about the lower-class character of the CTAS itself.[12] A Cork 'skillig' ballad[13] from 1840, lamenting the social death of a local rake, plays off the latter two prejudices:

> One old in iniquity, and young in years,
> I fancy still the public house resounds,
> With Tom thy boisterous mirth and 'calls for other rounds'
> Before your taproom drunken notoriety,
> Caus'ed you, my lad, to join the Tem'prance Society,
> At length you've found your proper level,
> With butter-snatchers, cleave boys, now you revel …
> For Tommy, who was once a dandy,
> HAS NEITHER WHISKEY, WINE, NOR BRANDY.[14]

Constable Brudenell Plummer's report from County Clare that 'persons above the rank of working class' were 'anxious to conceal' the fact that they had taken the pledge may represent an extreme position, but the unwillingness of many of the upper classes to involve themselves with Temperance was a serious concern for the early movement.

FATHER MATHEW IN DUBLIN

While enthusiasm for the Temperance cause was rapidly becoming very widespread, Mathew's missions had been restricted to only ten of Ireland's 32 counties. The vast majority of Mathew's converts were from the southwest and south central parts of Ireland. Parts of

Connaught and all of Ulster remained unconverted, while Dublin, Ireland's largest city, was largely untouched by the new wave of Temperance euphoria.[15] Success on the national stage that the CTAS's founders hoped for required a triumph in the nation's principle city. Demonstrations in Dublin on the same scale as those that had already occurred in the southwest would shake off any remaining suspicions that the movement was parochial. As Mathew explained later in 1840, 'the eyes of the whole kingdom are fixed on the metropolis; the good example given here will have double the effect produced in other parts of the country, and consequently the results will be more important.'[16] Mathew knew that the eyes of many Irish churchmen also would be fixed on Dublin's extremely influential Archbishop, Daniel Murray, whose endorsement of the cause would doubtless win over many wavering clergymen. Finally, Mathew hoped that an equally public embrace of Temperance by the Dublin elite, Catholic and Protestant alike, would inspire men and women of substance to join the CTAS across all of Ireland, thereby producing an army of patrons, ready and willing to assist the burgeoning numbers of local societies eagerly searching for musical instruments, band uniforms, reading rooms and funds for tea-parties. With all of this in mind, Mathew arranged a week-long mission to Dublin for the end of March 1840, by far his longest stay yet in any Irish city outside Cork.

Mathew was aided by the fact that many in Dublin, frustrated by continued intemperance, anxiously awaited his arrival and expected a grand triumph. As the editor of the *Dublin Evening Press* noted,

> Dublin, it must be confessed, is behind the rest of the country. If Father Mathew could give us six weeks – for a mere visit would not do here – he would accomplish greater wonders than he has as yet achieved. We know, indeed, very well, that the excellent Catholic clergy of this city are zealously engaged in the work – and that Father Yore and Father O'Connell have very thriving and constantly augmenting societies. What we want, however, is the general, the simultaneous impulse. We wish to get rid of drunkenness in Dublin as quickly and as completely as they have done in Waterford, Clonmel, and Limerick.[17]

The much-anticipated visit, once announced, was widely and fulsomely publicised. The *Freeman's Journal* was typically enthusiastic:

> Our city will be honoured on Sunday next by the distinguished presence of the great man, whose name and almost supernatural achievements have latterly become the universal theme throughout the entire kingdom ... the wonderful exertions of this singular man in eradicating from the country a vice which seemed to have seized upon its very vitals, have

> invested him with such a surpassing interest, and excited such a desire even to see him, as cannot fail to make thousands throng round the standard of his glorious cause.[18]

Mathew was to arrive in Dublin on Sunday, 29 March, and preach a ticketed charity sermon on behalf of '50 destitute orphans' at the Pro-Cathedral in Marlborough Street. The Dublin papers had also announced he would administer the pledge in Beresford Place, near the Customs House, the next day.[19] Mathew made a triumphal entrance into Dublin on Saturday, and on the following day many prominent Dubliners attended the sermon, including the Lord Lieutenant. Still, the *Freeman's Journal* observed that while the sanctuary area was packed, neither the nave 'nor the remaining portions of the building were crowded to the extent which the celebrity of the great apostle would induce us to expect'.[20] The enthusiastic scenes outside the church in the streets before and after the sermon, despite the presence of nearly 100 policemen, were further evidence that Mathew's strongest appeal, in Dublin as in the country, was to those too poor to pay the price of admission:

> On leaving the scene of his eloquence and getting into his carriage, the multitudes, who still remained outside in undiminished numbers, evinced such eagerness to behold the mighty advocate of charity and of abstinence from the intoxicating draught, was such as to temporarily impede his departure. His progress back to the hotel was attended by a countless throng, by whom he was cheered almost unceasingly, and who, after he had alighted, remained in the street in front of the hotel. Mr Mathew, after a short interval, presented himself on the balcony and briefly addressed the people below.[21]

The weather on Monday, 30 March, the first day of public pledging, was terrible: a 'heavy, drizzling, continuous rain'. Although many still came to gape, fewer than 4,700 (closely counted by both the police and the press) actually took the pledge. Even allowing for considerable exaggeration in less careful counts of the numbers who had pledged in other parts of Ireland, this was a remarkably low total. Mathew's exhortations (carried as the major news of the day by the Dublin papers) and better weather on Tuesday improved matters, but only marginally so, as some 8,000 took the pledge. By week's end, Mathew had extended his visit by several days and still had only enrolled some 50,000.[22]

The total does not seem to have disappointed Mathew. The relatively low numbers pledged in Dublin did not reflect a lack of enthusiasm for Temperance. During the week, the numbers enrolled mounted daily, and in fact there appear to have been many people each day who did not get an opportunity to take the pledge.[23] Mathew claimed that the steady influx of converts led him to extend his stay. As he explained to the last 'batch' he administered the pledge to on Saturday, 'he did not think that he should have remained there so long administering the pledge of temperance. He had supposed that two or three days would have sufficed for the purpose, and that he should have returned to Cork before going to Enniscorthy. But seeing them pour in so eagerly, and so continuously, induced him to remain during the entire week to receive them into the society.'[24] The day before, Mathew had noted that he would not be able to administer the pledge to all who sought it, remarking that 'he hoped, therefore, that they would all be ready when next they met'.[25] Finally, although Mathew had explained to the press and a crowd of disappointed postulants on Friday that, out of respect for Protestant feelings, Saturday would be the last day for pledging as he 'could, of course, not administer the pledge on Sunday, because it would be a profanation of the Sabbath', he nevertheless did administer the pledge on Sunday from a balcony window in Halston Street to several thousand.[26] Mathew's willingness to offend the scruples of stricter Protestants was not terribly surprising given his overriding zeal for converts, but the fact that he did so certainly indicated that many who wanted to pledge had not had the opportunity to do so. This curious fact is underscored by the ease with which Mathew proved later in 1840 that he could enrol large numbers in Dublin, when his two-day visit at the end of September yielded as many postulants as his week-long March/April mission had.[27]

The best explanation for the CTAS's modest enrolments in Dublin in March/April 1840 must recognise the unprecedented public opportunity for self-promotion which that mission provided the Temperance movement. Mathew's crusade, as it entered its fourth month of intense missionary activity, was receiving an inordinate amount of attention – from the government, the churches, the press, and the Irish people. Much of that attention was negative, as the movement threatened to disrupt the livelihoods of thousands, transform the meaning of sociability, and unite the Irish people, particularly the unpredictable peasantry, as they had never been united before. Mathew's correspondence reveals a lively concern for his movement's future, and a strong appreciation for the resourcefulness of many editorialists, not to mention publicans, brewers, distillers and spirit grocers, in undermining the cause. Mathew's first visit to Dublin as the Apostle of Temperance, therefore, was designed to provide a national pulpit for Temperance apologetics and propaganda. A closer examination of some of the details of the proceedings of Mathew's visit makes it clear that strategic concerns of legitimising and 'nationalising' the crusade, appealing for clerical support, and enlisting a higher class of total abstainer were paramount, and took precedence over the enrolment of vast numbers of postulants. If Mathew had focused on the mass enrolment of members at Limerick and Waterford, in Dublin he concentrated on elevating the tone and increasing the respectability of his movement.

It is easy to underestimate the Temperance movement's controversial aspect, but in March 1840, Father Mathew was keenly aware of it, and his words to a group of postulants in Dublin underscore his fear that Temperance's triumphs were threatened:

> He was now pushed on by providence and circumstance, at the head of a great revolution going forward. He had, in so being situated, excited the hostility and hatred of many thousands of people, many of whom, near connections of his own, would, he had no doubt, kindle bonfires in his own city of Cork, and light tar barrels, if they heard of his death in the city of Dublin.[28]

First and foremost, then, Mathew and the CTAS's supporters sought to avoid any event in Dublin that might provide ammunition for their numerous opponents, while the society enjoyed unprecedented attention from the national press. Mathew's concern for his life may appear melodramatic, but even if he was probably safe from interested violence, crowding and dangerous disorder, such as had prevailed at Waterford and especially at Limerick, were a very real and frightening possibility in a city several times their size. For this reason, the police presence in Dublin was very large, and owing to elaborate arrangements that included blocking off streets to control crowds, access to Mathew by postulants and admirers alike throughout the week was often difficult.[29] There seems to have been a great deal of time between the pledging of 'batches' at the Custom House, a situation alleviated only somewhat by the end of the week when separate groups were brought into the corridor under the portico while Mathew enrolled others in the open air in front of the steps.[30]

While these measures kept the number of postulants down, they also afforded Father Mathew his best opportunity yet to define his movement for the Dublin press, who were voraciously taking down his every word and reprinting them all the next morning for national consumption. For the most part he made substantial speeches to every 'batch' of postulants, something he had not done at Limerick, Waterford and other places. In this way, for an entire week Mathew dominated the newspaper columns, and took every advantage of the opportunity to present the most thorough case he could for his cause. Mathew considered his Dublin speeches so significant an apologia for his crusade that he authorised their editing and reprinting in pamphlet form shortly after his visit.[31]

While a well-ordered and well-reasoned appearance in Dublin could be expected to enhance the movement's national prestige immeasurably, its endorsement by the clerical establishment there was perhaps even more critical. In this regard, Mathew was aided by the fact that Temperance had influential proponents in Ireland's principal city. Mathew diplomatically protested on the first day he administered the pledge that

> his object when on this occasion he visited Dublin was not for the purpose of administering the temperance pledge. He came to this city on a different account, namely to forward the interests of charity, and seeing how much good work had been done in this cause by their excellent pastors here, he did not deem it necessary to come forward in it at present. However, having been advised to do so by the reverend and excellent gentlemen who presided over the Teetotaller's Societies in Dublin, he now did so.[32]

'The reverend and excellent gentlemen' Mathew deferred to were William Yore, the parish priest of St Paul's and the president of St Paul's Total Abstinence Society, and Andrew O'Connell, the parish priest of St Michael and St John's and the president of the Metropolitan Total Abstinence Society, both of whom joined him at Beresford Place to assist him in administering the pledge. He was also referring to the Carmelite John Spratt, who led a smaller society known as the Irish Total Abstinence Association, whose church Mathew visited on Sunday, and who would take Mathew's pledge at Swords the following August. Both Yore and O'Connell were priests of some influence in the archdiocese. Yore was the vicar general, while O'Connell was the archdiocesan treasurer.[33] By their commitment to assist him, O'Connell and Yore in particular clearly allied their organisations with Mathew's, and indeed many of their followers took the pledge a second time at his hands.[34]

Just as importantly, Mathew made a point of presiding over, or giving benedictions and sermons at, a variety of morning and evening services at Catholic churches all over the city throughout the week. His presence brought huge, happy crowds and overflowing collection plates, obliging many an influential Dublin parish priest. Still, it clearly interfered with his pledge-giving activities, as the pledge was usually not administered on these strictly religious occasions. As a result, Mathew, who presided over a series of 8:00 a.m. masses, never began administering the pledge before eleven o'clock or so, and he seems to have finished most days before five.

Despite this popularity, the public endorsement Mathew had hoped for from Daniel Murray, the Archbishop of Dublin, and the Catholic church remained elusive. While Murray must have privately supported the visit, he carefully avoided those explicit marks of approval that Mathew may have expected and doubtless hoped for. In Limerick and Waterford, Mathew had been invited publicly by Bishops Ryan and Foran respectively to visit their dioceses, and he was to travel on from Dublin to Enniscorthy as the personal guest of James Keating, the Bishop of Ferns. The powerful and influential Daniel Murray, meanwhile, remained non-committal, at least in public, on the Temperance question. No letter from His Grace was forthcoming in the Dublin press, welcoming Mathew. Murray does not appear to have attended any of the week's proceedings. The closest he came to noticing Mathew's activity was an offhand comment (eagerly snatched up by the press) at a Confirmation, when 'His Lordship observed on the occasion that, at all events, the evil example which led to one great vice, that of drunkenness, was now removed from them'.[35] If Mathew and the CTAS leadership sought a definitive stamp of approval for the CTAS from the archbishop of Dublin, they failed to obtain it.

Still, Mathew must have become even more aware than he had been of the ability of his personal popularity to enhance his crusade. Church doors throughout the city had been thrown open to Mathew, in part on the strength of his ability to raise money. However indifferently attended, his sermon at the Pro-Cathedral had produced the significant sum of £350, and the well-attended meeting at the Royal Exchange, which benefited the Mendicity Institute, also yielded a bountiful harvest for that struggling civic charity. Mathew knew that if the Dublin clergy welcomed him, he would find many pastors elsewhere who would soon do the same. In that sense, if complete endorsement eluded his crusade, the CTAS had nevertheless gained an air of respectability it may have lacked before.

Despite all this attention to clerical politics, no subject occupied a more important place in Father Mathew's Temperance discourses during the week in Dublin than the need to convert Ireland's upper classes to Temperance, as either patrons of, or, preferably, active participants in, local societies. He informed one group of postulants that

> The great success of his society was that it had been commenced by the poor. It was in order that the poor be comprehended that he adopted the

> plan of getting them to repeat the pledge after him. Formerly the course adopted was for every person to write down his name, but if he had followed such a course, he would never have done, as he would not be able to make as many members in 12 months as had been received during the last three days. The old plan was found to be a failure, because it originated in a mistake. They began at the wrong end. Their plan resembled the building of a steeple, by beginning at the top. They, to be sure, succeeded in getting a number of the rich and respectable to join them, but the plan was calculated to exclude the poor. Our Saviour began by teaching the poor, because He knew human nature, and was aware that the rich would always be obliged to follow in the end.[36]

As Mathew repeatedly explained throughout the week, the time had now come for the upper orders to stand up and be counted among the ranks of the temperate. He even went so far as to acquiesce to a separate meeting in the Royal Exchange on Saturday where he spoke to some 2,000 of the 'very respectable' (some 500 of whom took the pledge) who were unwilling to mingle with the crowds in the square, while 'some thousands' of poorer postulants waited for him in Beresford Place.[37] 'I endeavoured, as well as I could', Mathew informed the Beresford Place contingent upon his return, 'to impress on their minds the obligation imposed on them to protect and assist those of you who become teetotallers.' 'I told them', he added, 'their prosperity and happiness is interwoven with yours; and unless you are industrious and happy, they cannot be so.' Finally, Mathew remarked, he had urged the rich to join the movement because the very survival of Ireland's upper orders depended on their playing an equal part in their nation's regeneration. 'If they allowed you to become depraved', he pointed out to the crowds, 'their children would suffer from their carelessness. The ways of God are justice and truth, and the poor will inflict retaliation on the rich if they neglect to make them what they ought to be.'[38]

During Mathew's first visit to Dublin this appeal to the well-to-do was a failure. Although by the third day of his mission 'the postulants appeared to be also of a much more respectable class in society', and 'Father Mathew referred to that circumstance repeatedly during his several addresses with evident satisfaction', even on that day this 'more respectable class' of postulants was composed of 'tradesmen and mechanics' at best, and few above that rank pledged during the rest of Mathew's time in Dublin.[39] An evening visit to Trinity College at the invitation of the undergraduates was much noticed, but yielded only nine converts.[40] The separate meeting held at the Royal Exchange must have been a bittersweet encounter for Mathew, as his urgent exhortations there to a self-selecting and receptive crowd only converted one quarter of his audience, while the separate nature of the proceedings did more to reveal the divisions between rich and poor within the movement than to remove them.

Despite these disappointments, however, Mathew's Dublin visit must be accounted a great triumph. If the number of recruits had been lower than some had expected, order had been preserved at all times and many more had wanted to pledge than could be accommodated. If many of the well-to-do had resisted enlisting, all had spoken well of the crusade and the tone and profile of the CTAS had been improved. And, if Daniel Murray had avoided public praise, he had been sufficiently impressed with Mathew's visit that he was prepared to provide Mathew with even greater opportunities to gain the endorsement of the Catholic Church in Ireland. Meanwhile, invitations continued to pour in from around the country, popular enthusiasm continued to increase, and Mathew and the CTAS were still in a position to augment their numbers. The careful response of the metropolis, furthermore, had the practical effect of returning the initiative to Mathew and his growing legions of lower and middle-class postulants. If the people continued to take the pledge, hold mass meetings on behalf of the cause, and join active local societies, the CTAS could still hope to convince Ireland's wavering elites that their own future depended on co-operating in the moral regeneration of Ireland through Temperance.

MAYNOOTH

The Temperance crusade continued to grow dramatically as Mathew's missionary activity continued unabated through the spring of 1840. Later in the month of April, at a grand Easter procession in Cork, James McKenna headed thousands of marchers with a blue silk banner proclaiming 'Moral Freedom – Total Abstinence – Two million members'.[41] Once again McKenna was displaying his talent for exaggeration, but Mathew himself claimed 1.8 million by mid-June, and two million before the month was out.[42]

The numerical and geographical spread of the CTAS over the next several years will be examined in detail below, but what needs to be kept in mind is that this dramatic expansion and its accompanying proliferation of local societies would have been quite impossible without some degree of Church approval of the crusade. While the CTAS's initial growth had been aided and abetted by an enthusiastic cadre of clerics, these supporters were still a small minority of Ireland's priests. The opportunity to obtain broader acceptance for Mathew's cause came at the hands of Daniel Murray, and was one of the most significant fruits of the visit to Dublin. Sometime early in May, Mathew was invited by Murray, who had clearly been impressed by Mathew, and by John Montague, the President of Saint Patrick's College, Ireland's national seminary, to visit the college, and to preach the dedication sermon at the Church of the Blessed Virgin in Maynooth on Trinity Sunday in June 1840. So anxious was Mathew to be present that he cancelled a much-anticipated visit to England.[43]

The dedication service on Trinity Sunday was a particularly significant one. The *Freeman* glowingly referred to it as one of 'the most magnificent religious ceremonies which has taken place in this country in modern times'.[44] Daniel Murray presided at the Mass, which was the culmination of a visit by the archbishop that had also featured the ordination of 30 Maynooth graduates. Still, the Capuchin friar stole the show. After a visit to the college, which produced a bountiful harvest for his society of seven professors, 17 of the 30 newly-ordained priests, and 250 of the student body of some 600, Mathew was carried on the shoulders of part of a crowd of some 20,000 to the church to deliver his sermon.[45] Most of the crowd, who were reportedly filled with 'a desire to behold the great Apostle of Temperance', could not have been contained in the church, let alone afford the five shillings minimum charge to attend the service (some seats cost a pound), but they surrounded the church with bands and banners proclaiming their fidelity to the total abstinence cause.

Mathew's triumph was noted in many quarters. The *Freeman* reported that 'the visit of the great Apostle of Temperance to Maynooth has been an important epoch in the annals of teetotalism', insisting that Temperance had 'assumed a bolder and more proud position, not so much as regards the immense accession to the numbers of the society as the station, the dignity, and the talent of those who have been enrolled'. The anonymous author of 'A Tribute to Father Mathew', who wrote a glowing account of the visit that was reprinted in several newspapers and distributed by the CTAS in pamphlet form, echoed the assessment.[46] The author, probably a seminarian, was present on the occasion and insisted that Mathew's 'glorious' Maynooth triumph was merely 'the prologue to the future history of Ireland'. 'Whilst only the poor and illiterate flocked to your standard', he admitted, Temperance 'was seemingly ascribed to ignorance and superstition'. 'But', the author added, 'the self-refuted absurdity of representing ignorance and superstition as doing the office of heroic virtue, is fully silenced by the grave authority of Maynooth college. Their adherence to you was an act of judgement, guided by knowledge and prompted by exalted virtue.'

Mathew's Maynooth visit was witnessed by tens of thousands, while millions knew all the details a few days after. The invitation amounted to something approaching his Church's official stamp of approval. Mathew's triumphal reception in Ireland's ecclesiastical womb and his officially approved enrolment of seminarians and professors were great marks of his acceptance by the Church. Prior to this coup, it was still possible for Irish priests to treat his Temperance movement as a purely secular crusade, peripheral to the Irish Catholic Church as a religious institution. Mathew could no longer be ignored, nor could most of the many pastors who were ambivalent about his crusade continue to resist the urgent requests of their people that an official invitation be issued to the great apostle of Temperance.

A NATIONAL CRUSADE: TEMPERANCE GEOGRAPHY

For three years, from the beginning of 1840 until early 1843, Father Mathew's missionary Temperance ministry brought him to nearly every part of Ireland. While there were other important factors in establishing and maintaining strong local Temperance societies enjoying widespread approval and cooperation, Mathew's initial presence, and the galvanising force of the mass Temperance gatherings that resulted, were paramount. Mathew's energy and activity in the mercurial Irish weather in those pre-railway days of slow and difficult travel were nothing short of heroic. By January 1843, Mathew could report to an American correspondent that 'I have now, with the Divine assistance, hoisted the banner of temperance in almost every parish in Ireland'.[47] This was something of an exaggeration, but not as far from truth as might be suspected.

Mathew's precise movements were determined by a combination of expediency and opportunity. Requests from local clergy for visits were accepted and missions publicised, which in turn often produced additional requests from the same area that Mathew tried to accommodate as best he could. His missions were to some extent, therefore, controlled by the Irish clergy, and particularly by the bishops. The maps in the Map Appendix, together with the list of Mathew's missions, trace the expansion of the CTAS throughout the country from 1840 to mid-1843, by following, as closely as possible, Mathew's movements.[48]

Map A summarises Mathew's activities at the county level for the entire period 1839–43.[49] Again, the number of Temperance missions is only one measure (albeit an important one) of the movement's strength in a given area. Additionally, Ireland's counties were hardly uniform in area and population, so it is not surprising that some received more missions than others. Still, Map A does provide a clear indication of those parts of the country where Father Mathew was most active. Even though the number of missions most likely understated Temperance's strength around Cork city, as well as in Limerick, Waterford and Tipperary, the movement's firm grip on Munster is evident, as is its strength throughout most of Leinster, particularly in Wexford and Dublin, as well as Kildare, Kilkenny, Meath and Queen's County. Monaghan was clearly the movement's strongest outpost in Ulster, while in Connaught the large counties of Galway and Mayo were the sites of many missions.

Maps B, C, D and E break down Map A by year from 1840 to 1843. Beginning with the first three months of 1840 in a strong core region, which would be included in the area formed by drawing a line from Cork northwest to Ennis in County Clare, north to Galway, southeast to Abbeyleix in Queen's County, south to Waterford and then finally southwest back to Cork, Temperance spread rapidly to counties on the edge of this area – Kerry, Mayo, Kildare, Wexford and Dublin. Meath, West Meath and Sligo soon followed, and by year's end most of the country outside of Ulster had been visited. In early 1841, Mathew concentrated on the southern parts of Ulster, particularly County Monaghan, the southwest (Kerry and southwest Cork), and, especially, the province of Leinster – that part of the country surrounding Temperance's core region. Between April and June 1841, Father Mathew again laid siege to southern Ulster, and made additional short visits to Kerry and central Ireland. With the exception of a foray or two into unconquered parts of Ulster, in the two years between mid-1841 and mid-1843 the remainder of the missions were dedicated to revisiting areas where many had already taken the pledge, either in response to accounts of backsliding, or, more frequently, to give those who had been reluctant to pledge the first time another opportunity to do so. By 1842–43, a variety of factors had combined to reduce the number of missions, particularly in the west, as the maps, and the table below, clearly demonstrate.

Temperance's dominant position in southwestern and south central Ireland may actually have enhanced its national appeal and prospects.

Table 3.1: Temperance Missions, 1839–1843

Year	1839/40	1841	1842	1843*
Number of Missions	101	87	78	24

* The figure for 1843 represents missions over the period January–June.

While the CTAS enjoyed success in the north and west, it came later and less frequently to those parts of the country, for reasons that will be examined later. Mathew's movement, therefore, could not be primarily identified with the sectarian peculiarities of Ulster, the poverty and relative backwardness of Connaught, or the elitism of the metropolis. Rather, the CTAS was strongest, and was seen to be strongest, across much of the (relatively) prosperous south-central part of the country; in Counties Limerick, Tipperary, Wexford, Waterford and north-east Cork; and in the cities of Limerick and Waterford. Much of this area has been termed the 'culture hearth' of Ireland by one historian, and the cradle of the 'devotional revolution' by another.[50] It had already been the locus of 'national' mass movements since the 1820s, including the remarkable pacification campaign of 1828, and the anti-tithe movement of the 1830s.[51] More so than any other part of Ireland, this region benefited from a critical density of fairly substantial Catholic farmers, who constituted Emmet Larkin's 'nation-forming class', and Kevin Whelan's 'proprietors-in-waiting', and who, along with civic-minded shopkeepers and tradesmen in Waterford, Limerick and other towns, provided the lay leadership particularly capable of organising societies and bands, meetings and parades, as well as influencing local clergy to invite the Apostle of Temperance to the district.[52] While these groups may never have joined the Temperance movement in numbers proportionate to their percentage of the population, it was popular enough with them for them to provide the backbone that helped the CTAS to flourish best in those parts of the country where they were most influential. The success of their efforts was borne out not only by the number of visits made by Mathew to the region, but also by the steady increase in the numbers enrolled in the CTAS, and by a corresponding steady decrease in alcohol production through the early years of the 1840s.

A MORAL REVOLUTION ACHIEVED: A 'NATIONAL' VIRTUE

From its establishment in October 1842, the influential weekly newspaper, the *Nation*, strongly supported the CTAS. In December 1842, an early editorial proclaimed that Mathew's mission had been largely accomplished:

> We find in history no parallel to this temperance movement in Ireland. It is altogether unprecedented, and a solemn, soul-stirring spectacle it is! Nearly five millions of the Irish people have risen against a vice that was

> the curse and ruin of their country – have pledged themselves to wipe off the stain that which from ages has been fixed on the national character, and have adhered to this noble and unexampled pledge with a constancy as noble and as unexampled. Their pledge, so fervently taken and faithfully observed, is prophetic of a brighter era in the history of their native land.[53]

The figure of 'five millions' mentioned was derived from the CTAS's own claims. The actual numbers of Irish people enrolled in the CTAS at its height are impossible to determine with any degree of accuracy. In early 1843 Mathew claimed five and a half million devoted followers, a total (rounded up to 6 million by John Francis Maguire) that was certainly grossly inflated. The system of numbered Temperance cards issued on which the estimate was based had in fact broken down long before, with cards being sent indiscriminately about the country for parish priests to distribute.[54] Father Mathew's secretaries kept the membership book at Cork, but most who joined were never formally enrolled, nor could they have been as it was not unusual for tens of thousands to pledge by the hundreds over the course of a single day. Crowd estimates that appeared in the press for meetings across Ireland were unreliable at best, with the exception of a few that were carefully monitored, such as the first Waterford and Dublin meetings. Even Father Mathew acknowledged this, and once joked with a crowd of some 20,000 in England that 'in Ireland, such a gathering would no doubt be magnified into something like 150,000'.[55] Even granting, however, that attendance at meetings was often greatly exaggerated, and allowing for the fact that many who attended did not pledge, while others pledged at more than one meeting, given the scale of Mathew's missionary activity, and the active assistance given to the 'moral miracle' by many other clergymen, it is nevertheless appears that some millions took the pledge in Ireland. The actual total was probably a good deal below Mathew's five and one-half million offered in 1843, but, given that the entire population amounted to something over eight million, many of whom were young children, the only thing that is clear is that a very large percentage of the adult population was pledged at one time or another.[56] How large a percentage is debatable, but judging from the decline in alcohol production analysed below, and taking into account that a significant portion of the alcohol produced was transformed into 'temperance cordials', consumed, whether unwittingly or knowingly, by teetotallers, it must have at the very least approached half the adult Catholic population of some four million. Certainly there were parts of the country, particularly in the north and west, where very few took the pledge, but these were more than offset by large sections of the midlands where most, if not nearly all, for a time embraced the crusade.

Alcohol production figures for legal whiskey are available for Ireland from the 1830s, and clearly indicate the staggering rate of alcohol production there before Father Mathew's crusade.[57] The same figures also demonstrate just how dramatically production fell between 1838 and 1843. Between those years, as indicated below, licenced production fell nearly 60 per cent across the country, despite a significant increase in population. The duty charged on whiskey, added in Ireland at the point of production, is also provided as it was a crucial factor affecting legal production. Generally speaking, production declined as duty increased, as the dramatic increase in production after the duty was significantly reduced in 1834 indicates.

Table 3.2: Spirit proof-gallons * charged with duty in Ireland, 1833–1843, with population, per-capita consumption, and duty figures.

YEAR	GALLONS	POPULATION **	GALLONS CONSUMED PER CAPITA	DUTY PER GALLON ON IRISH SPIRITS FOR HOME CONSUMPTION
1833	8,168,596	7,891,867	1.04	3s 4d
1834	9,708,415	7,954,100	1.22	From 1/9: 2s 4d
1835	11,381,228	7,985,575	1.43	2s 4d
1836	12,248,772	8,017,250	1.53	2s 4d
1837	11,235,635	8,048,825	1.40	2s 4d
1838	12,296,642	8,080,400	1.52	2s 4d
1839	10,815,709	8,111,975	1.33	2s 4d
1840	7,401,051	8,143,550	0.91	From 15/5: 2s 8d
1841	6,485,443	8,175,124	0.79	2s 8d
1842	5,290,650	8,206,700	0.64	From 11/3: 3s 8d
1843	5,545,483	8,238,275	0.67	From 1/8: 2s 8d

* – A proof-gallon is an alcohol constant, and is 57.1 per cent by volume of alcohol.
** – Population figures for 1841 are from A.J. Fitzpatrick and W.E. Vaughn, *Irish Historical Abstract* (Dublin: RIC, 1978). Figures for 1834 are from the *First Report of The Commissioners of Public Instruction, Ireland* (London: HMSO, 1835), p. 74. Figures for all other years are estimates based on those figures and the 1831 census.

These figures must be qualified in a number of ways. The briefest glance at per capita consumption of spirits in Scotland (2.38 proof-gallons in 1831) strongly indicates that Irish spirit production was under-reported.[58] In fact, illicit distillation of whiskey, or *poteen*, was wide-spread in Ireland, particularly during the earlier years of the 1830s in the north and west, where conversion to alcohol was often the most profitable use of grain crops.[59] Variations in duty charged and revenue enforcement policies both had some affect on legal versus illegal production.[60]

Nevertheless, all indications are that the dramatic production declines of 1839–43 were real, and not just the result of a sudden shift in alcohol consumption from legal spirits to vast quantities of illegally produced *poteen*. Revenue police records, as the table below indicates, demonstrate a marked decline in detections of stills in the period from 1840 until 1843, despite a moderate fourpence duty increase in 1840 that, all other things being equal, might have been expected to encourage an increase in illegal production, and a corresponding increase in detections by the increasingly-vigilant and professional revenue police. The substantial increase in detections in 1843 probably resulted in large part from a depression in agriculture prices, and a shilling duty increase in May 1842, itself a reaction to declining revenue receipts as a consequence of the success of the Temperance movement.

Table 3.3: Detections for illicit distillation in Ireland, 1834–1843

YEAR	NUMBER OF DETECTIONS	DUTY PER GALLON ON IRISH SPIRIT
1834	8,223	3s 4d/from 1/9: 2s 4d
1835	8,192	2s 4d
1836	4,904	2s 4d
1837	3,323	2s 4d
1838	3,136	2s 4d
1839	3,248	2s 4d
1840	1,359	From 15/5: 2s 8d
1841	1,004	2s 8d
1842	881	From 11/3: 3s 8d
1843	1,895	From 1/8: 2s 8d

The table suggests that during the period of the Temperance movement's greatest success, illicit production of alcohol declined even more than legal production, by something approaching 75 per cent between 1839 and 1842.

Further confirmation, if any is needed, of the downward trend in alcohol consumption comes from all other quarters. Beer production, for example, while only a small proportion of Irish alcohol consumption in this period, followed a similar pattern, declining from 967,000 standard barrels in 1838 to 496,000 in 1842.[61] Liquor licenses held and issued to spirit grocers and publicans in Ireland manifest coinciding trends.[62] Moreover, extensive anecdotal evidence supports the proposition of a considerable decline in drinking. Those who had been away from Ireland for a time were most struck, including two Irish Protestants who had been living in London and returned in 1841 to find 'sobriety to be universal throughout Ireland'.[63] Paul Cullen, the rector of the Irish College in Rome, home for a visit in July 1840, reported Ireland 'greatly changed'. 'I have not', he went on to observe with some surprise, 'seen a drunken man since I arrived in this country.'[64] Other visitors were equally impressed. At the Royal Irish Agricultural Society meeting in Cork on 21 July 1842, a Mr Smith of Deanstown, Scotland, failed to discover the expected convention atmosphere, and told the delegates so, in tones of praise tinged, perhaps, with regret: 'In scenes such as Cork at present, he had expected to see, as in his own country, and in the sister country likewise, many indulging at least to some extent in perhaps intoxication. He had seen immense numbers from all quarters of the country, of all grades and classes; and in the entire congregation, he did not see a single drunken person.'[65] A Mr Grey of Gelston, another visiting member of the RAS of England, rose and added that

> he begged to unite with Mr Smith in congratulating them on the extraordinarily improved state of society, which carried sobriety and moral conduct into the lower orders. He had passed through towns in Ireland where fairs were being held, and he had seen the great gathering in town on the present occasion, and during all this he had not witnessed one man in a brutal state of intoxication.

Perhaps the most thorough testimony along these lines, however, came from Mr and Mrs S.C. Hall, the English travelogue authors who were by 1840 veteran observers of Ireland. They began their three-volume account of their latest tour in 1840 with a long discussion of the workings of Temperance, a phenomenon about which 'we had entertained, in common with many others, strong doubts', particularly about 'the actual extent of the reformation'.[66] Their observations, 'unbiased by prejudice' and 'the result of careful inquiry and close examinations', bear quoting at some length, as they convey the powerful impression Temperance's success made on those who witnessed it.[67]

> In reference to the extent to which sobriety has spread, it will be almost sufficient to state, that during our recent stay in Ireland, from the 10th of June to the 6th of September, 1840, we saw but six persons intoxicated; and that for the first thirty days we had not encountered one. In the course of that month we had travelled from Cork to Killarney – round the coast, returning by the inland route; not along the mail-coach roads, but on a 'jaunting car', through by-ways as well as highways; visiting small villages and populous towns; driving through fairs; attending

> wakes and funerals (returning from one of which, between Glengariff and Kenmare, at nightfall, we met at least a hundred substantial farmers, mounted); in short, wherever crowds assembled, and we considered it likely we might gather information as to the state of the country and the character of its people. We repeat, we did not meet a single individual who appeared to have tasted spirits; and we do not hesitate to express our conviction, that two years ago, in the same places and during the same time, we should have encountered many thousands of drunken men … Of the extent of the change, therefore, we have had ample experience; and it is borne out by the assurances of so many who live in towns as well as in the country, that we can have no hesitation in describing sobriety to be almost universal throughout Ireland.[68]

Reports from the police provide powerful official testimony of a widespread change for the better in public behaviour. The constabulary reports of March 1840, although administered at an early point in the movement's development, note dramatic changes in public drinking habits. A.B. Hill reported from Dunmore in County Kilkenny that at 'the fair of Kilkenny on Saturday 28th inst (where I attended purposely to watch the result of temperance) not a single case of intoxication came under my observation'. 'On former occasions', Hill elaborated, 'drunkenness and fighting were the order of the day. In this instance, notwithstanding the crowded state of the city the people quietly dispersed at a very early hour and at 6 pm the streets were nearly empty.' Even more remarkably, 'On visiting the public houses of my own district during that night I found them closed and the inmates in bed, a stranger proof of the working of the society I could not adduce.'[69] J.J. Thate in Charleville, Co. Cork, an otherwise hostile observer of the movement, did concede that Temperance 'certainly had the effect of producing a most orderly deportment amongst the people at fairs, etc.'. 'Previous to the pledge', Constable R. Power, stationed in Cork's West Riding, observed, 'on Sundays and Holidays several persons used to get drunk and generally had petty fights among themselves. Now the thing is quite changed for it's a rare thing to see a drunken person in the street on these or any other day.' In fact, every respondent who answered the question noted a dramatic, and occasionally miraculous transformation in public behaviour, with the exception of three who felt that it was too early to make any judgment.[70]

The State Paper Office holds a large collection of magistrates' diaries from various parts of the country for much of this period, most of which confirm that these changes persisted for some time.[71] Magistrates and police throughout Ireland had been required, for some years prior to the Temperance reformation, to attend fairs, races and other public gatherings in their district as part of the Whig government's aggressive attempt to suppress faction fighting and 'rioting'. The duty was often dangerous and particular problems were caused by the presence of 'whiskey tents' at all occasions in rural Ireland in the 1830s. In a typical incident, C.H. Tuckey, a stipendiary magistrate stationed in the County Carlow, attended Saint Mullin's Fair with 31 constables on 25 July 1839, and encountered 'considerable rioting'. The police were

> assailed with stones from after 4 o'clock. At 5 three prominent rioters were seized and at ¼ past 6 when the Chief Constable and 19 police marched towards the tents in order to desire the keepers to leave the field they were attacked front and rear and some of the men were cut and wounded with stones; the constabulary fired a few shots and dispersed their assailants.[72]

The diaries of the comings and goings of the men charged with keeping, or at least monitoring, the peace in Ireland provide independent confirmation of the fact that, between 1839 and 1843, drunken disorder on public occasions across much of Ireland was transformed from a pressing concern into a passing one.

C.H. Tuckey, for example, the magistrate at Carlow noted above encountered far fewer breaches of the peace after 1839, particularly after a visit by Father Mathew in April 1842 to Rathvilly.[73] John Barron, working out of Milltown Malby in County Clare, was, at least according to his official diary, particularly zealous in suppressing riots in his area, and seemed almost disappointed when he reported on 18 March 1840 that the fair at Mullough the previous day, 'formerly proverbial as the most troublesome in Clare from its being held on Patrick's Day' had been quiet, and 'thanks to temperance there was not the most distant appearance of a riot and only two or three persons who had any appearance of having drank one of whom we took into custody, he being a little noisy'.[74] The Ennistymon fair a week later also 'passed off quietly', as did the 'generally very troublesome' Lurloughmore fair and races in June ('altho' there was a vast assemblage'); the Lahinch patron in July ('there could not have been less than 15,000 persons there'); and the Miltown fair in August. Later that month the vigilant Barron decided his time would be better spent looking for trouble at impromptu local races and hurling matches 'as the fairs are very quiet'. 'The Rev. Mr Mathew', he conceded, 'has been of great service in this respect.' Neale Brown at Tullamore in Co. Kerry agreed, when he noted in March 1840 that the Cloghane fair, 'formerly remarkable and notorious for being very much disturbed by drunkenness rioting and breaches of the peace', had not produced 'one case of drunkenness brought before me nor any prisoner or complaint made by the police'.[75] 'This is attributed', he related, 'to Father Mathew having administered the pledge of total abstinence at Birr on the 2nd of March.' Many magistrates, in fact, appear to have stopped attending fairs altogether. William Cooke was told, for example, when he took up his post in Abbeyfeale, County Limerick, in June 1841, not to bother attending a local fair as 'it will be quiet'.[76]

Magistrates did not necessarily find that Temperance brought only peace. Their time was increasingly taken up with new kinds of problems they would have found impossible to imagine months, or years, earlier. A succession of dull fair days in Neale Brown's district, for example, was upset by the Tullamore petty sessions on 23 April 1842, when the magistrate heard an assault case 'where the offence was induced by the complainant being supposed to have broken the temperance pledge'.[77] The accused's parish priest wondered 'what measures could be taken against those whom he was credibly informed were going about seducing persons from observing the temperance pledge, and that the persons so acting were in the possession of money to a greater degree than their station in life would warrant'. Brown also heard the priest's complaint that 'there were some of the police officers in town in the habit of speaking very improperly of the teetotallers' and that 'their own conduct was base, that many of them were in the habit of drinking'. At Abbeyfeale, the new magistrate William Cooke's most pressing problem was complaints about the local society's band, who insisted on practicing on Sundays 'with music & in large numbers'. Little wonder that Lord Morpeth, then Chief Secretary for Ireland, wryly informed the House of Commons in 1840 that 'the duty of the military and police in Ireland is now almost entirely confined to keeping the ground clear for the operation of Father Mathew'.[78]

These accounts, and the multitudes of testimony and evidence that could be added to them, illustrate what was surely one of the most intriguing features of the CTAS's success. Every indication, from alcohol production to figures for illicit distillation and pub licences, indicates an actual decline of drinking in Ireland during the early 1840s, approaching 60 per cent or more. Public drinking, on the other hand, at least to the point of obvious intoxication, seems to have largely disappeared across wide sections of the country, particularly in those places and at those times when it had previously been ubiquitous.[79] Whiskey tents disappeared or were replaced by tea tents at most fairs and races, and the people themselves, as a later chapter will detail, found effective ways, as the pledge insisted they do, to 'discountenance intemperance in others'.[80]

The elevation of sobriety into a widespread public expectation in many places was, in fact, a phenomenon much remarked upon. In the constabulary reports, several respondents noted that even those who had not pledged had 'from example almost entirely given up drinking'.[81] The anonymous author of a letter to the editor in the *Freeman's Journal* in December 1840 marvelled that 'alcohol is now almost everywhere cried down', while in September of the same year, the anonymous author of an address to Father Mathew captured the spirit of triumphant Temperance when he noted that 'the odious and detested vice of drunkenness has almost entirely disappeared from public view; even those who had not resolution enough to take the pledge were ashamed to be seen indulging in the dangerous experiment of intoxicating draughts.'[82]

This establishment of general, rigorous temperance as a public expectation cut across class in ways that Temperance societies had difficulty in doing, and an appreciation of this new state of affairs is crucial to understanding the magnitude of the movement's success, and how it differed from Temperance elsewhere. Cyrus Clarke, an English Quaker Temperance advocate travelling in Ireland in 1840, commented on the phenomenon in a letter to the *Bristol Temperance Herald*. 'I was surprised', he noted, 'to observe how generally the fact of the great benefit produced by Father Mathew's labours was admitted and appreciated, even by those who are not themselves teetotallers.'[83] 'All parties', he added, 'appear eager to express the sanguine confidence, with which they anticipate the future fruits of this mighty revolution of popular feeling and habit.' If it remained rare for the prosperous to involve themselves in organised Temperance, it also became scandalous for them to scorn the new sobriety. Take, for example, this report from the *Waterford Chronicle*, complaining of the unacceptable behaviour of 'respectable' farmers who came into Dungarvan

> causing a great deal of scandal when they come here to market. In this they are very inexcusable, because they are a class of men in independent circumstances, who can afford a good breakfast and dinner, and take their tumbler at home if they choose, as many a respectable man does and will do without compromising his reputation for sobriety; but if they intend persevering in the public house muddling line – if they intend living the outlaws of the blessed reformation that has take place, let them, 'like the lepers of old, stand without the city gates' – let them form a tribe amongst themselves, like the Pariahs of India; as they refuse to go forth with the children of Israel in search of the promised land, why, let them remain in Egypt in their bondage – let them stop at home. To the townspeople, they are become an abomination.[84]

The farmers' crime was not so much their drinking, which, provided it was done in private, was common enough and still acceptable, if far from admirable, for men of their station. Their refusal to respect newfound conventions about alcohol, however, was regarded in a very different light, and earned them not only this very public rebuke, but also a not-so thinly veiled threat of popular retaliation in the form of a ducking: 'Let the Philistines beware in future', the editorialist warned, 'If caught napping here again, as some of them calling themselves respectable lately were, in all likelihood they will be introduced to intimacy with the pump, by no means congenial to the whiskified temperament.' Such admonishments were only rarely written down and administered by newspaper editors, but they were common, and probably not much less public, at the hands of neighbours, co-workers, Temperance activists, and enthusiastic clerics. Some of the social tensions resulting from the movement's success will be explored subsequently, but it bears noting that the establishment of an expectation of public sobriety and respect for Temperance, irrespective of the class issues that certainly kept many outside active Temperance societies, was clearly one of the most significant accomplishments of the CTAS in the early 1840s. If half, or something rather more than that, of the adult population actually took the pledge, even more appear to have significantly altered their drinking habits, and to such an extent that to call Ireland, as many did by 1842/43, a 'nation of teetotallers', was to indulge in only a very slight exaggeration. Thus was Temperance, at its height, even more a public virtue than a private one.

The astounding magnitude of the CTAS's success, and, indeed, the establishment through the first three years of the 1840s of a revolutionary national social movement on an unprecedented scale, made the position of Temperance in Irish society appear secure. There certainly were problems. Some of the difficulties with which this chapter began had not been resolved. The Temperance crusade still struggled mightily during these years to convince the Catholic clergy at all levels that the movement deserved their whole-hearted support, but was only partly successful. Just as significantly, in many parts of the country the CTAS was still failing to enrol 'the upper orders' in its active ranks in the kind of numbers that Mathew had hoped for. Father Mathew's colleague, James Haughton, who in early 1840 had expressed dismay at the failure of Ireland's upper classes to take the pledge (see above), perceived little improvement in that respect two and a half years later. 'I am happy to tell you', he informed his American friend, William Lloyd Garrison, 'Father Mathew goes on conquering.' 'Our people are with him', Haughton continued, 'and great and increasing are their happiness and prosperity; but the merchants, the traders, the gentry, and the great ones of the land are too proud and too foolish to lay hold of the simple mode he offers them for affecting their own and their country's regeneration.'[85]

Nevertheless, it appeared clear to many that a new period in Ireland's history had begun, a happy time of enjoying the fruits of the nation's new found virtue. The obstacles that remained, however serious, were minor compared to what had already been achieved, and more time would further erode the few remaining islands of resistance. The Dublin visit had firmly placed Temperance at the centre of the national stage, and Maynooth had provided the Church's mark of approval and paved the way for a period of remarkable expansion. The *Nation*, for example, approvingly reprinted an editorial from an English newspaper in December 1842 on the 'deeply-rooted, most glorious, most blessed moral revolution'.[86] 'We have no fears for its permanency', the editors insisted bravely, 'such effects as these do not spring from transient bursts of superstitious feeling; the good seed has germinated and rooted itself in the Irish heart, and we fervently hope and believe it will survive the shocks and changes of many centuries.' More significant testimony on the subject, perhaps, were many of the addresses to Father Mathew from local Temperance societies, nearly a hundred of which were carefully preserved by McKenna. As the anonymous and exultant author of the address of the Erris Total Abstinence Society in County Mayo explained late in 1841,

> Our anticipation for the *future* are founded on our experience of *the past*. We have seen intemperance, like the summer conflagration of our heath clad mountains, spread far and wide, and in its desolating course reach'd every class and grade of society, it corrupted and degraded its unfortunate victims – made Irishmen a disgrace to humanity and Ireland a bye word among the nations of the earth. But a change has come over the spirit of the people. Your voice went forth in the moral wilderness and roused the fallen to a sense of their misery. They awoke from their lethargy – looked with astonishment and horror at their degraded condition, and by one generous and gigantic effort, burst forever the ignoble fetters of sensual indulgence and walked forth in their might the free and triumphant followers of temperance and virtue.
>
> Since the first ages of Christianity to the present time, history affords no example of so general, so speedy, so pacific and so effectual a regeneration of any country. Ireland is now what she formerly was, and what she always ought to be, a land of peace and morality, an 'Officina Gentium' – an 'Insula Sanctorum' from Erris to Howth, from Fairhead to Cape Clear throughout the breadth and length of the land.[87]

Not surprisingly, James McKenna, who was, by 1843, busily composing a history of the movement, agreed, and no less fervently. A new era in Irish history, McKenna insisted, was now 'at hand'. When 'Mathew spoke – the fiend of intemperance, which so long rioted in her misery, was exorcised – the spell of her infamy was broken'.[88] Ireland had been freed, and now 'like the uncaged eagle she soars on high in the moral firmament'.

CHAPTER FOUR

The Rhetorical Consensus: The Ideology of Temperance

Previous chapters have suggested that the impassioned calls of Cork's Temperance activists and Father Mathew drew Irish men and women to the CTAS, giving them reasons to change long-established customs and personal habits. These appeals, repeated at hundreds of meetings all over the country and reproduced daily in the Irish press, not only attracted converts, they also provided the means by which these same men and women came to appreciate what the act of taking the pledge meant. Any understanding of the nature of the Temperance movement requires detailed examination of the crusade's rhetorical appeal.

It was unavoidable that so large and impressive a movement as the CTAS spoke with a variety of voices. Still, one of the most striking features of Father Mathew's crusade was the speed with which a coherent, recognisable rhetoric of Temperance emerged. It could be found not only in the words of the movement's own national leadership, and the speeches of Father Mathew and local activists, but also in contemporary histories and newspaper editorials, in popular ballads, and, perhaps most tellingly as regards the common currency of these ideas, in ritual addresses from local communities to Father Mathew. Irish men and women who joined the CTAS were conscious of enlisting in a *movement* as such; and one with particular objectives and defining characteristics.

PART I: THE CHALLENGE

With its network of stock phrases, recurrent images, and tried and true expressions, Temperance rhetoric, carried largely by (and to some degree originating with) the popular liberal press, gave distinctive, powerful, and widely accepted meaning to the act of taking the pledge, and acted as an essential catalyst for the causes' growth. In all its forms, this language centred around the core idea of collective and individual 'regeneration' from a 'degraded' state. In addition to this universally invoked conversion process, Temperance rhetoric can generally be characterised as 1) providential, in that God was understood to be directly involved in the Temperance movement; 2) transformative, in that the consequences of the Temperance reformation were held to be radical, fundamental and permanent, temporally and spiritually; 3) patriotic/nationalistic, in that the Irish people as such were supposed to be the particular focus of both the providential and transformative moral power of total abstinence; this dimension of Temperance rhetoric was sometimes, explicitly or implicitly, quite anti-English; 4) communitarian, in that the right of the community to expect the individual to conform to Temperance's radical ideology, and to punish deviation from the same, was typically maintained. In general, it can be said that this rhetoric was consistent and widely shared; that it was understood, responded to, and echoed by most of those who took the pledge; and that it had both explicit and implicit political consequences for the development of the CTAS as a national movement.

The Early Message

Before examining this language and its usage, it is helpful to explore in greater detail how it emerged, and how it differed from pre-existing Temperance rhetoric. Temperance meetings, as they had evolved in Britain and Ireland to 1838, and particularly in Cork, generally provided a platform for practiced advocates of moral reform to render dramatic appeals, most typically to a mix of the curious and the converted. These appeals were often structured as pseudo-scientific lectures on the injurious effects of drink (necessary in an era when conventional wisdom held that moderate and even heavy consumption of alcohol was needed to maintain one's constitution), but they were just as likely to involve emotional testimonials or humorous self-portraits of reformed drunkards.[1] Such presentations were essentially calls for personal conversion and individual responsibility in moral terms. While they often appealed to notions of social obligation, particularly to the family, they focused primarily on the personal, material, and moral/spiritual benefits that resulted from sobriety.[2] The Temperance society, as an active organisation, was useful because it aided in the creation and support of the temperate individual.

In Cork, the efforts of Temperance activists throughout most of the 1830s in exhorting the faithful and converting the unconvinced were energetic, but unexceptional. The efforts of William Martin, the elderly, physically imposing Quaker who had first recruited Father Mathew to total abstinence, the first agitator for the cause in Cork, and the founder of the CTAS, were typical. Martin, an active crusader for total abstinence from 1831, was known for his abrasive and colourful rhetoric.[3] Alcohol in all its forms was 'brewer's wash', 'poison', and, 'armed with the usual catch-words of temperance oratory', Martin represented 'a very homely old school' of public speaking and Temperance advocacy.[4] Fond of biblical quotations and a font of humorous anecdotes that inevitably portrayed drinkers as fools, Martin's platform rhetoric also usually included techniques such as a lengthy call-and-response dialogue invoking the more imposing members of the animal kingdom: 'What does the lion drink? Water! What does the elephant drink? Water!', etc.[5]

What is striking about the rhetoric of the CTAS after April 1838, however, was how little it depended on such tried and true techniques of earlier English, American and Irish activists. If Martin remained, with other 'old schoolers', an advocate, Mathew's own involvement was initially minimal in comparison with the contribution of lay Catholic members of the CTAS, many of whom were uncomfortable with the proselytising techniques of some of Martin's associates, and all of whom were keenly aware of the cause's failure to attract the Catholic poor.

These men, including John Francis Maguire, James McKenna, Frank Walsh, Thomas Lyons, John O'Connell and others, brought with them to their Temperance work a set of concerns quite different from earlier, mostly Protestant, activists. They were members of the rising Irish Catholic middle class, 'emancipated' since 1829 and brought to practical political self-consciousness in the decades before and since Emancipation by the Catholic Association, its leader Daniel O'Connell, and the long series of agitations he had engaged in, most recently the Tithe war of the mid- to late 1830s.[6] A strong sense of middle-class identity was for them also associated with activism and an obligation to elevate the entire community.[7] From their continual and early emphasis on mass conversion and enrolment figures (see Chapter 1) it appears they were much inclined to look beyond the laudable but narrow stories of personal and familial redemption resulting from sobriety. Alcohol was charged with meaning – an important source of imperial tax revenue, a shameful and characteristic Irish vice, and a mark or even cause of Ireland's degraded circumstances. Temperance, in addition to providing a path to spiritual and material self-improvement (the dominant message of Temperance advocates for more than a decade), also had a deeper potential as a means to collective kinds of ends: ends intertwined with developing ideas about progress, Ireland's own history, and her unsatisfactory relationship with Britain. Mathew, as shall be seen, was by no means uncomfortable with these themes, but even more importantly, his accession to the CTAS's presidency opened the door for these ideas to begin to find there way into public discourse in new and powerfully influential ways. In short order, Temperance was enmeshed in an intensely political, patriotic and fundamentally 'national' discourse, the vocabulary of which, while it did not downplay the individual temporal and spiritual benefits of Temperance, expanded on the logic of earlier efforts. The temperate man and woman was not the end of the CTAS, he or she was the beginning of a regenerated Ireland and a new social order.

James McKenna

James McKenna is of particular interest in tracing the early development and practical expression of some of these ideas. His influential role as an evangelist for the CTAS has already been made clear. McKenna also made extensive efforts to publicise the movement through newspaper advertising, the printing of posters, pamphlets and handbills, and by regular communication with the press, but the most comprehensive expression of his Temperance philosophy is preserved in his manuscript history of the movement.

McKenna kept voluminous records of the CTAS's progress in his *The History of the Temperance Reformation in Ireland, England and Scotland by James McKenna, Chief Travelling and Confidential Secretary to the Very Reverend Theobald Mathew*. This eclectic, meticulously hand-written collection of hundreds of outsized pages of transcribed addresses, newspaper articles, and correspondence was woven together in McKenna's own strident and highly charged presentation. McKenna intended to publish his account, as the definitive, triumphal and popular history of what, when he was writing, seemed a miraculous, permanent reformation. He confidently predicted his work would 'be found the most interesting ever presented to the literary world'.[8] McKenna's early death, and the Temperance cause's rapid retreat, probably combined to prevent the manuscript's publication. Although of dubious literary merit, the pages of this zealous history lay out certain themes clearly and dramatically, themes which occur over and over again in much of the rhetoric of the cause.

The true source of, and best explanation for, the success of Temperance in Ireland, McKenna insisted, was Providence. God Himself was acting through the Irish people and using them for His own purposes. 'It may not be', he pointed out, in a passage apparently written some time in late 1839 or early 1840, 'the least remarkable circumstance connected with this movement that the impulse did not begin from man. It came from a higher quarter. In Cork, for instance, so numerous have the numbers of our society become that it shows a higher power must have aided our endeavours. Since last September, so many have flocked to our society, that it is manifest we must have been aided from on high.'[9]

Early in his history, McKenna outlined three goals of Temperance. The first was 'unity among Irishmen'.[10] Temperance required not only 'abstinence from intoxicating drinks, but abstinence from drunken discords about nothing, or about that which is worse than nothing, namely, that with which we have nothing to do, of which we may take as an example the religion of our neighbours'. A second goal was the 'education of the popular mind'. 'To be sober and reflective', McKenna felt, 'are one.' McKenna was quick to point out that this education, related to sobriety, had a further political objective, as 'a drunken people will be immoral, ignorant and enslaved. A sober people must become moral, intelligent, prosperous, free and independent.' The third goal related to Temperance's role in enhancing prosperity. Yet even this objective was given a communal gloss by McKenna, who insisted that by improving the material circumstances of the people, Temperance would 'promote our national condition'.[11]

Temperance, for McKenna, was above all about regenerating the Irish people. Indeed, the scale of the movement's success and the magnitude of the reformation led McKenna to insist that Temperance could *only* truly be understood in its collective, transformative dimension. The Irish, McKenna maintained, were 'a people whom centuries of intemperance have degraded'.[12] 'The moral reformation in Ireland', he explained triumphantly,

> is the sublimest spectacle the world ever beheld, and no features in its brilliant history will so much excite the praise and admiration of future historians as that it develops a peculiarity in her people, marked and distinct from that of any other nation in the civilized world. For where can a parallel be found of a nation rising in the space of a few years from universal indulgence in a dangerous and destructive habit, to a rigid and equally universal abstentiousness?[13]

If the Irish people had achieved abstinence together, it was also in its collective dimension that this accomplishment had its deepest meaning:

> We are proud of the country – proud in the recollection of her past glories – proud that in later days her sons have maintained in the battlefield and the senate a position enviable, and an eternity of name. But prouder far

> are we, that Irishmen have presented to the nations of the world a spectacle of self-denying virtue that puts to the blush all yet read of Greek or Roman story – a spectacle on which earth must look with admiration, and hell with hate – the spectacle of a nation disenthralled and emancipated from chains that dazzled with their deceitful lustre.[14]

For all of these reasons, to fail Temperance was to fail Ireland. 'To stand aloof from teetotalism', McKenna asserted, 'is looked upon, not so much in the light of a personal, as of a national dereliction.'[15] This collective sense of Ireland's temperate destiny, was, in the end, from McKenna's standpoint, the real meaning of the pledge for an Irishman. 'When he takes the pledge', McKenna maintained, 'he gives security, not only that he will heretofore be a good man, but that he will be a good Irishman.'

McKenna's intensely patriotic vision of the Temperance reformation was built upon a romantic understanding of Irish history, and a forceful expectation of a new golden age that the reformation was establishing so rapidly. Ireland had once enjoyed, McKenna reminded his readers, 'from the voice of universal Christendom the appellation of the "Isle of Saints"'.[16] McKenna would 'weep for her departed greatness', if not for an internal 'voice of prophesy' telling him that '"Ireland will be greater yet ever than she has been"', a greatness that 'is already at hand' through Father Mathew's efforts.[17]

The implications of this vision became more apparent once it was understood that the degradation of individual Irish men and women through drink was no accident; it derived from social and political circumstances. In this way, the individual degradation of Irish men and women reflected an Ireland deliberately and systematically degraded by her political position. 'The Exchequer of England', McKenna remarked contemptuously, referring to the duty on whiskey, 'was enriched with the price of our individual degradation. Our national character was degraded in the eyes, not only of Great Britain, but of the world.'[18] 'We knew', McKenna had warned earlier in his manuscript, 'we had foes, numerous, active, alert foes.'[19] More than simply opponents of Temperance, these 'foes' were, by definition, traitors or foreigners, 'willing, eager, ardent to grasp, to torture, to vilify, the energies, the hopes, the intentions of Irishmen'. By their opposition, McKenna boldly asserted, they rendered Temperance 'a political position'; one that thrived despite 'the truculent enmity of such foes'. Temperance, as understood by James McKenna, had produced a national transformation that could be expected to shift the political balance of power away from these manipulative and exploitative forces and towards the morally 'disenthralled' Irish people.

John Francis Maguire

More could be said of McKenna's manuscript, but the real importance of his work was that it is reflective of widely held and oft-invoked ideas about Temperance. Other early activists also shared many of his convictions, which were evident particularly in the writings of John Francis Maguire. As a journalist, Maguire was intimately concerned with the pulse of public opinion, yet relatively little historiographical attention has been paid to the role he played in helping to shape as well as to articulate popular understanding of Temperance's objectives. Maguire's early advocacy of the cause in his pamphlet *The Cause of Total Abstinence Justified*, was touched on in Chapter 1, but it is important to note here that the pamphlet's general tone, and many of its specific arguments, reflected McKenna's. If McKenna highlighted the Providential and patriotic aspects of the CTAS, however, Maguire spoke most clearly of its transformative and communal qualities. The success of the CTAS to date could best be discerned, Maguire argued, by 'coolly and dispassionately' investigating 'the nature of the doctrine of Temperance'.[20] Maguire wrote the pamphlet, he explained in its preface, to combat the 'greatest curse of our unfortunate country, – that which has kept her far behind her sister – England, in refinement and civilization.'[21] Alcohol was 'the most powerful' source of 'degradation', the '*radix* from which a thousand branches, prolific in ills and bearing poisoned fruit, spring'.[22] A barrage of editorials in his newspaper, the *Cork Total Abstainer*, founded in February 1841 (the *Cork Examiner* after August 1841), also strongly echoed McKenna's vision of Temperance. Maguire also offered a fundamentally providential understanding of Temperance's accomplishments. In the first edition of the *Total Abstainer*, he insisted that 'God, through his earthly agent or minister, has raised up this new practice for the moral liberty and regeneration of Ireland'.[23] 'It was far beyond the boundary of probability – nay, it seemed of possibility', Maguire scoffed, 'to accomplish a total revolution in the habits of a whole nation' without the aid of God.

The 'great object' of this divinely-mandated revolution, Maguire noted in his new paper's first editorial, was the transformation of Ireland through 'a true and perfect union of all creeds and classes' in order 'to advance the cause of National Temperance'.[24] Intemperance constituted a 'stream of moral corruption flowing on, wave after wave, not only engulfing the happiness, the honour, and the character of individuals; not only sapping the foundation of every social, political or religious obligation, but, alas! bearing onward in its hellish course all trace of national character and fame!' 'Happy', Maguire insisted in concluding, 'is Ireland in her *cause*.'

Maguire described a movement which was held together by a widely shared understanding of its collective purpose. Early in 1841, for example, the *CTA* approvingly reprinted the remarks of a Mr Looney, made at a Temperance meeting in Mallow Lane on 17 February. 'It is necessary for all to join', Looney had insisted, 'it is no sacrifice at all. The Patriot must come forward for his nation's sake.'[25] Another editorial on 6 March reinforced the point by insisting that most of the millions who had pledged by that time had never 'previously exceeded the bounds of strictest moderation' in their drinking habits. They had pledged not to rid themselves of a bad habit, but 'for example and self-preservation, for character and country, to banish drunkenness forever from their shores, and to lift up into the magnificence of moral splendour old and loved Ireland'.[26] Because the Irish had pledged together, moreover, Maguire insisted they would surely keep the pledge. Fidelity was assured by 'a strong principal of honour, courage, and resolution seated in the hearts of the Irish people'.[27] Maguire's status as a principal confidant of Father Mathew's gave credibility to his journalistic efforts on behalf of the Temperance movement and rendered his vision of an Ireland transformed and united by Temperance enormously influential in shaping popular understanding of the CTAS.

Father Mathew

If McKenna and Maguire provide important examples of the coherent message of the CTAS in its early days, it is equally clear that Father Mathew, who soon became the movement's most prominent spokesman, was just as forthright in proclaiming the Temperance gospel. Father Mathew made hundreds of speeches during the course of his campaign around Ireland. During the movement's early years, many newspapers carried verbatim accounts of his appeals, which of course considerably amplified their effect.[28] Mathew's speeches, therefore, were intended not only for his immediate audience, but also for the entire country. Indeed, the broad outline of his Temperance message soon became almost too familiar. John Francis Maguire certainly appreciated this – not only did he change the focus of his own paper in 1842 away from Temperance and towards Repeal politics, he also, in his later biography of Father Mathew, described in detail the tendency of reporters to skip assigned Temperance meetings in favour of a day off.[29] They found it easy enough, he explained, to write convincing approximations of Father Mathew's well-worn words, or even to guess which of his stump speeches was most likely to have been recycled for the occasion. Maguire's anecdote reveals an important truth – Father

Mathew presented a consistent, well-known rhetorical vision of Temperance to the Irish people, replete with references to 'degradation' and 'regeneration'. With McKenna and Maguire, Mathew urged Irish men and women to join a divinely-ordained revolutionary movement that was both patriotic and all-encompassing.

To begin with, Father Mathew was clearly convinced that his movement was divinely directed. As he told Tobias Kirby, the vice-rector of the Irish College in Rome, in May 1842, 'The results of the great temperance movement are allowed by all to be miraculous, and to be the work of God.'[30] Nor did he hesitate early on in the crusade to make this conviction public. In Lismore on 29 January 1840, for example, he remarked that he was 'but an humble instrument in the hands of Providence'.[31] The following summer, while administering the pledge at Naas, he wondered why anyone refused to take the pledge when 'it is manifest that this is the work of God'.[32] 'No human agency', the Apostle insisted, echoing Maguire, 'could possibly cause such a mighty revolution in the habits of the people.' In fact, it was a rare Temperance speech by Father Mathew in which he did not make reference to the movement's divine mandate, a grace that the individual partook of when he or she pledged. Father Mathew consistently presented Temperance to the Irish people as nothing short of a Divine attempt at collective transformation.

Mathew also certainly believed quite deeply in the transformative power of his movement, and clearly viewed himself as creating a new race of temperate Irish men and women whose secular and spiritual salvation was thereby all but assured. In April 1840 he urged a Dublin audience to become 'impressed with the same spirit he observed in many of the country people who, when coming to take the pledge, say that they do not present themselves to become teetotallers, but to be converted'.[33] 'That showed', he assured his audience, 'they meditated making an entire change in their lives. They will be able to do so.' 'The members of our society', he told a crowd at Naas on 15 August 1840, 'have been changed, as it were, into new men by the virtue of this abstinence.'[34] In Dublin later in 1840, he suggested that those who became teetotallers were a kind of 'blank, or fair sheet in which anything may be written'.[35]

Yet there was very much more to Temperance than the mere transformation of individuals. Whatever salvation that resulted, however desirable, needed to be understood as part and parcel of a patriotic epiphany. Temperance was, a satisfied Mathew told postulants on 10 June 1840, 'becoming a national virtue'.[36] 'Every lover of his country', he informed a large Cork meeting some eight months later in February

1841, 'must be an advocate of the cause ... I consider the man who opposes temperance, an enemy to his country.'[37] Rejoicing over a sober St Patrick's Day the following year, he informed a Dr T. Ferrian in Wirthing that 'sobriety prevailed throughout the length and breadth of the land. Drunkenness is no longer the besetting vice of the Irish people.'[38] Father Mathew's platform relied a great deal on this evocative imagery of a new Ireland, remade by a movement 'pregnant with blessings for our country'.[39] In June 1842, at a meeting at Nenagh, he described his decision to begin his crusade in these patriotic terms:

> I had long reflected on the degradation to which my country was reduced, a country second to none in the universe for every element that constitutes a nation's greatness, with a people whose generous nature is the world's admiration. I mourned in secret over the miseries of this country; I endeavoured to find out the cause of those miseries and, if it were possible, to apply a remedy. I saw that those miseries were chiefly owing to the crimes of the people, and that those crimes again had their origin in the use that was made of intoxicating drink. I discovered that if the cause were removed, the effects would cease.[40]

Mathew had a particular fondness for asserting that a temperate Ireland would provide an example to other nations, as when he informed a crowd of some 20,000 at Swords, Co. Dublin, on 16 November 1840 that Ireland was 'giving the tone to the rest of the world'.[41] The Temperance movement 'was all that was wanted to make the Irish people, in every point of view, a truly great and exalted people'. 'Other nations', he insisted, revealing wounded national pride, 'would be no longer able to introduce on the stage, and in pantomimes of drunkards, the Irishman, as one of whom drunkenness was characteristic.' 'Temperance', he asserted patriotically, in Cork on April 1841, to a cheering crowd at a meeting,

> would proceed in its onward career, until Ireland, from one end to the other – from the centre to the circumference – would present the wonderful spectacle, in contrast with its condition three years hence, of an entire nation reclaimed from the most criminal and accursed propensity that had ever blighted and blasted the best interests of the people.[42]

Father Mathew's belief in the transformative power of Temperance found rhetorical expression in a vision of a long degraded but soon-to-be-regenerated Ireland. 'The long and dreary night of sorrow and degradation that oppressed Ireland', which Mathew mentioned in his published letter to the land agent W.W. Simpson, was in fact something of a mantra.[43] Late in January 1840, at Lismore, for example, he prophesied that 'glorious days are beginning to dawn on our long disserved and oppressed country', while he announced at the beginning of his first Dublin mission some three months later that 'the great object of the teetotallers was to elevate the people from a state of degradation to the highest scale of moral worth'.[44] On 9 May 1840, the occasion of his second visit to Waterford, he told postulants that 'before long Ireland will again be an island of saints, and not an island of drunkards'.[45] 'Heretofore', he explained to thousands in Callan the following month, 'the want of self-respect was a great taint upon the Irish character. We seemed anxious not to rise above a position of degradation.'[46] Ireland's rosy future was assured by the temperate 'rising generation', another recurring theme in Father Mathew's platform rhetoric and correspondence.[47]

For all his patriotism, Father Mathew's own tone seldom slipped into the boastful anti-English triumphalism quite common in other advocates of Temperance. Conscious of the vulnerability of his cause, as well as its susceptibility to accusations of politicisation, Mathew was very careful not to make enemies or alienate potential allies, particularly as some of his most faithful supporters, correspondents and, later, financial backers were English. In that sense, Mathew had an English constituency of which he was considerate. Because he was also aware of belonging to a movement that extended across national boundaries, he had little interest in building up Ireland at the potential expense of his 'sacred cause'. Indeed, he would have seen any such attempt as fundamentally misguided, as the crucial problem in Ireland from his point of view was divisiveness itself. Ultimately, he looked to England to recognise and reward Irish virtue, ushering in a new relationship between the two islands.

And yet Mathew, with McKenna, marked himself out as an opponent of the English government's willingness to raise revenue from Irish alcohol consumption via spirit duties and licensing fees. In June 1840, at Callan, for example, he complained about 'the constant drain on the capital of the country' caused by alcohol consumption.[48] 'Millions', he explained, 'have been going away annually in licencing and other duties.' A more explicit rendition of those remarks brought considerable controversy for Father Mathew later that summer. At Naas, in August 1840, as he often did, he spoke emotionally and forcefully against emigration, decrying the 'heart-rending scenes of human woe and wretchedness of the heart as I have witnessed on the quays of Cork … parting, perhaps forever, under circumstances exceeding the power of language to convey an adequate representation of.'[49] The money 'unnecessarily and wantonly lavished' on drink could, of course, have been used to keep families together, but instead 'a small portion of it goes to the profit of the publican, who sells the poisoned draught, while the remainder of it, swallowed up in duties, is transferred to a foreign country'. Well before this, it should be noted, the decrease in the excise revenue that Temperance was naturally causing had been cited gleefully by many, usually in terms that condemned England's willingness to profit from Irish degradation.[50] Mathew's comments identified him with this strain of explicit anti-English sentiment, particularly through his emotional association of the taxation of the poor man with the painful process of emigration.[51]

Finally, Father Mathew's conception of Irish Temperance also emphasised its patriotic, communal dimension. His oft-repeated goal for the movement was, after all, 'unity' among the entire Irish people under the banner of total abstinence. This produced practically, in Mathew's rhetoric, a blurring of the lines between the teetotaller, the community and the nation. As the national dimensions of his crusade grew, so his patience with those who impeded its inevitable progress diminished. Mathew's communitarian sense of the movement manifested itself in a lack of patience with backsliders. As Maguire explained, 'it was with a positive sense of pain that he became conscious of the desertion or backsliding of a single follower. He mourned over the loss of a stray sheep, and never rested until he had followed it back into the wilderness of temptation, and brought it back, and placed it safely within the fold.'[52] At Limerick in October 1841, at a special meeting convened for the purpose of re-pledging penitent pledge-breakers, he declared, 'It is not surprising that a few should fall away. Human nature is frail, and there will be found men who, like Essau of old, would barter their birthright for a mess of pottage.'[53] 'Oh, deep and deadly', he further lamented, 'must be the hue of that person's character who makes trifle of the solemn engagement he enters into, and worthy of no respect at the hands of his fellow mortals.'

The movement's great weapon against the twin evils of backsliding and indifference, the moral force of both the Temperance society and of the entire community, will be examined in detail in the next chapter. It bears noting here, however, that Mathew invoked such pressure at every opportunity, as he did in Cork in the course of a chiding new year's address to the Temperance societies there in 1841:

> He mentioned the case of a man who had called on him that morning for the purpose of returning his own and his son's medals. He regretted to see that the several teetotallers who were in the room at the time exhibited

> the greatest indifference to this. The unhappy mistaken man persisted, and he did not see the indignation amongst those present which was elsewhere felt at the violation or abandonment of the pledge. In those places, the man who was guilty of such a dereliction was looked upon as a kind of monster. In some districts there was not a man who had broken it. The people shunned and refused to associate with those who did so.[54]

A pledge-breaker, he had assured a Dublin crowd a few months earlier, brought 'degradation upon himself and upon three millions of people – yes, he certainly does by the breach disgrace not only himself, but, I may say, the people of a whole kingdom'.[55]

As for the unpledged, while Mathew urged his followers 'to entertain nothing but charity towards those who will not become teetotallers', in fact he endorsed a tolerance for drinkers so heavily laced with pity and contempt that there can be no doubt he sought (and encouraged his followers to seek) universal conversion.[56] There was, he assured teetotallers at Strokestown in October 1840, 'great importance to the community at large of abstaining from intoxicating drinks'.[57] In Cork a few months earlier, on 24 August 1840, he had been more emphatic. 'There is no way', he explained to a packed meeting at the Horse Bazaar, 'by which a man can confer more blessings on his fellow creatures than by inducing him to become a teetotaller.'[58] 'Fly, I say to you', he further exhorted, 'fly from the breath, the touch of the drunkard, no matter who he may be, for crime, sin, death – temporal and eternal – are all around him! Call that man your enemy who endeavors to dissuade you from joining this society, follow the example of others.' The pledge itself compelled the teetotaller to 'discountenance, by advice and example' intemperance in others.[59] Mathew's correspondence, as well as his eagerness to administer the pledge to women and children, amply demonstrate his determination that as many of the Irish as possible should take the pledge.

Promoting the Good Work

McKenna's, Maguire's and Father Mathew's own words tell only a part of the story of the promotion of Temperance in its early days. In addition to the thousands of leaders of local societies, and the bewildering collection of bishops, parish clergy, employers, controversialists, politicians, newspaper editors, travel writers and other opportunistic supporters, the cause had certain authorised advocates. Father Mathew believed in the value of advertising and spent thousands of pounds on printing. He also approved contemporary histories of the cause, most notably the incredibly popular early pamphlet history of the cause authored by

James Bermingham, the parish priest of Borrisokane, Co. Tipperary, entitled 'A Memoir of the Very Reverend Theobald Mathew, with an Account of the Rise and Progress of Temperance in Ireland', published in May 1840.[60]

Father Mathew was a careful reader of the Irish and English press, and he sometimes printed, at his own expense, copies of Temperance material he found there, or forwarded interesting articles to other papers for possible reprinting.[61] Articles and pamphlets printed for the teetotallers were then mailed to the officers of various local societies, to be placed in local reading rooms or otherwise made available to the membership, or to other individuals the CTAS believed might support the movement.[62] For the most part, this 'official' propaganda for the cause is lost to history, but one particularly striking piece can be identified, and reveals that Mathew was willing to endorse very forceful visions of Temperance in its providential, transformative, nationalistic, historical, triumphal and communitarian dimensions – rhetoric closer to James McKenna's than his own more careful language.

On 29 July 1840, a W. O'Connor in Fermoy wrote to Mathew, thanking him for forwarding a printed copy of an article entitled 'A Tribute to Father Mathew' authored by 'a Disciple of Father Mathew'.[63] O'Connor's letter revealed that he had drunk deeply of the movement's propaganda already, and he was confident the new piece would be 'taken up and digested, through Ireland, with the most beneficial effect'. 'My unfortunate country', O'Connor observed, was 'sunk to the bottom of depravity – by intoxication and immorality', a condition 'used as a political pretext to refuse us our national rights'. Temperance, that 'inestimable panacea', was a 'holy and nation-regenerating cause' which would bring the Irish to 'enjoy their national rights and comforts' with 'degradation, starvation and oppression totally removed'. 'If published', O'Connor concluded, apparently encouraging an even wider distribution for the new pamphlet, 'it would (as it should be) make an indelible impression.'

The piece O'Connor was referring to originally appeared in the *Freeman's Journal* the previous month, on the occasion of Father Mathew's triumphal visit to St Patrick's College and the village of Maynooth, described in Chapter 3.[64] Apparently written by one of the 250 students who took the pledge that day, the article bears careful examination, and quotation at some length. Not only did it reveal the sentiments of an articulate Temperance convert, it was also printed and widely distributed by the leader of that movement in order to provide a model for conversion to the cause.

The first section of the tribute to Mathew dealt with the historical dimension of the sudden rise of the CTAS, culminating (for the author) in the complete endorsement of Temperance by the Catholic church in Ireland.

> The glory of such a triumph will not be lost to you … the sacred fire you have kindled continues to spread, and like the hallowed flame of St Patrick, lighted up in view of Tara, it will not be extinguished until it has pervaded and sanctified the length and breadth of the island … the movement you have excited has no parallel in the history of any country except the first conversion of the Irish to Christianity. Your visit to Maynooth is the prologue to the future history of Ireland.

A second section addressed the composition and motivation of the crowd assembled from more than 30 miles around the village:

> The gentry as well as the poor, the priest as well as the people, kneeled before you in humility, under the canopy of heaven, with bared heads, to cooperate in this great movement of a nation … Whilst only the poor and illiterate flocked to your standard of temperance the movement was scribed to ignorance and superstition. But the self-refuted absurdity of representing ignorance and superstition as doing the office of heroic virtue, is fully silenced by the grave authority of Maynooth college. Their adherence to you was an act of judgement, guided by knowledge, and prompted by exalted virtue.

Another section considered the implications of Father Mathew's success:

> This business is pregnant with important consequences. It will work a total reformation in the whole body of the Irish clergy. By their talents, their virtue, their knowledge and their influence, they were hitherto very formidable to the enemies of truth and Ireland; this will make them invincible. The example of this day will mark the people. They will become sober, industrious and sensible alike of their social rights and moral duties. Their energy, their intelligence, their fearless spirit, will no longer be squandered in factions, feuds, illegal combinations, or political broils, but will be soberly and combindly exerted for the good of their afflicted country.

Finally, and perhaps most revealingly, the author explained his own decision to take the pledge in patriotic terms, despite the fact that he had not intended to do so:

> Yielding cheerfully myself to the many generous examples I had seen in the town and in the college, I did what an Irishman should do under the circumstances. I must be like them, I said; I will do as they have done,

> and, folding my arms in deep deliberation, I knelt amongst the crowd. I registered in heaven my solemn promise of total and perpetual abstinence, and got the benediction of Father Mathew.

Immediately, however, the author begins to question the wisdom of his decision, but notices a trusted friend in the crowd next to him:

> His account of himself confirmed my strong conviction, and, by a singular coincidence, expressed my own feelings and motives on that extraordinary occasion. 'This (said he, with the impassioned zeal of a convert) you may rely on it, is the precursor of some mighty change in this country! It will reform the people, it will give a new character to the clergy, it will wipe away many a tear of sorrow, and eventually give happiness to our country ... the regeneration of Ireland is now secure, Father Mathew has done it. In spite of bad laws and drunken legislators, Ireland will rise again, majestic as her hills, impregnable as her shores, and, shaking off the oppression of centuries, will regain the ascendant of learning and public virtue amongst the nations of the earth'.

The Temperance pledge, as it was presented here, was taken in response to both rational consideration and emotional circumstance. It embodied self-improvement, historical destiny, religious fervour, as well as national and community identity in the very act of self-denial. The language, of course, was dramatic, and betrayed, as it confessed, 'the impassioned zeal of the convert'. What it revealed was that for many converts, Temperance's true meaning, indeed the powerful, life-changing determination of the individual to take the pledge itself – could only be discovered in the collective nature of the Temperance meeting, and of the future 'Temperance society' that was to be all of Ireland.

The movement's best-known and most substantial piece of early propaganda was certainly James Bermingham's *Memoir of the Very Rev'd Theobald Mathew*. Bermingham's work of some 100 pages was the product of his own conversations with Father Mathew, and was composed in the month or so after Mathew's visit to Bermingham's parish in Borrisokane, County Tipperary in March 1840. Issued in pamphlet form at the modest price of one shilling (the proceeds were designated to help fund the building of a Catholic church in Maryboro), the history included a short biographical sketch of Father Mathew and an account of the movement's astounding growth.[65] Mathew warmly endorsed the finished product, 'apart from paragraphs complimentary to myself, which I should wish omitted', adding that 'the details of the progress of our glorious society is perfectly correct' and hoping that 'that your pamphlet, so well calculated to promote the sacred cause of

Tee-totalism, will be read by every lover of human nature and his country, without distinction of creed or politics'.[66]

Like so many other observers of Temperance, Bermingham saw the hand of Providence in the CTAS.[67] Passages discussing the nature of the movement also clearly emphasised both its transformative power and communitarian, national dimensions:

> In truth, not only were our countrymen remarkable for the intemperate use of intoxicating liquors, but intemperance had already entered into, and formed part of, the national character. An Irishman and a drunkard became synonymous terms. Whenever he was to be introduced in character, either on the theatre or in the pages of a novelist, he should be represented habited in rags, bleeding at the nose, and waving a shillalah. Whiskey was everywhere regarded as our idol ... A mighty change has come over Ireland, the night of Ireland's degradation is past; the foul vapours are scattered which obscured our best prospects; bright and peaceful, and happy days are opening upon us.[68]

In fact, Bermingham later noted, the suddenness of the collective change was astounding. 'We lie down', he wondered, 'a nation of drunkards; we rise a temperate people; and Ireland – sunken and degraded Ireland – with one bound again stands erect, to assume that position among the nations, to which the genius and warm-heartedness of her sons, and her own unfading beauty and fertility entitle her.'[69]

Just as Father Mathew did, Bermingham explicitly disavowed any 'political' agenda – again, in relation to ongoing party politics. Mathew and his teetotallers 'disclaimed all connection with politics'.[70] 'It is true', Bermingham admitted, 'that a peaceful and sober people may, with more hope of success, lay their just claims for equal rights before the legislature, and a kind and paternal government may regard sooner the constitutional struggles of such a people.' Still, Bermingham stoutly maintained, 'teetotalism was never intended, and we hope it shall never be made, an instrument to effect political purposes'.

Despite these reservations, Bermingham recognised with the movement's other advocates, that Ireland's moral transformation provided a jumping-off point for a new era in her history.

> Though a great deal has been attempted in favour of this country, and much had been effected, yet in the march of nations, Ireland should stand still or retrograde, until the foul stigma had been wiped off, which the habitual intemperance of her sons had cast upon her.[71]

Because of intemperance, 'our enemies sneered at us'. Furthermore, 'a frequent, if not strictly just argument set up against our claims for liberty was, that a people so enslaved to a base and demoralizing habit, could not be entrusted with civil rights or privileges'. That argument, Bermingham insisted, could no longer be sustained.

In order to emphasise this point, Bermingham indulged in a popular and effective historical analogy that modesty would not allow to Father Mathew. In a lengthy section he drew a careful comparison between Ireland's patron saint Patrick and the Apostle of Temperance; the similarities were, he claimed, 'striking'.[72] As the conversion to Christianity had been, Bermingham pointed out, the Temperance movement was also a turning point in Ireland's history, a history marked by 'worse than Egyptian servitude'.[73]

Bermingham's pamphlet was eagerly sought after, and sold well.[74] The degree to which its characterisation of the movement and its leader was generally accepted is, of course, open to question, but there can be no doubt that many of its themes found strong echoes in various other forms of popular expression. An anonymous miner from Bonmahon may only have been more scrupulous in his citations than later readers, for shortly after the pamphlet's publication, he wrote to the *Waterford Chronicle*, quoting from and praising Bermingham's work and agreeing that Temperance was the beginning of a great national regeneration, a 'happy deliverance'.[75] The *Chronicle*, in fact, ran extensive excerpts from the pamphlet on a daily basis in the first week after its publication.

Another prime example of the movement's official propaganda can be found in William MacNamara Downes' *Temperance Melodies for the Teetotallers of Ireland*, published in 1843, which included (in addition to an endorsement letter from Tom Moore) an introductory letter from Father Mathew, commissioning the project and designating Downes the 'poet laureate of the teetotallers'.[76] Mathew and other advocates of the cause had frequently called on music to replace the stimulation once provided by alcohol, as Mathew told teetotallers at Naas: 'It has been my wish to have music in our societies, as constituting a source of humble recreation and innocent enjoyment.'[77] Sheet music, Temperance ballads and even choral singing were very much the order of the day from an early phase in the cause's development. As a reporter noted on the occasion of Father Mathew's second major Temperance mission, to Waterford in December 1839: 'Ballad singers chanting temperance songs are heard in every street'.[78] An important result of this popular enthusiasm was a proliferation of ballad collections, and the *Temperance Melodies* was the CTAS's own attempt to use this enthusiasm to build up the cause and to 'catechise' Ireland's millions of teetotallers.

Enormously popular (the collection went through three editions in less than a year), Downes' songs were set to Moore's melodies and were designed to commemorate, as Downes claimed in a dedicatory epistle to the Apostle of Temperance, 'the triumph of moral worth among Irishmen'. 'I thought', he explained, 'the design would be the more appropriately national by associating the words with Irish airs.' The 'design' certainly was national, and like McKenna, Mathew, Bermingham, Maguire and other 'official' advocates of the cause, Downes' songs reinforced a particular view of the crusade. Degradation, regeneration, Ireland's glorious past (marred only by intemperance), her oppressed present, and her promising future, as well as the need for the Irish to embrace Temperance as a people all featured prominently in many of the songs, such as *Green Isle of our Fathers*:

I

Green Isle of our Fathers we love thee,
The cup of thy sorrow is past.
And bright is the sunbeam above thee
As long as thy virtue may last!

The minstrels may swell their proud pages
And wake the gay tones of their lyres;
For gone is the curse of the ages,
Had blighted the land of their sires.

II

Oh, what could so deeply degrade her,
Or fix on her sons such a stain?
It was not the hostile invader,
It was not the sword or the chain.

Ah, no – but the rank dregs of madness
She drain'd and that ill-fated bowl
Brought on all the woes and the sadness
That chill'd the pure fire of her soul!

Yet Erin, bright hopes are before thee,
Though gone are the days of your fame –
Thy children once more shall restore thee
The pride of a long-vanished name.

The ballad concluded:

Then blest is the vow we have spoken
That pledge which our country shall save.
Our children will keep it unbroken
When we shall be cold in the grave.

The chorus to another song, *The Reformer*, an ode to Father Mathew, warned would-be opponents of the cause that they defied divine will:

We'll faithful remain, let no Irishman stain
This glorious national movement.
'Tis seen from on high – and its motives defy
The foes of our moral improvement.

Father Mathew's favourite Temperance song, according to Downes' preface to the tune, was *We'll Drink No More O' the Barley*. Mathew was serenaded regularly by Temperance bands, and after *Hail the Conquering Hero* and *Patrick's Day*, *We'll Drink No More* was a popular choice. This simple song condemned whiskey drinking, but it also connected the practice to national failings and promised their remedy:

Of whiskey now we see no trace,
The cup that once betray'd us –
That burning cause of deep disgrace
No longer shall degrade us.
Twas Ireland's bane its dregs to drain –
Her curse both late and early;
It never more shall stain our shore;
We'll drink no more o' the barley.

PART II: THE RESPONSE

In order to transform Ireland, Mathew and other influential members of the CTAS sought, first and foremost, to mark out a public, moral dimension to Irish identity exclusive of class, creed and gender, bounded by the particular collective practice of total abstinence. As Mathew explained on many occasions, he was attempting to create new men and women, and by extension a new kind of public sphere. It is evident that there was widespread understanding between Mathew and his friends and allies regarding the nature of their mission. In the formative years of triumph for that cause – the crucial period between 1839 and 1843, when the vast majority of the millions who pledged formed their opinions about the movement, and made their decision to join it – Mathew and his articulate supporters spoke with one voice. What now needs to be examined is the response to that call. If, in fact, there was a coherent discourse of Temperance, with a vocabulary as laid out above, it remains to be demonstrated to what degree that voice was effective in conveying its message, and shaping the Irish people's understanding of their own association with the CTAS.

One important measure of the success of the crusade's leadership in promoting a particular vision of Temperance was the way in which the CTAS's local leaders and advocates described the movement to their own eager and enthusiastic followers. The surviving evidence indicates that most local Temperance activists in parishes all over Ireland did in fact partake of the common language of Temperance, promoting the cause in its own terms, as a dramatic effort at national regeneration from a state of collective degradation. To a striking degree, much of the rhetoric of local activists stood as a mirror image of the rhetorical challenge offered up by Mathew, McKenna, Maguire and others. As early as October 1839, for example, one C. Cockrane, addressing a meeting at Tullamore, Co. Kerry, 'wished that there were more such men as Father Mathew'.[79] On that day, Cockrane insisted, 'we would soon see Ireland as she ought to be. No more would it be represented to the English nation as if its inhabitants were savages, covered with hair, and having long tails wagging behind.' 'If whiskey were banished', he added, 'the misery, crime and cold blooded murder which characterise our nation would also be banished.' Nicholas Foran, the Bishop of Waterford, told his flock at a tea party in January 1840 that the CTAS was responsible for 'the moral regeneration of the Irish people' and that discerning observers of Temperance 'could not fail to recognise in the work the special intervention of Divine Providence who had created it for the benefit of his people'.[80] Justice of the Peace Daniel Clanchy's remarks at a tea party in Charleville, Co. Cork on Saint Patrick's Day, 1840, were unequivocal in their explanation of the movement's importance. 'Thus have Irishmen', Clanchy insisted, 'by casting off their evil passions, and by their fidelity in not again assuming it, exhibited to the world their steadfastness, and again we shall earn that glorious distinction, which in bye gone ages was the appellation of our native isle – the Isle of Saints.'[81] 'A halo of glory will be shed round our country', he concluded hopefully. Similarly, the following September, James McDonnell at a tea party in Boyle praised Ireland's 'regeneration' from a 'degrading habit' by which the 'national character was disfigured'. 'Even those who had not yet resolution to take the pledge', McDonnell insisted, 'were ashamed to be seen indulging in the dangerous experiment of intoxicating draughts.'

> May our beloved country, under the benign influence of temperance, once more become entitled to the enviable appellation, 'Island of Saints'. In this mighty revolution, which is now ... transversing the kingdom, and even extending itself beyond the boundless waves of the great Atlantic – in the devoted fervour with which our countrymen of all classes are everywhere thronging round the hallowed standard of temperance, and in the unparalleled fidelity with which they observe their sacred pledge, we recognise with gratitude the manifest indications of the finger of God.

Examples could be multiplied. Such language was commonplace, and could be found at most Temperance tea parties, dinners and meetings all over the country.

It is equally clear that the press, particularly the Liberal papers, played an important role in building up and maintaining enthusiasm for the Temperance cause. Contemporaries understood the press's power very well. As Maguire noted, of Mathew, 'It would be difficult to say whether he prized more, as a convert, a newspaper editor or a peer of the realm.'[82] Mathew could be effusive in his public praise or bitter in his private condemnation, but he never underestimated the press's influence on the popular mind. As he observed in Limerick, on 14 October 1841, their aid was 'powerful'.[83] 'The press', Mathew noted, 'after all, is the great palladium of human liberty – the great palladium of morality.' The opinion was a commonly held one, as the *Nation* explained in its first number:

> A newspaper is the only conductor to the mind of Ireland. Periodicals or books make no considerable impression, because they have no considerable circulation. Speeches are more effective, but we include them among the materials of journalism ... it is undeniable that the journals, with all their means and appliances, were, and are, and are to be for many a day, the stimulating power in Ireland.[84]

Independent of the important contribution to the CTAS's growth that more or less factual reportage of mass Temperance gatherings or other aspects of the movement made during the early days of the crusade, the Liberal press often repeated and amplified the CTAS's central message on its editorial pages, particularly in its patriotic and transformative aspect. Editorials endorsing the movement in glowing terms were common from the autumn of 1839. In October 1839, for example, the *Tipperary Free Press* termed the CTAS a 'moral and glorious revolution which every man who loves his kind and his country, must delight to contemplate', and urged it to 'spread its blessed influence all over our land'.[85] The influential *Southern Reporter*, which took up the Temperance cause early in November 1839, reinforced the communal and patriotic dimension of the crusade by observing, in an early favourable editorial, that 'it would better suit the purposes of the people's enemies that they should remain slaves to this debasing foible. A people abandoned to habitual drunkenness can never, of course, reach the same height of enlightenment and civilization which they might attain were they freed form this infirmity.'[86] By January 1840, the same newspaper unhesitatingly referred to the 'miraculous project which this truly blessed revolution is bringing about' and termed the CTAS a 'glorious NATIONAL SOCIETY'.[87] By Saint Patrick's Day, 1841, the *Freeman's Journal* was only reflecting the pro-Temperance consensus in the Liberal press when its editor encouraged 'the richer classes of our fellow citizens' to participate in Temperance demonstrations and accept their responsibility to participate in 'the moral regeneration of their countrymen'.[88] 'It is in their power now, by stepping forward and joining the ranks of *teetotal Dublin*, to give fresh stimulus to their work', the editor urged. There were those, the editorial continued, who would attempt

> to mar the progress of temperance by stigmatizing it as the result of momentary excitement, or, with their characteristic ignorance of the Irish heart, branding it as mere enthusiasm. That it originated and was sustained by enthusiasm we mean not to deny; but that enthusiasm is of a different character from what they would have us believe. It is the enthusiasm of Irish nature, that which was born with us, grows with our growth, and strengthens with our strength, and which when we shall have lost it, we shall cease to be Irishmen. 'A few weeks', and Temperance was to 'die a natural death.' Has it died? – Does it yet show symptoms of decay? We put it to you, and from the sincerity of your hearts answer, has not the experience of the past year convinced you that this cause is not that of momentary impulse, and that in the Irish people there exists a power of mind control hitherto unparalleled in the annals of the world?

The concluding exhortation, that the Irish people should 'with the moral courage of men make yourselves the advocates of national Temperance', only served to underscore the very evident fact that many newspaper editors drank deeply from the CTAS's nationalistic rhetorical wellspring.

If evidence indicates that certain elite groups (local activists and newspaper editors) identified with the CTAS's central message, and did their best to spread that message as widely as they could, there are also suggestions that this understanding of the purposes of Temperance was effectively diffused among millions of ordinary Irish men and women who joined the society. Much of the evidence for this is discussed in the next chapter, which examines popular behaviour and Temperance in closer detail. By taking the pledge together, by entwining their participation in the Temperance movement with a variety of dramatic public demonstrations and religious occasions, and by the communal ostracism or punishment of pledge-breakers and, to a lesser extent, the unpledged, the Irish people bore witness to their own understanding of the nature of the Temperance cause. Two indications of the enthusiastic popular reception of the CTAS's central message will be examined below, however, since they relate more particularly to the rhetorical elements described above.

One indication of the widespread appeal of the specific message of the CTAS can be found in the proliferation of popular ballad poetry that echoed the central elements of the movement's rhetoric. These unofficial Temperance hymns (as opposed to the sanctioned work of William MacNamara Downes examined above) typically circulated as ephemeral broadsheet ballads, sold in the streets for a few pennies, which were a regular feature of pre- and post-Famine Irish popular culture.[89] A few examples of the rhetoric of some surviving ballads are given here to demonstrate the message of the Temperance movement was very much in evidence in this popular medium.

Early in 1841, James Martin, who claimed that his 'station in life shuts me out from the high grades of society' and who insisted that 'the generality of my readers, with very few exceptions, are found among the lower orders', published a Temperance ballad collection at Kells, Co. Meath, which included a lengthy ode entitled *The Totallers Farewell to Whiskey*.[90] In it, the author described Temperance as a divinely ordained crusade destined to restore a degraded Ireland to her former greatness. Drunkenness, 'Sent hither, to Erin, her worst foes to please/Curst author of poverty, want and disease' was to be conquered by one

> Whose voice shall resound from the South to the North
> Ycleped Father Mathew, to whom it is giv'n,
> To preach to this nation the mandates of heav'n!
> By the special will of JEHOVAH, designed,
> To bring all my blessings with Grace to mankind.
> God saw, with regret, how ebriety taints,
> The once spotless name of this *Island of Saints*.
> And her matchless sons, who were once wont to shine,
> In learning and war, from the pole to the line,
> As palpable drunkards, of late stigmatized,
> By which they're degraded, nay: so much despised,
> … Her sapient rulers, unwilling to see,
> Her long-wretched children, rich, happy, or free;

Gave her, in abundance, all hopes to exclude,
Toil, rackrents, and whiskey, for justice and food!
Imposed, for their comfort, a duty on grain,
And gave distillation – a bait and a bane:
While all who got tipsy, to solace the mind,
If seen, were arrested, imprisoned or fined!
Half-starved, tightly fettered, grieved ragged and poor,
And fleeced with more taxes than they could endure,
And plodding thro' hardship – to lessen their grief,
They sought in the whiskey a fruitless relief:
To flee for a moment from gloomy despair,
And gain a short respite from anguish and care.
Then soon to be habit, first practiced by few,
On numbers the vice imperceptibly grew;
And brought on the nation, a byeword a curse,
But now FATHER MATHEW is sent to efface
The stain and that vice from the nation to chase.

Another popular poet, Philip Connell, published a collection the same year, because, he claimed, 'since the unprecedented success of Teetotallism I have heard several complain, that they saw nothing from the Poetical department worthy of the great cause' of 'the regeneration of Ireland'.[91] Priced at 6d and filled with Temperance ballads set to popular tunes, the collection was obviously aimed at the masses. Several poems in the collection are worth noting for their rhetorical content if not their artistic merit. The collection's title poem, *The Medal and the Glass*, in the form of a dialogue between a Temperance medal and a whiskey glass, painted a portrait of a degraded Ireland:

From a race of burly men,
Who once did fame and glory win,
A fallen, dwindled, wither'd race,
The name of Irish now disgrace;
Tis drunken Pat now wears the brand
Of slave, in every foreign land.
Degraded, sunk, and doom'd to bear,
Contempt, and labour, every where.

Another ballad, written to the popular tune *Neil Gow's Farewell to Whiskey*, also portrayed the movement in collective and patriotic terms, and struck an anti-English tone:

Then paddies to your promise stand,
Till peace and plenty, hand in hand,
Forever from our happy land,
To hell have chased the whiskey, O!
We'll then make teapots of our stills,
And change our jails to flour mills;
While Doctors with their pukes and pills,
May follow cursed whiskey O!
– The lawyers, bailiffs and police,
Who long poor Paddy's back did fleece,
May skulk about like half-plucked geese,
Lamenting after whiskey, O!
While old John Bull, the gutling drone,
For pork and beef may grunt and groan,
For Paddy'll shortly eat his own,
Instead of drinking whiskey, O!

Song, to the popular tune *Patrick's Day*, did not hesitate to demand the full participation of the entire nation in the Divine revolution:

A second Saint Patrick, by heaven's command,
The work has commenced with a powerful hand;
The aid and assistance of all, he demands:
And who e'er will refuse, is a sot and a villain,
Who still for his country's uprise is unwilling,
But have the poor Irish each other's blood spilling,
On Patrick's day in the morning –

The collection's concluding poem, *The Irishman*, began by lamenting Ireland's decline:

You friends of Erin who behold,
Your country hastening to decay,
Her freedom lost, her interest sold,
Her children wandering far away;
Each effort tried for Erin's weal,
You'll find but an abortive plan,
While cursed whiskey can prevail,
Against the wisest Irishman.

and concluded with a ringing endorsement of the CTAS:

Then Irishmen, awake, arise!
Revive the glories of your name;
Let happy homes, domestic joys,
Content and comfort be your aim:
Till commerce crowding sea and land,
Unite the Shannon to the Bann;
And fame, as formerly, demand,
Respect for every Irishman.

The content of the examples given above appears to have been typical of many other anonymous Temperance songs, a number of which made their way into the press. *A New Song to an Old Tune*, for example, popular around Christmas 1839, was reprinted in many Irish newspapers.[92] In it, Father Mathew beheld 'Temperance, spreading far and wide', which 'glads his patriot heart' while 'all the saints in heaven above/Pour blessings on his work of love'. The entire Irish people, meanwhile, were to enjoy the fruits of moral liberty and participate in its establishment: 'From north to south, from east to west,/We'll conquer all the land./For Ireland, old Ireland, this is the happy day!' Another verse promised that 'our faction fights are o'er,/All Irishmen are brothers now'. In 1841, a Christmas poem which appeared in the *Cork Total Abstainer* promised that 'As "drunken Irish" we no more/Are scorned by other nations;/Amongst the people of the earth/We take our proper stations.'[93] Another song, *Lays on Temperance*, proclaimed that 'Temperance now reigns absolutely here,/And gains fresh impulse each revolving year,/Roams o'er the country with majestic stride,/And spreads its heavenly precepts, far and wide. Want flies, crime ceases, and Draconic laws,/Are rendered useless, by the sacred cause.'[94] *Lines on the Very Rev'd Father Mathew* insisted that Mathew had 'his kind and country freed' by battling 'passions which prostrate left our own lov'd isle/The prey of viscous spleen,/And bathed the shamrock's leaves in red/That nature nurtured green.'[95]

The degree to which popular understanding of the CTAS matched that of the movement's leaders is clearly manifested in the addresses local societies presented to Father Mathew on his arrival at a mission site.[96] While the authors of these usually-anonymous addresses were sometimes the presidents and leaders of CTAS branches, often they were written by members of the society with a reputation for poetical composition or known for their public speaking abilities. The addresses were typically read to Mathew in front of the crowd that always greeted him when he arrived for his missions.[97] As such they were public odes, designed to represent the sentiments of the entire membership of the local branch of the CTAS to Father Mathew. Almost always comically lofty in tone and usually choked with sentiment, the addresses nevertheless provided wonderful insight into a given community's own sense of what elements within the Temperance message were most likely to resonate amongst a crowd preparing to take the pledge.

Perhaps the most intriguing characteristic of the addresses, coming as they did from societies all over the country and written over a period of at least four years, was the degree to which they made use of the same themes, stock phrases, historical imagery, and sense of destiny that characterised the other forms of Temperance rhetoric. The language of 'regeneration' and 'degradation' was very much front-and-centre, all of which makes it very evident that local Temperance societies all over Ireland were inclined to reproduce the very same image of the movement that the CTAS's leaders, and Mathew himself, had so consciously espoused.

Many addresses proclaimed the transformation of Ireland in historical terms that admitted the movement's divine dimension. The 'Citizens of Waterford', for example, confessed that 'the past history of our country has been in truth a narrative of woe, a recital of successive misfortunes', the most 'hideous' of which was 'an excessively indulged passion, under its influence we know that the finest dispositions of the Irish heart were perverted and debased'. 'The minister of God appeared amongst us', the address noted of Mathew, and 'he toiled and laboured; heaven blessed – and soon, before a few months had passed away, we saw the Irish heart reclaimed, the Irish character restored to dignity.' 'You have effected the conversion, that was at first so difficult, so incredible, and in its end so glorious, restored as the people of Ireland have been to happiness and esteem of this world, and to the favour and benediction of heaven.'[98] The Total Abstinence Society of Leixlip and Lucan, Co. Dublin also pronounced Mathew to be 'the moral regenerator of our country', and rejoiced at the prospect of 'Ireland deserving of the appellation formerly bestowed upon it, that of being an Isle of Saints', a sentiment echoed by many societies including the teetotallers of Carrick-on-Suir, Co. Tipperary, who prayed that Mathew would continue his 'sacred mission until the great work is consummated until the beautiful island of our birth is regenerated and be dignified amongst nations as she formerly was the abode of peace harmony and brotherly love, the seat of arts and learning and the Island of Saints'.[99]

Many others saw the movement in patriotic terms. John Norris, writing on behalf of the Ballina Total Abstinence Society in County Mayo, not only praised Mathew for his 'apostolic exertion for the regeneration of your country', but also identified him as the 'Chosen

Delegate of Almighty God'. Mathew was destined to oppose the 'devastation committed by the arch-fiend thro' the fields of St Patrick', manifested in 'the maudlin orgies of the shebeen, the smut-begrimed votary of intemperance croaking the ribald ballad, echoed by the blasphemies and encored by the oaths and imprecations of the stuttering, stammering, staggering company that "rapped the table, and called for the other jug"'. Norris assured Mathew that 'This, Rev'd sir, is not the language of exaggeration, it is the *vox populi* and consequently the *vox dei*'. For their part, the men and women of Ballina had been faithful 'with the exception of some few individuals who have long since forfeited any claim to character'. The teetotallers of Glentees, Co. Donegal believed that that day had already arrived. Ireland 'exhibited to the world the extraordinary fact of a whole nation practicing sobriety and self-denial to a degree of perfection scarcely ever thought of'. In the same vein, the teetotallers of Wicklow urged Mathew to 'continue the noble work of regenerating your country and raising her to a rank not only with the nations of the earth but far above them'. At Passage, Co. Waterford, intemperance was termed 'our national foe', while the Callan Total Abstinence Society in Co. Kilkenny praised Mathew's 'labours for the moral regeneration of your country' and Newry teetotallers commended Mathew's 'important work of national redemption'.

Many addresses also emphasised the communitarian nature of both the Temperance movement and the emerging sober Irish nation. The teetotallers of the parish of Lady's Island in Co. Wexford hoped that 'our country may be as one family of Teetotallers, a pious and moral nation', while the teetotallers of Corofin, Co. Clare insisted that there were 'no pledge-breakers among us'. At Charleville in County Cork, teetotallers urged that Temperance be 'universally adopted by our fellow men'. At Mallow, also in Cork, teetotallers were encouraged that the movement had 'awakened Erin's sons in the remotest parts of our Isle to a sense of their duty and caused them to fly to the standard of sobriety and good morals that floats triumphantly in the breeze'. Belfast and Lisburn teetotallers likewise hoped 'that every Irishman whose heart beats true to his country, will now hasten to take his part, in this great and glorious struggle ... We bless God that this is a cause free from sect and party, that it is a great national question, calculated to be beneficial to all in its ultimate bearings and injurious to none.'

Just as importantly, many addresses emphasised the popular and bottom-up nature of the Temperance crusade. At Ennistymon in Clare, teetotallers believed the movement was 'a revolution unheard of and unknown among any other people or clime, without precedent and without parallel, exhibiting all that is vast in the idea of the countless masses, all that is imposing in the mighty reflex of the popular will'. At Erris, in County Mayo, the address spoke of the enthusiastic 'spirit of the people'. At Drumcondra in Dublin, teetotallers insisted that it was 'the people of this country who through an innate conviction have responded to your call'. Ballylangford teetotallers noted that 'as a people we have assumed a new character', adding that God had seen to it that 'we have been regenerated'.

Conclusion

Temperance rhetoric made a vital contribution to the making of the CTAS's moral revolution. The CTAS had a consistent, coherent and clearly expressed ideology which centred around the complete transformative regeneration of a particular people and nation, all accomplished as an expression of the will of God. The cause's call was widely and effectively diffused through the country through speeches, newspapers, pamphlets and poems, and was understood and shared by participants at all levels. The attractive power of this message was a crucial component in the conversion of more than half of the Irish Catholic population to total abstinence, and of an accompanying dramatic transformation of public behaviour.

Ultimately, however, the widespread acceptance and embrace of the CTAS's message described above must be understood in terms of gain and loss for the Temperance cause. The fact is that the Temperance movement's rhetorical consensus was not conducive to the consolidation of moral revolution, and actually aided and abetted the breakdown of the movement at the pinnacle of its success. The crux of the problem was that the CTAS's rhetoric, so effective in attracting the Irish people to the cause, reflected no similar consensus about what was to be done once the desired transformation of Ireland was actually accomplished. The initial message contained little or no coherent or consistent explanation of what a transformed Ireland would look like, or how its relationship to the rest of the world, and particularly England, could be made more reflective of the new balance of moral power. Simultaneously, the transformative aspect of Temperance's rhetorical appeal in particular had promised that mere Temperance, however universal, was not the end of the CTAS. The movement's expansion, to make matters worse, encouraged the rapid proliferation and reproduction of Temperance rhetoric from a variety of sources, and Father Mathew and his closest disciples therefore lost much of their control over the CTAS's meaning even as the cause achieved its greatest success. In this way, the speed with which the movement achieved its initial objective – near-universal public sobriety – produced unintended negative consequences that worked against the consolidation of the cause.

In conjunction with these problems, powerful claims of central aspects of Temperance rhetoric proved in the long run to be a two-edged sword for the movement. The CTAS's assertion of manifest divine authority, for example, was threatening to some and made many influential but cautious churchmen, Protestant and Catholic, nervous. Just as threatening to the cause's long term viability was the degree to which its rhetorical appeal depended on building up and encouraging Irish nationalism. By placing questions of patriotism and particular historical understandings of Ireland's past and present at the centre of the CTAS's rhetoric, the movement's leadership risked reducing Temperance to a supporting role in the principal task of uplifting the nation. This was especially dangerous given the fact that Mathew's commitment to avoiding associating partisan politics with his movement was not shared by many of his followers.

CHAPTER FIVE

Temperance Ritual and Practice

If Temperance was promoted and advocated by its leaders through the press and the platform, it was also lived by millions of Irish men and women as a network of behaviours, rituals and practices. Mathewite Temperance took the commonplace associational premises of early Temperance reformers and grafted them onto a resolve to convert an entire people to the observance of total abstinence. Structures designed for small urban societies in America, England and Ireland were ill-suited to millions of transformed peasants. Father Mathew's teetotallers demonstrated both flexibility and ingenuity in adapting Temperance to local circumstance. While the practices they developed were local, they shared certain essential characteristics. Most importantly, they gave Temperance its particular appeal and meaning within Irish society.

In the wake of its mass meetings that publicly mobilised a critical mass of men and women, local branches of the CTAS invented or modified an array of events and venues to organise and sustain themselves as teetotallers. These included dinners and tea-parties, dances, reading rooms, and coffee-houses. Such clubbish behaviour and organisation, however, were never the end of the CTAS. In the spirit of the meetings which had converted so many, teetotallers kept Temperance in the public realm through their holiday parades and funerals, through their pilgrimages, religious festivities and 'visiting' customs, and their attempts to enforce sobriety on public occasions. In this network of collective behaviours, many consciously designed as spectacles to encourage people to join the movement and thus demonstrate its strength, Temperance became an integral, dominant part of people's lives, including even those who did not 'take the pledge'. The 'national regeneration' Temperance's supporters spoke so consistently about was no abstract potentiality. It was occurring daily within the context of these changes.

THE MASS MEETING

Teetotalism began with public conversion. The vast majority of Father Mathew's teetotallers took the pledge in connection with one of his hundreds of Temperance missions between late 1839 and early 1843. Evidence from a variety of sources indicates that, despite the large number of local priests willing to enlist teetotallers in Mathew's society, most of the people preferred to take the pledge at his hands, on display and surrounded by thousands of other postulants.[1] In short, taking the pledge was understood to be a public act – the more public, the better. Allowing for some degree of local variation, this act followed a certain formula.

Once a parish priest arranged a date for a mission by Mathew, it would be publicised. Not only was the visit announced from the alter for a number of weeks prior to the meeting, but local activists would also post notices and newspapers would carry advertisements, while articles on recent missions frequently announced Mathew's schedule for the next several weeks.[2] The vast majority of Mathew's visits partook of two established practices that most postulants were already familiar with and had most likely participated in in the past – the charity sermon, and the mass meeting.[3]

The ongoing financial crisis in the resource-starved pre-Famine Irish Catholic church meant that there was little money for much-needed church building and upkeep, let alone the support of a rapidly increasing network of religious charities.[4] Charity sermons were an important part of the Church's response to this crisis. Father Mathew, like many other regular priests, was an accomplished preacher long before he became a Temperance advocate. Whatever Mathew's speaking talents were, there can be little doubt that he was at his best making charitable appeals. He instinctively and perfectly managed the mix of drama, emotion and sincerity. His style was replete with anecdotes of the virtue and generosity of the Irish poor, and a compelling confidence in the fundamental goodness of his audience. One observer found his sermon on behalf of the Widow's Asylum in Dublin in September 1840 to be the most effective charity sermon he had ever heard, singular for 'the pure and extraordinary spirit of Christian charity and love' that 'breathed in every word he uttered'.[5] 'Every sentence', the reporter marvelled, 'was calculated either to arouse to the utmost extent the fear of the rich man at the awful responsibility to which he is subjected, or to afford those who have been humbled by the hand of affliction and misfortune consolation of the strongest and most exalted kind.' Interestingly, Mathew almost never mentioned Temperance during his charity sermons, although, given as they so often were on behalf of the widowed, orphaned, destitute and fallen, they afforded a superb platform for encouraging conversions. Instead he focused on the charity at hand, only mentioning where the pledge would be administered afterwards. While Father Mathew was concerned with calling well-to-do listeners to account, many of whom were not teetotallers, his approach had the effect of heightening anticipation for the subsequent Temperance meeting, usually outside the church.[6]

Public meetings and demonstrations were already a familiar part of life for most of the people, particularly outside Ulster. A peculiar devotion to spectacle had been carefully cultivated by Daniel O'Connell, who found in the massed peasantry Ireland's only real strength. The mass Temperance meeting, held out of doors, partook of a ritual that was, by 1838, a generation old. The Irish people were used to being asked to gather in numbers, often on a historically significant spot, to listen to speeches, and to respond to a call – to generate petitions for or against legislation, to protest against tithes, or to end faction fighting. These meetings depended for their success on the existence of a cadre in every town and village of local notables willing and able to organise committees, print placards and make speeches. In the year prior to the first mass Temperance meeting in Waterford, for example, there were a number of large-scale anti-tithe demonstrations in Ireland. One at Boylagh, Co. Donegal, in late September 1838, allegedly attracted some 25,000 people.[7] These meetings were understood to be, whatever their immediate object, displays of strength, determination, and collective solidarity, all directed at the political authorities. They were also popular and entertaining 'events' for all concerned.

The pageantry of a Temperance meeting therefore overlaid many of the 'rituals' that had marked these earlier, explicitly political gatherings. For all their similarity to a pre-existing tradition of public meetings, however, it must also be recognised that Mathew's Temperance gatherings were absolutely unprecedented in at least two significant ways. In the first place, their size was several orders of magnitude greater than anything seen before in Ireland. If O'Connell's Catholic Association meetings of the 1820s drew their thousands, and if sympathetic reporters claimed ten, twenty or thirty thousand for anti-tithe gatherings a decade later, the eighty, ninety and even hundreds of thousands that many of these same astounded observers counted at Mathew's Temperance meetings were still unprecedented. Secondly, Temperance meetings demanded much more of their audiences than these earlier gatherings had. Active participation was expected, as was the willingness to enter into a solemn public commitment before family, friends and neighbours.

The attractive power, promised excitement and inspirational importance of the mass Temperance meeting cannot be overestimated. Temperance gatherings were events few of the peasantry could resist. What began as curiosity often ended in conversion. A reporter at a meeting at Kilbeggan, Co. Westmeath, assured his readers that many who attended 'for the mere purpose of looking, not having the least idea of pledging, left as teetotallers'.[8] In fact, no observer of Mathew's crusade failed to be moved by the spectacle of mass conversion the meetings offered. 'To those at a distance', an overwhelmed reporter observed of the first mass meeting in Waterford, 'the details we have endeavoured to collect and embody may appear exaggerated and the work more of fancy than fact.'[9] 'It was', he added, 'a truly glorious sight, and one that can never be effaced from the memory of those who witnessed it.' Nor were the people themselves unmoved by these enthusiastic accounts. In August 1840, for example, Dean J.P. Lyons, parish priest of Belmullet, Co. Mayo, informed Father Mathew that his parishioners were 'hesitating between their passions and their duty' until 'the recent wonderful scenes at Castlebar'.[10] This mission 'had so powerful an effect on the public mind' that many of Lyons' parishioners 'were now importunate to become members of your temperance society and to abandon, at once and forever, all attachment to intoxicating liquors'.

Temperance missions to larger towns usually began on a Sunday, and often lasted for three days. Smaller towns might be visited mid-week, as the Capuchin travelled between weekend destinations. Crowds began to gather the night before a meeting, and swelled to tens of thousands on the day itself. If Father Mathew arrived the night before, as he usually did before Sunday meetings, his carriage was met by hundreds if not thousands, while the town would be illuminated with lights in windows and bonfires lit in the streets. The day of the meeting, a festival-like attitude pervaded the town. Young, old, men and women – all turned out in force. The physically afflicted and their attendants were particularly in evidence, as many believed that Father Mathew and his pledge had healing power. Ballad singers sang Temperance songs, while cacophonous, notoriously atonal brass bands competed for attention. Members in good standing of the town's Temperance societies proudly exhibited medals suspended from ribbons (usually white or green); many members carried white wands as emblems of authority and to aid in marshalling the crowds, serving as unofficial stewards. By 1842, one reporter described a meeting of some 20,000 at

Lucan, Co. Dublin, attended by a dozen elaborately costumed local bands as 'a pageant, or review of his armies of followers'.[11]

Another long established convention of Irish mass meetings as developed by O'Connell was the leader's triumphal entry procession; the crowd attempted to divine his arrival time and his route, and huge delegations – often led by a parish priest or curate – went miles outside of town and waited for the Bianconi car that might contain the celebrated man of the people. Mathew, concerned about criticisms that his crusade was an exercise in self-promotion, resisted this tradition, and often chided the crowd for their laudatory behaviour during his entries. If he came to town on the day of the meeting, this studied modesty often became a sort of game. To avoid the inevitable reception committee, Mathew frequently attempted to arrive incognito in a private carriage of some well-to-do local supporter of the cause, or better yet to slip in quietly the night before. At Galway, for example, in January 1842, he 'disappointed' the local society 'and indeed the public at large' by 'arriving privately' a day ahead of schedule, forcing the abandonment 'of the idea of a procession'.[12] Counter-measures on the part of the local societies were also often employed, ranging from the use of watchmen to – as at Navan, Co. Meath, on St Patrick's Day, 1842 – taking the precaution of erecting 'triumphal arches at every entrance to the town'.[13] If Mathew failed to avoid the people, or if he were discovered attempting to do so, he often could not prevent the crowd from unhitching the horses and pulling his carriage, or even carrying him into town on someone's broad shoulders, while a band attempted 'See the Conquering Hero Comes'. Usually, a gushing address prepared by members of the local society was read, to which Father Mathew always replied equally effusively.

After the inevitable charity sermon (usually a less plebeian event) Father Mathew proceeded to the designated spot to administer the pledge. Traditionally, O'Connell's meetings were held, as noted above, at locations that had notable national or local historical importance. Mathew seems to have discouraged this in connection with Temperance, perhaps because of a distasteful sectarian scandal that occurred prior to his visit to Cashel in early 1840. There, local activists attempted to obtain permission to hold the meeting at the Rock of Cashel, but the town's Church of Ireland minister, Rev. Whitty, refused to allow the use of the site for so 'diabolical' a purpose.[14] Petitioners, like those from Athenry, Co. Galway, who addressed Mathew at a meeting in Loughrea in January 1842, might request that he hold a mission in their town soon, and 'ascend the steps of the old cross at Athenry, that ancient monument of the faith of our forefathers', but in general Mathew seems to have gone out of his way to avoid this kind of symbolism.[15] He preferred to make use of open spaces convenient to the churches where he preached. In the larger towns, the front steps of some public building served well, but Mathew often used chapel yards, particularly when gates might be used to control 'batches' of postulants. A platform was often erected, in order that the local clergy and other notables could preside above the peasantry. One such platform, at Boyle, Co. Roscommon, was 4 feet high, 24 feet long and 16 feet wide.[16]

Because Mathew's method of administering the pledge was time-consuming, his speeches on these occasions were short and to the point. Sometimes he made a general address, but more often, particularly if the weather was bad or the numbers were great, Mathew made short speeches to smaller groups of postulants, usually several hundred at a time. After his remarks, the people knelt as Father Mathew enunciated the pledge, which the people repeated. He usually made a point of touching each new member of his society, marking them with the sign of the cross, although occasionally he might make the sign of the cross over groups of the converted. This procedure went on until nightfall, or until the mail coach on which Mathew was to depart left, or until all present had taken the pledge. Most newspaper accounts mention the physical exhaustion Father Mathew contended with, standing, speaking and being jostled by boisterous crowds for hours on end, usually without any pause for rest. At the end of the day, Mathew was serenaded once again by local Temperance bands and escorted by vast crowds on his way out of town or to the local hotel, or the home of a clergyman or well-to-do supporter.

The importance of the rituals associated with Father Mathew's comings and goings is obvious when the efforts local societies took to prepare for these occasions are considered. In fact, all members were involved in one way or another. There were addresses to be drawn up and approved, banners and costumes to be finished, medals to be polished, platforms to be constructed, and handbills and posters to be distributed. Bands practiced for hours (however fruitlessly) while evergreens for arches and wood for bonfires needed to be collected. Small wonder Lord Lorton issued a proclamation 'strongly exhorting and enjoining' his tenantry to 'attend to their harvest work' and 'recollect that a poor man's wealth is his time' rather than participate in Father Mathew's visit to Boyle, Co. Roscommon in September 1840.[17] Given that people often travelled 20 or more miles to see Father Mathew, who toured constantly until 1843, a typical local society might have gone through some degree of furious preparation for meetings a half dozen times during a year.

LOCAL SOCIETIES: CUSTOMS, PRACTICES AND VENUES

More important than what happened on the few occasions when Father Mathew was present was how local societies practiced Temperance when he was absent. The quotidian nature of drinking meant that the temperate constantly faced the need to adapt and transform behaviour. Most in fact seem to have developed many ways of doing so, some of which modified pre-existing behaviours (dances, for example) while others significantly transformed established custom (such as pub and shebeen culture, and gender relations, if not roles). By providing attractive educational, recreational and convivial opportunities, local Temperance societies often succeeded in placing themselves at the centre of Irish social life.

Temperance dinners were essential features of the movement, and put local organisation, prosperity and respectability on display. When Mathew arrived in a town, he was nearly always invited to attend the kind of formal meal or banquet, along with all the local notables who could be induced to appear, that was an inescapable feature of Irish public life during the nineteenth century. Such dinners were also regular events for local societies, particularly on the anniversary of their foundation. Johan Kohl, a German traveller, described the elaborate preparations for a Temperance dinner at Kilrush, Co. Clare, in 1842:

> Round about the walls hung the banners of the several corporate bodies of the town, surrounded by mottos well-calculated to please the popular tastes of the time ... Garlands and festoons were wound about the hall. A large horse-shoe table stood in the centre of the room, and boards resting on empty casks and blocks of wood were arranged as seats. At the head of the table were two armchairs, one for Father Mathew, and one for the principal Catholic priest of the place who was to act as chairman. Behind these chairs a giant cornucopia was represented, with a multitude of shamrocks falling out ... On side tables stood countless hosts of teapots and teacups, and huge piles of bread and butter.[18]

In keeping with traditional Irish hospitality, abundance was the most consistent characteristic of these dinners, at least if one is to believe the many newspaper accounts. Tables were inevitably described as near collapse under the bounty of the feast, while the diners were 'filled to the bursting point'.[19] Dinners were predominantly ticketed middle-class affairs, although it was not unusual for attendance to reach well down into the ranks of local shopkeepers, farmers and mechanics. Music from newly-formed Temperance bands and speeches masquerading as toasts were the order of the evening. Inescapably, the Queen, the president and patrons of the local society, the local clergy (from the bishop on down, often one by one) and Father Mathew himself, were toasted in turn, producing an endurance test of the sort that, a few years earlier, had caused Alexis de Tocqueville to flee Kilkenny at the prospect of a public dinner in his honour.[20]

Such dinners often preceded 'tea parties', or 'soirees', but in general the Temperance tea party, the hallmark of an active local society, was a more casual and novel affair. Attendance at dinners was usually two or three hundred at most, and was limited to those who could afford the food and entertainment; tea parties might take place anywhere on the slightest pretext and tended to be free unless they followed a dinner. In Waterford, in June 1840, a large tea party was held 'in honour of the Queen's delivery from assassination'.[21] Sixteen hundred had attended a tea party in the town hall six months earlier.[22] At Tulla, in County Clare, more than a thousand attended a party hosted by the local curate, James Dinan.[23] Five hundred took 'immense' rooms in Tipperary, 'brilliantly lit up and decorated with evergreens'.[24] There was a sense, in the accounts of tea parties, of a more relaxed atmosphere than at some dinners. Singing and story-telling were common, as at Kanturk, Co. Cork, where, in 1841, one reporter decided that 'it would be impossible, in this brief sketch, to give any idea of the varied amusements that gave zest to the evening's festivity'.[25] The company was 'kept in roars of laughter' by the Rev. J. O'Donoghue, 'by his humour and anecdotes'.

The high point of the tea party for most occurred after the presiding clergy retired. In Killenaule, Co. Tipperary, 'the festivities were kept up until 2:00 o'clock, when the chairman and other gentlemen withdrew, highly gratified with the evening's entertainment; but the dancing was continued by the juvenile portion of the assembly until the day appeared.'[26] In Athlone, Co. Westmeath, at a tea party whose attendees 'were nearly all working class', at 10:00 pm 'they sent for three fiddlers in order to have a dance'.[27] In Leitrim town, dancing continued until 7:00 am.[28] In Oranmore, Co. Galway, they 'danced till the small hours'; at Athenry, Co. Galway, they lasted until 8:00 am; while in Limerick 'music and dancing kept up until the Aurora'.[29]

Such antics were not always well-received; this was a period marked by growing Church interest in regulating the habits of the faithful, and unsupervised all-hours dancing did not sit well with many. John McHale, the influential Archbishop of Tuam, was one who took exception to tea parties, a stance which sparked a public controversy with Father Mathew and went some way towards undermining his societies' influence in Connaught.[30] Such criticism irked Father Mathew, well-known for his fondness for entertainments, who happily presided over occasional tea parties and dinners where dancing and other amusements occurred. In an angry mood at a Limerick banquet on 14 October 1841, he lashed out at critics: 'I have been blamed', he noted, 'for many matters connected with the temperance societies, for which I think no blame should be attributed to me, or to those who are blamed with me.'[31]

> I cannot express the sentiments of sovereign contempt which I entertain for those who thus betray the feelings that agitate them. Some say I should prevent females to attend soirees, while their own daughters and wives, perhaps, mingle in the crowded ballrooms and whirl in the maze of the profane waltz, and enjoy each other's society in that respect, whilst they themselves, the victims of drunkenness, may be seen reeling through the streets to their homes after spending their nights in the taproom or tavern.

As the controversy over dancing revealed, Temperance societies created a new context for interactions between the sexes.[32] Because it so radically associated what had been the private moral realm with public, patriotic and communal transformation, the CTAS could not and did not avoid considering the proper place of women (and children) in the new social order. Father Mathew and other Temperance advocates eagerly enlisted women in the cause, and employed a variety of particular rhetorical techniques to attract female converts.[33] The regeneration of the Irish was to be marked by a changed social climate, centring around public events at which the sexes mixed freely. In Mathew's opinion, the movement offered a new basis for interaction between the sexes, and a new era of emancipation for both men and women. Removed from the morally corrupting influences of alcohol, Irish men and women were better fitted to enjoy each other's sober and rational company, since alcohol constituted the virtuous Irish people's only real vice. Tea parties were to be the forums for this new freedom.

The precise ratio of women to men in the crusade is unknown, but there is evidence that in its early days the cause was not as successful as it would have liked in recruiting women. The constabulary reports, compiled in March 1840, for example, addressed the subject directly, albeit only partly successfully due to the confusing nature of the question posed to police inspectors. Constables, asked 'How many women, or men above working class' had pledged, appear in many cases to have answered as if they had been asked how many women above working class had pledged; thus Mathew Cashman in Galway reported that three 'respectable women' had pledged and Henry Blake counted 'several' postulant above working class, men and women.[34]

Taken as a whole, however, the responses indicated that women participated in significant numbers in many areas, albeit in fewer numbers than men did, and were very much in attendance at the first mass meetings.

Soon, however, the CTAS became successful in pledging vast numbers of women as well as men. Indeed, the presence of women in large numbers at Mathew's meetings was an element of the Tory critique of the movement, as when the *Waterford Mail* condemned a Temperance gathering as 'thirty or forty thousand people individuals of both sexes tumultuously assembled'.[35] Another reporter from the *Limerick Standard* referred contemptuously to drunken men at an early mass meeting in Clonmel 'seen staggering towards the courthouse in groups, supported at either side by their wives and female friends'.[36] But the women were not present merely to support the men, the reporter noted with ambivalent curiosity:

> The pledge was administered to no less than some thousands of all sexes, ages and conditions. Amongst them we perceived very many young females, apparently farmer's daughters, who were very respectably attired, and who betrayed the greatest possible zeal in urging their male friends forward to take the pledge.

Supporters of the cause also remarked on the presence of women at meetings with satisfaction, inevitably noting the power of female 'moral influence'. At Mathew's second meeting, at Waterford, 'it was observed with pleasure that females outnumbered males by about 25 per cent. This has not, we believe, been the fact elsewhere. Here it speaks trumpet tongued of the stability of the society, for it scarcely need be said that the influence of the fair sex is well-nigh omnipotent.'[37] Some nine months later, at Freshford, County Kilkenny, the *Waterford Chronicle*'s reporter also observed vast 'numbers of peasant girls who came to set a beneficial example to their fathers, brothers and sweethearts, by taking the Pledge'.[38] Similar asides and observations are common enough in newspaper accounts of meetings, particularly during the first year or so of the crusade when it was considered worth noting. Women usually pledged alongside men, although on occasion they pledged in separate batches or even, as was the case in Dublin, in a separate meeting, out of deference to the fact that, as Mathew later explained, 'a lady becoming a member of our society was considered as being a sort of reproach on her character, as if she had been previously addicted to the use of intoxicating drinks and many, for fear of incurring such a stigma, were deterred from taking that step'.[39]

Still, it has been argued in this chapter that, though pledging was a crucial part of Temperance, the real measure of the movement's impact and place in Irish society was found in the changed daily lives of the pledged, and in the interactions fostered by local Temperance societies. On that account, the place of women in the Temperance revolution as it was lived out became more complex. Irish Temperance, while it certainly advocated personal moral reform and made much of the benefits to individual families of temperate behaviour, placed a particular premium both on public sobriety and on the public celebration of the virtues of sobriety. For this reason the movement had the practical effect of emphasising women's place in a transformed public sphere and downplaying (although by no means ignoring) their stereotypical role as the guardians of domestic sobriety (and the principle victims of domestic inebriety).[40] Women were usually welcome at Temperance tea parties and dinners, although they did not attend all these functions.[41] They also marched in Temperance parades and demonstrations, albeit usually in smaller numbers than the men, while the deaths of female members of societies appear to have been marked by funerals, as described below.[42] We can assume women were deeply involved in the hectic preparations for all these events. This public presence of women in the movement was, however, constrained. There is little evidence that women addressed meetings or acted as leaders of local societies.[43] Although their incorporation into the movement was significant, therefore, women's part in the crusade was by and large viewed in traditional terms. Nevertheless, it is clear that the public dimension of participation applied to women as well as men, and the active involvement of women in the movement was understood to be of critical importance. Women came to represent a large proportion of Mathew's disciples, and they responded enthusiastically to the CTAS's call to participate in the mission of national regeneration. Temperance was revolutionary in many senses, but none was more remarkable than the way in which women as such were actively incorporated into a public, patriotic mass movement for the first time in Irish history.

READING ROOMS AND COFFEE HOUSES

The new social landscape that temperate Irish men and women found themselves a part of was one dotted with Temperance reading rooms and coffee houses established by local Temperance societies. Temperance reading rooms were particularly common, and were directly associated with particular branches of the CTAS. In these spaces, teetotallers gathered in the evenings, amidst collected books, pamphlets, newspapers and popular magazines. From the beginning, the CTAS in Cork had sponsored such rooms, while the handbill issued to new members who made their way to Cork urged converts, on their return home, to 'become a subscriber to the committee rooms' as a way of making contact with other teetotallers.[44] These rooms soon were extremely popular, with the ready availability of so expensive a commodity as newspapers and books adding to the appeal of company and conversation. By December 1839, over 200 used the Church Street Temperance Reading Rooms in Cork City nightly.[45] As early as April 1840 the *Freeman* reported that there were at least 20 Temperance reading rooms in Cork City alone. By late 1842, after a Repeal tour of Munster, T.M. Ray noted, of the Irish, that 'temperance has made them a reading and a thinking people. There is not a town in the province in which there are not temperance rooms established, where useful books, periodicals, and newspapers are received, and eagerly perused; for though poor, he found wherever he went that the great majority of the people could read.'[46]

Reading rooms could be a source of tension as well. Thomas Carpenter, Dingle's head constable, noted the disgust of 'the father of a tradesman in this town who was formerly of intemperate habits', who complained that 'his son earned more money before he took the pledge, his time being now chiefly devoted to attending meetings'.[47] Other problems were brought to Father Mathew's attention. One 'R.J.L.' wrote to inform Father Mathew that three teetotallers in his society played cards in the society's rooms 'for gain', often for six hours at a time and much to the detriment of religious and family duties.[48] 'I think', R.J.L. primly observed, 'that when men shake off their drunken habits and become teetotallers they ought also to shake off all other sinful habits.' This amusing and revealing letter concludes wonderfully, as Mathew's scrupulous informant begs for a dispensation for his sodality's upcoming anniversary dinner, 'as *I will have to pay for it* and it will be the same expense'. Mathew was besieged by similar letters.[49]

Reading rooms were not the only social centres for the movement. In many communities, public houses were replaced by coffee shops, which soon became popular locations for informal tea parties. These venues were privately owned, but many local Temperance societies held meetings, band practices, etc. in coffee shops. Much evidence indicates that many continued to frequent coffee houses much as they would have the local pub, and that the distinction between public houses and coffee houses was not always clear. Many of the former began to sell coffee and tea and some of the latter sold alcoholic 'cordials' or even whiskey, albeit illegally.[50] William Fitzpatrick, an irate

Dublin grocer, pointed out at a trade meeting on 26 August 1840, that 'one half, at least, of the publicans have been obliged to give up their trade, and by whom had their places been taken? Why, by the proprietors of what were called teetotal shops.'[51] Such shops were, he alleged, 'places where persons were entertained at all hours of the night, and where gambling, illicit drinking and every species of immorality was suffered to be practiced'. Despite Fitzpatrick's outburst, the authorities did, at least on occasion, insist that coffee shops follow the same closing rules that public houses adhered to. In Newportstreet, in Dublin, where Elizabeth Dwyer kept the 'Coffee Teetotal Tavern' at number 1, Constable William Bayes twice had to break up a loud after-hours Temperance party on the night of 8 June 1840.[52] According to his testimony, 40 persons were packed into the tavern, some of whom 'were seated around a table of ample dimensions, and presenting a good show of bottles and glasses, the contents of which were rapidly circulating'. Meanwhile, 'at least a score of lads and lasses' were engaged in 'making the floor tell'. Although the bottles turned out to contain only water and 'temperance cordials', the proprietress was fined anyway.

TEMPERANCE, PUBLIC BEHAVIOUR AND MORAL FORCE

Coffee houses, although venues for the recreation of local societies, were also open to the public, and it was in the public sphere that the behaviour of Temperance societies was on display in its most dynamic form. The mandate of Temperance demanded that teetotallers inspire, cajole or compel the conversion of those who might otherwise choose to remain in a state of degradation. It also required that the moral force of the Temperance reformation be demonstrated in forceful ways to all interested observers, especially those across the Irish Sea. The CTAS can only be understood, therefore, through the conscious public behaviour of its branch organisations and their millions of members.

PARADES AND FUNERALS

The popular Temperance bands that featured prominently in entertainments such as dinners and tea parties were the unifying centrepieces of another ubiquitous Temperance event – the parade. A defining feature of the movement was the rapidity with which it involved itself with public celebrations. Temperance demonstrations did not co-exist with other displays; they quickly became the only show in town, almost from the beginning of the crusade. St Patrick's Day and Easter, standing as close as they did in the calendar, nevertheless became the two great Temperance festivals. Father Mathew gave prominence to the latter; the societies themselves seemed anxious to celebrate the former. Nor were these the only occasions that warranted a parade. In addition to Father Mathew's arrivals and departures, there were Temperance demonstrations at Christmas, on 'pattern' days, and, indeed, on practically any public occasion.

While there were countless Temperance parades in Ireland, the one that took place on 19 November 1840 at Ballyshannon, Co. Donegal was perhaps typical: the Rev. Daniel Coyle, president of the local branch of the CTAS, led some 4,000, divided into men's, women's and boy's societies, in procession behind their band, which attempted such local favourites as 'We'll Never Get Drunk Again', and 'Neal Gow's Farewell to Whiskey'. Asked by Coyle to avoid party-coloured ribbons, the people were bedecked with their medals suspended from white ribbons. Three hundred marshals, armed with long white wands, kept the pace on the five mile march to a meeting at Kinlough, while thousands more lined the parade route and cheered.[53]

In many urban areas, there were fierce rivalries between various Temperance societies. St Patrick's Day demonstrations in Dublin became particularly elaborate. In 1841, Father Mathew's society placed 'a chaise with Brady, the blind harper, dressed in the costume of the ancient Irish bards, and playing on the national instrument' just behind the band, while another society carried elaborate banners and 'a long pole, surmounted by a loaf of bread, decorated with ribands, beneath which was a reversed, broken whiskey bottle, with a noggin and a glass also suspended from a cross stick still lower down'.[54] Not surprisingly, the whole arrangement was 'a prominent object of remark throughout the day'.

As Temperance parades became more frequent, Father Mathew became less and less enthusiastic about them, probably because he knew they were widely regarded by Protestants and those in authority as threatening demonstrations, particularly as the Repeal campaign gathered strength in the early 1840s. This was especially the case in Ulster, where Temperance parades were often attacked by Orange mobs.[55] All over Ireland, many local magistrates and constables were certainly very uneasy about them. Two extant letters of W.T. Hamilton, writing on behalf of the Chief Secretary, to the High Sheriff of County Kilkenny and to the Petty Session magistrates at Ballinasloe refused local authorities' requests to ban Temperance processions.[56] Magistrates' diaries and constabulary reports made careful notes of Temperance processions.[57] The remarks of Sub-Inspector Mark O'Malley Burke at

Kenmare, Co. Kerry, that Temperance parades there were lamentable 'scenes of triumph and excitement' which 'occupied the exclusive attention of the vulgar', were harsh but typical of many.[58] 'Virtue', the Sub-Inspector added contemptuously, 'is modest and unostentatious. It does not stand in need of medals, banners, committees and parades.' William Kelly, a sub-inspector in Father Mathew's home town of Thomastown, Co. Kilkenny, was particularly suspicious of the society, noting that 'I have seen persons acting as officers upon the occasion of members marching in procession, having long wands and using words of command as "quick march", "forward", "halt".'[59]

These concerns were not the stuff of paranoia. Given Ireland's long history of secret, oath-bound societies and the surreptitious drilling of the discontented, not to mention the current climate all over England of popular civil unrest and threatened Chartist violence and revolution, they were understandable. Whatever Mathew's intentions, the degree of his control over his teetotallers was always a question, and the intentions of thousands of local activists were even more unclear. Whatever else they were, Temperance parades were certainly designed to demonstrate popular organisation and discipline to those in authority, along with the implicit (and sometimes explicit) message that the people had every intention of making their weight felt in the New Ireland they were participating in creating.

On 7 July 1840, a government proclamation forbade marching with banners and emblems. Several Temperance processions were immediately cancelled, including one at Clonmel, Co. Tipperary, where Father Mathew was holding a mission; others were modified to remain legal. The proclamation was directed more at Orange marches than Temperance processions, and was never vigorously enforced, but the ban drove something of a wedge between the cautious Father Mathew and his more enthusiastic supporters. In July 1840, for example, his announced visit to Duleek was to be made on the condition that 'no banners or emblems be in evidence'.[60] In an undated letter to Father John Spratt, the Carmelite Temperance leader in Dublin, Mathew wondered if the 'great risk' of holding an Easter procession was worth the benefit; warning that 'upon your head rests the responsibility'.[61]

Local activists knew that the parades were compelling displays whose pageantry was in no small degree responsible for maintaining enthusiasm among converts as well as witnessing to those still unwilling to join the society. Writing on 11 July to protest the ban, 'Amicus Temperantice' reminded the *Waterford Chronicle*'s readers that processions were 'designed to entice from their evil ways those who still reveled in intemperance' by means of 'heart-stirring music'.[62] That paper's editors also decried the government's proclamation, noting that 'the moral effect of such a procession was calculated to be productive of a great amount of good on the apathetic and the wavering', not to mention 'those who may have been tempted to abandon the cause'.[63] Several days later, Nicholas Foran, the Bishop of Waterford, warned teetotallers in his diocese to obey the proclamation, acknowledging that it had caused 'considerable dissatisfaction'.[64]

One variety of Temperance procession that continued unabated in the face of the ban was the elaborate funeral demonstrations mounted by many local societies. Because of their quasi-religious character, these events took place legally in the face of government anxieties and proclamations, and served just as well if not better to demonstrate popular organisation, discipline and determination. In fact, there was no more powerful, solemn and dramatic an event in pre-Famine Irish public life than the funeral of a member of the CTAS. If the mass Temperance meeting was Mathew's triumph and drew many to join the organisation, the elaborate funerals they provided for their members were the particular glory of local societies, and had a dramatic effect on the unconverted in every corner of Ireland.

Drink and death were closely connected in pre-Famine Ireland, particularly given the still-strong tradition of waking the corpse with gallons of whiskey. Temperance intruded on this important and deep-seated connection in ways that need to be appreciated. The nature of the problem may present itself best in the comments of one amazed observer, at Dunmanway, Co. Cork, in a letter on the spread of Temperance dated 16 March 1840, to a constable friend, telling of a poor acquaintance, one R. Roche, who died a teetotaller:

> A member of the family, fearing the public would dispute the absence of the usual refreshment on these occasions, had a large quantity of whiskey brought to the wake; but the entire people refused to take any part of it, and highly commended the advice of the deceased, whose memory they held in great estimation. I have heard that there, and all such gatherings, the chief topic of conversation recently has been the benefits, and progress of temperance.[65]

Roche's death strengthened the crusade around Dunmanway in ways that his life never had, but also demonstrated the movement's need for a ritualised response to these tensions. If Temperance societies were to establish a meaningful hold on the hearts and minds of the people, it was incumbent on them to find ways to make the new connections between Temperance and death every bit as strong as long standing links between whiskey and death.

From their beginnings, therefore, Temperance societies forged an immediate connection with the deaths of members, as most quickly established mortality funds that paid benefits to widows, widowers and orphans and financed a decent burial. Mortality societies connected with working men's associations and mechanics' institutes were common enough throughout the British Isles by the nineteenth century, particularly for certain classes of tradesmen; the Temperance society sought to bring this powerful conveyor of respectability down to the lowest rungs of the social ladder. They succeeded in doing this, often in spectacular fashion. The *Waterford Chronicle* described the funeral of a labourer, 'poor Ned Shanahan, the teetotaller' in Thurles on 21 May 1840:

> [About 105] teetotaller boys ..., decently dressed and with their medals appended, walked two by two, and preceded all the other teetotallers ... The committee and leading men of the teetotallers, about fifty ... dressed in scarves and hatbands, and some carrying white wands, next followed, walking two and two. Immediately after these, eight priests, then following the corpse in a black coffin, very decently mounted, and carried on the shoulders of the teetotallers ... stationed just at the coffin and with black wands surmounted with crosses, were two of St Paul's Total Abstinence Society, dressed in black scarves, and hatbands, tied with large satin ribbons. These two men were followed by 44 other members of the society dressed in a similar manner, some bearing black wands with crosses. All the other teetotallers with medals, followed three deep – in all, it is said, by some one thousand persons.[66]

Teetotal funerals of this size were not unusual in the early 1840s; a carpenter named Regan was carried to his resting place by 800 in Limerick; over 150 buried Mrs Alley Higgins in Athenry; over 800 attended the burial of a blacksmith's young son at Thurles; and nearly 1,000 teetotallers buried their parish priest in Tipperary town.[67] These funerals were almost certainly intended as spectacles to encourage others to join the society; as the *Dublin Evening Press* acknowledged approvingly: 'The moral effect of such interesting proceedings on the minds of those not already connected with this society must be very considerable.'[68]

FAITH, FAIRS AND FACTION FIGHTING

Parades and funerals were spectacular but occasional events. Irish public life was composed of religious practice and the regular rhythm of the fairs, patterns and races that occurred in some combination several times each month in a given area. There is much evidence, in the newspapers of the period, of the many ways that Mathewite Temperance, although theoretically non-sectarian, was involved in specific religious practices of the common people. Masses and prayers were offered for local societies, particularly on their anniversaries. Some priests and even bishops forbade members who broke their pledges to receive the sacraments.[69] The journey to a Temperance meeting, or to see Father Mathew in Cork, often lasted a day or more, and took on some of the aspects of a pilgrimage. In Carrick-on-Suir, 'a portion of the humblest classes of the people' began to use the rock where Father Mathew first issued the pledge as a pilgrimage site.[70] Temperance cards and medals were often treated as relics or talismans by a people comfortable with the idea of sacred objects.

Probably the most significant indication for the average Irishman of the new place of Temperance in Ireland, however, was the peace that began to prevail at fairs and patterns. This peace was manifest in two related developments. The first of these was the decline in rioting and faction fighting; the second was a more general decline in public drunkenness and disorder.[71] Magistrates, who were used to attending with dozens of policemen to sweep up dozens of drunks and remaining late waiting for brawls and riots to break out, were particularly conscious of the transformation.[72] Neale Browne, a stipendiary Magistrate at Tullamore, attended the fair of Cloghane on St Patrick's Day, 1840 with 35 policemen, the fair being 'remarkable and notorious for being much disturbed by rioting and drunkenness and disturbances of the peace'.[73] 'Today', he noted in his official diary, 'there was not one case of drunkenness brought before me nor any prisoner or complaint made by the police. This is attributed to Father Mathew having administered the pledge of total abstinence at Birr on the 2nd of March.' Similar accounts are legion, not only from magistrates but also from observers in the press, who found in this sudden peaceable public behaviour the greatest proof of the people's regeneration.

It would also be remarkable if Temperance had failed to engage that other well-known, if under-studied aspect of Irish rural life – the network of local rivalries and contentions that often manifested itself in faction fighting. Large scale faction fights characteristic of certain parts of Ireland in earlier decades of the century were certainly in decline long before the Temperance crusade began in earnest, although of course they were still common enough.[74] Many of the local rivalries that contributed to them were still very much in evidence, and Temperance, with its rhetoric of unity and cooperation, developed some of its own practices in this context. The *Cork Standard* noticed, on the occasion of Father Mathew's first visit to Lismore, Co. Waterford in

January 1840, that 'the "Gows" and "Poleens", two opposing factions whose deadly feuds and fights have long been notorious in this county, shook hands with each other on this occasion'.[75] In the absence of violence, rivalries were given other outlets, as at Clifden, Co. Galway, in August 1840, when the teetotallers engaged whiskey drinkers in a leaping match, or at the Murrisk pattern some weeks later, where running and wrestling were added to the mix.[76]

In place of faction fighting, Temperance also offered, in addition to tea parties and competitions, 'visiting'. 'Visits' were not uncommon for some societies, and consisted of paying formal calls, usually on a Sunday, to some neighbouring society. Both bands would usually play, and the occasion often ended in a joint tea party. Thus, on a fine June day in 1840, 800 Limerick teetotallers, with banners flying and bands playing, took the steamer *Dover Castle* down the Shannon to Kilrush, where they called on that town's society.[77] The day ended with speeches, lunch and a concert. The same month, Clare teetotallers marched to meet with the Kildysart society.[78] In November 1842, a visit by the Monaghan society's band to Dungannon to play at a tea party was considered remarkable only because a magistrate forbade it.[79]

MORAL FORCE

The Temperance movement in most parts of Ireland came to be held together less by the close solidarity of tight-knit local organisations and more by the overwhelming weight of public opinion. This was in part a consequence of the scale of the movement's own success, but it derived largely, it has been argued, from a widespread understanding of the collective and communal character of the crusade's ultimate objective of national regeneration. The force of that public opinion was most evident in the changes in behaviour noted above. It was also manifested in demonstrations of strength by teetotallers, as well as in the great lengths some went to in order to continue drinking in ways that did not offend public opinion, and in the unhappy circumstances of those 'backsliders' who chose to reject their own pledge.

Teetotallers were not above using their numbers aggressively on public occasions. In Carrick-on-Suir, a 'teetotal mob' attempted to arrest two intoxicated policemen they caught leaving a pub on a fair day; a riot resulted when other policemen tried to rescue their comrades.[80] At Kanturk, Co. Cork, after a Saint Patrick's Day fair in 1840, 'at the close of the day a few of the temperance men passed through the street, and carried to the police a few people they found turbulent and intemperate'.[81] The Lasser pattern was, according to the *Freeman*, 'perhaps unequalled' for its 'scenes of riot, debauchery and drunkenness'.[82] Faction fights were common, even in the late 1830s, and 'the revel seldom ended without the sacrifice of human life, and the myriad of dislocated arms, broken bones and contused heads ranked among the least of its abuses'. Patrick O'Gara, the parish priest of Ardcarne, gathered thousands of teetotallers 'comprising the bold and athletic men of Croma and Cooteshall ... and marched in processional order to the pattern ... Instantaneously, the whiskey tents are deserted – peace succeeds to violence – conciliation to social animosity.'

The drinking of cordials (unpleasant-tasting concoctions that masked their principle component, whiskey, with other exotic ingredients), meanwhile, particularly in coffee houses, became commonplace even for many teetotallers in the wake of the movement's success.[83] The *Freeman's Journal* reported on 30 August 1841 a raid on Donnybrook coffee houses during the annual fair, where 25 persons, 'the majority of who declared themselves to be teetotallers', were brought before the magistrate and fined. Fifteen were taken up in a raid on a Dublin coffee house the same week, where 'vessels containing intoxicating drinks' were hidden. 'Several of the prisoners', the paper indignantly reported, 'had also the appearance of being recently drinking. Nearly all the prisoners solemnly assured the magistrates that they were teetotallers, and that they had gone into the house merely to take cordials, or other temperate refreshment.'[84] Similar anecdotes from smaller towns are rarer, but policing was of course much more efficient in Dublin. Judging from the consternation of many Temperance activists, cordial drinking in pubs and coffee houses was common.

From 1840 on, Father Mathew and other advocates of the cause were particularly outspoken on the subject of cordials. A typical condemnation occurred at Limerick, on 14 October 1841, when Father Mathew described them as 'devices that should be abhorred' and 'snares of Satan ... laid for the people'. He later told a Wexford audience that 'he would prefer the open pledge breaker to the cordial drinker'.[85] Dublin Temperance activist Richard Haughton found that cordials he tested were one half whiskey mixed with what was 'probably vitriol, or some equally injurious material'.[86] Haughton also warned teetotallers serious about their pledge to stay out of pubs. One particularly fierce critic took it upon himself to distil a collection of popular cordials with the assistance of a chemist and also found that they were composed primarily of whiskey. His report, in the form of a letter to the editor of the *Freemen's Journal*, condemned many coffee shops as 'dens of the worst infamy and guilt, where scenes are acted out befitting pandemonium itself'.[87]

The creeping habit of cordial drinking is interesting for many reasons, but for none more than the light it sheds on the social importance of the line between members in good standing of a local society and pledge-breakers. The lengths that so many went to in order to drink in a way that would not offend family, friends and neighbours, let alone their own sense of participation in the crusade, was a very telling dimension of the effect of the Temperance movement, and brings home the fact that the real force that discouraged backsliding and held the cause together was the moral weight of the wider community who had taken the pledge. The ways that Mathew and the CTAS leadership urged members to 'discountenance intemperance' were explained in Chapter 4, but it must be noted here that the people took up the advice with enthusiasm.

By all accounts, outright pledge-breaking (as opposed to the surreptitious sipping of cordials) was quite rare in the crusade's early years. The Constabulary Reports of March 1840, for example, indicated very low rates of backsliding, despite the fact that many of the respondents did not like the movement, and no doubt would have been delighted to expose rampant hypocrisy. Of 69 responses, only two reported that more than ten people had broken their pledge, while most listed zero, one or two and could often name them, so notorious were they in their communities.[88] Shunning, public ridicule, and other forms of ostracism were the rule for pledge breakers, just as Mathew and other leaders of the cause recommended, to such an extent that even Mathew at various points tried to rein his followers in. At Kilkenny in June 1840, for example, he cautioned 'against over-zeal, and against using rough means of expressing dislike towards anyone that might break the pledge. They should remember there had been a Judas among the Apostles, and they should not wonder if they found one amongst themselves so base as to violate the pledge.'[89] Instead of 'taking the law into their own hands', they should bleat like sheep 'when they saw a teetotaller who abandoned his promise, and they would effectually punish him'.

The caution was warranted. In some areas, at least, local societies encouraged members to keep careful watch on each other, and entering a pub placed people under suspicion. Criticism of the time-wasting and family-corrupting features of tap-room culture, a common opinion in temperate circles before and since, not only indicated that social transformation in Ireland was by no means a complete success, but also revealed the uncomfortable reality that Temperance had the power to divide as well as unite. The rules of St Mary's Temperance and Mortality Society, published in 1839, were typical of other societies'. They required members, should they 'discern another member violating his pledge' to 'proceed forthwith to the society room, and have it entered into the blotter, specifying the name, time and place, and in what way violated'.[90] At Clonmel in 1841, a 'Committee of 18' published notice that they would provide employers with the names of backsliders.[91] The author of a pamphlet on the state of the Temperance cause near Knockmahon among local miners objected strongly to a similar practice there of 'coercion and espionage' carried out by 'some half-dozen zealous spies' in league with the local curate and employers.[92] Their activities had not only prevented the Knockmahon band from 'practicing in a respectable house in the village, where they were allowed a room to themselves – a blazing fire in cold winter weather, together with comfortable seats around it, and a table on which to place some bottles of "Moore's Celebrated Stomach Beverage", or "Conways's Effervescing Antiscorbutic Spruce"', they had also forced the closing of local grocers 'stocked with general merchandise' who deigned to sell spirits.[93] This pamphlet also sheds light on the actions of Nell Casey, a frustrated publican in Kilrush fined for dousing one Dan Dempsey as he lingered outside her establishment checking on the identity of customers.[94]

If reports in the popular press and elsewhere about the trials of pledge breakers are reliable, Nell Casey's behaviour was in the best interest of her patrons. Isaac Robinson, a Limerick meat cutter who broke his pledge shortly after Mathew's visit to that town, was expelled from his stall at the meat market.[95] Such ostracism was common, and so were duckings, which quickly became the preferred public punishment of pledge-breakers. At Carrick-on-Suir, a woman who broke the pledge was 'taken to a pump and treated to a shower bath, after which they carried her to the banks of a river, where they very quietly gave her a plunge bath'.[96] Another Carrick-on-Suir man who broke the pledge was taken out of his place of employment, a stockyard, and doused with buckets of water as he was led away. Novelist Maria Edgeworth, a close observer of Temperance, reported that the very few who broke the pledge in her area were 'completely shunned and disgraced, so that they are awful warnings to the others'.[97] 'So long as public opinion is upheld in this matter', she opined, 'we may hope that this great power, this inestimable moral blessing to Ireland in particular, will continue.' The *Kilkenny Journal* agreed, when it noted that 'the backslider incurs the utmost contempt and obloquy on the part of his neighbours'.[98] Little wonder that in Westport in 1840 two men who had broken the pledge 'begged public forgiveness off the alter, last Sunday se'nnight, for the scandal they had caused', and that many who violated their pledge hastened to take it again.[99]

CONCLUSION

The CTAS was held together by the glue of public opinion. The movement's collective strength depended, not on a well-integrated network of organised cooperative branch societies, but rather on the compelling, compounded moral force of the entire community. The power of this moral force should not be underestimated. Temperance transformed social relations in so many ways that the words of Temperance activists, including Father Mathew, who insisted that the temperate were 'new men', cannot be dismissed as so much propaganda. The change in the people was tangible, and it gave many a thoughtful contemporary reason to pause. What had seemed to many at its inception to be a passing enthusiasm had proven to be a powerful agent of social change. The Irish people were remaking themselves. Perhaps Thomas Davis, editorialising in the *Nation* in December 1842, put it best:

> A great moral wonder has come to pass in our day, and in the midst of us, upon which all lovers of their race will look with not inconsiderable interest. The redemption of the Irish people from the debasing bondage of intemperance deserves to be ranked among the most notable events of this age … let [its] history be studied among the homes of the Irish peasantry … Amongst the lowest classes in Ireland, the entire social life is undergoing a blessed change … and a worthy feeling of national pride and manly independence is beginning to rise in the popular mind on the ruins of a reckless indifference or a degraded sensibility.[100]

Davis's comments, made at the movement's high water mark, brought home the fact that the impact of Mathew's movement could be found in public conversion, and in the public behaviour that maintained the moral and communal authority that ultimately held the cause together. The nature of Mathew's 'moral wonder' was best discovered by examining the common people's transformed way of life.

POISED FOR DECLINE?

Despite the fact that by 1843 Temperance had transformed Ireland, the movement's failure to consolidate its gains would prove disastrous sooner rather than later. It is clear from his correspondence that the

Apostle of Temperance was extremely anxious about his cause's future, and with good reason. In a sombre mood in Limerick in October 1841 Mathew observed

> I have suffered much and severely in this great cause. All has not been bright and sunny and pleasant and joyous. My pathways have been crossed, on more occasions than one, and various are the arts that have been used to destroy the good resulting from the glorious movement. Though a friend of mine, the editor of the *Belfast Vindicator* [Charles Gavan Duffy] has said that 'Father Mathew must be rejoiced at his success, and that no man should feel more satisfaction than he,' little did he know that my cup was dashed with gall and wormwood, and that I had to taste of bitter draughts.[101]

Father Mathew had always been suspicious of the machinations of those who opposed his 'sacred cause', but the Temperance crusade was in fact undone by a combination of factors. Temperance leaders trumpeted their intention to establish 'a true and perfect union of all creeds and classes' that would transcend existing political and religious divisions, and promised an entirely new era of national progress and improvement. At any juncture of Irish history, such a mission would have been a contentious and troubled undertaking, but amidst the growing political agitation and the multiplying religious difficulties and disputes of the early 1840s, it proved to be an impossible one. Father Mathew's stunning successes had only for a time eclipsed the troubled nature of the CTAS's position in relation to powerful religious and political forces in Irish society, forces that lost little time in reasserting themselves.

It is, then, ironic that even as Davis and the other Young Irelanders (including Mathew's friend and enthusiastic ally Charles Gavan Duffy) lauded Temperance, they, in conjunction with Daniel O'Connell, were endeavouring to harness it to partisan purposes that went a long way towards unravelling the cause. Their success in this regard depended on an acute understanding of both Temperance rhetoric and Temperance behaviours and practices, and they had indeed looked on the movement's progress 'with not inconsiderable interest'. The crusade's very success provided a blueprint for other social and political movements, the success of which in turn fuelled the CTAS's rapid decline.

However much the movement's manifest political utility eventually undermined its position in Irish society, the CTAS's uneasy coexistence with the Catholic Church proved to be fundamentally troublesome. In Mathew's eyes, the ambitious mandate of the CTAS to remake Ireland promised a great flowering of religion and ensured the salvation of countless souls. Many churchmen agreed with him, but others viewed things quite differently, and were deeply suspicious of Father Mathew and of Temperance enthusiasm. Because both the CTAS and the Catholic Church claimed divine authority and because they both claimed moral authority over the Irish people, they were bound to have a complex relationship, a relationship which now requires explanation.

CHAPTER SIX

The Cork Total Abstinence Society and the Church

Like any popular movements in nineteenth century Ireland, the success of the Temperance crusade depended in large part upon the attitude of the Church towards it. The national scale of the CTAS's progress cannot be understood without an appreciation of the particular realities of pre-Famine Catholicism in Ireland. If Temperance's initial magnificent success, however, was tied to these realities, so too was its ultimate failure. While the CTAS enjoyed much enthusiastic support within the Church at all levels, because the CTAS sought to transform the people themselves rather than their drinking habits, it is not surprising that the movement disturbed many churchmen. Charged with safeguarding the souls of the people and protecting the Church and her mission, many cautious Irish clerics resisted being caught up in Temperance enthusiasm. For reasons that need to be examined in detail, the CTAS, despite the best efforts of Mathew and his many clerical allies, remained outside the Church as an institution. The consequences of this exclusion were very serious to the movement in the long run because in many places it prevented the CTAS from consolidating its position in terms of the principle focus of the daily life of most of the Irish people – their parish.

The real strength of the Temperance movement, it has been argued, was found in the zeal and activity of thousands of local societies. The vitality of those societies itself relied, in very many ways, upon the Catholic church and its clergy. For all his ecumenical inclinations, Father Mathew was also a priest who understood this quite clearly. Not only was Father Mathew restricted in his movements by the necessity of holding his Temperance meetings only in parishes where Catholic bishops and priests invited him, his societies themselves were nearly always parish-based, and dependent on local clergymen to inspire, control, and lead them.[1] Mathew's determined efforts to enlist the support of the local clergy, the Irish bishops and the Roman authorities were at best only partly successful. Most of the parish clergy, in fact, did not rally to the standard of Temperance. To make matters worse, the Irish bishops as a body avoided any formal endorsement of his movement, and in fact disowned the crusade. The long term consequences of the bishops' collective coolness towards the CTAS cannot be overstated, for without their active encouragement, the bulk of the parish clergy, so vital to the movement's success, could not be relied upon.

The chapter that follows is divided into four sections. Section I explores Mathew's sometimes troubled relationship to his Church. Section II treats of some of the theological and practical problems that Temperance presented to many clergy in the Irish Church. Section III examines more closely the relationship between the CTAS and its potential grass roots leadership, the parish clergy of Ireland. Finally, section IV addresses Mathew's particular difficulties with some of the Irish bishops, and explains why these difficulties arose, and what their consequences were.

SECTION I: MATHEW AND HIS CHURCH

The clergy of all persuasions are not our friends.
– Theobald Mathew to James Haughton[2]

To note that Father Mathew was a very complex and interesting personality is, at this stage, only to state the obvious. Not only a man of considerable intelligence, refinement and charm, Mathew was tolerant in politics, ecumenical in religion and charitable in everything. In brief, he was a very attractive character. He could also, on occasion, however, be impulsive, wilful and even imprudent. These traits, as shall be seen below, weakened him as a leader, particularly in the eyes of the Irish clergy. In Cork, where he was a favourite of all creeds and classes, his faults were masked not only by his obvious virtues, but also by his considerable energy and accomplishments, and, it must be conceded, the uncontroversial scope of his various activities. While there was little in his early career to indicate that this compassionate and affable man was not the equal to any occasion or challenge that might arise, nothing in his prior experience could have prepared him for the unprecedented and awesome responsibility of leading the CTAS. As a well-known local figure, Mathew had overcome whatever prejudices might have attached themselves to him within his Church on the basis of his class or educational background, or, more importantly, the fact that he was a friar. As the leader of a national movement, however, Mathew was once again vulnerable on these accounts, and had far less time and opportunity to disarm his critics.

To begin with, there was no mistaking Father Mathew for a typical Irish priest. The wealth and status of the Mathew family in Tipperary distinguished him in terms of class from many of his clerical peers, who were by and large the sons of shopkeepers and strong farmers.[3] While by no means rendering him unpopular, Mathew's gentlemanly speech, manners and dress gave him the bearing and assurance that was remarked on by virtually all who met him. The English novelist William Thackeray, for example, who met Mathew in 1842, observed approvingly that he did not 'wear the downcast, demure look, which, I know not why, certainly characterizes the chief part of the gentlemen of his profession',[4] an observation that was echoed by Charles Constantine Pise, an American priest who visited Cork in the same year and who noted Mathew's 'elegant manners' and 'high-toned gentlemanly reserve'.[5]

If Mathew's family background distinguished him from his clerical peers, his early training may have inspired some real misgivings. Mathew suffered the stigma of having, in 1808, as a young seminarian, departed St Patrick's College at Maynooth under threat of expulsion, ironically enough for hosting an unauthorised party in his room.[6] Father Mathew never spoke publicly about this incident, an indication of his own uneasiness on the subject, despite the fact that the confession of alcohol-related sins was a common technique on Temperance platforms. Of course the story would have been fairly well known in clerical circles. His leaving Maynooth was particularly significant as the Irish Church was becoming dominated increasingly by its graduates, and that seminary had already established an enviable reputation for producing a very disciplined and correct body of clergy. By the time Mathew launched his movement, most of the bishops and about half of the priests serving in Ireland had been educated at St Patrick's College.

At the time he began his career as a Temperance missionary in April 1838, Father Mathew had been Provincial of the Franciscan Capuchin order in Ireland for 17 years.[7] While this office gave him a great deal of personal autonomy, it also placed him in a particular position in relation to the wider Irish church. As a friar, or a member of a 'regular' order, as distinguished from the 'secular' or parish clergy, Father Mathew was peripheral to the ecclesiastical power structure. Among the some 200 regulars in Ireland in the early 1840s (less than 10 per cent of the total number of priests), moreover, there were only 13 Capuchin friars, and the order was, according to John Francis Maguire, the 'lowliest and least influential'.[8]

The regulars were frowned on by many bishops concerned about their independence and lack of discipline, not to mention the drain they placed on scarce financial resources.[9] Disputes had often arisen over the bishops' attempts to increase their jurisdiction over the activities of regulars, and as a consequence the power and influence of the friars had been in rapid decline since 1800.[10] Father Mathew's own career illustrates some of the underlying tensions. As a young priest, for example, he had been transferred from his first assignment in Kilkenny in the diocese of Ossory to Cork after having been charged with violating the regulations imposed by the Vicar Capitular concerning the administration of the Sacrament of Communion by friars.[11]

Certainly Mathew's subsequent career in Cork had been exemplary in many ways, and his reputation for selfless good conduct was spotless. Nevertheless even here there were grounds for concern, especially among those inclined to be suspicious of the independence and accountability of friars. In the early 1830s, for example, Father Mathew had resolved against all advice to begin the building of a new church in Cork along the north bank of the river Lee at Charlotte's Quay, across from the old Capuchin friary. He was warned that the ground was too soft to allow for construction, but his determination to have a church that would be visible to sailors and those working along the river near his old friary was unshakeable, and led him to reject the offer of a more attractive site further east, on Sullivan's Quay across from the Grand Parade.[12] The construction of Mathew's gothic church during the 1830s, which involved elaborate and expensive drainage and foundation projects, became something of a white elephant, diverting scarce resources from other urgent diocesan church-building projects and spawning a series of lawsuits, government loans and appeals for funds. By 1840 it was still unfinished and at least £3,500 over its £10,000 budget (already a very high figure for a pre-Famine church), while public accusations that revenue from Temperance medals was being diverted to the project led Mathew to suspend its construction in 1841 for the duration of his crusade.[13]

Although there was not a partisan bone in his body, as his popularity increased and his sermons and speeches were widely quoted, Father Mathew's positions on questions of the day became well-known, and inevitably alienated potential allies. In this sense his moderate politics and his broad ecumenism, both of which were part of his appeal in Cork, were less useful on the national stage. Mathew was a supporter, for example, of the controversial government-sponsored national education system.[14] He spoke out forcefully and emotionally against emigration and alcohol taxation, and in favour of land reclamation projects.[15] He refused to vote in elections, out of, as he explained it, a distaste for clerical involvement in politics, a position that many priests would have taken as a criticism of their own ready participation.[16] Though his position on Repeal was not generally known, the unpopular fact that he adamantly opposed the participation of Temperance societies and bands with the Repeal campaign was.

Mathew was a theological liberal who, as a preacher, preferred to exhort congregations to follow their better natures than to threaten them with eternal damnation. Long before his involvement with Temperance, Mathew was renowned for his compassion as a confessor, a fact that led many to the Capuchin friary rather than their own clergy for consolation and absolution.[17] If his popularity may have led some to suspect Father Mathew of emphasising God's mercy at the expense of His justice (Mathew once admitted to Michael Blake, the Bishop of Dromore, that he would rather 'be damned for mercy than severity'), his embrace of Temperance led others to question Mathew's orthodoxy.[18] Some particular Catholic theological objections to the practice of Temperance will be raised below, but it needs to be noted here that many were uneasy about Mathew's liberal theology.

The need to end sectarian controversy was certainly one of the most persistent themes of Mathew's message, often manifested in urgent appeals for cooperation and toleration, and reinforced concerns about his doctrinal soundness. Typical, perhaps, was a letter Mathew wrote to W.W. Simpson, a land agent for the Marquis of Landsdowne, which culminated in an appeal for unity among Christians:

> Is it not distressing to see two persons wrestling the significance of some isolated passage – say from St Paul – from one side to another, until their variances generate ill-will between themselves, which often extends to their friends and neighbours, while they forget the simple Divine precept, 'Love one another', that would settle all differences and heal animosities?[19]

The same tolerant message was often part of Mathew's Temperance speeches, as in Lismore in County Waterford, when he had openly longed for the day when 'all sects and parties, being children of the same Omnipotent Father, the Great God of all, redeemed by the same Saviour, believing in the same gospel of peace and love would forget their jars and turmoils, and spend the days that remained to them in the blissful bonds of charity and concord.'[20] Charity and concord, many of the clergy felt, were laudable Christian ideals, but in a period marked by aggressive Protestant proselytisation countered by a vigorous Catholic defence of the faith, few were willing to see them achieved at the expense of orthodoxy.[21]

The CTAS was avowedly non-sectarian. Not only had all of its' founders been Protestants, but the meetings of Father Mathew's branch were, from their earliest days, mixed affairs that often featured Protestant speakers. The widely-promulgated rules of the society forbade religious discussions and controversies at meetings. In the crusade's early months, Father Mathew attempted to avoid administering the pledge on Sundays, and, except in a few cases of severely inclement weather, he would not administer it inside Catholic churches.[22] He often repeated a story he told first at Dublin, in September 1840, about a man who came to see him in Cork: 'The moment he entered my room, he said, "Father Mathew, I am an Orangeman!" to which I replied, "I don't care what you are, but let me make a teetotaller out of you".'[23] The anecdote reveals the real delight with which Father Mathew greeted his rare Protestant postulants, while his ideal view of the collaborative nature of Temperance societies was summed up in the letter to W.W. Simpson quoted above:

> Let men differ as they may, and their differences be every shade and colour of the rainbow; but let them join in expressing their approbation of teetotalism, and in supporting the system. We have been too long estranged from each other by mistaken views and sectarian jealousies; rather let us unite as true friends and Christian brothers, and throw oil on the troubled waters of society.[24]

In practice, of course, Mathewite Temperance was a far cry from this ecumenical ideal. By 1843, even Mathew had to acknowledge some failures on this account. After a letter critical of Temperance societies was printed in the Protestant *Cork Constitution*, for example, Mathew informed the editor that he was 'proud to be still a fellow labourer with many' Christians 'of all creeds'.[25] 'I fondly hoped to erect, in union with them', he explained, 'on the broad basis of fraternal charity, a great association, having for its glorious object the happiness of the whole human family.' He was obliged to concede, however, that 'the sublime ideal has not been worked out in its fullest extent in Cork and in a few other localities'. Mathew blamed 'those who, by appealing to the worst passions of the human heart' had 'to a certain extent made the temperance societies, in appearance, sectarian'. 'Every motive, human and divine', he concluded passionately, 'has been urged to prevent the members of other Christian sects from uniting with Roman Catholics in the great temperance movement.' In private, Mathew admitted to Edward Bullen that 'the parish priest or their co-adjutors are almost in every case presidents and vice presidents' of local societies.[26] In a bitter letter to his estranged friend James Haughton, he confessed that 'you are well aware the Teetotallers of Ireland are a Roman Catholic Body – There are not fifty Protestants united with us, though I have made every effort to induce them to associate with us'.[27] Mathew exaggerated Protestant apathy, as Haughton was quick to point out, but there were numerous features of the movement as it evolved that served to discourage Protestants, including its clerical leadership and the fact that Mathew's charity sermons were nearly always in support of Catholic causes. Some other features that were discouraging to Protestants were also countenanced by Father Mathew, who was willing on occasion to sacrifice principle to expediency where winning converts was concerned. These included the pledge itself, the kneeling posture adopted by most postulants, and Mathew's habit of signing each of them with the cross as he prayed that they would have the strength to keep it. As one angry Mayo Protestant clergyman complained in 1840, in a public letter to Mathew eloquently denying reports that he had taken the pledge,

> It would be impossible for me with my principles, to sanction your mode of operation, especially at Claremorris. I could not renounce my liberty in Christ Jesus, by bringing myself within the bondage of a voluntary vow – I could not sanction the superstitious veneration attended to your medals by the ignorant populace of the country – I could not bend the knee to a fellow worm of dust – I could not yield a momentary countenance to the delusion so widely spread of your reputed miraculous power, which, though verbally disowned, is yet upheld by your touching the ulcerated, crippled, etc. Nor could I, in especial, have appeared as your disciple in support at Claremorris, where your visit was avowedly solicited for the purpose, and rendered tribute to the enlargement of a chapel, in which a worship I have sworn is idolatrous is wont to be offered. I do not say these things offensively but in explanation.[28]

Practicality dictated that Father Mathew acknowledge the Catholicism of most of his postulants, whether in pledging them on Sundays or accepting, for the sake of 'order', the practice of their kneeling while pledging, or by encouraging their clergy to lead local societies. These compromises, however, were never matched by any willingness to subordinate his movement or his own authority within it to the Catholic Church.[29] If the CTAS was too Catholic in its practice and membership for many scrupulous Protestants, Mathew's often and loudly professed desire to keep Temperance and sect separate, an ideal firmly rooted both in the CTAS's ideology and his own temperament, was certainly not helpful in winning the confidence of the many clerical partisans within his own Church. Indeed, for many of the Catholic clergy, Mathew's close friendships and alliances with many Protestants inspired intense suspicion. If Mathew's background, the high profile of his controversial political and theological positions, and his ecumenical views combined to render him suspect in the eyes of many churchmen, his own behaviour as the leader of the enormously popular crusade, as will be seen below, did little to allay those concerns. Mathew's enormous popularity, his single-minded attachment to the Temperance cause, and his evident willingness to put the well-being of that cause before all else, led many of his fellow clergymen to conclude that the CTAS posed a real danger to authority within the Catholic church, and that Mathew's leadership increased rather than reduced that threat. The Capuchin's over-reaction to opposition to Temperance made it apparent to many that he was temperamentally ill-equipped to deal with the difficult responsibilities of his role as the leader of a radical national movement.

SECTION II: THEOLOGICAL OBJECTIONS

The prejudice that pervades Maynooth College, in favour of strong drink, is a mystery to me, and I do not know how to account for the delusion except by attributing it to the machinations of Satan – he ranges like a roaring lion against Teetotalism, and all his hellish powers are excited against a Teetotal priest or student, knowing the many brands that Teetotal preaching would snatch from the burning.

– Father Mathew to Rev. James Clarke, who wished to renounce his pledge, c. June, 1843.[30]

Beyond whatever reservations they may have had about the CTAS's leader, there were a number of principled objections, which will be termed 'theological,' (although they partook in varying degrees of established theological debates), that overlaid the reluctance of many within the Catholic Church to endorse the Temperance cause. These concerns were widespread, and by their nature strongly held. Their cumulative weight, while it did little to slow Temperance's initial expansion, reduced clerical enthusiasm for the CTAS and therefore increased its vulnerability to reaction and decline.

Although the tip of this iceberg of concern appears from time to time in Mathew's correspondence and in a number of contemporary discussions and events, most theological discussions about Temperance were private. Scattered evidence demonstrates that the nature of the movement was at least occasionally the subject of heated debate at the highest levels of the Irish church. John O'Sullivan, the parish priest of Kenmare in the diocese of Kerry, for example, in his private journal described participating in a theological argument over the society 'at the Bishop's table in presence of some fourteen or fifteen priests' where 'the Bishop turned on me most angrily' when O'Sullivan voiced reservations concerning the CTAS.[31] Because of the popularity of the Temperance cause, however, and the fact that it was embraced publicly by a number of prominent churchmen, priests and bishops who were troubled by the movement's theology usually kept their misgivings to themselves, or, as was the case with the opinionated O'Sullivan, within clerical circles. Those who opposed or were suspected of opposing the movement not only opened themselves up to questions about their own sobriety, but also to very public condemnation, particularly during the movement's period of exponential expansion. The *Waterford Chronicle*, for example, early in 1840 condemned 'an isolated portion of another neighbouring county' for its 'dissolute and scandalous example', and blamed in part the apathy of the local clergymen. 'If one or two of the Leinster parishes should withdraw from this grand moral revolution', the editor thundered, 'and continue to wallow in the mire and misery of drunkenness – if they should spurn the dictates of an honest and honorable pride, leaving conscience and duty entirely out of the question, and remain a stigma on the face of this fair island, we cannot help them.'[32] After P. Magrath, the parish priest of Ardmore, accosted the editor and accused him of spreading scandal by these harsh, barely-concealed references to his parish, his sacred office did not shield him from subsequent, still more explicit reprobation:

> [Temperance] is an open question, not bounded by the limits of parochial jurisdiction; as open to public discussion as the China question, the Franchise question, or the Repeal question itself, *and infinitely of more importance to the interests of the country than all these questions put together*. I also hold that the opinions of men holding authority, and exercising influence, such as the Catholic clergymen do, when publicly promulgated, are open to be publicly commented on, either through the press or otherwise. I differ with the Reverend gentleman on this subject; he preaches the doctrine of sobriety-moderation, or, in other words, semi-abstinence. I, on the other hand, am an humble advocate of teetotalism.[33]

Not even Bishops were safe from popular indictment. In September 1840, handbills and posters were widely circulated in Dublin, probably by distillers or publicans, containing anti-temperance remarks allegedly made by William Kinsella, the Catholic Bishop of Ossory.[34] In the uproar that followed, Father Mathew denied that the comments had ever been made, while the bishop insisted that, although he had refused to bless Temperance medals, he did not oppose the crusade. John MacHale, the Archbishop of Tuam, who became well-known as an opponent of Mathew, if not of Temperance, was subjected to a number of scathing condemnations in the press as a consequence.[35] Many of the clergy at all levels were understandably unwilling to endure controversy or blistering personal attacks. Those who opposed the popular movement risked undermining their authority and influence.

Precisely because of these widespread fears and concerns, it is difficult to reconstruct the nature of principled objection to Temperance. The movement was so strong in Ireland, and became so nearly universal so very quickly, that clerics made few anti-Temperance arguments in print even though, according to Mathew and other observers, many were far from sympathetic. However, considered criticism of Catholic total abstinence societies on the Mathewite model, so rare in Ireland, has survived in the candid memoir written by Father Joseph Prost, an Austrian Redemptorist priest who was stationed in the United States during the period of Mathew's greatest success.[36] Many of the American Catholic clergy at the time were Irish-born, and enthusiasm for Temperance was very widespread, particularly among the bishops, at least one of whom had attended several of Mathew's meetings in Ireland.[37] As Prost described it, Mathew's achievements 'took on an electric quality for Catholics in England and America'. Prost's comprehensive arguments against teetotalism were formulated in the United States, and great care, therefore, is required in considering them in relation to Irish circumstances. Nevertheless, his memoir serves as an invaluable introduction to appreciating the potential range, and even the vehemence of contemporary Catholic opposition to teetotalism.

At the American Church's Provincial Council in Baltimore in 1840, Joseph Prost stood alone in arguing against a proposal to endorse Mathewite Temperance societies. His solitary opposition reveals more about the divide between German and Irish influences in the American church than about the real prevalence of Catholic objections to Temperance. While he admitted drunkenness in America and the British Isles was a serious problem, Prost spoke for many of the clergy on both sides of the Atlantic when he listed seven reasons 'among others' for opposing Catholic Temperance societies.[38] They are therefore worth quoting at some length:

> [1] The whole thing is a Protestant invention and it does not seem proper to follow them as if they were our teachers.
>
> [2] The Protestants have no other method to convert people. They are forced to use such novelties, and they have to take refuge in the fascination people have for the current fashions in order to achieve an 'effect', and this 'effect' is further diminished by the fact that drunkards remain what they are and decent people are instead

tormented by this. Moreover, the Protestants had no permanent success in this matter and once it failed them, we took it up.

[3] The entire Catholic Church is a temperance society and it is the duty of every father-confessor to forbid anything that will become *occasio proxima* and to refuse the sacraments to all those who refuse to avoid the *occasio proxima* … If the father-confessors do their duty, then all will soon improve.

[4] The whole temperance society will be a fiasco as it was with the Protestants without prayer and the frequent reception of the holy sacraments, and those who pray and frequent the holy sacraments will be moderate drinkers even without a temperance society. And why should I deny people who drink moderately the benefit of what God gives them?

[5] We should not try to be wiser and better than Jesus Christ and the Apostles. There are temperance fanatics who assert that wine is the creation of the Devil; they are total Manichaeans.

[6] Everything good can be misused. Even the razor, for there are many persons who have used it to cut their own throats. To be completely consistent one ought not to take a razor in one's hand.

[7] The most important point that I made in opposition was the following: If someone wishes to associate this good work with a vow, then such a vow must be given voluntarily and with considerable thought. Such a vow would only allow for holy persons who would strengthen themselves constantly through prayer and the frequent reception of the holy sacraments. What happens usually? Passionate speakers try to persuade people to become members of the temperance societies. The Irish have ardent temperaments and allow themselves to be convinced by fiery speeches … Those who attach themselves to the temperance societies thought they had made a vow. The speakers for the temperance society, who were Catholic priests, reinforce this attitude in that they threaten people who break the vow with the wrath of God. Thus incited by fiery speakers, some people, who rarely if ever pray, and who have not received the holy sacraments for a long time, believe they have taken a vow. What happens when the excitement is gone? For a short time they are able to control themselves, but then they begin to drink again. If they did not take a vow, they could drink without sinning, as long as they did not become drunk. Now they do it, though bound by the vow, and they consequently commit a sin, *ergo multiplicantur pecatta* [*sic*] [thereby multiplying sin] … one thereby places a burden on them without giving them the means to support it.

Prost's objections were serious, and not only deserve some careful consideration, but also require an assessment of their relevance to Ireland. His first and the second criticisms were based on what would have been very common suspicions about Protestantism, and the Protestant roots of the current movement, which were well-known. It would be a serious mistake to underestimate the influence of this criticism in an Irish context. While explicit public condemnation of Mathewite Temperance on these grounds does not seem to have been made, in the increasingly sectarian atmosphere of 1830s and 1840s there would have been little need to make the argument at all. There can be no doubt that many of the Catholic clergy were extremely suspicious of Temperance, which was initially seen by many as just another cloak for proselytisation. The CTAS's strong desire to enlist the Catholic clergy as leaders of local societies and, indeed, Mathew's own recruitment were designed to disarm precisely this kind of sectarian hostility. While the overwhelming success of Temperance under the direction of Mathew and other priests may have changed many minds, doubtless some of the clergy who refused to support Temperance did so because they viewed it as a dangerous Protestant idea best left to its originators.

Prost's third and fourth objections centred on a Catholic understanding of the role of the Church and its sacraments in promoting moral conduct and ensuring the salvation of souls. Prost essentially claimed that the means to combat drunkenness were already available to the clergy, and that the real problem for the faithful was not drink, but failure on the part of many to submit themselves to the sacramental discipline already offered by the Church – namely, confession and communion. Sin in all of its manifestations, and not merely drunkenness, was the real enemy of all Catholics. Once again, public expression of this opinion in Ireland is elusive, if not quite unheard of, but certainly the movement's counterpoints – that, manifestly, Temperance was a work of the Holy Spirit, and that members of Temperance societies were far more likely to take their religious duties seriously than those who continued drinking – were frequently asserted.[39] Very real efforts were made by many to convince the clergy that Temperance could enhance (and indeed must advance) the practice of religion. As Mathew had explained at Lismore, the site of one of his earliest meetings, members of Temperance societies 'seemed to vie with each other in fidelity to the laws of God and society, and seemed animated with a spirit of self-respect of which they were entirely ignorant before.'[40] On 5 May 1842, responding to clerical critics of his crusade in a letter to Tobias Kirby, vice-rector of the Irish College in Rome, Mathew elaborated on this point, pointing out that 'the most moral, most religious persons in every community are the teetotallers, and this should content the prelates and pastors.'[41] Temperance's role in reviving religion was a particularly common theme among clerical supporters of the movement, and was cited frequently as the movement's greatest achievement.[42]

Behind the argument that Temperance improved religious practice and that members of Mathew's society were more likely to frequent the sacraments was the determination of many Temperance priests and bishops (although never Father Mathew) to use the organisation as an instrument for directly effecting a change in the religious habits of their flocks. Links between Temperance societies and religious practice, such as special masses for societies, Temperance pilgrimages and religious processions, etc., have already been noted. Quite a few priests, however, and at least one Irish bishop went a good deal further by requiring members of Temperance societies to frequent the sacraments. Nicholas Foran, for example, not only 'ordained that his clergy throughout the diocese should refuse sacraments to any person breaking the pledge' unless 'they make public atonement for doing so'.[43] He also insisted that 'every Catholic who is a member of the society shall attend to the duties imposed upon him at Christmas and Easter, and should he not do so he ceases to be a member of the society'. The members of the Temperance society at Ballyheigue, County Kerry, were encouraged to confess and receive communion 'en masse', and 'their appearance and demeanour was most edifying'.[44] The 'Rules of the St Mary's Temperance and Mortality Society' were drawn from Father Mathew's Cork model, but 'the Very Rev. President' in Limerick had added the requirement for Catholic members of 'confession at least within the period of six months, and that a book be kept in the sacristy ... in which each member complying with the request will insert his name; this book to be examined every six months'.[45] As a part of the government's investigation of Temperance in March 1840, the rules of the St Mary's Society in Limerick were surreptitiously copied by Wilson Kitson in faraway Co. Clare 'while speaking in a casual way' with an Ennistymon curate. It may be assumed, therefore, that they circulated widely in the country and were adopted elsewhere. It was not uncommon for pastors to connect Temperance more directly than Father Mathew chose with the Church's sacramental life.

Prost's fifth and sixth objections (that Christ drank wine, and that many Temperance supporters seemed to hold, heretically, that alcohol was a creation of the devil or that God had deliberately created something inherently evil) were common among the Irish clergy. At bottom, these objections sought to distinguish between use and abuse of alcohol. As James Dowling, the parish priest of Multyfarnham, Co. Westmeath, sensibly expressed it to Father Mathew in July 1840, 'The idea of having the whole people of a country bound for life to abstain from a thing lawful in itself has startled many, and has hindered some of the priests from joining or giving full sanction to your society'.[46] For his part, in 1843 Frederick Lucas, in his influential English Catholic journal, the *Tablet*, attempted to distinguish between good, 'Catholic' Temperance, that recognised no inherent evil in wine and honoured its sacramental employment, and 'Protestant Manichaeans or Tatians', who were 'fanatics who go far beyond this line of prudence and wisdom, and strive to establish temperance itself on principles of heresy and error'.[47] Lucas spoke for many when he warned Mathew about becoming the unwitting 'dupe' of 'this breed ... of old standing' whose 'extravagance' had long before 'sickened us of teetotalism'. He urged Mathew to alter the pledge in order 'to exclude from this society all those who take it in a heretical sense; all those who take it under the belief, and intending by the pledge to confirm themselves in the belief that intoxicating liquors are in themselves evil and unlawful'.[48]

This had in fact become an old charge by the time Lucas had made it. Father Mathew had already addressed these concerns directly, either by allowing, as he did from the beginning, a 'sacramental exception' for the reception of communion wine, or through attempts to clarify or qualify his opinions on alcohol, and apologise for the excesses of some Temperance advocates. This was particularly the case after 1841–42, when the movement's expansion had slowed and certain structural weaknesses were becoming apparent. 'I never asserted that the moderate use of these drinks was sinful', Mathew protested to Tobias Kirby in February 1842, 'but I affirmed that total abstinence was safer and better.'[49] At the Cork meeting in February 1843, and a month later in Dublin, Father Mathew took great pains to point out that he refused to condemn those who did not pledge as sinners, but insisted that the temperate achieved the 'perfection of moderation'.[50] He referred his critics to Romans 14, a Pauline passage addressing the early Church's internal disputes over Jewish dietary practices, as responsible for forming his own opinion on the matter, which concluded:

> Everything is indeed clean, but it is wrong for anyone to become a stumbling block over eating, it is not good to eat food or drink wine or do anything that causes your brother to stumble.[51]

Mathew also approved of the sentiments of the first verse of chapter 15 of Romans, 'We who are strong ought to put up with the failings of the weak, and not to please ourselves', and often made the same point in his Temperance speeches and private correspondence. As he explained to Kirby, 'Saint Paul would neither eat or drink if it would be a cause of scandal to any'.[52] In other words, Mathew conceded that, according to scripture and Catholic teaching, alcohol *per se* was not evil, but it certainly constituted, in an Irish context at the very least, a stumbling block to virtue for many and therefore ought to be renounced by all on that account, for the sake of the weak. This was particularly true of the clergy, the force of whose example, he knew, was paramount. Given this, as a matter of charity the blistering condemnations of alcohol by Mathew and others needed to be understood, not as expressions of theological convictions, but as well-intentioned attempts to prevent the destruction of souls. 'A little exaggeration', he protested to Kirby, 'is allowed when all is at stake.'[53] He observed to Kirby that the peculiar circumstances in Ireland made total abstinence practically a moral duty. 'Nothing but total abstinence', added Father Mathew, 'could stem this rushing torrent of woes.' 'If my renouncing forever the use of intoxicating drinks', he insisted, 'induced but one individual to become a teetotaller who would have otherwise persevered in the use of these at best dangerous liquids and become a drunkard, the acquisition is worth any sacrifice.'

Still, if Mathew was at times capable of restraint towards those who opposed the pledge out of conscience, many of his supporters were not. The moral vision of a universally temperate Ireland that was at the heart of the movement's ideology (as critics such as James Dowling recognised) made little room for conscientious objectors, and the overall tone of the crusade was harshly critical towards those who continued to drink in public, or to advocate a right to do so, a fact that Lucas in particular complained about.[54] It was this edge of fanaticism present in the Temperance crusade that so discomfited many among the clergy, who read Romans differently from Mathew, as a condemnation of divisive extremism on open questions, particularly as the early Church had in fact determined that Jewish dietary law had been superseded by Christ's message. As Patrick Dorrian, a curate in Belfast, complained in 1846, 'if teetotalism be even sure of removing drunkenness, but willing to substitute this forcing of consciences to its own views, I think it might fairly be questioned if the old state, with all its faults, would not be preferable to the new one, and less a scourge to society in the long run.'[55] Or, as Josef Prost put it, 'If someone wishes to deny himself the use of spirits in order to be a good example to others, he should be praised for this holy action. But it cannot be made a commandment for others'.[56] Even if William Kinsella, the Bishop of Ossory, never made the remarks so widely attributed to him in 1840 when he refused to bless

Temperance medals, and quoted below, many (including Prost) would have privately approved of them:

> The pledge should only be taken by persons unable to control their appetites by reason or moral feeling ... virtuous, moral or well-instructed persons did not require such constraints to keep themselves from drunkenness. That the pledge may prove useful for drunkards, or persons of weak understanding, unable to control themselves, he did not deny ... he did not see any reason why the working classes in Ireland should preclude themselves from the use of what might add to their social enjoyments or what might be necessary to preserve the health of persons exposed, as the working people of Ireland were, to the effects of cold, damp or other privations.[57]

Prost's final, and 'most important' objection centred on the question of whether or not the pledge constituted a religious vow, or a promise made to God. There were really two aspects of this theological concern. On the one hand, if the pledge was regarded by Mathew as a religious vow, it was clear that at least some if not most who took it did so without adequate preparation and reflection, and were not strong enough spiritually to keep it. As Prost explained, 'One thereby places a burden on them without giving them the means to support it'. When they broke the pledge, as many surely would, their sin of drunkenness would be compounded by the even more serious sin of having broken a vow. If, on the other hand, the pledge was not a religious vow, but a mere moral resolution or promise, then that fact needed to be made clearer to those who pledged, because those who took it assuming it was (or were later convinced of the fact by local clergy) still committed serious sin by breaking what they believed to be a sacred promise.

This question became the subject of open controversy in Ireland in the 1840s. James Dowling, for example, Multyfarnham's scrupulous parish priest noted above, passed on to Mathew the 'great anxiety' of many priests of his acquaintance to 'know whether you regard the obligation of the pledge as a obligation of honour or whether you regard it as binding in conscience *per se*'.[58] John O'Sullivan, the parish priest of Kenmare in the diocese of Kerry, noted his own opinion in his diary, observing that 'the promise of abstaining from intoxicating liquors (*provided one did not mean to make a vow*), was one that could be violated the moment they wished to cease being members' of the CTAS.[59] Mathew's various statements on the subject make it clear that, much as he wanted to avoid the issue, it was too controversial for him to remain silent. When pressed he was willing to admit explicitly that he did not consider the pledge the equivalent of a religious vow. 'I do not consider the promise to abstain from intoxicating drinks a vow', he explained in a public letter in September 1840.[60] 'I look upon it as a simple resolution to perform a moral act.' He repeated himself in Dublin two months later, after having obviously grown frustrated by the debate:

> To be sure, some may still object to the pledge, as such might be a violation of moral liberty; while others would be found alleging that the temperance pledge was a religious vow, and as such that no one ought to take it. But I say to you that taking the temperance pledge constitutes no religious vow whatever, it is a simple moral resolution ... So that it is not, my friends, by any means a religious vow, and those that assert that it must be, I can only observe, know my intentions in administering the pledge better than I do myself ... I am bound to say this – that I never for a moment thought that anyone who broke the pledge was thereby guilty of violating a religious vow.[61]

Mathew then went on to insist, however, that he still considered pledge breakers a disreputable set who ought to be shunned.

Mathew's caveat brought up a still-more complex issue which Prost never considered. In an Irish context, the pledge was also widely understood to have a collective, communal dimension. Mathew was consistent in insisting that while those who pledged incurred no direct obligation to God, they did incur a social obligation. He explained this notion most clearly in the summer of 1843 when he became embroiled, while in England, in a dispute with Frederick Lucas over the nature of the pledge. At a Birmingham meeting in September, Nicholas Wiseman, the Vicar Apostolic of the Midland district, presented the case in this way, with Father Mathew affirming it:

> A great outcry has been raised against the promise as being administered in the form of a vow ... many were scrupulously afraid; lest they should involve themselves in a vow which they might possibly violate. Now, the whole question depended upon this – to whom the promise was made? A vow had ever been considered by Catholics as a solemn promise to God alone, and were the words of the pledge to involve a sacred obligation, it would unquestionably be a solemn vow; but Father Mathew did not urge a promise to Almighty God. They promised society – they promised their wives – they promised their children – they promised themselves – no longer to continue what had proved to them a dangerous and degrading practice. In Ireland, the promise was understood to be made to the people, and if the party making it broke it, the people knew how to resent it. He [Dr Wiseman] would appeal to Father Mathew if this was the sense in which the pledge was understood? Father Mathew—Precisely so. The Bishop – The party taking the pledge appealed not to the tribunal of the Church, but to the open tribunal of the whole world.[62]

Even this understanding of the pledge, however, was problematic to many. It was evident to many priests that, if the pledge was a public vow, not only was pledge-breaking certainly sinful, but it was perhaps even more sinful than breaking a private vow. In 1840, Nicholas Foran, the Bishop of Waterford, explained to the teetotallers of his diocese that, as a public vow, the pledge could not be broken without sin unless it was renounced publicly first.[63] The following year, William McLaughlin, the parish priest of Donahedy and Leek in the diocese of Derry, told his parishioners that 'the solemn pledge of temperance, although not an oath, was an obligation voluntarily undertaken before God, and in the presence of hundreds of their fellow-beings, to practice strict sobriety'.[64] 'It ought to be deemed, if possible', McLaughlin carefully explained, 'more binding than a private oath, and observed with the most honourable and religious fidelity.'

In 1842 Michael Slattery, the Archbishop of Cashel, issued a printed circular to his clergy on the subject of Temperance pledge-taking and breaking (not 'to be read publicly as coming from me, nor allowed by any means to get into the newspapers') designed to help clergy in the confessional, which acknowledged that the public nature of the pledge imposed certain moral duties.[65] No one, the document noted, 'was obliged to practice perfection', except those who 'had taken an obligation on themselves' to do so, such as the Temperance pledge. Teetotallers 'gave a public and formal expression to the resolution made by them, not merely to the person who administered the pledge, but also to the body they were joining and to society at large'. Members of societies 'entered, then, into an engagement, as it were, with society'. They were, therefore, 'amenable to the tribunal of public opinion for the fulfilment of their compact', and needed to be 'regarded as contracting not only a personal but a social obligation, and thereby incurring a great *social* responsibility'. It was this social obligation, not the nature of the pledge itself, that imposed moral duties, which themselves 'may thus become a matter of conscience and be binding under sin'. Slattery ominously concluded that 'the generality, nay perhaps all of those who violate the pledge, do so under the impression that its violation is sinful, and consequently are really guilty of sin by acting against their conscience'. Thus, while according to their own consciences pledge-breakers might break no religious vow, their evident disregard for their social responsibilities was in itself widely seen to be sinful. In response to Wiseman's explanation in 1843, for example, 'A clergyman in the South of Ireland' revealed his own understanding of the pledge in vague but strident language.[66] Whatever Mathew might say about the nature of the pledge, he insisted, pledge-breaking in his parish was seen to be 'a most barbarous crime, not only against society but against high heaven'. 'Of this fact', he insisted, 'I am quite certain, and so is every clergyman with whom I have discussed the temperance movement.'

Many priests then, it seems clear, despite Mathew's assertions to the contrary, were convinced that the pledge partook of the nature of a vow of one kind or another. Quite a few priests, for example, refused the sacraments to those who broke the pledge, until they either renounced the pledge formally or retook it. Among them was Nicholas Foran, who, in the summer of 1842, ordered priests in his diocese to 'refuse sacraments to any person breaking the pledge, without they make public atonement for doing so'.[67] John O'Sullivan, the parish priest of Kenmare in the diocese of Kerry, actually insisted that pledge-breakers in his parish return to Cork to pledge again before he would 'readmit them to the temperance hall and to the sacraments', even though he recognised that the obligations imposed by the pledge were strictly social.[68] During his dispute with Mathew in 1843, Lucas cited this case as a particularly confusing and dangerous one, given Mathew's determination, 'which we neither approve nor condemn', to run his Temperance society outside the Church. Lucas further demanded that the pledge's language be altered to make its nature as a mere promise clearer.[69]

Lucas's point was a crucial one. It represented a widespread and considered opinion that the movement was quite intertwined with religious practice and observance, and intimately connected with many Irish Catholics' own sense of being in (or not in) a state of grace. Given the mode of administering the pledge, it is not surprising that many other clergymen were convinced that most of the people *believed* the pledge to be a kind of religious vow, which, as Prost had noted, made the breaking of the pledge a very serious matter regardless of what its true nature was. When, for example, Cardinal Franzoni, the Prefect of Propaganda, wrote from Rome in 1842 to Daniel Murray, the Archbishop of Dublin, and to Michael Slattery, the Archbishop of Cashel, requesting a report on Mathew's movement, he specifically inquired if the breaking of the pledge was considered to be a sin.[70] Murray noted that returning the medal relieved one from the pledge, but also observed that the pledge was administered while kneeling amidst immense crowds by priests who marked postulants with the sign of the cross. 'Most people', Murray conceded, 'believe that it cannot be broken without fault.' Slattery was somewhat more cautious, and noted that 'whatever indeed it may be about the method and rules by which men are brought into this society, by no oath, properly speaking, are they obliged, just as the founder of the society himself has declared'. However, he pointed out, the violation of the promise that was made often became sin 'from circumstances, certainly by reason of scandal or evil that would follow from it', from the drunkenness itself, or 'from the fact that when men are able to think that they sin from such a violation, they do indeed sin by acting against their own conscience'.

As was the case with disputes about the need for Christians to retain their liberty of conscience on open questions, Mathew was clearly frustrated by the controversies about the nature of the pledge. Although he considered Temperance to be a 'sacred' cause, he did not want to make the theologically dangerous assertion that the pledge was a binding oath made to God. Still, he also wanted to take every opportunity to impress all who took it with a sense of solemnity and import, and was perfectly willing to make use of religious rituals and symbolism to do so. Attempts to force him into repeated public declarations that his pledge was non-binding in the religious sense seemed to him mean-spirited and uncharitable, as they were sure to undermine the will of many to remain temperate. In an exasperated moment in October 1843, in the wake of Lucas's blistering attacks on his movement, he referred such questions to his audiences' consciences, remarking that they were 'entirely a matter for their own consideration', but that, given the practical benefits of Temperance, he was 'surprised that persons with the facts before them could trouble themselves about the nature of the pledge'.[71] Mathew, so fond of referring to his crusade as a 'sacred cause', never seemed to grasp that the influence that it claimed over the consciences of its members could be seen as threatening or dangerous by the men charged with saving the souls of the Irish people.

The damage done to Temperance by these various theological objections is difficult to measure, but it was probably considerable. One example of how demoralising they could be occurred in 1843, when many of the students and priests at Maynooth wrote to Mathew to renounce the pledge, apparently as a result of a theological controversy at the college about the pledge as a religious vow.[72] To one doubting seminarian, Mathew acknowledged that pressure was being brought to bear on his followers, admitting that 'the circumstances in which you and my other dear brother Teetotallers are placed in Maynooth, are well known to me, and I deplore the privations you have all suffered'.[73] He dispiritedly accepted the resignation of John Barry at Maynooth 'without alluding to the theological opinion you have quoted, for there are a great many Maynooth letters to answer and little time to devote to that painful task'.[74] For the sake of Temperance's image, Mathew requested that some of the students at least observe their pledge outside the college walls. In a moment of frustration, he candidly confessed to one student that the 'six million' other Irish teetotallers had 'not caused me so much affliction as the few timid backsliders of your college'.[75]

The Maynooth controversy is more important to an understanding of the Temperance crusade's fundamental weakness in relation to the Catholic Church than the mere numbers involved would indicate. Although unreported by the press, the mass resignations must have become widely known in clerical circles, and doubtless did much to undo Mathew's moral triumph of a few years earlier at the college. More significantly, the dispute did not represent an isolated, academic occurrence, as the similar but far more public controversy in the *Tablet* a few months later proved. Mathewite Temperance and Catholicism, in the minds of most priests and bishops, whether or not they supported the movement, were connected in the most intimate and important ways imaginable. Given this, the power that the movement had over the consciences of the Irish people needed to be either brought under the control and influence of the Church, or otherwise contained. The range of theological objections raised by Prost in America and echoed in various ways by the clergy in Ireland, particularly those concerning the nature of the pledge, made the latter solution more attractive to many. Taken as a whole, the objections greatly weakened the support of that crucial group of men Mathew relied upon to lead the Temperance movement and make his moral revolution.[76]

SECTION III: THE PARISH CLERGY

> *If the priests would nobly come forward in other parts of Ireland to cooperate in the glorious struggle, as they have done in Meath, Carlow, Dromore, Kilmore, Killaloe, Cavan, etc., etc., before the end of this year there would not be a drunken Catholic in Ireland.*
>
> – Theobald Mathew to Tobias Kirby, 5 May 1842.[77]

The influence of priests in pre-Famine Ireland has been commented upon at great length in many places. Alexis de Tocqueville's observation that there existed 'an unbelievable union between the Irish clergy and the Catholic population' is widely attested to.[78] Father Mathew found the Temperance movement's most powerful supporters, as well as its most determined opponents, among his fellow priests in the Catholic Church. As Father Mathew's above comments to Tobias Kirby demonstrate, he firmly believed that his society could only flourish where parish priests and their curates 'came forward'. Father Mathew nearly always noted in his addresses when local clergymen took the pledge, and he rewarded them when they did with special silver Temperance medals. By insisting the clergy lead the Temperance movement, Mathew was simply recognising what was taken for granted by his contemporaries – that any successful social or political movement in Ireland depended on committed clerical participation. The 'universal consummation' of Temperance, its 'rearing up into a mighty, a national harvest', one Waterford journalist pointed out in December 1839, 'depends wholly on the exertions of the clergy'.[79] Given the nature of social relations in rural pre-Famine Ireland and the priest's place in them, the communal pressures associated with taking, and particularly with keeping, the pledge could not be sustained in the face of clerical opposition, or even indifference, and could only succeed over time with strong clerical support. The opinions and actions of their clergy were therefore of critical importance to the success of local Temperance societies over the long run.

While there were as many opinions on Temperance among Irish priests as there were priests, in the most basic terms the clergy chose between actively supporting the movement and refusing to do so. In the eyes of Temperance's advocates this was the critical decision, because those who did not support such a radical crusade might as well have been opposed to it. The consensus that had been established among the Irish people in favour of total abstinence during 1839–41 needed to be reinforced by an equally determined consensus among those who had emerged as their natural leaders if the cause was to truly triumph. Isolated pockets of stubborn opposition or scattered back-sliding could in time be dealt with, but a critical mass of priests in favour of Temperance was indispensable.

A large number of Ireland's priests were active supporters, organising and sustaining local societies, inviting Father Mathew, preparing the way for his visits, and distributing cards and medals afterwards. Just how many is difficult to determine, although Father Mathew claimed at a meeting in February 1841 that 700 priests had taken the pledge, or about one-third of the nearly 2,200 in the country at that time.[80] Because Mathew was prone to exaggeration when it came to the numbers of his supporters, this figure was likely an overestimate. While more priests certainly pledged after early 1841, there were defections as well, particularly as the intensity of principled objection to the crusade increased in 1842–43.[81] Still, allowing for the fact that some supporters may not have taken the pledge at all, and recognising that there were varying degrees of dedication, enthusiasm and fidelity among those who did, it is reasonable to suppose that perhaps one-third of Irish priests were, at one time or another, strong enough supporters of the reformation to take the important symbolic step of pledging. Impressive as this figure at first appears, it must be noted that it represents a significantly lower proportion of pledge-takers among the clergy than among the adult population as a whole.

Clearly, much of the good that resulted from the Temperance movement was a consequence of the efforts of those priests who did all they could to further the cause. Many, with Mathew, believed that drunkenness was at the root of most of the social ills of Ireland, and was primarily responsible for crime and poverty. Some had been advocates of temperance, if not total abstinence, for many years. J.P. Lyons, the parish priest of Kilmore-Erris and dean of the diocese of Killala, for example, claimed in a letter to Mathew that he had done all he could against intemperance during his clerical career. 'When I came among them 15 years ago', he reported of his parishioners, 'the degrading vice of drunkenness was so habitual with persons of every class, grade and persuasion that it ceased to be considered discreditable before men or even before God.' Hundreds of priests did all they could to organise, strengthen and lead local societies. Nicholas Cantwell at Tramore in the diocese of Waterford, for his part, frequently gave pro-Temperance sermons and had 'nearly every adult' in his parish enrolled in the CTAS.[82] J. Fitzpatrick, a curate in the bishop of Cloyne and Ross's mensal parish of Skibbereen, organised a tea party and led a procession in that town in January 1840 to discountenance the local custom of 'drinking in' the new year.[83] Determined advocates such as Lyons, Cantwell and Fitzpatrick could be found all over Ireland. Many others became enthusiastic supporters of the movement when they witnessed, first hand, the spectacle of mass Temperance gatherings and the transformative effects of Temperance on public behaviour.

There is a great deal of evidence that indicates, unsurprisingly, that Temperance flourished best when local clergy enthusiastically endorsed the cause. In the early days of CTAS expansion, many local priests began enrolling members into Mathew's society in anticipation of future visits by Temperance's great apostle. Early in 1840, for example, Patrick O'Davern, a curate at Donoskeigh in the archdiocese of Cashel, took it upon himself to enlist 'preliminary' members who could not wait for Mathew to arrive.[84] There were probably, in fact, several dozen priests scattered through Ireland, even before Mathew began touring in earnest, who distributed his cards and medals, although it needs to be kept in mind that not all who administered the pledge were necessarily zealous teetotallers themselves or even strongly in favour of the movement. Many more began to do so during the course of 1840–41.

Accounts of Temperance meetings in the early 1840s, moreover, reveal the active role taken by many of the clergy in local societies. Temperance processions and funerals were invariably headed up by parish priests and curates, while no tea party was complete without priests at the head table and a toast to the clergy of Ireland. The zeal of James Maher, a newly-appointed curate at Mallow in 1842, was by no means unprecedented, and the account of the priest by a local admirer submitted to the *Cork Examiner* demonstrated the potential impact of clerical leadership in the temperance cause. Father Mathew's visit to Mallow, where drunkenness had been a longstanding and serious problem, had produced a tremendous initial response, but 'there was an active leader wanted'.[85] Arriving in town and discovering its Temperance society to be moribund, Father Maher

> practiced what he preached, by becoming a teetotaller himself, and then went about discovering those who violated the sacred pledge, and inducing them, by word and example, to retake it. In short, he organised the scattered and fallen membership into a respectable and inseparable body, consisting of five hundred. He then took a spacious news-room, in which they assembled in hundreds after their day's toil.

The fundamental problem for the Temperance movement was that there were never enough Father Mahers to go around. Individual priests could and did organise and galvanise strong local societies inspired by Father Mathew's example, but their activity only underscored the fact that many others did little or nothing to advance the cause.

Although the unwillingness of a majority of Irish priests to endorse fully the crusade was of a piece in the sense that it crippled the movement, non-commitment to the cause was in fact composed of a spectrum that included perhaps two-thirds of Ireland's priests. The upper and lower limits of the spectrum ranged from outright hostility, principled or otherwise, to downright apathy, often tinged with scepticism, towards Temperance. In between were hundreds of doubting, traditionally-minded, overworked or opportunistic priests who would or could not allow themselves to be convinced that a universally temperate Ireland was possible or desirable. Taking these not-necessarily-mutually-exclusive positions in turn, and beginning with the movement's decided opponents, it is important to remember that the CTAS was too popular in many areas to make out-and-out condemnation wise. While Mathew complained to Tobias Kirby of the 'melancholy truth' that 'very many' priests 'exert[ed] all their influence to oppose the progress of temperance, and induce the teetotallers to violate their pledge' by means that included refusing the sacraments to members of Temperance societies, as well as 'forbidding them to take or keep the total abstinence promise, or to attend temperance meetings', he was reacting to the outspoken opposition of only a few.[86] Still, the movement had many determined clerical opponents, only a small number of whom, it can be safely assumed, ever allowed their opposition to become well known. Father Mathew was convinced of the influence of his foes, and regularly complained, as he did in another letter to Kirby on 20 September 1842, of 'the unholy, and, I may say, cruel opposition which I met with from very many of my clerical brethren'.[87] 'Hundreds of hitherto faithful teetotallers', he insisted, 'have been in a manner compelled to break the pledge', while 'as many more have received dispensations from them.' Worst of all, 'millions are deterred by their sarcasm and sneers from joining our glorious society'.

Father Mathew had a rather sinister explanation for the behaviour of his brother priests. He was 'perfectly well aware', he explained in 1841 to Paul Cullen, 'that intemperance was the predominant sin of the Irish priesthood, and that there would not be a purer and more efficient body of ecclesiastics in the Church of Christ, if they had been free from this besotting vice'.[88] In correspondence with Tobias Kirby the following year, he attributed the 'violent opposition of the clergy' to the fact that many were 'deep drinkers themselves' who 'openly encouraged the people to follow their example'.[89] He repeated the accusation the following September, observing that 'Many, too many alas, of our clergymen drink deeply to excess of intoxicating liquors'.[90] Heavy drinking was endemic in Irish society, and drunkenness was a common failing of the clergy, just as it was among the people.[91] An awareness of the reality that most priests drank, and some were doubtless, as Mathew alleged, 'deep drinkers', makes it unsurprising that a significant percentage of the clerical population opposed the Temperance reformation.

Other priests, probably a substantial number, were theological doubters of the virtue of total abstinence. However unwilling they may sometimes have been to be identified as opponents of Temperance, these principled men subscribed to some combination of Josef Prost's theological objections to total abstinence, and were unwilling to bind either themselves or their parishioners to so doubtful an obligation. Theological opponents of the cause have already been explored in some detail above. It needs to be reiterated here, however, that the controversies at Maynooth and in the pages of the *Tablet*, not to mention Mathew's own repeated attempts to justify his position, despite his evident impatience with what he viewed as theological quibbling, all indicate that there was widespread doubt among Irish priests about the orthodoxy of the CTAS during the early 1840s.

Another elusive but probably numerous class of conservative priests thought there was nothing wrong with moderate social drinking. Not to be confused with their harder-drinking colleagues, these traditionally-minded critics of the movement appreciated the fact that pre-Famine Irish culture was closely associated with alcohol. While they may have been critics of drunkenness, their sensibilities about alcohol were determined by the fact that moderate (by period standards) social drinking was absolutely customary for the clergy. Alcohol, furthermore, was intimately bound up in religious practices such as stations and, indeed, the expectation of a clerical presence at most social and religious events, where of course the consumption of alcohol was presumed. Mathew was aware of this kind of opposition, and complained in 1842 to Kirby of the 'scandalous profanation of the Sacrament of matrimony that takes place at weddings where all the parties are nearly drunk', urging that 'marriages in Ireland should be henceforward celebrated in the parish church, and in the morning'.[92] Clerical incomes, furthermore, although by no means large, were sufficient (unlike those of many of their parishioners) to allow for the regular provision of wine, brandy and whiskey punch at and after meals, and many priests were unwilling to change ingrained habits. In common with other members of the middle and upper classes, because their patterns of consumption tended to be private, habitual and casual, abandoning the use of alcohol seemed, paradoxically, both less necessary and more onerous. The private comments of John O'Sullivan, Kenmare's parish priest, are once again instructive. 'I have not taken the pledge', he noted, 'though I seldom, very seldom, exceed one tumbler of punch, and I do not see why I should deny myself so much.'[93] The statements attributed to William Kinsella, the Bishop of Ossory, in 1840, and already quoted above (that 'virtuous, moral, or well-instructed persons did not require such constraints', and that 'he did not see any reason why the working classes in Ireland should preclude themselves from the use of what might add to their social enjoyments') might also be fairly said to represent this way of thinking.[94]

Many other priests, moreover, were simply too busy to serve the Temperance cause in the ways that Father Mathew hoped they would. Diligent service as the president of a local society involved attending numerous meetings, dinners and parades, and could be enormously time consuming. Additionally, society presidents needed to keep track of pledge-breakers, mediate disputes over the distribution of musical instruments and the use of the society's rooms, and serve as conduits for medals and cards sent from Cork. Any Irish priest in the 1840s who took his calling seriously was already subjected to an exhausting workload. Given the sacramental character of the Catholic faith, and with an overall priest-to-people ratio that approached 1:3,000, it was all many priests could do to keep up with the pastoral demands of ministering to their flocks.[95] In a period when these demands were actually increasing, the undermanned Irish clergy were often understandably reluctant to become part-time Temperance advocates.

The opportunists among the clergy were well-represented, and while they cannot be considered to have been opponents of Temperance in all instances, their usefulness as leaders must be called into question. Mathew certainly complained, again to Kirby, of the 'sordid and base motives' of some of his opponents.[96] 'Drunkards at weddings and christenings give the best offerings', he complained, 'and distillers and spirit-dealers were their most generous money-giving parishioners.' Mathew was well aware that these facts were countered by the fact that he was the most successful charity sermon preacher of his day. His practice of separating the administration of the pledge in the open air from his delivery of sermons in the church had the added benefit of allowing local parish priests to take the one and leave the other, as their consciences required. Mathew could generally be relied upon not to mention Temperance to the audiences he asked for charity. His charity sermons usually filled the local church with both the curious and the well-to-do, and if the £350 he raised at his first Dublin sermon was an unusually large sum, £100 in smaller towns was not unusual.[97] Given his great propensity for giving away money as fast as (indeed, a good deal faster than) he acquired it, Mathew's visits also produced an additional windfall of at least £10, and often as much as £40 or £50, for the parish priest to apply as he thought fit.

The attractive power of this largesse in so poor a country cannot be overestimated. These much-needed funds appear to have been desperately sought after, and Mathew's charity sermons played carrot to the stick of popular demand in driving Temperance forward despite widespread clerical reservations in the early 1840s. The enthusiasm of parishioners, the opportunity of a lucrative sermon, and Father Mathew's own private largess, undoubtedly overcame the objections of most of the more unenthusiastic clergy, who were willing to invite him to their parish if their bishops approved.

It is therefore no surprise that the tone of many surviving requests from parish priests for visits was quite mercenary. N. O'Connor, the parish priest at Maryborough and a vicar general in the diocese of Kildare and Leighlin, for example, reminded Mathew of a 'promise to preach for the finishing of my chapel'.[98] 'It is a good building but without an alter piece', O'Connor noted, and 'wanting some improvements.' 'I am sure no one of your Lieutenants in this county will get inside of me as they say or anticipate me', O'Connor observed, since he was 'a little jealous and would be greatly disappointed.' O'Connor's was a common theme, as priests in some cases seemed to be anxious for first visits to an area in order to ensure a good turnout at the charity sermon.[99] John Kenyon, curate at Ballinaclough in the diocese of Killaloe, was deputed 'by his Principal' (Edward MacGrath) 'to annoy you on the score of a half-promise which you made, it seems, in a confiding moment' to preach a charity sermon in their parish church.[100] Kenyon had already thought long and hard about Mathew's largesse, for earlier that year a letter of his had appeared in the *Limerick Reporter* praising Mathew and Temperance, and noting Mathew's practice of donating significant sums of his own to the charities he preached for.[101] 'Such a rate of expenditure betrays a very determined resolution, on his part', observed Kenyon at the time, 'not to grow rich on the agency of cards and medals.' Kenyon's own request for a visit also included the suggestion that Father Mathew avoid the neighbouring parish of Toomevara 'like a fit of drunkenness until it be accomplished'. 'So might your cause prosper', Kenyon amusingly concluded, 'our schoolhouse be floored, and Toomevara enjoy its subsequent good luck without being envied or overlooked by Father MacGrath.' Kenyon was, in fact, a principled supporter of the movement, but Edward MacGrath was probably typical of many priests who were unenthusiastic about Temperance in every respect except for the good the cause might do their chapel roof or schoolhouse floor.

Finally, some number of sceptical or suspicious Irish priests were quite simply devoid of the kind of reforming zeal that was so characteristic of their pro-Temperance brethren, and in any event could not convince themselves that human nature could undergo so dramatic a transformation. The Cork priests who 'did not entertain very sanguine hopes as to the final result of this great movement, which all admit has done infinite good', met by Charles Constantine Pise, a visiting American priest, in 1842 were another species of this sort.[102] 'I am very much prejudiced against Mr Mathew', John O'Sullivan, Kenmare's parish priest confided to his journal.[103] 'I have taken up as opinion that there is an immense share of acting and humbugging about him, and I cannot look upon him with the same eyes as the public do.' Indeed, reluctance to be swept up in Temperance enthusiasm appears to have been the most typical position of the Irish clergy in relation to the CTAS, although many of these passive priests invited Mathew to visit their parishes, and some, like the Cork priests encountered by Pise, or O'Sullivan for that matter, were impressed by the movement's accomplishments.

Despite the enthusiastic support of a substantial minority of Irish priests during the early years of the Temperance crusade, therefore, the majority of the clergy were at best lukewarm advocates, continuing to drink (at least in private) despite Mathew's pleas and the example of Ireland's teetotalling millions. Taken as a body, the priests failed to provide the Temperance crusade with the powerful and committed leadership that Father Mathew and the CTAS so craved. The consensus in favour of Temperance that was a marked feature of popular opinion in the early 1840s never existed among the clergy. This was a sad fact from Mathew's point of view, as well as other supporters of Temperance. Early in 1844, when James Haughton composed a public letter to the clergy which took them to task for failing the crusade, Mathew begged him not to publish it. 'The address you suggest, to the clergy of Ireland', Mathew warned, 'would be productive of much evil.' 'The clergy are the most jealous of all men', he lamented, 'and would not submit to anything like advice or remonstrance.'[104] Still, Mathew bitterly conceded that 'the clergy of all faiths are, to put it mildly, unfavourable to total abstinence'.[105] 'Under these untoward circumstances', Mathew added, 'it is a great cause of thankfulness to the Lord, that so many millions continue faithful.'

The dissatisfaction that Mathew repeatedly expressed on the subject of clerical resistance to Temperance is very revealing, both in terms of his own understanding of the nature of the moral revolution he was leading, and in relation to the eventual disintegration of the crusade itself. Not only did Mathew believe he was largely dependent on his fellow priests to further the cause, but he was also dismissive of the level of support that he did receive, which was after all considerable. Clearly Mathew expected nothing short of a total endorsement of the crusade by nearly all, if not all, of Ireland's clergy. His sense of frustration at the failure of the priests as a body to establish the same consensus in favour of total abstinence that their people had was palpable, and must be taken into account in any assessment of the decline of the Temperance movement.

SECTION IV: THE BISHOPS

> *The teetotallers of your city have more support, than any other portion of our society – would to God, we had in other places Bishops as zealous for our sacred cause as your beloved Dr Foran.*
>
> – Father Mathew to Brother Joseph Murphy in Waterford.[106]

A national moral reformation such as the CTAS aspired to be depended on the unqualified commitment of the people's spiritual leaders. This was doubly true given the mixed response of the rank-and-file clergy to the crusade. This irresolution might have been overcome if the Catholic hierarchy had enthusiastically taken up the Temperance cause. Father Mathew and the CTAS were largely successful in obtaining episcopal approval of his missionary activity, although for reasons which will be discussed later, there were occasions when Temperance's Apostle was unwelcome in parts of Ireland. A more important objective – the bishops' active endorsement of the movement, particularly by encouraging the involvement of their parish clergy – was attained in only a few dioceses. As Mathew complained on 15 September 1842 to Tobias Kirby in Rome, 'many Bishops are privately opposed to the spread of temperance, partly to gratify their priests, who do not wish to see the people triumphing over a passion by which they themselves are enslaved, and partly for other motives'.[107] This failure to achieve the wholehearted endorsement of the hierarchy compounded the movement's already weak position in relation to the Catholic Church. To make matters worse for the CTAS, the intensity of influential opposition to the crusade eventually led the Irish bishops, in their collective capacity, to do what they could to distance the Church from the Temperance movement.

If it is accepted that Father Mathew adhered to his oft-stated principle of only visiting dioceses where he had been invited, and if it is assumed that parish priests would not invite him if their bishop did not approve, the number of bishops who at least tacitly approved of the Temperance movement can be determined. If each of Mathew's 282 Temperance missions undertaken between late 1839 and mid-1843 (see Chapter 3) is identified with a particular diocese it becomes clear that, at one time or another during those crucial years for the Temperance crusade, all but three of Ireland's twenty-three bishops and four archbishops permitted Mathew's visits. On this basic level the CTAS's crusade was accepted by the bishops, which is not to say that Father Mathew was satisfied with the general level of enthusiasm and practical assistance he received.

It is important, however, to distinguish between various levels of support for Temperance among the Irish bishops during the period of the movement's rapid expansion from 1839 to 1843. Ten of the 27 bishops were, to one degree or another, active advocates of teetotalism. Seven other bishops also supported the movement, but with reservations. Ten other bishops, finally, ranged from lukewarm to hostile in their reaction to the CTAS. Included in the group of active advocates were George Browne of Galway, Patrick Kennedy of Killaloe, John Ryan of Limerick, Nicholas Foran of Waterford, and Thomas Coen of Clonfert, all of whom endorsed local societies even before Mathew began to tour.[108] During Mathew's first four months of Temperance missions, 16 of his 24 missions were to parishes in those five dioceses. These early supporters were joined by other bishops who quickly became confirmed Temperance supporters, namely James Keating of Ferns, James Browne of Kilmore, Michael Blake of Dromore, and John Cantwell of Meath.[109] Patrick McGettigan of Raphoe also took the pledge from Mathew, and encouraged his priests to follow his example.[110]

The support of Nicholas Foran of Waterford deserves special mention, as it demonstrates both how much an activist bishop could do to further the cause, and, by comparison, how little most other pro-Temperance bishops actually did to strengthen the movement. In Waterford, Foran took his role as patron of the CTAS very seriously. He boasted of his part in inducing Mathew to undertake his missionary activity in the first place, and led numerous Temperance meetings in the early 1840s, chastising backsliders, encouraging the reluctant, and, perhaps most importantly, strongly urging his priests to do the same.[111] During his visitations in 1840 and 1841, Foran turned Temperance preacher himself, and 'in every parish through which he travelled [his lordship] with his assured zeal for the cause of Temperance, preached most powerfully in support of the cause to which he has ever been "a tower and pillar of strength"'.[112] He was known to ask parish priests in public 'how your flock stands in relation to the mighty moral revolution', and to react angrily if the answer was unsatisfactory.[113] He took every opportunity of praising Mathew and Temperance to the skies, and was adamant in his opinion that the movement was the work of God. 'I have reflected deeply and earnestly on the subject', he explained at one Waterford tea party,

> to see whether it might not be ascribed to the agency of natural causes or human means, and after all the attention I have been able to bestow on the subject I have arrived at the conclusion that the finger of Divine Providence is distinctly legible in this almost miraculous movement – that it could not be achieved through any human agency – and that some great blessing is, I humbly hope, in store for a people to whom this great good has been revealed.[114]

Foran was the ideal Temperance bishop as far as Mathew was concerned, and it was no coincidence that Temperance thrived in Waterford and Limerick, where John Ryan was nearly as zealous. The other bishops noted above were willing to offer wholehearted approval, as, for example, when James Keating of Ferns, with Mathew at a church dedication at Bree in 1842, led the crowd in three cheers for 'divinely inspired' Temperance and its apostle, adding his hope that 'every man, woman and child would be enrolled under [Mathew's] banner'. 'Then indeed', Keating concluded, 'would Ireland truly be the envy of the surrounding nations and admiration of the world.'[115] For all these bishops' occasional effusiveness, however, their support was not nearly as practical or as persistent as that offered by Foran and Ryan.

Seven other bishops offered only modest endorsement, but nevertheless publicly indicated their approved of the crusade. The most important of these were Daniel Murray, the Archbishop of Dublin, and Michael Slattery, the Archbishop of Cashel. Murray demonstrated increasing confidence in the crusade over the course of 1840, first by approving Mathew's visit to Dublin in March, then by sharing the altar with him at a church dedication at Maynooth in June, and finally by allowing the fact that he had personally invited Mathew to revisit Dublin in September to be published.[116] Later that same year, Murray attended a Temperance banquet in Mathew's honour given by the Earl of Glengall.[117] As late as the autumn of 1841, he also praised Mathew's 'good work' in his correspondence with Paul Cullen.[118] Slattery, for his part, invited Mathew to stay with him during his first mission in his diocese in January of 1840, very early in the Temperance crusade.[119] Mathew was particularly active in Slattery's archdiocese in 1840–43. Both Archbishops had certain reservations about Mathew's crusade, which grew stronger over time, and which will be explored below, but their initial willingness to cooperate with the movement was vital to its early success. At least five other bishops gave at least some public indication of support for the Temperance crusade, including Cornelius Egan of Kerry, who spoke favourably of the 'moral reformation' during his diocesan visitations in August 1841, and Bartholomew Crotty of Cloyne and Ross who did the same while making his visitation rounds the year before.[120] Egan was also one of only five bishops who participated in the Mathew Testimonial early in 1843, and spoke well of the cause among his priests the same year.[121] William Kinsella of Ossory, as noted above, had reservations about the CTAS, but he also praised Temperance, allowed Mathew to tour his diocese, and even invited the Apostle to stay with him during one of his visits.[122] Although Francis Haly of Kildare and Leighlin and Edward Kernan of Clogher do not appear to have been active in the crusade, Mathew was a frequent visitor to their dioceses and they were also among the contributors to the Mathew Testimonial.

Ten bishops, meanwhile, were not inclined to offer the crusade any particular mark of approval, or in any way to urge their priests to further the cause. These included William Crolly, the Archbishop of Armagh, John MacHale, the Archbishop of Tuam, William Higgins, Bishop of Ardagh and Clonmacnois, James McLaughlin of Derry, Cornelius

Denvir of Down and Connor, Patrick McNicholas of Achonry, Thomas Feeney of Killala, Patrick Burke of Elphin, Edmund French of Kilmacduagh and Kilfenora, and, finally, John Murphy of Cork. Part of the explanation for the reluctance of these bishops to endorse Temperance was no doubt related to geography. The movement, as we have seen, was strongest in Munster and Leinster, and of the ten bishops above, nine had dioceses in Ulster or Connaught, where both archbishops were opposed to the CTAS. All three of the bishops (Higgins, McLaughlin and Denvir) who actually kept Mathew out of their dioceses entirely were from the province of Armagh, where, unsurprisingly, William Crolly seems to have only allowed one visit to the archdiocese of Armagh.[123] Presumably, suffragan bishops in the archdioceses of Tuam and Armagh were under somewhat less pressure from their people and priests to support the Temperance movement, and more from their archbishops to be sceptical about the cause. Other reasons for their lack of support were no doubt related to the same spectrum of resistance that many of the parish clergy exhibited in relation to the movement.[124] Compounding matters, some bishops were unwilling to support a cause they knew at least some of their priests opposed.

Among these ten Irish prelates, as among the clergy more generally, Mathew had few overt opponents, but those he did have were uniquely positioned to do immense damage to the Temperance cause. To begin with, the prophet had no honour in his own county. Although in Cork the bishop, John Murphy, who was related to a prominent distilling family, did not prohibit Mathew's meetings, he made a point of serving wine at diocesan synods and was known, according to one contemporary, to 'tease Father Mathew in his pompous way about his temperance movement, towards which ... he was never very cordial.'[125] While these were only small gestures of disrespect, they contributed to the fact that Father Mathew's influence in his own diocese, particularly among the clergy outside of Cork city, never equalled his influence in other parts of Munster and Leinster.

William Crolly, the Archbishop of Armagh and the Primate of All Ireland, has already been mentioned as having discouraged Mathew from visiting his diocese, and other parts of the Protestant heartland in Ulster. This reluctance has been usually ascribed to a cautious unwillingness to heighten sectarian tensions, which was no doubt contributed to the archbishop's ambivalence. In 1841 he told a delegation of teetotallers from Aughnacloy that he did not oppose Temperance, but only wanted to see if Mathew's other visits to Ulster resulted in violence before extending an invitation.[126] Crolly's opposition did not soften, however, even after a number of peaceful visits by Mathew to the North.

When Mathew finally did visit Drogheda, Crolly's mensal parish, on 8–9 May in 1842, none of the diocesan clergy appeared to have been active in the Drogheda Total Abstinence Society. Another large Temperance society in that town, the Drogheda New Total Abstinence Society, with Thomas Burke, the prior of the Dominican convent there, as its vice-president, though it did claim Crolly as a patron, may have been a rival organisation.[127] Mathew did complain of rival Temperance societies full of 'pledge breakers' in Drogheda. His correspondence also reveals that at one time he had to defend himself against the charge of having deputed a priest in Drogheda to administer the pledge against the bishop's wishes, an indication that something was at work in Crolly's opposition beyond his concerns about sectarian violence.[128] The Drogheda incident in particular provoked Mathew to a bitter private condemnation of his prelatical opponents. 'It is not for me, for the sake of a paltry triumph over the prejudices of a few Ecclesiastiks, which are daily disappearing', Mathew scornfully explained to James Haughton of his clash with the archbishop, 'to expose the Temperance Movement to the hostility of in Ireland an all powerful body.'

Father Mathew's real nemesis, however, in the 'all powerful body' of the Irish bishops was the Archbishop of Tuam, John MacHale, who was aided and abetted by his alter ego, William Higgins, the Bishop of Ardagh and Clonmacnois. Fierce opposition to the crusade by both these men was rooted in the deep dislike they took to Father Mathew after several unpleasant encounters. Not only did these clashes alienate MacHale and Higgins from the movement, they also ultimately rendered Father Mathew a controversial figure among the bishops and a potential source of division in the Church, which seriously reduced his influence even among those members of the hierarchy who were initially inclined to support him.

With the possible exception during this period of Daniel Murray, no one in the Irish Church was more influential than John MacHale. MacHale's fiercely populist and anti-English nationalism, his passion for the Irish language, his suspicion of Protestantism, his stern resistance to any form of mixed education, along with his domineering personality earned him the sobriquets 'The Patriarch of the West', and 'The Lion of the Fold of Judah', and made him a natural antagonist for the politically cautious, genteel, ecumenical, and independent-minded Father Mathew.[129] Still, initially relations between the two were promising. On 23 March 1840, Joseph Burke, a curate at Ballinarobe, Co. Mayo in MacHale's diocese, excitedly informed Father Mathew that he had informed MacHale 'that you had promised to visit this town', after which the archbishop 'publicly at conference declared that nothing could give him greater pleasure than that you should visit his diocese.'[130] Up until 29 July 1840, when he visited Claremorris, Co. Mayo, Mathew was quite active in Tuam.

Shortly after Mathew's July visit, however, MacHale publicly broke with the CTAS. The archbishop had requested of Mathew that the revenue from the sale of medals resulting from his proposed appearance at Balla in the Fall be at the disposition the archbishop, and Mathew apparently refused.[131] Joseph Burke provided some details of the incident in a letter on 4 September 1840 to Mathew.[132] 'I have heard the other day from Dr MacHale', he reported, that the Temperance movement thrived on '*great sums of money* brought out of the country to the serious injury of the people.' As he explained to Mathew, Burke immediately protested to MacHale that 'there was more money dispensed in charity than could have been received for the medals', but could not shake the archbishop from a determination to 'separate us from you as our president and our Father, the moral regenerator of our long degraded country'.

There were two important sub-texts to the archbishop's change of heart. In the first place, MacHale appears to have been deeply suspicious of Mathew. Not only did he resent the money he imagined Mathew extracted in return for Temperance medals, but he also knew that the friar's charity sermons occasionally benefited the national schools. The archbishop was engaged in a furious struggle with Archbishop Murray and most of the other Irish bishops over the proposed national education system, which Mathew was known to support while MacHale was its bitterest foe. MacHale's rejection of government-funded schools left him scrambling for resources among the generally impoverished Catholics of the archdiocese of Tuam to finance an alternate system, and he was therefore doubly opposed to Mathew's mode of operation. MacHale was perfectly capable of rejecting Mathew's Temperance crusade as a consequence. In the second place, during his first visit to the diocese of Tuam early in July, Mathew had visited Westport, where he stayed with the dean of the diocese, Bernard Burke. Burke was a friend, and a warm supporter of Temperance, but Burke and MacHale had been engaged in an acrimonious rivalry that dated back at least as far as 1834.[133] Their animosity was compounded by the debate over national education, as Burke did all in his power to establish a National School in Westport.[134] By staying in Westport as Burke's guest on his first visit to Tuam, therefore, Mathew could not have chosen a better way of alienating the 'Patriarch of the West'.[135]

Late in August 1840, MacHale wrote a letter to the priests of his diocese directly ordering them not to invite Mathew to Tuam.[136] To make matters worse for the CTAS, the archbishop was also supposed to have offered dispensations to all those who took the pledge in his diocese, and founded his own Temperance society, complete with cards and medals, as well as a limited pledge that only bound for a period of six months or a year.[137] In addition to its evident role as a fund-raising vehicle, therefore, MacHale's society also reflected concerns about Protestant influences in the CTAS, and the nature of Mathew's pledge. There is no evidence that it was particularly successful or active.

Over the course of 1841, relations between MacHale and Mathew worsened, and actually became a feud with serious consequences for the CTAS. Sometime in March, MacHale, no doubt antagonised by jibes in the press and determined to assert his own authority within his diocese, made some uncomplimentary remarks in public about Temperance tea parties held in Tuam, probably on St Patrick's Day, 1841.[138] The criticisms were published in a local paper and forwarded by a teetotaller to Father Mathew, who mentioned his surprise at the 'curious prejudice' of MacHale in a letter the same month to John Kirwan, a teetotaller in Glan, Co. Galway. Unfortunately for Father Mathew, that letter, despite its being marked 'private', found its way into the Tory press in MacHale's diocese. The *Mayo Telegraph*, in particular, aggravated matters by using the letter as a weapon to attack MacHale's opposition to the national school system, charging that the archbishop sought to keep his flock 'in ignorance and drink'.[139] Father Mathew realised the seriousness of the situation, but his immediate attempts to repair the damage through a public letter of explanation and apology failed to assuage the archbishop. According to one press report, by June 1841 MacHale had increased the pressure on members of Temperance societies affiliated with the CTAS within his jurisdiction by directing at least some his clergy to refuse the sacraments to those who attended their meetings.[140]

The situation controversy was greatly aggravated by a retaliatory resolution passed by Bernard Burke's branch of the CTAS at Westport in June 1841, and widely reported in the press:

> *Resolved*. That, believing from information we have received, that Dr MacHale is determined to prohibit his clergy all over his diocese from co-operating with us in the temperance movement, we hereby resolve to contribute to the support of them only that will aid us in promoting the interest of our Society, by attending our meetings.[141]

So bold a challenge to episcopal authority set a very dangerous precedent, and the Metropolitan Total Abstinence Society in Dublin, affiliated with Mathew's society, but led by Andrew O'Connell, the parish priest of Saint Michael's and Saint John's (and, significantly, the treasurer of the Chapter of the Archdiocese), promptly passed their own resolution on 28 June 1841, also reprinted in the press all over the country, which repudiated the Westport statement. Father Mathew, however, appears to have been touched by the display of loyalty in Westport, and was equally offended by O'Connell's condemnation. Extremely unwisely, on 5 July he scathingly and emotionally rebuked O'Connell in a letter sent to the press but not, O'Connell later complained, to him. The letter is worth quoting at some length:

> These resolutions [of the MTAS] I read last night with the deepest sorrow in the *Dublin Evening Press*, and contending emotions so agitated me that repose fled and, after a sleepless night, I write this letter at half past three in the morning, my eyes dimmed with tears. I do not complain of your want of courtesy to myself, not to allude to higher, holier motives which should have influenced you, to consult me before you publicly denounced the Westport Branch of the Cork Total Abstinence Society. If you had not given in your resolutions these characteristic remarks, I might conclude you were not aware of my connection with this faithful portion of the temperance body. Absent from Cork during the last seven weeks, toiling from the rising to the setting sun, I knew nothing about what had occurred in Westport, for if I had, I would have instantly advised these helpless beings to retract their impotent threats. By what statement you excited the high-minded teetotallers of Dublin to pass with acclamation such a sweeping censure on their Brethren in Mayo, without investigating the merits of the case, or allowing time for inquiry, I know not. I am ignorant myself of everything respecting the painful affair except your newspaper report. 'A Man is a man for all that.' And if the poor worm in its agony turns upon the proud foot that tramples upon it, why should you add the weight of your hand to crush the writhing victim, and be in on the death? I can scarcely credit the evidence of my senses, and believe that the Very Rev. Andrew O'Connell, a member of the venerable chapter of the Most Rev. Catholic Archbishop of Dublin, would have thus arisen in his might and rush with more than railway speed to Westport, in the archdiocese of Tuam, to 'break the bruised reed'.[142]

This controversy with the much respected O'Connell probably did even more harm to Mathew's reputation with the bishops than his increasingly public disputes with the Archbishop of Tuam.[143] Profoundly disrespectful towards MacHale, the letter also displayed the emotionalism of Father Mathew and his sensitivity to perceived injustice. Moreover, it also made quite clear Mathew's startling lack of diplomatic skill, as well as the circumspection that his position as the leader of a fledgling national crusade required. Such spirited and unforgiving criticism directed at O'Connell, an influential priest who had done much to further the cause in Dublin, and who might have been relied upon to do more in future, would have been ill-advised even if Mathew had not been so dependent on the goodwill of his Church to further his cause.

O'Connell's response two days later on July 7 criticised Mathew for the public nature of his attack, and insisted that the Westport resolutions were 'calculated … to sever that attachment between the priesthood and the people, which for ages had been the proud boast of the Irish Church'.[144] The consequences, he insisted, of not condemning the resolution, which was 'unworthy of any cause, however good, and subversive of all ecclesiastical authority', would have been 'disastrous'. Although the Westport resolution was withdrawn, and apologies were offered by the local society to MacHale, the damage to the larger movement had already been done.[145]

The Archbishop of Tuam, for his part, abandoned all restraint. MacHale became, an appalled and intimidated Father Mathew informed Paul Cullen on 20 September 1841, an 'implicable [*sic*] enemy' of the cause, applying 'the most disgraceful epithets to me and the teetotallers' and 'dispens[ing] with all in his archdiocese in the total abstinence pledge'.[146] To make matters worse, Mathew explained, MacHale had denounced the Temperance movement and Mathew during a Sunday sermon in August at his mensal parish at Kilmeena before 'a large and astonished' congregation.

> After a long tirade in Irish against the society, he said that I was a vagabond friar and that I went about with a *woman*, that she sold medals for me charging a shilling for bits of Birmingham pewter which cost only two pence, and that we spent the money drinking brandy and water, laughing at the poor dupes whom we robbed … a thrill of horror ran through the whole congregation at the awful assertion that Father Mathew was living in sacrilegious Guilt with this woman, and that he was a brandy drinker.

Unsure of which accusation offended him more, Mathew denied them both. The assertions, moreover, he complained, were repeated at 'private dinner tables, amongst the rest at the Right Reverend Dr McNicholas's, the bishop of Achonry, in the presence of the Very Rev'd Dean Durcan and other clergymen'. Mathew explained to Cullen that it was 'impossible to conjecture how far the wrath of His Grace of Tuam might lead him', but some intervention might prevent MacHale's having 'recourse to the newspapers to attack me'. 'I tremble lest these accusations should get into the public papers', Father Mathew finally concluded.

At least according to Mathew's account of the sermon, MacHale had levelled extremely serious charges against Mathew. Mathew was a greedy friar, not to mention a mercenary outsider. MacHale's allusion to sexual misbehaviour on the part of Mathew was particularly baseless, but nevertheless served well as a means of further undermining popular respect for his priestly office. The brandy-drinking reference was not only an accusation of rank hypocrisy, but also, among the whiskey-drinking Irish-speaking peasantry, a slur on Mathew's aristocratic airs. MacHale, who thought of Mathew less as a prophet of God and more as a potential troublemaker, had far less to lose than the Capuchin did in the dispute. The archbishop took the opportunity to assert his control over the clergy and the Catholic people of Tuam, and, by sponsoring his own Temperance movement, to raise some revenue in a very poor diocese.

Mathew correctly understood that the sermon at Kilmeena was a warning, albeit a vicious one. The fact that MacHale's speech was in Irish was important, reducing the likelihood that it would appear in the press, or, if it did, leaving more room for the archbishop to disavow the more outrageous parts of his remarks.[147] The implicit threat, of course, accentuated by MacHale's repetition of the accusations to clergy who he must have known would pass them on to Mathew, was that the next time the attack might be made more directly and explicitly. Mathew's concern that this might happen runs through his letter to Cullen, and indeed he wrote yet another letter the very next day (21 September 1841) to emphasise that he wanted to avoid trouble with MacHale, and that he lived 'in hourly terror' of attacks in the press from him.[148] In fact, this exchange appears to have ended the public dimension of the Mathew/MacHale feud. Although a more direct attack never materialised, Mathew's concern was warranted given the Archbishop of Tuam's long-established reputation as a pugnacious writer of fractious public letters.

Another bishop who opposed the CTAS was William Higgins of Ardagh and Clonmacnois, a close friend and ally of MacHale's in the Irish church. The evident cause of Higgins' initial difficulties with the CTAS was money. In 1840, Higgins had laid the cornerstone of an overly-ambitious cathedral in the town of Longford, which was designed as the 'largest Roman Catholic place of worship in the United Kingdom'.[149] 'The erection of the noble structure', the *Freeman's Journal* reported, 'had been long a favourite project with the Right Reverend Dr Higgins, the zealous, revered, and patriotic bishop of Ardagh. It formed the subject of his constant thoughts, and the whole happiness of his life seemed involved in its completion.' Higgins was no early advocate of teetotalism, and in fact the public dinner celebrating the laying of the cathedral's cornerstone in May 1840 was distinguished by a 'great abundance' of fine wines.

Higgins later attributed his initial reluctance to have Mathew visit to 'extreme caution' and suspicions about 'the stability of the movement', but during the summer of 1840 the growing popularity of Temperance apparently led the bishop to reconsider, at least in part in the light of Mathew's proven talent as a fund-raiser.[150] At the end of July 1840, therefore, Higgins deputed Richard Davys, a curate in his mensal parish of Longford, to meet Mathew at Castletown-Delvin in Westmeath as the Capuchin returned to Dublin from a series of missions in Mayo. The interview went very badly, according to a retrospective account Davys sent to Mathew some two weeks later, on 12 August, in an attempt to clarify points of dispute.[151] According to Davys, he had brought Mathew a written invitation from Higgins to administer the pledge in Ardagh provided that, after expenses, 'the proceeds of the Temperance Movement in Ardagh should be available for the building of the Cathedral Church already commenced'. Higgins's demand was unusual. His representative acknowledged that 'nothing but the peculiar circumstances of so heavy an undertaking in a very poor and persecuted part of the country could induce him to propose such conditions'. Higgins certainly presumed what no other bishop had in their invitations to Mathew, namely that the friar was making a profit from his missions, and Mathew was clearly much offended. Similar accusations were already appearing in the press, and Mathew was acutely sensitive to them. At Castletown Delvin, again according to Davys, Mathew 'distinctly and repeatedly refused to accede' to Higgins' proposal.

The unsuccessful meeting had two immediate consequences. The first was that Davys' letter notified Mathew not to allow any expectation of an invitation from Higgins to 'interfere with your future arrangements in visiting other parts of the country', and Mathew never did visit the diocese of Ardagh and Clonmacnois. The second consequence was Higgins' decision to yield 'at last' to 'pressing and repeated solicitations to administer himself the temperance pledge in the Diocese of Ardagh'.[152] 'I am instructed by his Lordship', Davys informed Mathew, 'to convey to you his determination of giving the pledge himself in even the humblest locality of his Diocese.' Given the nature of Higgin's dispute with Mathew, mercenary motives obviously loomed large, as a local priest informant explained in a private letter to Mathew on 4 September 1840, noting that 'the bishop seems to think that he will be able to amass large sums of money for the cathedral by the temperance movement.'[153]

Far from disavowing Mathew in public, however, Higgins, in a series of meetings around his diocese in August 1840, alluded to 'the successes of all those who have gone before him in propagating the virtue of temperance', particularly the 'respected and venerable clergyman, whose name and untiring zeal in spreading wide the blessings of temperance, were already so familiar to them'. Higgins also borrowed standard CTAS rhetoric about 'national regeneration' and a second conversion of Ireland rivalling that of St Patrick. There were also indications that Higgins had other concerns about Mathewite Temperance. He emphasised at every turn the Catholicity of his society and the need for Temperance to be more closely connected to the Church.[154] Higgins encouraged his priests to enrol and he pledged seven of them at Moate in August to serve as an example.[155] As he told a crowd at Carrick-on-Shannon later in the month, he 'earnestly hoped that the day was not far distant when every person of influence – clergymen in particular, with their bishop's sanctions – would lend their time and labours at once to this happy movement'.[156] Higgins took care to administer the pledge on Sundays, immediately after mass. Father Burke also pointed out to Mathew on 4 September 1840, that Higgins 'has deigned to distribute medals and cards purely Catholic so that the Protestants who are very edifying members of our society cannot wear them'.[157] He also repeatedly warned postulants not to associate any superstitious beliefs with his Temperance medals.

Despite these efforts, it appears that Higgins's society was a failure. Although several thousand joined initially, there seems to have been little consistent effort to consolidate this limited initial enthusiasm, and there are few references to Temperance meetings held by the organisation after August 1840. Father Burke reassured Mathew in September that 'the people will have no other medals than those with your name and the usual stamp on them'.[158] Furthermore, members of Higgins' society travelled outside the diocese when opportunities to receive the pledge from Mathew presented themselves. One reporter describing a Temperance parade in September 1840 at Lasser in County Roscommon scornfully mentioned thousands of members of the CTAS being joined by 'the few whom the Bishop of Ardagh could induce to join his society'.[159] When Mathew visited Kilbeggan, Co. Westmeath in the diocese of Meath the following year, many of the postulants there had travelled from Ardagh, and were described as members of Higgins's society who were filled with a 'fervour and anxiety' to 'take the pledge from the Reverend Gentleman'.[160]

By the autumn of 1841, Mathew's clashes with bishops had put the CTAS on the defensive, not only in terms of Mathew's relationship with

MacHale (and his suffragan bishops, over whom the archbishop exercised considerable influence) and Higgins, but with the Irish hierarchy generally. The Temperance movement of the early 1840s was so popular and emotional a social crusade that to some observers at least it bore within it the seeds of potential schism. Several years later, in 1847, an overwrought Higgins would give explicit voice to these fears in a letter to Cullen opposing Mathew's episcopal nomination to Cork, when he accused the Capuchin of 'riding roughshod over all episcopal authority, pitt[ing] people against priests, and well-nigh introducing a schism into Ireland', but there were more contemporary indications of concern.[161] To be sure, the movement's own rhetoric could be perceived in this light, particularly its oft-stated objective of creating a common ground for all Irish men and women, transcending sectarian animosity and oblivious of 'creed and class'. As early as 1840, one of Mathew's correspondents warned him that he must at all costs avoid a 'schism' in the Church, and that 'the bishops and priests' needed to be enlisted '"*ad unum*" to support temperance' or the cause would 'like a fire-globe or meteor' be of 'short duration'.[162] Andrew O'Connell's response to Mathew's rebuke over the condemnation of the Westport resolutions, moreover, made it clear that he understood Temperance to be a force capable of endangering and dividing the Church, and that others did as well.[163] In 1842, in a letter to Kirby, Mathew alluded to a pastoral letter issued the previous Lent, probably in Tuam, in which the teetotallers 'were designated schismatics'.[164] When the influential editor of the *Tablet*, Frederick Lucas, turned against Temperance in September of 1843, he did so on precisely this ground. A movement, determined on insisting that its 'mission was not of the Church', but nevertheless intimately bound up with religious practice, devotion and sacramental life, Lucas pointed out, was unacceptable. 'Never', he warned, 'was there a more pregnant instance of the danger of allowing a religious movement to escape out of the hands of the Church, and become a matter of popular, undisciplined enthusiasm.'[165]

On one level, Mathew's difficulties with various Irish churchmen were simply particularly glaring demonstrations of the fact that in many places the Temperance movement had already by the early 1840s served to divide the Church on many levels. In these clashes, especially those that occurred in public with MacHale and O'Connell, Mathew had shown his passionate, proud and stubborn streak, not to mention an unrepentant willingness to put his crusade first and Church discipline second. The disputes served to demonstrate even to the CTAS's friends Temperance's enormous power to divide and to weaken further a Catholic Church already riven by division over mixed education and under siege from aggressive, well-organised and well-financed Protestant proselytisers. The manner in which Mathew defended his cause certainly did little to assuage concerns about its potential divisiveness.

Mathew was aware that some considered his movement a threat, and he was extremely concerned that the CTAS not be seen to be challenging episcopal authority in any way. 'For however they might differ in opinion', he noted in a letter to James Haughton, referring to the bishops as a body, 'they would all unite, in what they consider the maintenance of ecclesiastical discipline.'[166] To be sure, Mathew was no wild-eyed schismatic. Long after his dispute with MacHale, Mathew remained popular with many bishops, most of whom understood from personal experience how contentious MacHale could be. Nevertheless, their collective response to the developing movement, once decided upon, reflected an overriding interest in maintaining an ecclesiastical discipline under pressure from many sides.

After his running dispute with Mathew over the nature of the pledge and the CTAS's relationship to Catholicism, in September 1843 a frustrated Frederick Lucas demanded in an editorial that the Irish bishops 'do what they have not done' and 'publish some joint resolution' as to 'the sense in which this pledge is to be taken, and the extent to which it was to be allowed'.[167] 'The disorder', he insisted perceptively, referring to the Temperance movement more generally, 'has grown up from underneath; the remedy must come from above. We need a strong exercise of episcopal authority.' Lucas, publishing the *Tablet* in London, however, ignored what the Irish bishops could not afford to – the popular consensus in favour of Mathew and his crusade, and the powerful support Mathew was still receiving from an energetic and enthusiastic minority of priests and bishops. Had Lucas been more alert, however, he might have noticed that just such an underlying sense of responsibility in regard to maintaining discipline in the Church had already caused the Irish bishops to act. Long before Lucas's appeal, they had effectively closed ranks against the CTAS, albeit in a much more prudent and cautious manner than the one Lucas proposed. The considered opinion of the Irish hierarchy on the CTAS was best discerned not by what they did, but by what they did not do at three crucial junctures. In 1841, the bishops studiously ignored Father Mathew's elevation to Commissary Apostolic. In 1842, they checked his campaign for indulgences for members of the CTAS. Finally, in 1843, the episcopal body refused to endorse efforts to place the movement on a firmer financial footing.

To understand the significance of the first two of these rebuffs, it is necessary to examine the Roman dimension of the Church's

Temperance problem. Mathew's reaction to the outright opposition to the CTAS of MacHale and Higgins, and the continuing non-cooperation of Crolly and other unenthusiastic bishops, was to use his correspondence with Paul Cullen to solicit from Rome an open endorsement of the movement and other marks of its approval. Cullen was the normal channel through which the Irish clergy communicated with the Roman authorities, and if he could be brought to exert his considerable influence on Irish affairs on Mathew's behalf, Mathew's opponents would find it difficult to resist the movement, while his more half-hearted supporters might become more enthusiastic. Papal support could serve as the hammer, which, in conjunction with the anvil of popular enthusiasm, would forge a universally temperate Ireland. Initially, there was reason to believe that the strategy might prove effective. Daniel Murray's correspondence reveals that Mathew's activities were much discussed in Rome by early 1840, and that the Pope took a personal interest in the crusade.[168] This may explain why, on a visit to Ireland in the summer of 1840, Cullen spent some time observing Mathew administer the pledge.[169] By all accounts, he was impressed with the proceedings and with the great change in the Irish people.

Mathew appears to have believed he had gained an important ally, and began regularly forwarding 'all the papers containing information on the temperance society ... to Dr Cullen'.[170] In December 1840 Mathew asked for a very unusual favour, requesting that Cullen solicit Pope Gregory XVI on his behalf for 'a transfer of my obedience from my Religious Superiors to the Sacred Congregation' in order to permit him to dedicate all his time to Temperance work.[171] Mathew was, of course, by then aware that it would be impossible for him to fulfil his duties as Provincial of his order in Ireland and at the same time lead the Temperance crusade. In effect, he wanted a public mark of papal approval of his crusade.

On 28 August 1841, just as his feud with MacHale threatened to boil over, Mathew was named a 'Commissary Apostolic' by the Pope, or, as one of his biographers described it, 'a missionary force' directly subject to papal authority.[172] According to the *Freeman's Journal*, the commission itself was 'couched in terms the most complimentary and affectionate, evincing the high regard entertained by the head of the Church of Christ towards the great benefactor of his fellow man', a fact confirmed by Cullen in a congratulatory letter in which he noted that Gregory XVI perceived 'the finger of God' in Mathew's success.[173] Curiously the Pope, who according to Cullen had consulted with the Director-General of the Capuchins, also requested that Mathew continue, at least for a time, as the Provincial of his order. Father Mathew's initial reaction was one of delight, and, as he wrote Cullen on 20 September 1841, the honour was 'all I could have wished, and more than I expected'.[174] The appointment had 'completely rescued me out of the hands of such as may feel inclined to oppress me, and thus impede the glorious cause'.

The press reports that soon followed made it clear that Mathew's new title was expected to transform his position in the Irish Church.[175] John Francis Maguire's *Cork Examiner* explained that it represented the 'Father of the Faithful's' full 'approbation and sanction' of Mathew's 'Apostolic labours in the great cause of Temperance'; the 'high dignity' of the office 'confers very great ecclesiastical privileges and immunities'. The *Freeman's Journal* was even more impressed. The honour, it seemed, had resulted from 'the anxious and expressed desire of Pope Gregory the Sixteenth to have an opportunity of conferring some distinguished mark of his esteem and admiration on the man whose heavenly exertions in the great cause of temperance has drawn down blessings on the heads of so many millions of his followers'. Mathew was now, it was asserted, 'subject to no spiritual authority whatsoever save that proceeding directly from the sovereign pontiff'.

In practice, however, the title meant little. Commissaries Apostolic traditionally were active in missionary territory, where episcopal control was impractical or impossible, and what the designation was supposed to mean in an Irish context was unclear, perhaps deliberately so. Even if, in theory, it permitted Mathew to come and go as he pleased throughout the country, in practice this would have proved imprudent, and Mathew continued to seek permission from the clergy and bishops for all his visits. He complained to a clerical correspondent that the Bishop of Ossory 'did not condescend' to acknowledge the designation, while his ultimate verdict was that the title was 'not the least advantage to me, not being recognized by the Prelates of Ireland'.[176]

If his new Roman laurels may have given MacHale reason to pause, they did little to inspire additional enthusiasm among the Irish clergy for Temperance. Mathew was encouraged in his relationship with Cullen, however, and later in September, thanking him for his efforts, he forwarded more articles on Temperance and newspaper accounts of meetings.[177] This letter, marked 'Private', also contained Mathew's complaints to Cullen about MacHale's bitter opposition to the movement. Though MacHale knew, Father Mathew charged, that drinking was 'the predominant sin of the Irish priesthood', he 'suffers vice' and has 'encouraged many of his priests to return to the vice of intoxicating drinks'.

Cullen's reply several weeks later warmly congratulated Mathew on his new title, and encouraged his Temperance work, but it also struck a number of cautionary notes that indicated that Mathew already had lost a crucial ally. The letter reveals a great deal about why many bishops may have hesitated to endorse actively the Capuchin or his movement after the conflicts with MacHale and Father O'Connell became public. Cullen wished the Apostle of Temperance well, but warned him that opposition from within the Church should be expected, and that Mathew must 'on no account' enter into public controversy, even when ecclesiastical authorities 'are not acting as they ought'.[178] 'The mischief that is done by dissensions between ecclesiastics', he observed, no doubt alluding to Mathew's exchange with O'Connell, 'can scarcely ever be remedied.' He thanked Mathew for forwarding the articles on Temperance, but expressed distress that 'the editors seem desirous to promote and foment dissension'. 'It would be better', he maintained, if 'some of them would let controversy on temperance alone.' He asked Mathew to exert his influence with them to 'leave such matters to yourself'.

Even more significantly, Cullen endorsed one of the most serious criticisms MacHale and others were levelling at Mathew. In a long postscript, he noted that 'you appear to entertain sentiments too liberal towards Protestants in matters of religion', who were, after all, 'strayed sheep from the one fold'. Mathew should avoid 'really violating charity' by 'lull[ing] Protestants into a false sense of security in their errors'. Cullen particularly referred to Mathew's sermons, but it is difficult to know which remarks Cullen may have found distressing. The censure may have resulted, however, at least in part, from the sermon Mathew delivered at his most significant appearance, the dedication of a new church at Maynooth in June 1840 during his visit to St Patrick's College (see Chapter 3). On this occasion, with Daniel Murray present, Mathew had made a passionate plea for a toleration that to many seemed to border on latitudinarianism. While it was usual at church dedications to acknowledge the generosity of Protestants who had contributed to the building funds, at Maynooth Mathew transcended such platitudes by praying for their prosperity and salvation, but not for their conversion:

> He thanked them in the name of God to whose worship they did such service. He prayed that Almighty God would pour down every blessing upon them for their kindness to their poor fellow countrymen. He earnestly beseeched the King of Heaven to make them more prosperous in the concerns of this life, and to grant them the eternal Glory of Heaven; and that these blessings might be extended to their children and their children's children of the remotest generation.[179]

For all the good effects of Mathew's crusade, which he happily acknowledged, the movement was clearly becoming worrisome to Cullen, who had little interest in supporting ecumenically-minded friars who were also publicly involved in acrimonious challenges to episcopal authority.

Despite what he told Cullen at the time, Mathew became less content with his new title. The formal text of his new commission had not mentioned what Cullen and others had reported informally to Mathew – that the Pope was a supporter of his Temperance movement and saw 'the finger of God' in it.[180] Early in October, a report appeared in the *Belfast Vindicator*, edited by Mathew's friend Charles Gavan Duffy, at that time himself an enthusiastic teetotaller, that Pope Gregory XVI had, 'in a recent lengthened interview with a distinguished priest, expressed himself delighted beyond measure to find the Catholic clergymen of this country were, as an order, taking the teetotal pledge'.[181] 'Nothing more', His Holiness was reported to have observed, 'is required to make them *the best* and most efficiently zealous priests in the *whole world*.' Father Mathew, meanwhile, had written to Kirby on 6 October 1841. He complained that MacHale was 'exerting all his efforts to dissolve the temperance society', and enclosed a gold medal 'for His Holiness'.[182] The Pope apparently accepted it, since it was reported in the press in February that Father Mathew had received a letter confirming that the Pope was wearing the medal.[183] Later that month, Mathew wrote to Kirby to thank him for his efforts, and declared himself 'exceedingly delighted' at the 'honour'.[184]

Although Kirby's letter to Mathew apparently had taken pains to point out that the Pope had taken no pledge, Father Mathew was convinced that 'if his Holiness was aware of the awful state to which this country was reduced by the use of intoxicating liquors, He would not hesitate'. Mathew also took the opportunity, in this moment of exhaltation, to reply indirectly to Cullen's earlier complaints. He denied that he had ever been guilty of 'lulling Protestants into a false sense of peace'. 'I have never', he insisted, 'made a single concession.' He claimed, in fact, to have 'reconciled more Protestants to the Holy Roman Catholic Church than any other priest in the Kingdom'. Mathew made no secret of the fact that he knew at least some of the bishops were working against him. He told Kirby he 'was well aware whence these accusations against me have been sent to Rome', but he also assured him that he would do all he could to avoid giving 'the enemies of the Catholic Church a cause for triumph by vindicating myself against the foul calumnies of dignified Eklesiastics'.

Supporters of the CTAS made much of the Pope having 'taken the medal', which meant one thing in an Irish context and quite another in a Roman one. Reports in the press indicate the confusion was widespread. At Skibbereen, Co. Cork, for example, in mid-February, the local Temperance society toasted the Pope at a tea party, while its president, Joseph Malony, maintained that 'the venerable Pontiff of Rome wears the temperance medal, and is a member of the Cork Total Abstinence society'.[185] As a consequence, an embarrassed Father Mathew had to write to Kirby again on 25 February 1842, explaining that the acceptance of his gift had, in some reports, as Kirby had feared, been 'magnified into the Holy Father's having become a teetotaller'.[186] Father Mathew suggested helpfully that it would perhaps be best not to contradict such rumours in public, because that might induce 'many to return to drunkenness'. The best reason for tolerating them, he added, was 'the belief that His Holiness has thus sanctioned our sacred society and has softened down the violent opposition of the clergy.' It is not known what Kirby replied, but Mathew was not above using the popular misconception to bolster his crusade. On at least two occasions in 1842, he reportedly told crowds at his Temperance missions that the Pope was a teetotaller and wore his medal, although at Kilmacthomas, Co. Waterford in April he also conceded that 'His Holiness the Pope has no occasion to take the pledge'.[187]

Ultimately such gestures of papal approval were insufficient to improve Mathew's status in the Irish Church. He seemed to have realised this, for in May 1842 he made a still-more ambitious request, this time of both Kirby and Cullen. 'I am well aware', he observed to Kirby, 'of the infinite advantage it would be to Teetotalism to have my system approved by His Holiness, myself recommended to the Bishops and Clergy, and a Plenary Indulgence with the usual conditions granted to Teetotallers at the hour of death.'[188] What Mathew sought, then, was not only indulgences for members of his society, but also an official Roman recommendation and endorsement of his activities, which he could use to secure the quality of support he was still having so much trouble obtaining in the Irish church. He repeated the request to Cullen, adding that he 'confidently hope[d] that you will be able to procure these favours for me'.

It is not clear how Cullen or Kirby acted on Mathew's plea, but the following autumn, Cardinal Franzoni, the Prefect of Propaganda, wrote to at least two of the Irish archbishops, asking them to assess Mathew's movement, and in particular its worthiness as a medium for indulgences.[189] Franzoni, who pointed out that his inquiries were in response to requests from the American bishops to allow indulgences for their Temperance societies, nevertheless asked specific questions about Mathew's pledge-giving activities, including his societies' objectives, the mode of the pledge's administration, its wording, and whether or not the breaking of it was considered to be a sin. The replies of Murray and Slattery, archbishops generally considered to have been friends of Mathew and supporters of his Temperance movement, indicate just how far, even by 1842, episcopal support for the movement had eroded. The letters contain many similarities; it seems possible that a joint response had been worked out between the two archbishops.

While both Murray and Slattery praised the movement, Murray for what it had done 'to reform custom and benefit religion', and Slattery for its role in '[bringing] about a reform in the morals of our nation that ought to be admired', they both expressed reservations about the pledge, noting that although Mathew himself made it clear that the pledge was not a religious vow, many of his followers were confused on the subject.[190] Murray described, as has been pointed out, how it was often given accompanied by the sign of the cross, by postulants on bended knee surrounded by great crowds, and he concluded that 'most people believe that it cannot be broken without fault', and worried that 'not all can keep so difficult a promise'. Slattery, for his part, explained that, whatever Mathew said on the subject, in many cases the breaking of the pledge was sinful 'from the circumstances', including the 'scandal or evil' that pledge-breaking caused, 'or from the fact that when men are able to think that they sin from such a violation, they do sin by acting against their conscience'.[191]

Most importantly, both archbishops strongly opposed the idea of indulgences for members of Mathew's society, and for similar reasons. Murray argued that the organisation was not 'exclusively Catholic' by the choice of its leaders. 'It is not a religious society', Slattery also observed, 'for many of the Protestants have gone into it. Thus it seems to be held by men as a merely civil society, and indeed in my opinion the Sacred Congregation ought to regard it the same way'. Furthermore, both archbishops took pains to point out that, should the CTAS receive indulgences, the movement might be seen by the government to be 'political'. 'It would be inadvisable for the Pope to openly patronize the Society which would be the case if indulgences were granted', Murray pointed out, because then 'non-Catholics would consider it political and a danger to the state, especially now when people are politically agitated.' Slattery echoed him: 'Many of our enemies falsely represent the society of temperance as if it were a dangerous political society', and if indulgences were granted 'perhaps they may seize the occasion' to attack the Church. Murray suggested that indulgences might be granted for American societies and withheld in Ireland. Slattery thought it 'much better' that 'matters continue as they have gone'. The idea of indulgences for Temperance 'seems to me superfluous, when Catholics amongst themselves are able to gain so many', although he had no objection if 'those so inclined ... belonged to this society'.

These letters are important because of the role they must have played in undermining Mathew's request for indulgences. It seems plain, furthermore, that by 1842, at least some influential churchmen who had supported the Temperance movement were looking for ways to limit the Church's involvement. In this instance, Mathew's ambition was frustrated by the two archbishops in Ireland who were most favourably disposed towards the CTAS, but who were nevertheless concerned about Temperance's theology, the lack of episcopal control over the movement, and their own sense that, by 1842, Temperance was too open to charges of politicisation to risk connecting the Church to its official organisation.

Mathew, for his part, seems to have sensed which way the Roman wind was blowing on the indulgences question, and decided to take what he could get from the Pope. In September 1842 he explained to Kirby, 'Should you find any difficulty in obtaining the grant of a Plenery Indulgence for my teetotallers from His Holiness, I do not urge you to persevere in the supplication'.[192] He still hoped, however, for the granting of the second part of his request, that is, the explicit commendation of his society by the Pope. 'A letter from His Holiness', Father Mathew pleaded, 'expressive of His satisfaction at the glory given to God, exaltation given to our holy religion, and the immense happiness to millions of beings by this great moral movement would be exceedingly useful.' 'The necessity for this interference of the Holy Father', he explained, was due to the opposition of the bishops. 'Obtain this letter of recommendation for me', the Apostle promised, 'and our pure and spotless banner of Temperance will soon, with Divine Assistance, wave over the length and breadth of the land.' Obviously anxious, he wrote again some two weeks later on 28 September 1842, to repeat his complaints about the 'evil opposition' that was undermining his work.[193] The letters from the Irish archbishops would have arrived in Rome about the same time, and there is no evidence that either Kirby or Cullen ever attempted to procure the Papal letter, or the indulgences.

His relations with Kirby and Cullen appear to have cooled after 1842, and Father Mathew wrote less frequently. Certainly a bitter tone characterised subsequent letters. In October 1845, for example, Mathew forwarded £150 in mass stipends to Cullen, and apologised for 'presuming to address you again, my last letter not having been acknowledged'.[194] Two months later he wrote again, enclosing an additional £170, while admitting to Cullen he was 'was no politician'.[195] Given the disastrous state of his own finances by that date, it is difficult not to view the letters and their enclosures as clumsy attempts to retrieve a fall from grace.

The Irish bishops, meanwhile, though some remained friendly with Mathew, appeared increasingly comfortable with their unspoken policy of collective neutrality. The movement had proved to be too divisive, and the angry and emotional opposition of MacHale and Higgins, as well as the quieter, but equally determined antipathy of William Crolly, had the practical effect of weakening the support of those bishops whose endorsement of Temperance had never been unreserved. Just how dramatically his support had declined may be seen in the bishops' very tepid collective response to the requisition for the Mathew Testimonial in early 1843.

By the time the request for signatures for the national requisition to honour the Apostle of Temperance was circulated, in October 1842, Mathew's financial difficulties were already widely known. A well-organised collection was planned, and the active cooperation of the Church was probably the best way to secure funds on the scale required to relieve the Capuchin of his rapidly mounting debt. According to Mathew, however, when the bishops met in Dublin in early November, they adopted a resolution 'not to attach their names to the testimonial', a decision Mathew felt he 'did not deserve' and one that 'cost me many a pang'.[196] 'I'm well aware of the names of the prelates who influenced the rest, to enter into this combination', Mathew noted. 'There were, it is true', he conceded, 'a few illustrious exceptions. Some of the bishops … nobly expressed their approbation of the great Temperance Movement.' If Mathew's account of their behaviour was correct, and there is every reason to think it was, the bishops had clearly decided to sacrifice the Temperance movement on the altar of unity, probably in response to threats from MacHale and others to enter into yet another bitter public controversy on the subject. In the end, for whatever reason, none of the archbishops and only five bishops supported the effort, which was a remarkable failure. The five included Browne of Galway, Egan of Kerry, Haly of Kildare and Leighlin, Kinsella of Ossory, and Kernan of Clogher, but, curiously, none of Mathew's oldest and most reliable allies, a certain indication that some ulterior force was at work in restraining their actions. To blame the bishops alone for what did not happen in 1843 – the financial rescue of Mathew and the CTAS – would be unreasonable, but it is fair to say that they played a major part in the failure of the first Mathew Testimonial. Considered together, the three episcopal decisions examined above – not to acknowledge Mathew as a Commissary Apostolic; not to support the indulgences appeal; and to ignore the Mathew testimonial – amounted cumulatively to a pointed rejection of Mathew and the CTAS by the body of the bishops, and to disaster for the Temperance movement.

CONCLUSION

The CTAS was a complex social movement. Most of the millions who took the pledge did not undertake a private resolution; rather, as Mathew and most churchmen realised, they assumed a commitment that they did not disassociate from their other communal moral obligations. Mathew used this fact to help expand his crusade, linking Temperance, and allowing his supporters to link it, with the religious practices and beliefs of Irish Catholics. This association was both natural and enormously helpful in the crusade's early days, but the Church proved, in the long run, a reluctant and, finally, an unwilling fellow-traveller. For the many within the Church who did not view intemperance and its consequences as the ultimate threat to religion in Ireland as the CTAS's founder and supporters did, the association could not be allowed to continue. Unfortunately for the CTAS, the near impossibility of achieving the degree of organisation and leadership sufficient to maintain the movement without the enthusiastic participation of the Catholic clergy at all levels became evident very quickly.

Mathew's own relationship to his Church, and the ways in which his religious and political convictions combined with his emotional leadership, may have undercut support for the CTAS. Theological objections to Temperance were widespread and influential in turning many priests and bishops against the movement. Despite a strong core of active supporters, there was no consensus in favour of Temperance among Ireland's priests, most of whom either opposed the movement or remained ambivalent. The Irish bishops, for their part, although some welcomed the crusade, were even less effective as Temperance leaders than their priests. Over the course of 1840 and 1841, a series of unpleasant disputes (some of them very public) with several influential bishops soured the hierarchy on the Temperance movement. Paul Cullen, remarkably influential at Rome, who was originally a warm supporter, was also eventually alienated. By 1842/43, the Irish bishops as a body disowned the crusade. As a consequence, they opposed efforts to shore up the movement spiritually (in the form of indulgences) and materially (by fund raising), with very serious ramifications for the movement's long term viability.

Clearly there was an element of naïveté evident in Father Mathew's dealings with his church. The triumph of Temperance embodied in the CTAS, Mathew firmly believed, was a direct expression of the will of God, with which 'no one ought to interfere'.[197] Convinced his own role in the crusade was divinely ordained, Mathew was surprised and frustrated when others disagreed and he found himself embroiled in worldly disputes. The tension that resulted between the Temperance cause and many members of the clergy became more pronounced over time as problems arose and Mathew's unwillingness to compromise the CTAS's vision became more evident. The CTAS strove to maintain its ecumenical, 'national' focus and its independence from ecclesiastical control.

In the long run, as the movement began to disintegrate, Mathew's frustration level rose, and he eventually became extremely bitter about the failure of his Church to seize the extraordinary opportunity he believed they had let slip through their fingers. A bitter assessment of the depth of that failure survives in a fragment of Mathew's correspondence which may serve as a fitting conclusion to this chapter:

> Our bishops and clergy have indeed lost most providential opportunities of promoting the Glory of God and the happiness of the flock committed to their care *by paltry* [equivocations. By] practicing a little self-denial, they would have given an example that would have been invariably followed by the laity and intemperance and all its crimes and miseries would have been forever banished from our country. The Lord in his mercy sent forth the spirit amongst the people: but it was rejected by their pastors and upon them be the blood + Guiltiness.[198]

CHAPTER SEVEN

The Confluence of Temperance and Repeal

The most widely commented on aspect of Father Mathew's Temperance crusade on the part of historians of nineteenth century Ireland has been its connection to the contemporary Repeal movement.[1] The overall tendency of these works has been to view Temperance as a more or less powerful auxiliary to the Repeal campaign, but the relationship was in fact a complex and symbiotic one.[2] The Temperance movement served less as an auxiliary, and more as an inspiration for the Repeal campaign. Daniel O'Connell did not politicise the Temperance movement; rather, he succeeded in channelling the inherent political energy of the CTAS in a particular direction. The rhetoric, tactics, leadership and membership of the intensely patriotic and emotional Temperance and Repeal campaigns came to overlap to a degree that appalled Father Mathew even as it inspired O'Connell and intimidated and angered conservative opponents of both movements. O'Connell's Machiavellian attempt to marry the crusades succeeded in its Irish context, but ultimately could not be made to bear any political weight on the other side of the Irish Sea. This failure speaks to a growing disconnect between mid-nineteenth century English and Irish notions of the nature of political authority. The ultimate consequences of this association were also very important for the Temperance cause. If the failure of the Catholic Church as an institution to support the CTAS may be said to have virtually guaranteed the eventual decline of the Temperance crusade, its entanglement with the Repeal movement not only further contributed to that decline, but also ensured that it would be a swift and sure one.

Before examining the confluences between Temperance and Repeal as social movements, however, it is important to understand how they became essentially entangled. This in turn requires not only an examination of the Repeal campaign, but also, first and foremost, an appreciation of the degree to which Irish political life in the 1830s and early 1840s revolved around the relationship of one man, Daniel O'Connell, to the critical mass of Ireland's overwhelmingly Catholic peasant population. While it was true that O'Connell was a member of Parliament and the leader of a political formation closely allied with the Whigs in the House of Commons ('O'Connell's Tail'), his real power was rooted in his unparalleled ability to marshal and direct the collective energy of millions of Irish men and women toward his chosen political ends. This ability resulted from the people's loyalty to O'Connell, itself a consequence of his remarkable empathy and charisma.[3] In the early 1840s, therefore, Mathew and O'Connell were joint possessors of a remarkable degree of popular support. As the Dublin Quaker, Richard Webb, explained to an American correspondent in 1842, O'Connell's 'word is almost law with nine-tenths of the Irish in this country—and that of Father Mathew is nearly as great'.[4]

The rise of the CTAS coincided with the last great effort of O'Connell's magnificent political career, the failed campaign for Repeal of the Act of Union that had united Britain and Ireland since 1801. O'Connell was relentless in his attempts to enlist the teetotallers, and, indeed, teetotalism, into his developing political campaign. Father Mathew, unwilling to allow the CTAS to become a pawn in the game of partisan politics, did what he could to keep his growing network of total abstinence societies distinct from Repeal agitation. While he was successful in preventing any formal union, O'Connell's influence, combined with the nature of the Temperance movement's own appeal, ensured that there was little Mathew could do to keep most of his followers from consciously associating their recent moral transformation with O'Connell's projected political one.

In 1838, it must be pointed out, there was no reason to expect that Daniel O'Connell would become an advocate of Temperance. He was personally involved in the liquor trade, having in 1833 invested some £2,000 in a Dublin brewery bearing the family name, an operation managed unsuccessfully by his son Daniel.[5] A popular ballad from the 1830s described the O'Connell product enthusiastically:

> Some folks adulturate their drink
> With liquorice ball and treacle
> But Dan's brown stout is strong and tough
> Made of the best material,
> 'Tis genuine beyond a doubt,
> It won't create disorder,
> Not like some brewer's poisoned drugs,
> It's staunch Reform Porter![6]

In 1834, O'Connell had ridiculed the pro-Temperance conclusions of the *Parliamentary Report of the Committee on Drunkenness*, chaired by the teetotaller James Silk Buckingham, the radical member for Sheffield, observing scornfully at the time that Buckingham's 'appearance is that of a man who drinks nothing but water'.[7] O'Connell was a vigorous defender of the Irish brewing and distilling industries in the 1830s. In parliament, he had resisted all the Liberal efforts to control more closely the licensing and regulation of public houses, including legislation in the 1838 parliamentary session that proposed stricter provisions for Ireland's 'spirit grocers'.[8] In August 1838, while meeting with a delegation of spirit grocers and publicans, O'Connell claimed to have been disgusted by 'more than the usual quantity of cant made use of by the supporters of this bill'.[9] He criticised those supporters of Temperance who 'attributed all the crimes that were committed in the country to whiskey drinking, without going back to first principles, or looking to the causes that make men drunkards or idlers'. He made no secret of the fact that his position resulted from practical considerations. 'By whom have I been better supported', he asked rhetorically, referring to the spirit-grocers and publicans, noting that 'they subscribed liberally at the last election for the purpose of having my voters brought up to the poll.' In 1838, therefore, there existed a close political alliance between O'Connell and spirit grocers, distillers and publicans, who together composed an important segment of the Irish Catholic middle class.

PRECURSORS, NON-CONSUMPTIONISTS OR REPEALERS?: AUGUST 1838 TO AUGUST 1839.

By the summer of 1838, O'Connell felt that the political situation in Britain warranted the first steps in his long-anticipated and oft-threatened campaign. In August he cautiously established the Precursor Society, an organisation publicly committed to advocating repeal should proposed reforms of British policies toward Ireland be rejected. The Liberator's preference for repeal to reform evolved gradually and in response to his own growing frustration with the political process at Westminster, and was by no means complete by August 1838. By that date, however, O'Connell was a more advanced repealer than many of his more important and influential Irish allies. Many Irish Liberals and Whigs quite correctly discerned that Parliament was completely unwilling to grant repeal, and preferred to nurture reform within the union over the long term, and to garner, meanwhile, the patronage and places that were increasingly available to them. The Precursor Society balanced uneasily and ultimately unsuccessfully on the edge of a dilemma, between the need to organise a radical popular movement and the serious practical consequences of rejecting the current political system. If, on the one hand, O'Connell abandoned his Whig allies and advocated repeal too abruptly, he risked alienating many men of substance in Britain and Ireland. On the other hand, too gradual an approach was unlikely to inspire the masses who O'Connell knew constituted his only chance for pressing any government into either repeal or reform.

The birth of the Precursor Society coincided with the early stifling, by O'Connell, of an alternate political programme in Cork, with roots in the fledgling Temperance cause. The 'Non-consumption' movement, proposed on 8 August 1838, in the form of an anonymous open letter to Daniel O'Connell accompanied by a supporting editorial in the *Southern Reporter*, urging the collective rejection of all excisable goods by all of the Irish people, 'particularly whiskey and beer'.[10] Asserting that the 'struggle for equal rights under the Union' had been a failure, the editorial noted that the cause promised to 'exhibit the union – the determination – the moral power – the heroism, and the injured feelings of an entire people'. Clearly, even at this early date, the urge to associate the Temperance reformation with politics was irresistible. Although the campaign was condemned by the *Cork Standard* as an attempt 'to obtain what they specify from the legislature by this *ultra-teetotalism*', it rapidly gained support in the Cork Chamber of Commerce, where many local notables reportedly supported it.[11] A number of papers in the south of Ireland reprinted, with expressions of support, the letter and accompanying editorial.[12] By reducing tax revenue, the non-consumption movement was supposed to create sufficient pressure on the government to force political change. The open letter to O'Connell implied that Repeal of the Act of Union and legislative independence for Ireland would be the natural consequence of such a moral reformation:

> From England, no justice can be expected. To ourselves, and ourselves alone, must we look for working out peaceably, constitutionally, but determinedly, the regeneration of our country ... Through the instrumentality of this great national abstinence, Ireland may yet, within the period of a single year, work out her political regeneration. It requires but the will. If she refuses, let her abandon the repeal of the union, for she has not sufficient moral resolution to be free.

In fact, it was widely believed that the non-consumption movement was a deliberate attempt to establish a moral justification for repeal.[13]

Non-consumption's supporters, however, had underestimated O'Connell's unwillingness to endorse this particular form of agitation. Not only was he still struggling with the repeal/reform dilemma, O'Connell was fundamentally unwilling to support a policy which promised to be at least as injurious to his publican and spirit-grocer allies as it was likely to be to the English exchequer. He received the non-consumption letter, it was reported, 'with courteous coldness', but, 'were he to speak his sentiments, he would deprecate this step'.[14] Shortly after meeting with Dublin publicans and spirit-grocers on 15 August O'Connell visited Cork for a public meeting and dinner on the 27th, a visit designed as much to derail non-consumption as it was to promote the newly-established Precursor Society.[15] By the end of August 1838, both the *Southern Reporter* and the *Dublin Evening Post*, the two strongest advocates of non-consumption, ceased discussion of the subject and published editorials in favour of the Precursor Society.[16] O'Connell, therefore, acted forcefully in August 1838 to prevent any popular linking of Temperance to his political programme.

Unfortunately for O'Connell, his Precursor Society was a political failure. O'Connell's open letter to the Irish people in March indicated the depth of that failure. 'We have not precursors enough', he complained on 1 March to T.M. Ray, the society's secretary.[17] 'I asked for two millions', he noted, and 'I have not as yet got more than one-twentieth of that number.' The situation did not improve, and by the end of the parliamentary session in August 1839, O'Connell was deeply discouraged. Ireland had not produced the requisite agitation, the Whig government was weaker than ever, and the Precursor Society was all but ignored in Ireland, not to mention England. O'Connell was uncharacteristically pessimistic and depressed about his political future. 'I am, I believe', he informed Fitzpatrick from London in August 1839, 'on the verge of an illness – the illness of despondency.'[18] He wrote again to Fitzpatrick on 25 August that 'at no period of our history was the cause of Ireland more friendless', lamenting that 'the country has grown tired of supporting me'.[19] In September, O'Connell determined to dissolve the Precursor Society and retreated into a policy of Liberal voter registration that was officially neutral on the question of Repeal.[20]

O'CONNELL AND TEMPERANCE: SEPTEMBER 1839–MARCH 1840

Dejected, O'Connell returned from London in the autumn of 1839 to an Ireland undergoing a moral transformation through Temperance. Almost immediately, the burgeoning movement's energy, enthusiasm and popular appeal seem to have fascinated him. At a public meeting in Killarney on 29 September, he reminisced about an earlier linkage of Temperance and politics: 'In Clare, in 1828, I saw that, during eight of the sultriest days that a Summer's sun shone down upon that country, not one drop of ardent spirits entered the lips of the virtuous and brave electors on that memorable occasion (great cheering). That was the election that carried the emancipation.'[21] Three days later, on 2 October, at a meeting in Macroom, Co. Cork held in honour of Cork's MPs, O'Connell not only took his first public notice of the CTAS's remarkable success, but also indicated that he had decided to begin the process of associating that success with his own political programme.

> He next adverted to the Temperance Society, which, he said, was the greatest blessing ever bestowed on this country, and hoped that every man whom he was addressing, who had not yet joined it, would immediately do so (hear, hear). He had heard that the Rev. Mr Mathew had brought over no fewer than 50,000 persons to join this society, many of whom before had rendered their homes and their families miserable by habits of drunkenness, and would anyone tell him that the Irishmen capable of such exertions over their passions had not moral energy to achieve liberty for their country?[22]

Some three weeks later, on 21 October 1839, O'Connell was just as effusive about Temperance when he addressed another audience which included eight Irish bishops at a Cork banquet.[23]

This early decision to endorse the CTAS at meetings in Cork in October 1839 indicates that O'Connell shrewdly anticipated that Father Mathew's remarkable local success was likely to spread. His open willingness to antagonise his allies in the liquor trade also indicated his own frustration with the failure of his Precursor Society and his growing awareness that popular enthusiasm in Ireland would be focused increasingly on the Temperance reformation. O'Connell's intuition was confirmed with the spectacular success of the first mass Temperance meetings at Limerick and Waterford in late November and early December. The early attention he had paid to the cause increased in direct proportion to Temperance's expanding ranks.

At a public meeting in Bandon, Co. Cork, on 5 December, O'Connell made remarks of crucial importance indicating how important a place Temperance had come to occupy in his political calculations. At the height of the great rush of public excitement that followed the Limerick and Waterford meetings, O'Connell asked all in his audience who had taken the pledge to raise their hands.[24] After half did so, O'Connell insisted that the CTAS would provide the foundation for any future popular Repeal movement:

> But I tell you plainly, before I re-organise the country for the attainment of the repeal of the union, I shall watch the progress of that mighty moral institution, now running through every corner of the land with a power and effect not to be repressed. I shall watch, I say, the gigantic influence wich the temperance societies will inevitably effect, before I again unfurl the banners of Repeal; and then, despite the world, Repeal will be carried.

O'Connell clearly recognised that the widespread embrace of the Temperance movement's message of moral regeneration had crucial political implications. Even at this early stage, O'Connell appreciated that Father Mathew's cause could energise and organise his lower and middle class base of supporters even while he continued to build support for repeal more carefully and deliberately among sceptical Liberals in Ireland and England. All O'Connell needed to do was associate himself with the Temperance reformation.

O'Connell's new-found enthusiasm for Temperance did not please all his friends. Two weeks later, at Tralee in Kerry on 19 December, after noting the problem of popular apathy in political matters, as he launched into what was quickly becoming his characteristic endorsement, O'Connell was interrupted by a Mr Newell, an 'an eminent distiller of the town' seated at the head table.[25] 'The less you say about the Temperance, sir', Newell pointedly noted, 'the better you will be liked at this end of the room!' O'Connell joined in the laughter this caused, but took advantage of the opportunity to underscore the importance of Temperance:

> Whatever may be the effects of the Temperance Reformation, with respect to his private affairs, I am convinced [Newell] will sincerely rejoice in anything that conduces to the welfare of his countrymen, and I doubt not that he can find numerous methods of employing his capital and ingenuity, that will amply repay him for any loss … (hear) I resume, then, and ask what other part of the globe witnesses the tens, and the twenties, and the thirties of thousands of people setting off on long and arduous journeys, to take the pledge of total abstinence from an Apostle of Temperance? What has hitherto been our reproach? Why, the intoxication of the lower classes. Those amongst our enemies who acknowledged the wretchedness of Ireland ascribed all her misery, all her destitution, and her crime, solely to the habit of intoxication amongst her inhabitants. (Hear, Hear) In this, to be sure, there was an immense deal of exaggeration; but there can be no doubt, that great numbers of the populace were unfortunately slaves to this degrading propensity. I venture to predict that in a few years the exhibition of a drunken man will be as rare as that of a serpent after the mission of St Patrick.

Such comments were no solace to O'Connellites such as John Dower, a county Waterford brewer and political activist, who one week later, on

30 December, 1839, echoed Newell's concerns and complained angrily to O'Connell that his brewery 'ceases to be of any value to me on account of the Temperance Society which has become now so formidable in this ... district that the loss sustained thereby cannot be far short of ten thousand pounds'.[26]

Despite these notes of disapproval, the impact of the Temperance movement became a dominant theme in O'Connell's speeches.[27] Aware that any successful Repeal movement would require an even closer alliance with Temperance, for example, O'Connell tried to cushion the likely blow to his allies in the drink trade by presenting an unsuccessful petition to parliament on 29 February calling for indemnification by the government for their losses at the hands of the crusade.[28] Two weeks later, when in Galway attending the assizes at the same time as Mathew held a meeting there, O'Connell witnessed his first full-scale Temperance gathering. He was no doubt as impressed as the editor of the *Connaught Journal*. 'No language could describe the enthusiasm displayed by the multitudes that thronged into town over the last few days', the *Journal* proclaimed, a spectacle so 'truly astonishing, we could not have believed it, had we not ocular demonstrations.'[29] Mathew foiled an attempted joint public appearance by declining an invitation to attend a dinner in O'Connell's honour.[30] Early in April, François Guizot, the French ambassador to Britain, met O'Connell at a London dinner party and found him consumed with excitement about the Temperance cause.[31] O'Connell, Guizot later related, talked of little else, and 'detailed the progress of temperance in Ireland, the drunkards were disappearing by the thousands'.

TEMPERANCE AND POLITICAL ALIGNMENTS TO APRIL 1840

As Mathew's movement continued to expand exponentially in early 1840, culminating in the Apostle of Temperance's successful mission at the end of March and early April in Dublin, the fact of its increasing politicisation was also widely recognised. Perhaps the clearest indication of that fact can be found in the Constabulary Reports on Temperance, gathered in March 1840, which asked local constables and magistrates if Temperance in their district had any 'religious or political object'. Of the 49 useful replies (20 others were either non-responsive or non-committal) 12 implied that there might be, or likely would be, some connection, while ten others insisted that the connection certainly existed, and the other 27, although they denied any connection between politics and Temperance, often did so in a manner which indicated that such concerns were common. Some respondents feared armed insurrection.[32] Others, perhaps less inclined to paranoia, nevertheless viewed Temperance as deeply politicised, if not quite revolutionary.[33] Most common of all were respondents who viewed the movement as a potential 'political engine'.[34] Overall, there was a clear consensus in the reports that the movement was in grave danger of becoming caught up, if it was not in fact already entangled, in partisan politics, and most constables would have agreed with one Constable Lewis, stationed in county Galway, who was 'of the opinion' that the CTAS was 'gradually merging' into a political organisation.[35]

These responses reflected an active debate that had developed in the press in preceding months over the 'politicisation' of the crusade, due in part, no doubt, to O'Connell's open support for it. Early Tory critics of the CTAS had derided it for fostering disorder and superstition, but from December 1839 they increasingly condemned it for its politics. In general, unsurprisingly, the movement was seen as a Catholic conspiracy directed against the Protestant Ascendancy. The conservative *Limerick Standard*, on 24 December 1839, for example, pointed out that the Irish were not taking the pledge out of any sudden hatred for whiskey.

> Never, in the history of the country, were political parties so nearly balanced in the house of commons as at present. The stronger only hold the reigns of power by the aid of the Irish traitors, and now that power is on the eve of passing into other hands as a consequence of the accession of the Conservatives to office, we are *openly menaced with rebellion in Ireland*. We now repeat, it is in aid of such an event that the Mathewite reform, as it is called, is so much lauded by the Irish priesthood and the Popish press.[36]

Early in January, the *London Times* reprinted a recent article from the *Dublin Gazette* that similarly ridiculed the idea that the CTAS advocated only 'mere abstinence from the use of ardent spirits'.[37] The problem with Temperance, 'in plain language', was that it 'band[ed] together and badge[d] the multitude into a universal conspiracy, ostensibly and temporarily against a flagrant evil, but capable, at an hour's notice, of applying its enrollment and ensignry to any purpose'.

Daniel O'Connell, never one to miss an opportunity to heap scorn on Orange paranoia, responded to these speculations on 10 January 1840. 'It has been said', he noted, that 'there are political effects in [Temperance]. The *Mail* speaks openly and says there is. The *Standard* re-echoes the *Mail* and Gin-drinking Barnes of *The Times* says that there is some horrible and bloody consequences against Protestants on foot.'[38]

'Why', O'Connell scathingly observed, 'was there ever heard such non-sensical stuff? The Protestants and the Catholics have united in working for the temperance cause, yet the Orange gang say there is some horrible conspiracy on foot.'

If government and Tory observers were increasingly suspicious of the CTAS's politics, and if O'Connell continued to deny, disingenuously, that it had any, editorials and letters to the editor in the Liberal papers from early 1840 were also inclined to associate Temperance and politics, albeit in a more positive light. The *Southern Reporter*, for example, on 9 January 1840, praised the 'truly blessed revolution' and linked that revolution to 'great and important ... political objects which our country has in view'.[39] 'We are of the opinion', the editor concluded, 'that this happy and well-timed spread of Temperance will be a mighty auxiliary in the promotion of every measure of benefit.' Several days later, 'A Teetotaller' wrote to the *Waterford Chronicle* to complain of 'the misery and wretchedness of a great portion of the people of Ireland' which was 'owing to a long series of years of misrule and misgovernment'.[40] 'Ireland', the letter-writer insisted, was now prepared to 'hurl back with contumely on their slanderers, the foul and now disproved charges that have been so often made – that the Irish were unreclaimable from the sin of drunkenness, and consequently unfit for liberty.'

Similar observations abounded in the press. Saint Patrick's Day, 1840, and the near-encounter in Galway between O'Connell and Mathew, produced an outpouring of musings on the implications of Temperance's success for Ireland's political future. The *Waterford Chronicle* could not resist comparing Mathew and O'Connell: 'No one has done more for his country than Father Mathew, we scarcely except the Liberator himself. – One has been the great moral regenerator – the other the political.'[41] Of Mathew, the editor added, 'May his works be lasting, and may Ireland reap from them, in its moral and political condition, happiness and prosperity!' The *Southern Reporter*'s editor, praising the region's first sober St Patrick's day, found the occasion 'cheering to the patriot's heart', and was pleased to note that 'whilst heretofore, Ireland's intemperance constantly kept the fire kindled, and the iron hot, which the British Minister, with a ready hand, forged into chains for her oppressions and subjugation, and all favours were showered on happy England – that now the scenes are shifted, and Ireland is haughty England's model!'[42] However pro-O'Connell many enthusiasts may have been, none were bold enough as yet to link Temperance directly to particular political campaigns. J.P. O'Reilly, the superior of the Capuchins' house in Kilkenny and president of St Mary's Total Abstinence Society in that town, exemplified this cautious approach when he carefully toasted O'Connell at a St Patrick's Day banquet, but only 'in his capacity as an encourager of teetotalism'.[43]

In April 1840, O'Connell prepared to return to Ireland to launch a new phase in his campaign for popular support for Repeal. Mathew had decided, meanwhile, in the face of so much speculation to the contrary, to attempt to reassert his movement's apolitical nature. During his much-publicised visit to Dublin at the end of March, he told crowds on the first day of his mission that the CTAS was not a political organisation and that its members, furthermore, should avoid politics.[44] When a voice from the crowd replied that teetotallers need only avoid 'unlawful politics', Mathew insisted that his societies 'should not have any politics, lawful or unlawful, connected with them'. Two days later, Mathew insisted that he 'did not give a vote' and was utterly uninvolved 'in any political matter', a fact he restated a few days later.[45]

TEMPERANCE AND THE EVOLUTION OF THE REPEAL MOVEMENT, APRIL–AUGUST 1840

Unfortunately for Mathew, his attempts to counter the politicisation of the CTAS flew in the face of equally determined efforts by both the opponents and the allies of O'Connell, who were intent on fanning the flames of controversy. In April, an editorial in *The Times* was harshly critical of the CTAS, particularly of the public processions of local societies and other displays of strength.[46] 'Is it any less substantially political', the editor demanded of teetotalism, 'because it assumes a namby-pamby name?' Meanwhile, on 4 April the popular Catholic controversialist, Tom Maguire, the parish priest of Aughterah, in the diocese of Kilmore, became perhaps the first public figure to link Temperance and Repeal in explicit terms. In a speech delivered at a Reform Club meeting, Maguire, in a remarkable moment of enthusiasm, promised to

> Pledge myself to have three million of teetotallers before three months – that I will place myself at their head, and unfurl the flag of repeal, and not cease to agitate until we put the Tories and Whigs out of office, and achieve the liberties of eight millions of people. (loud cheers)[47]

At the same meeting, Henry Grattan, the member for Meath, also spoke approvingly of enrolling teetotallers as Repealers, noting that 'the people are rendered steady and united by teetotalism'.[48]

Mathew, at Wexford on 9 April 1840, condemned Maguire's comments in 'severe terms', castigating him for 'endeavouring to injure the great and good cause'.[49] At New Ross, Co. Wexford, the following day, Mathew cuttingly alluded to Maguire's reputation as a drinker by observing that 'he was at a loss to know where the Rev. Gentleman would procure the 3 millions of men mentioned; for certainly he believed the Rev. Mr Maguire was not a teetotaller, and he hoped he did not mean to include any of the Temperance Society, which was not a fighting one'.[50] Several days later, however, Maguire, in a public letter, only repeated his promises.[51]

Both *The Times* article and Maguire's comments contributed to a sudden rush of politically charged commentary on Temperance. Ballads ridiculed Tory fears of a Temperance rebellion, as expressed by one wit in 'A New Song to an Old Tune',

> And now when our water has spread,
> A convulsion volcanic they dread!
> Their terrorists teach, should the water but reach
> Our combustible stratum or bed –
> 'Tis said that eruptions would burst from our head![52]

At least some in the Liberal press partook of the popular mood. A correspondent for the *Waterford Chronicle* challenged Temperance's opponents with rhetoric that echoed that of Cork's non-consumptionists of 1838:

> Let the Tories bear in mind, that for a nation to be free, it is sufficient that she wills it. What people so fit for freedom as those who have had the resolution, the moral fortitude, as if by one impulse, to shake off the bonds of this insidious vice. *The Times* says the Irish were teetotallers in the year '98 ... – the destinies of Ireland perhaps, were in the scale – but the love of whiskey prevailed. Were the insurgents of those days teetotallers, in all human probability, the rebellion of '98 would be known by quite another name.[53]

On 7 April, the pro-Repeal *Freeman's Journal* was bold enough to approve of and amplify Maguire's remarks, and their editorial is worth quoting at length:

> The Irish were heretofore considered a drunken people, incapable of overcoming cool and steady enmity. Yet, with all their faults, which resulted from their addiction to the one great vice, they have triumphed over more obstacles already than the most sanguine amongst them could have foreseen twenty years ago ... what glorious victories over oppression may we not expect them to achieve, now that the great barrier to the effective display of their moral power is forever removed? While the

> thirst for whiskey was a national evil and a national disgrace they won emancipation much as their reckless habits had weakened their strength. But now that general SOBRIETY has been established – that temperance has taken deep root – that the avoidance of intoxication has become the point of honour amongst those classes which constitute the strength of the nation – must not the united struggle for repeal become irresistible? Englishmen may smile at the expression of these hopes; but they also smiled at the notion of suddenly converting millions from the use of that stimulant to which they had constant resource … they have thrown off the yoke of sin, and we are now fitted to struggle against the remaining fetters of slavery. We have proved ourselves fitted for freedom.[54]

Much of the rhetoric was familiar, but the editor's willingness to connect the new moral order with the Repeal campaign, as Maguire had a few days earlier, represented a new departure, and one that was to have influential imitators, principal among them the Liberator himself.

O'Connell returned to Dublin on 12 April and, significantly, chaired a Temperance dinner as his first public act.[55] Hinting that he was experimenting with teetotalism himself, O'Connell once again praised the cause, and crept ever closer to linking it with an anticipated new wave of agitation. 'The mighty Temperance Movement now going forward, which makes festivities of this kind no novelty in the land', O'Connell maintained, 'gives a moral power, a magical intellectual force, which I trust will yet produce that happy realization of those hopes we have so long entertained for Ireland (hear hear and loud cheers).' Two days later, on the eve of O'Connell's proposing his new organisation, the *Waterford Chronicle* announced that the Liberator had 'intimated his intention of subscribing to the total abstinence pledge'.[56] 'He would have done so earlier (he says)', the reporter explained, 'but he was anxious not to give the appearance of "party" to the present temperance movement in Ireland.'

O'Connell's speech on 15 April establishing his new pro-repeal organisation, the 'National Association of Ireland for Full and Prompt Justice or Repeal', climaxed in an invocation of the CTAS that eloquently summed up his earlier remarks about the crusade:

> I am counselor for the moral, the religious people of Ireland. I am aware that, unfortunately, too many of them were sunk in the abyss of intoxication. They too often fled from the evils of scanty food, the taunts of the oppressor, and all the evils to which poverty is heir, to the transient enjoyment of ardent spirits, and thus they rendered their condition worse … But the period of their delusion is gone by – the pleasure which they took in the gratification of their animal passions is abandoned, and

> thank God there will soon be three millions of teetotallers (tremendous cheering) to dignify their native land, and to place Ireland in the high rank she should hold among the nations of the earth. (Immense cheering)[57]

O'Connell took these sentiments one step further, however, when he approvingly observed that 'my friend Mr Maguire spoke of organizing the teetotallers'. Maguire, O'Connell argued, had proposed only 'moral organisation', but 'in the moral magnitude of the people he saw the means of their regeneration'. There was little Mathew could do in response beyond reasserting his society's apolitical objectives. Because he was aware that processions were provoking to many Tories, Mathew unsuccessfully attempted to cancel Cork's grand Easter parade.[58] When James Bermingham published his *Memoir of the Very Reverend Father Mathew* in May, this first history of the movement, prepared in cooperation with Father Mathew, contained a fairly explicit condemnation of the machinations of O'Connell and his associates.[59] So anxious was Mathew to underscore this point that he publicly wrote to Bermingham on 28 May, praising the author for 'having studiously avoided political allusions'.[60]

By early June, O'Connell, recognising that 'the complex and contingent objective, or pseudo-objective, of "Justice or Repeal" roused no one outside the circle of his own particular acolytes', had decided to transform his organisation into the 'Loyal National Repeal Association'.[61] Once again this tactical shift was preceded, accompanied and followed by extensive appeals to Ireland's teetotalling millions. On 9 June, at a Dublin meeting, as O'Connell explained, 'the great temperance movement will give us all the good and virtuous'.[62] On 4 July, just prior to his return to Dublin to announce the adoption of his new strategy, O'Connell had addressed the South London Catholic Total Abstinence Society on the subject of 'his darling ambition to enroll himself with those who are engaged in the great, glorious and holy cause of temperance'.[63] In a speech lasting more than an hour and a half that was prominently reported in the *Freeman's Journal*, while maintaining that he had 'always been a temperate man', he admitted 'I have not yet taken the pledge' but promised 'I intend to take it'. That information produced 'tremendous cheering'. O'Connell insisted that he 'would never ask from others a sacrifice I am not prepared to make myself'. All that had prevented him from enrolling, he explained archly, was a fear of 'exposing the temperance society to the imputation of politics'.

A few days later, O'Connell launched the Loyal National Repeal Association and began the Repeal effort in earnest at a Dublin meeting.

His opening remarks acidly noted that the English were pledge-breakers for having reneged on the promise of emancipation and justice offered to Irish Catholics at the time of the passing of the Act of Union: 'They have not done one thing towards redeeming the pledge, the solemn pledge given by the King, Lords and Commons – and all this solemn pledge turns out to be a base lie.'[64] 'Father Mathew (immense cheering) has raised the standard', O'Connell went on to point out, 'and two millions of Irish men and Irish women are pledged to perfect sobriety.' 'Can such a people', he insisted, 'continue constantly as slaves?'

O'Connell planned to follow this initiative which he termed 'an entire development of the national mind', with 'four great provincial meetings', and began by visiting Connaught.[65] For the second time in six months O'Connell's visit to the west coincided with Mathew's own missionary visits there. O'Connell was aware of the fact (indeed, he attended at least one of Mathew's sermons) and jocularly inquired of crowds at Castlebar, Co. Mayo on 26 July if the fine weather was given 'to me or to Father Mathew'.[66] He concluded his inaugural meeting in the west by insisting that 'when we have five or six millions of repealers, the repeal is as certain as if we had it'. The fascination with membership figures was a link with the Temperance movement, and one that O'Connell drove home in his closing exhortation.

> My worthy and most revered friend, Mr Mathew, told me that before he came to Connaught his society contained two million and a quarter. Before he leaves he'll have a million more – cries of 'he will, and more'. I call upon you then to rally with me for Ireland – respect the saintly man who is leading you from intoxication to temperance – let there be peaceful combination in the open day – be true to your religion, faithful to your country, and then we may say of Ireland, in the words of the poet, 'The nations have fallen but thou art still young/Thy sun is rising whilst others have set/And though slavery's gloom round thy morning has hung,/The full moon of freedom shall beam round thee yet'.

In these remarks, O'Connell not only appropriated a poem of Thomas Moore's that had been popular in Temperance circles for some time, he had also directly appealed to Ireland's teetotallers on the authority of Father Mathew to enlist themselves as repealers. Similar appeals and remarks were a dominant theme in O'Connell's subsequent speeches in Tuam and Galway.[67]

Galling as it must have been for Mathew to see his movement and his own person exploited for Repeal recruitment, he could console himself with the fact that the response in Connaught to O'Connell's appeal was 'unenthusiastic, perhaps even apathetic'.[68] Enthusiasm for

Temperance ran high, and according to pro-O'Connell editorialists still eclipsed budding enthusiasm for Repeal. 'We believe the repeal of the Union of Punch and Paddy', the editor of the *Freeman's Journal* playfully conceded on 28 July, 'is making much swifter way than the repeal of the union of England and Ireland. Father Mathew has a longer following than Mr O'Connell, and we rejoice at it most sincerely.'[69]

There were, however, disturbing indications that O'Connell was succeeding in at least some quarters. At a Repeal banquet in Galway on 2 August 1840 with O'Connell present, B.J. Roche, the parish priest of Saint Nicholas East, observed that 'the temperance movement, which he did not mean to connect with politics, produced sobriety, peace and order'. 'The people of Clare', Roche nevertheless reminded his listeners, 'gained emancipation by temperance'. Now a new generation had 'obtained a victory over their passions; and will it be said that they cannot obtain a victory over their enemies?' Early that same month, at least two Temperance societies contributed funds to the newly established Repeal Association, including one which noted that they did so knowing that 'it was laid down that their members should not interfere in politics, yet on so great and good an occasion, they embarked on the troubled waters'.[70]

Once again, Mathew responded to O'Connell's overtures and the erosion of orthodoxy among his own followers by taking every opportunity to emphasise the CTAS's political agnosticism. 'We have no politics in our body', he insisted at a meeting at Naas, Co. Kildare on 15 August. 'We permit no such. True it is we seek not to deter any man from entertaining whatever political sentiments he may individually think fit, but, as a society, ours knows no politics ... I have disclaimed, over and over again, the mixing up of politics in any possible manner with us as a body, and I now again repudiate it.' Two weeks later, in Dublin, he called the CTAS 'a neutral ground – an oasis in the desert of life'.[71]

O'CONNELL'S 'CONVERSION', SEPTEMBER–OCTOBER 1840

Unfortunately for Mathew, O'Connell still had a trump card to play. At least twice in 1840, O'Connell had intimated that he was about to join the Temperance society. On both occasions, his excuse for not doing so was that he wanted to avoid opening the CTAS to accusations of politicisation. By September 1840, however, as the Whig government continued to totter, and the response to his Repeal initiative remained tepid, O'Connell's sense of urgency increased.[72] While passing through

Limerick in September on his way to his annual autumn holiday at Derrynane, Co. Kerry, a frustrated O'Connell had publicly berated local activists, demanding to know 'why should there be apathy amongst you?'[73] During his month-long stay at Derrynane, O'Connell decided to make the dramatic gesture of becoming a teetotaller. To pave the way, two pieces of correspondence were published. The first was a letter dated 16 September 1840 to Thomas Hurley, the president of a branch of the CTAS at Tralee, Co. Kerry, which was fulsome in its praise of the cause and included O'Connell's subscription to provide that society with a reading room.[74] The second, dated 19 September, accepted an invitation from the teetotallers of Limerick to attend a Repeal banquet in that town on 7 October.

O'Connell's proposed visit to Limerick was to be part of a tour he undertook that month through Munster, Ireland's Temperance heartland, designed to energise the Repeal cause. At his first stop in Cork on 5 October, O'Connell addressed the Trade Union Association in terms that reinforced Temperance and Repeal connections. He was, he insisted, 'pledged to repeal', with 'that pledge as part of his being'.[75] O'Connell followed these remarks with an announcement.

> He then alluded to the vast spread of the temperance society, and the moral wonder affected on the people's habits by the Rev. Mr Mathew, and declared that he had himself become a teetotaller, and never had he, since then, felt the least inconvenience or bad effects arisen to his health for having done so, and he would, therefore, to the end of his days, continue a teetotaller, and never again taste one drop of fermented liquor; and concluded by expressing a fervent prayer that the day was not far distant when he should see the Repeal of the Union crowning the happiness, the prosperity, the tranquillity, and the liberty of Ireland.

O'Connell made no reference to his conversion at the banquet that followed the meeting, perhaps because it was chaired by the brewer Crawford Beamish, although O'Connell and Father Mathew were toasted as the political and moral liberators of Ireland.[76]

O'Connell, now a teetotaller, albeit without recourse to any formal pledge, was determined to make the most of his conversion, and the Repeal meeting at Limerick on 7 October, at the site of Mathew's first dramatic mass meeting less than a year earlier, provided the perfect occasion. Before a cheering crowd of some 60,000, not one of whom, according to the 'gratified' *Freeman's Journal*, 'suffered the slightest degree of intoxication', O'Connell devoted much of his speech to singing the praises of 'the moral miracle of temperance' and of the reformed Irish people themselves.[77]

> Now the people have become my preceptors. I have long been their tutor – now I am become their pupil – I have taken a lesson From them – I have profited from their glorious example, and I now declare myself a teetotaller in honour of them (loud cheers, which lasted several minutes). The men of Limerick have been my instructors; I owe the lesson to you; I appear before you on this occasion to thank you heartily for it, and request of you to take a lesson of me in return. We will carry the Repeal!

At the dinner that followed the Limerick meeting, an inspired O'Connell, flushed with success, gave an account of the day's events that provided his clearest statement to date of the way in which the spectacle of mass meetings, inspired by the Temperance movement and the model of the 1828 Clare election that had forced Catholic emancipation, might produce Repeal of the Union. That account is worth quoting at length, as it indicates that O'Connell had become convinced that the Temperance movement alone could provide the manpower and the moral force that might transform a hopeless cause into an irresistible crusade, even with minimal support from Ireland's Liberal elites.

> Did I not see them today, with physical force capable of overpowering any that resisted – with spirit and daring capable of setting at defiance any power – did I not see them today comport themselves with a degree of propriety which the upper classes might well endeavour to imitate? (cheers) But, the question is, which are the upper classes? (cries of 'the people!) You are right. The people. In fact, an infant might have ruled that 60,000 that assembled together ... There was never such an exhibition in any nation as that today – Oh! Blessed be God! We have educated the Irish nation! (Cheers) What danger is there to trust men with such power – I say it is dangerous not to trust such a people with power – and, moreover, it is thoroughly unjust! (hear, hear) Would John Bull show such an exhibition as that of today? (cries of 'no, no!') And yet he is treated as a freeman, while you are his slaves. (Long continued cries of no, no) Allow me the benefit of an 'if'. (great laughter) If you are capable of acquiescing in the degradation that is now politically pending over you, you would deserve to be slaves ... We saw about that time [1829] a calm and quiet exhibition of the power of the people: not exactly quite the same, but resembling it, in the county of Clare. (Cheers) We saw, during that exhibition, the anticipators of Father Mathew abstaining from the use of all liquors in the name of their common country, but it was only for one week! (Laughter) But it was the abstinence of a week that beat down Wellington and Peel – It was the water drinkers of Clare that carried emancipation – it was the moral dignity of those men – who could triumph over their habits and conquer their passions, who could overcome every passion but their love of their country, that enabled us to carry that measure ... All I want is that England should understand

> the scene of today ... suppose this happens – that in every town and county of Ireland, such a number of the population joins with us as you did this day in Limerick ... If the inhabitants turn out peaceable in the open day, and petition parliament to repeal the union, where is the man insane enough to think that the prayers of our petition would be refused?

For O'Connell, his own conversion to Temperance seemed to provide the leverage that would allow him to join Temperance enthusiasm to the Repeal cause. In subsequent days and weeks, at meetings in Clonmel, Kilkenny, Waterford, Dublin and Drogheda, the new teetotaller reiterated nearly daily the impression that Limerick had made on him.[78] While setbacks, doubts and tactical hesitations would continue for O'Connell in the months that followed, Repeal and Temperance were now bound up in his own powerful relationship with the Irish people.

Even as Ireland's political Liberator was preparing to tour Munster, on 29 September 1840 her moral Liberator was in Dublin, administering the pledge in the pouring rain. With O'Connell's manipulations very much in the forefront of his mind, Mathew issued a particularly urgent and pointed warning to Ireland's elites, who he observed were neither taking the pledge in satisfactory numbers, nor providing leadership for local societies. 'Many persons seem to apprehend that some system of combination or reorganization may arise out of the temperance system', Mathew admitted to an assembly of 8,000, alluding no doubt to O'Connell's Repeal campaign.[79] 'The thing, though unlikely', Mathew conceded, 'is not impossible.' 'The teetotaller', he explained, was a kind of '*tabula erasa* [sic]'; a 'blank, or fair sheet on which anything may be written.' 'If the landed gentry do not', he warned, 'write the proper sentiments in their hearts, they will be themselves to blame for any evil which may ensue.'

O'Connell, meanwhile, had demonstrated that he understood the power inherent in Temperance, even if the gentry did not. In December 1840 he was the guest of honour with 1,500 others at a Temperance banquet in Dublin hosted by the Carmelite, John Spratt, who had allied his Temperance society with Mathew's. In a candid mood, O'Connell admitted that his presence at the function was unavoidably political. 'Indeed it would be a great affectation in me', O'Connell conceded, 'if I attempted to conceal what everybody already knows – that I am a kind of walking mass of politics.' 'I must confess that in speaking to you so often I feel like a fish out of water', he went on to lament, 'being restricted, very properly, from any political allusions.' O'Connell still could not resist characterising Irish Temperance in national terms that had clear political consequences. 'It is not merely a few individuals of philosophic minds, or some persons devoted to ascetic virtues, who have come forward', he remarked, 'but we find an entire nation rising against their only vice – abandoning their only excitement to crime and guilt – giving up all that tended to demoralize and debase them as individuals.' Like Mathew, O'Connell had noticed the reluctance of the upper classes to take the pledge, and contrasted their behaviour with his own eagerness to take a lesson from the people.

> After so many of the moral people of Ireland have taken the pledge, it is highly disadvantageous to the gentry – for I'll use no stronger term – that they do not do likewise. (hear, hear) They are too rich, I suppose, to follow the current, and imitate the morals held up for their imitation by public opinion; but it ought to be our duty to make that opinion operate on all … any man who resists public opinion is not a good man – nay, I will go further and say that he is a bad man (cheers) because the fellow who says, 'I don't care for what my neighbour thinks of me', is a blackguard (Loud cheers) And now I'll take my leave of you, assuring you, that I never spent a more delightful evening, unmixed as it was even by politics, but solely for the cause of temperance.

The 'reorganisation' that Mathew had feared on the eve of O'Connell's conversion, in terms of the allegiance of his followers, was well underway before the year was out.

O'Connell's dramatic transformation from a brewer and the defender of the Irish liquor industry into Ireland's foremost teetotaller is much more than a story of cynical political opportunism or a testimony to the hypocrisy inherent in political gamesmanship. The transformation carried with it a great risk and even sacrifice, and O'Connell's confident willingness to brook both is a testimony to his political perceptiveness and to the nature of his relationship with the Irish people, as well as the powerful place that Temperance had come to occupy in that people's self-conception.

THE TIGHTENING OF REPEAL'S GRIP ON TEMPERANCE: NOVEMBER 1840–JANUARY 1843

Over the course of the next two years, O'Connell moved with emboldened confidence to subordinate Temperance to Repeal, both symbolically and practically. Mathew's resistance, although at times spirited, was handicapped not only by his need to remain respectful publicly of O'Connell, but also by his own unwillingness to acknowledge the extent of the danger for fear of providing impetus for a government backlash against his movement. John Francis Maguire's later explanation of Mathew's position in the early 1840s, while it overestimates support for Repeal and underestimates the political content of Temperance's appeal, was nevertheless essentially accurate:

> Father Mathew had, on a hundred different occasions, proclaimed, and most truly, that his society was unsectarian and unpolitical, and that temperance had nothing whatever to do with politics or polemics; though he well knew, at the same time, that nearly nine-tenths of those who had taken the pledge at his hands were Repealers, more or less advanced in their opinions, and that there was another man in Ireland who divided their admiration and affection with himself – and that man was Daniel O'Connell. If Father Mathew were ever so much inclined to interfere with the political belief or action of his followers, he was too prudent to think of carrying his action into practice; for he well knew that however great and deserved was his influence … if he attempted to impose restraint or check upon their free action, they would have burst the bonds of allegiance to his moral leadership.[80]

Although Mathew's correspondence reveals that he was privately very critical of O'Connell's machinations, in public Mathew was unfailingly polite and respectful in his dealings with the Liberator.

If Mathew avoided public criticism of O'Connell and Repeal, he continued to condemn vigorously the direct politicisation of Temperance. His remarks after O'Connell's conversion generally echoed much of what he had said before – that Temperance societies could not become a forum for political debates, and that Temperance parades and bands needed to remain staunchly apolitical – but they increased in frequency and urgency.[81] Mathew's friends could afford to be even more explicit in their public condemnations. Richard Dowden, a Cork Temperance activist, wrote to the *Southern Reporter*, on 16 November 1840, 'to correct a mistake into which some people have fallen, respecting the O'Connell's repeal tea party', referring to a Temperance gathering in Cork that O'Connell had agreed to attend at the request of the 'sober men of Cork'.[82] '*It is not a temperance movement*', Dowden forcefully asserted, adding that, 'Teetotallers may attend in numbers, but the members of those societies refuse peremptorily to mix politics with their proceedings.' John Shiel in Ballyshannon, Co. Donegal, a regular correspondent of Father Mathew's and later the author of an official history of the crusade, was just as vehement a few months later. In a letter published in many Irish newspapers, Shiel recounted Mathew's admonitions during a recent visit to Ballyshannon in January 1841, urging teetotallers to avoid all politics. 'Father Mathew', Shiel added, 'seems to be most anxious to keep teetotallers from entering into any political association; and, I am certain, from having conversed with him, that nothing would give more pain to his benevolent heart than to see the teetotal system turned into a plan for promoting the repeal of the union, or any other doubtful political views.'[83]

From 1841, the increasing reliance of O'Connell's emerging Repeal campaign on mass meetings and public demonstrations placed intense and ultimately irresistible pressure on Mathew and the political 'neutrality' of his teetotallers. The bands Mathew patronised so assiduously as part of a broader plan to replace drinking with more wholesome activities were invaluable auxiliaries in the Repeal cause, and the parades, banquets and communal demonstrations that were such a hallmark of the movement as it was lived by millions of the Irish were also marked increasingly by association with Repeal. 'I suffered much anxiety from the efforts made to induce the temperance bands to play at Repeal meetings', Mathew confessed to a friend in an undated letter about this time, and his further correspondence confirms the fact.[84] Mathew sometimes attempted to downplay the level of involvement, as when he reassured one William West at Wexford that he was 'happy to be able to calm your fears respecting the attendance of our temperance bands at political meetings'.[85] 'The writers of newspaper paragraphs for their own purposes, exaggerate and misinterpret', Mathew noted, adding that 'there are many bands, in Ireland, called temperance bands, which are not under my control.' In any case, he confessed to West, 'many vigilant and religious parents have to lament the disobedience of their children'. At other times, however, Mathew seemed resigned to the situation, as when he noted defensively in an undated letter to John Shiel, 'I feel surprise at your remarks on speeches at Repeal Dinners and the performance of Temperance bands at such parties and at political processions – you must be well aware that I cannot prevent what you complain of'.[86]

Mathew's comments to Shiel represent a realistic appreciation of the degree to which the causes became entangled after 1840. Newspaper editorials and accounts of Repeal meetings and banquets are replete with accounts of the performances of Temperance bands, references to Father Mathew and Temperance, and invocations of the political consequences of the success of the CTAS. A brief inventory of some of the involvement of Temperance repeal activities over a six month period from January 1841 is presented here to give the barest impression of the degree of overlap that became commonplace.

As this table demonstrates, distinctions between repealers and teetotallers became increasingly blurred. All over Ireland, Temperance societies toasted O'Connell and celebrated his membership in the movement as openly as the Liberator himself did. Temperance bands

Table 7.1: Temperance and repeal connections, January–June 1841

DATE	PLACE	EVENT	COMMENTS	SOURCE
10/1/1841	Oranmore	Tea Party	O'Connell toasted.	*FJ* 15/1/1841
14/1/1841	Waterford	Repeal Meeting	O'Connell addresses crowd as 'teetotallers and repealers'.	*FJ* 16/1/1841
?/2/1841	Kilcock	Repeal Dinner	T.M. Ray urges the 5 million teetotallers to yield 2 million repealers.	*FJ* 23/2/1841
8/3/1841	Dublin	Repeal Meeting	Letter from O'Connell; 'The mighty moral temperance movement blesses and secures the peaceable and crimeless demeanor of our patriotic exertions.'	*FJ* 9/3/1841
?/3/1841	Curragh	Repeal Meeting	Strong pro-temperance theme in O'Connell's speech.	*FJ* 11/3/1841
17/3/1841	Galway	Temperance Parade	O'Connell and Bishop Browne lead, O'Connell wearing a silver temperance medal. Three cheers given for O'Connell and Mathew.	*FJ* 21/3/1841
29/3/1841	Dublin	Repeal Meeting	O'Connell discusses his conversion to temperance.	*FJ* 30/3/1841
?/5/1841	Mitchelstown	Tea Party	Bust of O'Connell exhibited with a temperance medal around his neck.	*CTA* 18/5/1841
26/5/1841	Dublin	Repeal Meeting	Held in temperance hall.	*FJ* 28/5/1841
?/5/1841	Dublin	Repeal Meeting	Letter from a teetotaller contributing to Repeal rent read.	*FJ* 31/5/1841
9/6/1841	Dublin	Repeal Meeting	Letter from a Repealer read designating Repeal the 'new Mighty Moral Movement'.	*FJ* 15/6/1841
10/6/1841		Address	Address to 'teetotallers of Ireland' as the country's 'moral regenerators' promised before the next election.	*FJ* 10/6/1841
12/6/1841	Dublin	Repeal Meeting	Letter from a teetotaller Repealer read critical of apathy; 'what are the teetotallers about?'	*FJ* 15/6/1841
14/6/1841	Dublin	Repeal Meeting	O'Connell defends temperance; 'pledges' himself as a candidate in elections.	*FJ* 15/6/1841
20/6/1841	Rathvilly	Election Meeting	O'Connell asks for a show of teetotaller hands.	*FJ* 22/6/1841
22/6/1841	Carlow	Election Meeting	O'Connell claims 10 teetotal bands in attendance; asks for a show of teetotaller hands.	*FJ* 24/6/1841
25/6/1841	Dublin	Election Meeting	O'Connell urges all who vote for him to become teetotallers; calls for lower duty on coffee, tea and sugar.	*FJ* 26/6/1841
26/6/1841	Kilkenny	Election Meeting	O'Connell is processed into town by a parish temperance band.	*FJ* 1/7/1841

paraded O'Connell and other Repeal dignitaries into Irish towns for political meetings. Temperance societies and individual teetotallers contributed to Repeal funds and attended Repeal meetings, often in their capacity as members of the CTAS. The above period was unusual in that it included the general election of 1841 that was a consequence of the collapse of the Whig ministry in June 1841, but then again it was no coincidence that O'Connell used the campaign to test and exploit, as well as expand, his newfound connections with the Temperance movement. In 1841 the strategy backfired, as O'Connell lost his own Dublin seat at least in part because his increasingly vocal support for Temperance kept many of his traditional allies in the liquor trade away from the polls.[87] Still, given the inevitability of the Tory parliamentary majority that O'Connell so dreaded, the Dublin seat was a small price to pay for increased popular credibility as a teetotaller, and for the demonstrable success of teetotal organisation in producing powerful political demonstrations in Carlow, where O'Connell spent most of the election.

By 1842, O'Connell had clearly established a strong link between the Repeal cause as a popular mass movement and the CTAS. In the process, it has been argued, O'Connell's own sense of political possibility had been affected by the zeal, enthusiasm, organisation and order that Irish teetotallers had brought to the Repeal cause. The new political reality of a hostile government made it clear to O'Connell that the time had come to escalate the Repeal campaign. An organised, mobilised, peaceful but defiant Ireland would be in position to extract concessions and might even gain Repeal, either in the event of unrest or rebellion in England, or perhaps as a consequence of some foreign war. Both appeared to be possibilities, as Chartist organisation continued on a large scale in England, while relations between England and France, as well as America, were often tense.[88]

Much of this organisation, however, remained unaccomplished. 'Let every man become a repealer', O'Connell had exhorted on 21 July 1841 in the wake of the Tory victory. 'Do not talk to any man that is not one. Let no woman look at any man that is not a repealer. Every man, woman and child must join our ranks, and become repealers.'[89] Despite some recruiting success in 1841, Repeal's expansion had been 'slow', and O'Connell's primary object for 1842 was to 'widen his appeal'.[90] If many teetotallers had become Repealers, too many others continued to waver, and O'Connell sought yet another dramatic gesture to bring them on board.

That gesture occurred on 28 March 1842, when O'Connell finally achieved what had eluded him for two years – a public, symbolic, joint appearance with Father Mathew. The occasion was the Easter parade at Cork, which attracted 52 Temperance societies from around the southwest with more than 8,000 marchers.[91] O'Connell, uninvited, sent last-minute notice to Father Mathew that he would be present in his official capacity as the Lord Mayor of Dublin, and informed the Repeal Association in Dublin on 25 March that he expected to be 'honoured by the company of that great and good man, Father Mathew', who, he observed archly, 'never interfered in politics in any way', adding that it was nevertheless clear that the 'people of Ireland were too good, too virtuous, too moral to be treated long with contumely and insult'.[92]

Mathew, Maguire vividly recollected, was horrified by the impending visit. If he 'could have adjourned the procession, or got rid of it altogether, he certainly would have done so; but Easter Monday was the day specially devoted to such demonstrations'.[93] The two men walked part of the route together, and O'Connell at one point knelt and received Father Mathew's blessing. As Mathew feared, the importance of O'Connell's participation was missed by no one. The Tory *Dublin Mail* termed the encounter 'an insulting exhibition', while Maguire's *Cork Examiner* gleefully described 'the wild, the joyous shout that rent the very air as the two great men of Ireland, the political and moral emancipators of her people, met together'.[94] The *Freeman's Journal*, for its part, described at great length the encounter between 'Ireland's greatest sons', a 'fine subject for reflection' for 'the philosopher or philanthropist'.[95] 'The objects of both', the editor observed, 'are the same – the amelioration of their native land', adding that the 'mighty moral revolution in which each is engaged, having the same object in view, can never clash or become inconsistent.'

The two men reacted characteristically in the days and weeks that followed the encounter. On 7 April 1842, a distressed Father Mathew, in a public letter to the Quaker Temperance activist Richard Allen, complained of 'insidious efforts designed to give our movement a political colouring'. 'I utterly disclaim any political object', added Mathew, without mentioning O'Connell by name.[96]

O'Connell was not so circumspect. After the Cork parade, he returned to London, and addressed the Saint Patrick's Total Abstinence Society, describing in vivid detail his march with Father Mathew in Cork, whom he gushingly compared to the society's namesake.[97] Back in Dublin on 16 May, O'Connell attended a Dublin Temperance meeting where a Mr Brennan urged the crowd to adopt Repeal medals to go with their Temperance ones, insisting that 'if every man in the country had these two medals about him Ireland would be, and should be, soon an independent and prosperous nation'.[98] At the beginning of July, upon hearing that Father Mathew was scheduled to visit Tralee in Kerry, O'Connell wrote privately to him, and requested a visit to Derrynane, where he 'hoped to receive you'. 'There have been some lapses in this neighbourhood', O'Connell lamented, 'and the effects of *your* presence in bringing back the few who have fallen would be immediate.'[99] 'Let me remind you that you have beneath this roof four young teetotallers', O'Connell added, referring no doubt to his own grandchildren, 'who are as determined in their abstinence as the strongest minded' and 'whose constant demand of me is when will Father Mathew come here.' It is not known how Mathew responded to the note, but he did not visit Derrynane that July, and his speech at Tralee was devoted to expounding on his society's two 'fundamental' rules, 'to abstain from all intoxicating liquors, and to avoid all political and religious controversy'.[100]

Although O'Connell could not compel Mathew's acquiescence in his movement's politicisation, by the end of 1842 he had little need to do so. While the overlap between the two causes was by no means total, enough teetotallers had become ardent repealers that Mathew's objections were becoming more damaging to Temperance than to Repeal. Limerick and Waterford, the centres of Temperance activity, were not coincidentally the best organised for Repeal as well, while in Dublin Father Mathew's strongest supporters were also ardent Repealers.[101] While in Cork Father Mathew could control better the behaviour of his societies, in Dublin he had no such influence.[102] Dublin's most active societies were headed by two popular priests, Andrew O'Connell, the parish priest of St Michael's and St John's, and the Carmelite John Spratt, both of whom had aligned themselves with Mathew but who also had disagreements with him.[103] The national profile of the Dublin press, and the ease with which Repeal themes were introduced into Temperance meetings and vice-versa, concerned Mathew enormously. By the end of 1842, the links were very much in evidence, as when O'Connell attended another meeting of Spratt's society at Harold's Cross in October and gave 'one of his best and happiest speeches on temperance and on the horrors of breaking the pledge'.[104] 'As usual', the correspondent added off-handedly, 'he did not avoid dwelling upon the great national question which agitates the people.'

Mathew's anxieties about the politicisation of Temperance in Dublin manifested themselves in a barrage of complaints to (and about) John Murphy, the superior of the Capuchins in Dublin and, as Mathew viewed it, the man responsible for seeing to it that Dublin's societies avoided politics. 'As you are aware', he wrote Murphy on one occasion, 'of recent attempts, to introduce politics and contention into the

Temperance Society of Dublin, you will not be surprised by my addressing you on this subject.'[105] 'Greater exertions than heretofore are necessary on your part, to counteract the efforts of the individuals to whom I allude.' Mathew did not mention names, but he insisted that 'great injury has been inflicted on our sacred cause – by the divisions, introduced at the very commencement, but all would be now united were it not for individual efforts to the contrary'. 'For the sake of the great moral movement that has accomplished so much good, and that is manifestly blessed by God', Mathew urged Murphy to assume a more active role as 'I have often requested you to take, as my representative.' 'Call one or two public meetings to *give the pledge* before my visit', Mathew suggested, adding that 'this being the proposed object, it will prevent observations from being made.' He also urged Murphy to 'visit several of the temperance halls as often as possible'. On another occasion he urged Murphy to 'support your own dignity and you will soon hold your proper place amongst the teetotallers of Dublin'.[106] Still another letter warned Murphy that 'temperance affairs are not going on well in Dublin'. 'Mr Haughton and his friends', Mathew added, referring to the well-known ardent Repealer and Temperance activist, 'are exerting themselves, and you must not be idle. Call public meetings at Halston Hall and the other rooms. Publish your proceedings in the papers, and do not allow enemies to triumph over us.'[107] To an unnamed correspondent, Mathew alluded to the problems in Dublin by noting that 'the best way to put a stop to the union they have been long endeavouring to form is to withdraw the teetotallers from their meetings – this can only be done by holding frequent meetings ourselves'.[108] 'I have often endeavoured', he lamented, to impress 'the necessity of this mode of acting to Father John Murphy but he withdrew from the agitation except in private – He even strengthened their hands.' He urged another Dublin friend to 'counteract the plans of certain individuals' by visiting Temperance halls himself.[109] 'If you could infuse a portion of your animation into Father Murphy', Mathew pleaded, 'all would soon be well. He allowed their power to get too far ahead. It is not too late to recover what has been allowed to get into their hands.' 'There is no man more kind hearted than Mr Spratt', Mathew admitted, but 'he is led away by artful men.' 'As I do not wish to leave any memorial of my writing on this painful subject', Mathew added revealingly, 'I entreat you to burn my letters – I have committed all yours to the flames.' Unfortunately for Mathew, his own influence in Dublin was slight when compared to O'Connell's, and there was little he could do to keep the Liberator from essentially uniting the Repeal and Temperance movements in Ireland's principal city.

Perhaps the clearest indication of O'Connell's increasing confidence in his influence over Ireland's teetotallers can be found, paradoxically, in his own increasingly relaxed and confident behaviour towards teetotalism. Sometime before the summer of 1842, O'Connell appears to have given up the pledge.[110] His 'pledge-breaking', for obvious reasons, did not become public knowledge, and O'Connell continued to champion the cause, but he seemed more inclined to do so on his own terms. Increasingly, except on those occasions when he addressed Temperance societies, 'Ireland's teetotalling millions' were removed from centre stage to supporting roles in his public speeches on behalf of Repeal. Perhaps even more significantly, he took advantage of the Mathew Testimonial Banquet in Dublin in January 1843 to make a long keynote speech which, while effusive in its praise of the Apostle of Temperance, centred on politics and also afforded the opportunity for some complaints to surface.[111] Father Mathew and his supporters, O'Connell opined, for example, had 'passed too heavy a censure' on the Irish people, whose drunkenness was a consequence of oppression, and, in any case, was no worse than that of the other peoples of Britain.

1843: THE REPEAL YEAR, TEMPERANCE AND THE POPULAR MIND

The notion that Temperance was best understood as the partner of Repeal in the regeneration of Ireland, a reforming and repentant prelude to a penultimate political moment, with Father Mathew preparing the way for Daniel O'Connell, reached its highest expression during 1843, O'Connell's 'Repeal Year'. Not only did the Temperance movement resume centre stage in Repeal rhetoric at 'Monster Meetings' held all over Ireland, but a variety of sources indicate that the connections between the two causes were equally clear to most of the participants at these remarkable demonstrations. 'The mighty moral miracle of five millions of men pledged against intoxicating liquors has come from the hand of God, and I hail it as the precursor of the liberty of Ireland', O'Connell told an enormous crowd of Repealers at Roscommon on 20 August 1843, and much of his audience believed him.[112]

In terms of their pageantry and scale, O'Connell's meetings over the course of the Repeal year resembled nothing so much as Temperance gatherings, a fact that was emphasised by the Temperance bands and sobriety that marked the occasions. The meetings, over 40 of them in the six months between late March and late September, were designed as massive peaceful demonstrations of a totally mobilised population determined to achieve Repeal.[113] The Temperance of the people was a recurring theme for O'Connell at the gatherings, most obviously manifested by renewed and frequent requests for shows of teetotaller hands. 'How many teetotallers have you among you?' O'Connell asked a huge gathering at Sligo on 4 May, who were supposed to have replied with 'loud cries of "we are all teetotallers"'.[114] At the Curragh in Co. Kildare, three days later, O'Connell told a crowd of several hundred thousand that 'he really believed they were teetotallers to a man' and asked everyone who was to raise his hand.[115] A 'myriad' did so, and O'Connell wryly remarked that he had 'conjectured with a miraculous accuracy'. The fact is that O'Connell made effusive references to teetotallers and teetotalism in practically every speech he gave at these massive Repeal gatherings. One foreign observer took particular notice of the electrifying emotional effect that the hand-raising had on the crowd at a meeting at Athlone on 18 June.

> Almost every one amongst the thousands present raised his hand, whilst the joyful cry burst forth 'High! for Father Mathew'. It was a moment of great excitement – a scene calculated to make a great impression; and I would wish if it were possible, that Old England might have beheld those thousands upon thousands of labour-hardened hands raised up, as if making a solemn appeal to heaven.[116]

The same source emphasises the place that many participants in the meetings gave to the Temperance reformation. Venedy shared a journey to one meeting with a 'workman, a teetotaller', who insisted that Temperance was 'the seed, which will yet bear the crop of freedom'.[117] 'He said it to me', Venedy related, 'and I heard it from a hundred others, and saw it on the countenances of a hundred thousand more.' The connection so fascinated Venedy that he made enquiries of another Athlone artisan, who told him that teetotalism 'was constantly on the increase', and that 'he regarded the mission of Father Mathew as one that was divine – that was providential; for it was only with the aid of the teetotallers of Father Mathew that Daniel O'Connell could secure the freedom of Ireland'.[118] In their comments, Venedy's workman and artisan only reiterated what O'Connell and other enthusiastic Repealers had so frequently insisted on over the years – that Temperance and Repeal were of a piece.

Too many of the popular sources make precisely the same point of the Monster meetings, and of Temperance/Repeal connections more generally, for it to have been anything but a very widespread conviction. One reporter, present at a Temperance meeting at Rosslea, Co. Fermanagh in March 1843, described 'mingl[ing] with the crowd' in an attempt 'to overhear the sentiments of the Great Apostle, after passing through the shrewd intellect of an Irish audience'.[119] A dominant theme in the people's own conversations, he discovered, was a firm belief in the utility of Temperance as a weapon against 'a rich oppressor, who would quail before the united determination of the people'. Ballads provide a particularly fertile source for exploring these popular connections, particularly when the fact that singing was a regular pastime in Temperance reading rooms is appreciated. For just this reason, the *Nation*'s first collection of nationalist ballads, published in 1843, was 'especially recommended' to 'the teetotal societies', and included several on Temperance themes.[120] One popular ballad, *The Glorious Repeal Meeting at Tara Hill*, by an anonymous author, began a description of that meeting by emphasising the presence of Temperance bands: 'On Tara Hill the other day,/Five hundred thousand did assemble;/Teetotaller's bands did sweetly play/Our foes for to make tremble.'[121] Another balladeer had a more light-hearted view of Repeal meeting proceedings; he imagined what might have happened if soldiers at the proclaimed meeting at Clontarf in October had been met by a flanking fire 'of cordial and mulled soda-water'.[122] Another ballad was more explicit on the subject, describing the meeting at Tara on 15 August as 'A forest of banners, displayed in their hands,/ One hundred and fifty sweet temperance bands – / The tall harp of Tara reviv'd and played on,/ This day proves to Europe that Erin is won'.[123] Temperance's role was clear: 'By moral influence and temperance aid/ We'll rise like the flower and bloom in the shade – Hear, men of Ultonia, the shout of Repeal/ That floats to the summit, and dives to the vale – / From the high hills of Mourne to sweet Ennishone,/ Hurragh for Repeal, and the nation's our own.'

The same author published another ballad collection in October 1843.[124] *The Star of Repeal* pointed out that 'We have talent, wealth and might/ Bold, to carry on the fight,/ By the shield of moral power, and temperance drums;/ And like Washington we'll stand,/ By our own sweet "Father land,"/ And proclaim that our great Liberator comes'. *The Voice of Erin* praised Father Mathew but also urged all to 'join Repeal, and greet O'Connell,/ Freedom's mirror – Erin's guide'. *Erin's Redemption* made the connection between a politically and morally degraded and regenerated Ireland as clear as any speech by O'Connell. 'By penance dear Erin, redemption is thine;/ O'Connell and Mathew obey heaven's call,/ Like Moses and Aaron, their powers divide,/ Selected to guide you, and triumph o'er Baal.' Another collection of 'Repeal Melodies' contained an ode to the 1828 Clare election entitled

Ireland's Regeneration, which was introduced with a note that 'they were the first men of Ireland who made a vow of Total Abstinence; and nobly did they redeem their pledge: setting a bright example to posterity'.[125]

Tory critics of Temperance could sing as well, of course, and it is no coincidence that a few of their surviving musical satires thrived on delightfully muddled renditions of the rhetoric of Repeal and Temperance.[126] One balladeer offered *St Patrick's Day 1840. Written for the Ribbon Societies of Ireland*, which portrayed Temperance parades as political demonstrations: 'We true sons of Erin can assemble/ And proudly our green and white banners display/ Parade forth in thousands whilst Orangemen tremble/ And dread the approach of St Patrick's Day./Our priests in the van with their crosses before us,/In Dublin can march now as bold as in Rome.' The poem parodied the uses to which Temperance, and its language of degradation and regeneration, was put to by Repealers:

> The Mathewite medal a regeneration
> Is causing from bleak Malin Head to Cape Clear,
> And soon will make Erin become a great nation,
> Relieved from the curse of both whiskey and beer
> Our secrets we then may impart to each other,
> And all be united the cause to maintain;
> Bound closely together each true Ribbon brother
> Will stand by his chieftain with courage elated,
> And under a standard at Rome consecrated,
> Retrieve in one battle the land confiscated
> By Cromwell, who hated St Patrick's Day …
> The Union repeal, and the chains break asunder
> That binds to Great Britain this old Irish nation,
> Which should 'mong the kingdoms of the earth take her station,
> And not, as at present, in deep degradation,
> In vassalage be on St Patrick's Day.[127]

There are other indications besides pro- and anti-Repeal ballads that many understood Temperance as an adjunct to Repeal. Letters to the Repeal Association often mentioned Temperance. When Peter Connolly from Tynagh in Co. Galway sent a small contribution in 1841, for example, he pointed out that Ireland's drunkenness had long provided England an excuse to dominate Ireland, and had rendered Ireland passive.[128] 'We are sure', he insisted, that such 'crimes are at an end' now that the people had been 'delivered' by Father Mathew and O'Connell, 'the Great Regenerators of the age'. A few days later, one Reilly wrote to the Repeal Association from Ballymote, Co. Sligo, that he 'hoped for the final regeneration of my native land' through the Repeal movement, adding that, in his area, '20,000 teetotallers have pledged their sober words' to aid the cause as best they could.[129] Many similar examples could be provided.

The mere mention of Temperance at provincial Repeal gatherings even before 1843 could provoke a spontaneous response. A Mr Jagoe, for instance, addressing a Skibbereen Repeal meeting in September 1840, pointed out that, while 'some seem to think that the repeal of the Union is impossible', Temperance's success proved otherwise.[130] 'Irishmen', Jagoe explained, 'are preparing themselves to be fit to receive their freedom'. Similarly, at Carney in Tipperary in September 1841, the local curate Michael Bugler's remark that the people were 'now blessed with temperance', and would 'adhere to their pledge' provoked long and sustained spontaneous cheering for Father Mathew.[131] When a Mr Sullivan, an old veteran of 1798, told a Repeal gathering at Kilmacow that same month that Father Mathew's presence on that occasion 'would have been fatal to England', he was also met with loud cheers, while a Repeal meeting at Kill the following year, held under a 'triumphal arch' from which was suspended 'a rusty beer gallon without a bottom, a battered quart and noggin, and a broken whiskey glass', concluded with three hearty cheers for Repeal, O'Connell and Father Mathew.[132] Again, examples of such remarks and reactions could be multiplied, but those noted above help to make it clear that strong associations between Repeal and Temperance were a given for many participants in the Repeal movement.

Just how strong those associations could be, and how far Repeal might go in subordinating Temperance, might be best judged from the particularly eloquent words of one anonymous Repealer from Cove, Co. Cork, who sent a contribution to the Repeal Association in September 1840 accompanied by a letter composed in the Temperance rooms of that town. The teetotaller, the author noted,

> has already succeeded in emancipating himself from the degrading vice of intoxication and is determined, with the blessing of God, to use every constitutional means to correct the life-sapping effects of the 'Union'. We, sir, never intended teetotalism as a spell to lure us into the belief that all happiness centres in it. We designed it as a companion meet for patriotism – as a quality worthy of freedom – as a stimulus to our moral exertions – to deck our country with the dignity of a nation.[133]

TEMPERANCE AND REPEAL: CROSS CURRENTS

By 1843, then, significant areas of overlap between Temperance and Repeal had been effected, in terms of leadership, membership, tactics and, finally, rhetoric. In none of these areas, it must be noted, was the overlap total, but taken all together, their cumulative effect was to establish a curious kind of union between the movements. A closer examination of them gives credence to the idea that O'Connell had effectively, in the words of Elizabeth Malcolm, 'captured teetotalism and securely harnessed it to the chariot of Repeal', at least in the sense that, for many, the political logic of Repeal was bound up in its close and complex relationship to Temperance.[134]

There was a great deal of overlap between Temperance and Repeal leadership, on both the national and local levels. Many if not most of Mathew's most vocal and eloquent supporters became ardent repealers. Leaving aside O'Connell, the most influential advocate of Temperance in the country besides Mathew himself, two of the most important were John Francis Maguire and Charles Gavan Duffy. Maguire's crucial role in the CTAS from its earliest days has been examined in detail elsewhere. His importance as the cause's principle propagandist was confirmed when he established the *Cork Total Abstainer* in February 1841, and a cruel (and very public) blow it must have been when, a mere six months later, he renamed his paper the *Cork Examiner*, admitting that his original mandate, under the 'special patronage of the Very Rev. Theobald Mathew' to promote Temperance while steadfastly 'avoiding all discussions, such as party politics or religious controversies', had prevented him from pursuing 'the full realization of Irish liberty' through political action and the promotion of Repeal.[135] For the CTAS, the loss of its only official journal was serious, and for this reason alone Maguire's dual loyalties proved very costly indeed to Father Mathew.

If Mathew had another forceful supporter among the liberal press, it was in Charles Gavan Duffy's *Belfast Vindicator*. Not only was Duffy an influential advocate of Mathew's society, he was a personal friend who took an intense interest in attempts to establish the CTAS as a permanent social institution. Duffy's own plan, proposed after consultation with Mathew at a Temperance banquet in Newry on 29 September 1841, advocated 'Temperance Institutes' as a natural outgrowth of existing reading and meeting rooms which would serve places dedicated to 'improving the morals and cultivating the understanding of the people'. 'There', Duffy suggested, 'the artisan might be taught the principles of mechanics, the farmer the latest improvements in agriculture, and everyone something that would make him a better man and a better citizen.' Duffy's grandiose plan offered a vision for the future that Mathew heartily endorsed at the time. Mathew distributed 30,000 copies of the speech at his own expense, and used the model when he established the 'Cork Temperance Institute' in 1845.[136] Although Duffy continued as an advocate of Temperance after he joined the newly-established *Nation* in October 1842, his energies and talents, like those of Maguire, were increasingly caught up in advocating Repeal and still more radical political action. The *Nation* was certainly pro-Temperance, particularly initially, owing in large part to Duffy's influence, but was also prone to explicit linkages between Temperance and Repeal that Mathew did not approve of.

Other nationally prominent Temperance leaders also became Repealers. John Spratt and James Haughton in Dublin have already been noticed; to this list could be added John O'Connell, Peter Purcell and even, later, William Smith O'Brien. Perhaps even more influential were the Catholic bishops who came to support both movements, including many of the most active advocates of Temperance: Nicholas Foran of Waterford, who was as determined and ardent a Repealer as he had been an advocate of Temperance, Michael Blake of Dromore, Patrick Kennedy of Killaloe, George Browne of Galway, John Cantwell of Meath, Thomas Coen of Clonfert, and James Keating of Ferns.

Leadership overlap on a local level is much more difficult to discover in any great detail, particularly for rural areas, but its importance cannot be overestimated. Members of local Temperance societies could not help but be influenced by the fact that, in many cases, the same men who addressed them on the subject of Temperance at a tea party one day might preside over a Repeal meeting the next. This was often true of the parish clergy, who so often acted as Repeal wardens and as presidents of local Temperance societies. Close examination of newspaper accounts of both movements' gatherings reveals many of these dual loyalties. In Cork, Frank Walsh, Richard Dowden, Thomas Lyons, William Joseph O'Neill Daunt, and of course John Francis Maguire were both teetotallers and repealers. In Waterford, in addition to Foran, men like P.J. Murphy, vice-president of a local Temperance society, William Sullivan, a Repeal warden and the trades association president, Benjamin Morris, Alexander Sherlock, James Delahunty and Nicholas Cantwell, the parish priest of Tramore, spoke on behalf of both causes, sometimes at the same meeting. In Limerick, a few of the prominent men active in both causes included William Leary, mayor for a time and an ardent teetotaller and Repealer, and Patrick Darcy, a curate in Bishop John Ryan's mensal parish of St Michael, as well as John Raleigh, who chaired a local citizens' club and was also president of one of Limerick's Temperance societies. Practically every town in Ireland had its share of local leaders who wholeheartedly endorsed both crusades and whose public lives bore witness to the case argued so eloquently by Daniel O'Connell – that Temperance societies and the Repeal Association were often two sides of the same coin.

What was true of the leaders of both movements was also true of the rank-and-file membership as well. Much of the detail above bears out the degree to which many teetotallers became active Repealers. Both mass movements drew the bulk of their membership from the same Catholic population, and as both movements were more popular among the lower and middle classes than the more well-to-do, and as both at their height involved millions of the people, the overlap in membership was obviously considerable. 'How can it be otherwise', the *Freeman's Journal* had pointed out on 27 March 1841.[137] 'The people are Repealers – the people are Teetotallers; the two bodies must be composed of the same individuals.' The remark was optimistic in 1841, but as the Repeal ranks swelled in 1842 and, more dramatically, in 1843, it became more and more apt. The precise degree of overlap varied from place to place, but by 1843 when a government questionnaire on Repeal was distributed to stipendiary magistrates and county constabulary inspectors, nearly all responses noted that the two causes were very strongly connected in their area.[138]

If the leadership and membership of the CTAS and the Repeal movement overlapped to a substantial degree, it is equally important to note that the intersecting tactics (or, perhaps, public characteristics) of the two social movements did little to prevent their further conflation. Both movements thrived on display, and indeed relied upon their representational power to assert moral authority within the community, and to increase and maintain membership (see Chapter 5). This is particularly evident in their mutual primary reliance on enthusiastic mass meetings and their inescapable corollaries, public dinners. The former events were characterised by the ritualised parading of the leader before enormous crowds, complete with bands, banners, triumphal arches, evergreen boughs, and floats, replete with huzzahs, addresses, replies and speeches. The latter were marked by distinguished guests and public notice of the regrets from equally distinguished absentees, decorous toasts and lengthy responses.[139] In adopting both these events, of course, Repeal and Temperance were partaking of a ritual that was by no means original and one that had, at least in its present extravagant form, been carefully refined by O'Connell over the course of the previous decade or so. If Temperance had been aided in its early days by a well-established tradition of public meetings, however, Repeal benefited from the CTAS's instrumental encouragement of spectacle, particularly in developing strategies of stewardship and crowd management that allowed ever-increasing numbers to meet with a great deal of order. Total, or near total, sobriety was Temperance's original contribution to the ritual, and it quickly became indispensable.[140]

The presence of bands, almost inevitably designated as teetotal bands, despite, as Father Mathew noted, an occasional lack of official affiliation with the CTAS, was another ubiquitous feature of these events. Both movements also made use of membership rolls, parish-based local organisations, reading-rooms, and even outward markers of affiliation – Temperance medals and cards, Repeal caps and cards.[141] Most of the people experienced their connection with Repeal and Temperance in much the same way. They engaged in the same kinds of public preparations and interactions for both purposes, observed identical standards of public comportment at meetings, and, for that matter, followed the progress of both movements simultaneously in the same medium – by reading the newspapers, or, more likely, by having them read to them. Many would have responded as John Irwin, a 'plain, homely looking man, apparently a mechanic, but of shrewd and intelligent countenance' reported having done in October 1841 when he and a group of men were approached by a Chartist agitator named O'Higgins as they sat by a roadside in county Dublin 'engaged in reading the *Weekly Freeman's Journal*'. At a Repeal meeting, Irwin later related that he and his companions had rebuked O'Higgins by insisting that 'we are all Repealers and Teetotallers besides that', and had no time for Chartism.[142] In this sense, those who participated in Repeal and Temperance (and many who did not) had an instinctive understanding of the intimate connection between both causes, precisely because those connections were themselves practical and personal.

Finally, the degree of rhetorical overlap between the two movements was remarkable. Temperance rhetoric has already been examined in terms of its providential, transformative, patriotic and communitarian dimensions. Repeal was presented in much the same way to the Irish people. As with Temperance, Repeal, it was claimed, represented God's will for Ireland, could be relied upon to transform the nation economically and socially, offered the ideal means by which she could achieve her national destiny, and demanded the united efforts of the entire people. Just as importantly, Temperance was an indispensable component of Repeal rhetoric because it provided not only justification for the moral imperative of Irish freedom, but also much of the self-confidence that lent credence to the possibility of Repeal in the first place. If the 'modern miracle' of Temperance had already occurred in Ireland through the leadership of one man and as a consequence of the moral resolution of the people, who could deny the possibility that Repeal might follow? As O'Connell expressed it on one occasion, at a Repeal meeting in Galway in August 1840,

> when you submit to hold yourselves up as such an example to all other peoples on earth – when you voluntarily hasten to resign one of the greatest luxuries of the rich, and one of the greatest comforts of the poor – when you do all this, and when you cannot furnish any example of such sincere self-devotedness among any people that ever lived – when I see such enthusiasm in so good a cause, and that not among a few, but among millions – for already two million have joined Father Mathew – I cannot help expressing my conviction that any just cause in which you are engaged, no matter how difficult or serious, must finally yield before you.[143]

As a consequence, the association between Repeal and Temperance rhetoric was closer than might be assumed through a simple reading of direct references, although such reading reveals extensive overlap. In fact, Repeal rhetoric was believable in 1840–43 in ways that it had not been earlier, precisely because the Temperance revolution, predicated on a similar rhetoric and understanding of Ireland's place in the world, had been so unexpectedly successful.

On another level, furthermore, the connection was still more fundamental. The fact that the rhetoric used to promote the Temperance movement was directly connected to widely held pre-existing myths about Ireland's political and social degradation has already been demonstrated. Repeal partook of precisely the same notions of parallel personal and political degradation, and with Temperance promoted the counter-ideal of national regeneration, not in opposition or as an alternative to the Temperance regeneration but in conjunction with it. Both terms were as common at Repeal meetings as they were at Temperance gatherings. Thus O'Connell could be proclaimed 'Liberator and Regenerator of Your Country' on a banner at a Repeal meeting at Kilcock, Co. Kildare in 1841, while at the same gathering T.M. Ray could indict the Union for producing nothing but 'poverty stalking through the land, and degradation to the dregs (hear)'. 'Poverty', Ray insisted, 'Irishmen might endure, but degradation I hope they will not.'[144] Likewise, early in 1840 the *Waterford Chronicle* could speak of Father Mathew and O'Connell together, one as 'the great moral regenerator – the other the political', and be echoed in the comparison a few months later at a dinner toast in Cork on the day when O'Connell declared himself a teetotaller.[145] Examples of similar rhetoric are legion; nor did O'Connell avoid the subject.[146] In the sense that Temperance and Repeal both made use of the same powerful and pervasive sense of collective degradation, and both proffered a dramatic regeneration rooted in the moral authority of a reformed and organised people, Repeal and Temperance presented a united rhetorical front.

CONSEQUENCES AND CONCLUSIONS

This close association was severely damaging to the Temperance cause. It is useful to think about this damage as occurring on a number of levels simultaneously. To begin with, Mathew's position as the leader of a mighty movement was seriously undermined by the events of 1843, and indeed by O'Connell's repeated public efforts to undercut his authority among the CTAS's disciples. Additionally, the morale of the CTAS's membership, of no small importance in so emotional a crusade, was affected in significant ways by the connection with Repeal. Finally, and most practically, the CTAS's finances, shaky at best, were rendered all the more vulnerable by the financial successes of Repeal in 1842–43, and by the politicisation of the Temperance cause.

The significant inroads that the Repeal movement made in regard to the loyalties of many teetotallers often placed Mathew's disciples in the position of having to ignore much of what the Apostle of Temperance had to say about the proceedings of his own organisation. Many, if by no means all, local branches of the CTAS were, in various ways, actively involved in supporting Repeal. Mathew was compelled to speak out frequently against this, owing in part to his own understanding of Temperance's proper relationship to politics. 'Political feelings', he fretted in an undated letter to James Haughton, 'have raised a wall of separation ... in most parts of Ireland', while '*your own Repeal opinions* have proved injurious in this respect'.[147]

Perhaps even more importantly, Mathew feared the long term consequences to Temperance that too close a relationship to partisan politics was bound to produce. His correspondence and public comments on the subject of Temperance and politics were replete with references to the danger that any close connection, or perception of any such connection, might pose to his movement. He was well aware, he informed one correspondent in 1844, 'how closely the Temperance Society is watched and how glad some people would be to hear a proclamation read against our bands and public meetings'.[148] Mathew's fears were not unreasonable. He had seen political organisations suppressed over the years, and he knew well that oath-bound Irishmen were a red flag to many Tories. Rumours already abounded that Temperance parades were mere excuses for military drilling, and that many teetotallers were enthusiastic 'Ribbon-men'. But Mathew's desire to protect his crusade led him on occasions to attempt to resist widespread popular behaviours in ways that could only have weakened his cause and undermined his position among the teetotallers. His virulent attacks on the much-loved Father Tom Maguire, and his evident reluctance to meet O'Connell, are two obvious examples, but tensions with individual teetotallers or teetotal bands over acceptable political behaviour were a recurring theme, particularly as the Repeal campaign gained strength.

Again, by 1843 these tensions had reached a boiling point. Father Mathew wrote letters to local priests recommending that they lock up band instruments for a time, because their unauthorised use at Repeal meetings would be 'ruinous' to the cause.[149] One band leader in Limerick reacted angrily, demanding Mathew's assistance in liberating a drum, bought with their own money, from their parish priest, in order that they might 'bum it as they please'. The band, their leader vowed, was ready to give up the pledge to a man if their parish priest refused to comply.[150] Other unpleasant incidents also occurred, such as the one at a teetotal soiree on 6 March in Ennis, Co. Clare. With Mathew present, John MacMahon, a curate in the parish of Inch, responded enthusiastically to a toast of O'Connell and launched into a pro-Repeal speech. Mathew, interrupting, angrily admonished MacMahon, noting that 'it would have been better, sir, had you stopped at home'.[151] Each of these encounters, and there must have been many that went unrecorded, no doubt told and retold among the people, weakened Mathew's control over the CTAS, and more importantly, his moral authority among his disciples.

Early in June 1843, Mathew informed his supporters in Ireland that he was 'obliged in consequence of the late domestic calamity, to postpone his visits to the counties of Wexford, Tipperary and Clare'.[152] The domestic calamity alluded to was the death, in May, of his brother Frank, but the fact that Mathew spent July, August and September touring in England indicates that, whatever else was at work, he first and foremost wanted to distance both himself and his movement from Repeal. The announcement of his postponement of all Irish missions came just as the government, responding to the increasing size of O'Connell's 'Monster Meetings', dismissed all magistrates connected with Repeal, placed their troops on alert, and began to fill Ireland with as much of the British army as could be spared from other duties.

Mathew feared any violent confrontation in Ireland would be blamed on his society. Certainly, while in England, he did all he could to dissociate himself from Repeal agitation, making much of a letter containing Peel's sanction of his visit and insisting, somewhat disingenuously, in a speech at Leeds on 10 July, that

> the question of Repeal is never mooted in a temperance room … It is imagined in England that the teetotallers of Ireland, as such, have mixed themselves up with the great agitation that at present prevails in that country. Why, to be sure, when nearly all the population have taken the total abstinence pledge, it is not very likely that 300,000 persons could assemble without a few Teetotallers being amongst them.[153]

Father Mathew not only remained in England for nearly three months, but upon his return he confined himself to Cork and its vicinity for the remainder of the year 'with very rare exceptions'.[154] There is no doubt that this self-imposed period of exile and circumscribed activity did little to advance the cause in Ireland, and Mathew himself later lamented the 'twelve months' during which 'the Repeal agitation damaged our cause'.[155]

If Repeal succeeded both in undermining Mathew's authority and restricting his movements, it must also be remembered that the Repeal campaign ended in a demoralising political failure.[156] The great danger, of course, was that its' failure would weaken the confident communal consensus Temperance depended on. The sudden and humiliating end to the 'Monster Meeting' strategy in October after the proclamation of the Clontarf gathering, and the subsequent arrest and imprisonment of O'Connell, had an extremely negative effect on Temperance, because the two causes had been so intimately linked in the minds of the people. In this sense, it was doubly unfortunate for Mathew that the collapse of Repeal coincided with his own absence from the public stage. Mathew ascribed his veto of plans for a meeting at Trim, Co. Meath early in 1844, for example, not to 'inclination but timidity', although he was 'fully aware of the grand effects that would follow the demonstration you contemplate'.[157] 'Delay a little longer with the hope of having Mr O'Connell liberated and tranquility established', Mathew advised the organiser, and look forward to the day when, 'God willing, we will be able to assemble without apprehension.' With its vital meetings and public gatherings so circumscribed, Temperance lost, at a critical period, not only popular momentum, but also the opportunity to reassert its independence in the minds of most Irish people. By its inactivity in 1843 and especially early 1844, the CTAS failed to distinguish clearly and definitely its own agenda from that of Repeal.

Finally, the Repeal campaign peaked at the same time that the CTAS's financial problems reached a crisis in 1843–44. While the following chapter will examine Mathew's pecuniary difficulties, it is important to note here that Repeal undermined attempts to stabilise the CTAS's finances in several ways. To begin with, Mathew was certainly aware that O'Connell was Ireland's premier fund raiser, and was well aware of the fact that O'Connell's 'Repeal rent', which financed his political organisation, had first claim on the popular purse. 'A general appeal cannot with safety be made until after the 2nd Sunday of Lent, when the O'Connell tribute will be collected', Mathew advised one ally in an undated letter dealing with fund-raising matters.[158] 'It would produce a bad effect', he added, 'to clash with his interest.' Mathew's later charge – that O'Connell had 'caused the failure of the Mathew Testimonial Subscription' in 1843 – is too harsh and ignores other factors such as the studied apathy of the Bishops and his own unwillingness to make public appeals, but nevertheless there was some truth to it.[159] O'Connell's long and heavily charged political remarks at the inaugural meeting of the Mathew appeal in January 1843 also had a chilling effect on subsequent attempts to collect funds from the subscribers it particularly targeted – well-to-do Irish and English landowners. Mathew's remark, however, may have been a reference to a more malevolent incident. In a curious and intriguing undated letter, Mathew directed a supporter to work with Patrick Vincent Fitzpatrick, O'Connell's confidant and financial manager, in collecting for the Mathew subscription. 'Mr Fitzpatrick has intimated his willingness to afford confidentially all the aid in his power to the present appeal, now that the O'Connell tribute for this year has been collected.'[160] Fitzpatrick would, Mathew added, 'name to you the laymen and clergymen in the different parts of Ireland, who would make efficient collectors'. Despite this letter, and another in which Mathew alluded to an as-yet unfulfilled promise by O'Connell to 'call for a simultaneous collection for me on some future Sunday', Ireland's political Liberator appears to have been ultimately unwilling to provide practical assistance in collecting funds for her moral saviour.[161]

Mathew bitterly attributed this recalcitrance to O'Connell's ongoing ties to the Irish liquor trade. As he observed to one supporter, 'very much of the provincial collections and contributions of the rent were distillers, brewers, publicans, and we were sacrificed.'[162] Another undated letter to the same correspondent contained a similar accusation. 'Distillers, brewers and spirit dealers are the best contributors to the Repeal fund', Mathew cynically noted, adding that 'whiskey drinking prevails to an awful degree under the auspices of the greatest agitator in the whole of Ireland.'[163] To yet another, he complained that 'the repeal wardens throughout the country hold their meetings in public houses and many publicans are wardens and hundreds of our faithful teetotallers have *violated* and yielded to the temptation.'[164] Mathew also appears to have believed that his own unwillingness to endorse Repeal had made O'Connell and his Dublin allies reluctant to do much to uphold the CTAS in its hour of need. In retrospect in 1846, he told the publisher Luke Hansard that, had he endorsed Repeal, his 1843 collection would have 'amounted to £30,000'.[165] 'I have very little influence with Mr O'Connell', he curtly explained to the place-seeking Thomas Cooke the same year, 'not having thrown myself and the Temperance Society into his hands'.[166]

If Mathew's stubborn opposition to formalising the link between Temperance and Repeal was successful in preventing their complete union, the achievement was a pyrrhic one. The CTAS paid a very heavy price indeed for its attempt to maintain an independence that eventually meant little in practical terms. There was in fact little that O'Connell could have used in the Temperance movement that he did not in the end obtain. His actions confirmed the assessment of one observer of the Irish political scene who found O'Connell 'sincere on great questions of civil and religious liberty' but 'would wonder at nothing mean, paltry, or roundabout in the mode of his carrying out the details. He is a politician'.[167] Mathew was keenly aware of the consequences of O'Connell's behaviour and actions. In a private letter he insisted that 'the evil that has been caused by the association of our people with drinking repealers is inestimable'.[168] In another, he condemned 'the false idea that Mr O'Connell had the most intimate connection with the total abstinence society – He never pledged himself to the observance of our rules, and never observed them. To obtain the support of the teetotallers he boasted of being a member and even walked in one Procession wearing a medal'.[169] O'Connell had succeeded 'despite my utmost efforts to exclude his agitation from our halls'.

Despite Mathew's manifest bitterness, in all of this there was more at work than mere expediency or manipulation. O'Connell's Repeal campaign was not so much an attempt to 'agitate' in order to affect British policy as it was an ambitious effort to give political form to the CTAS's moral revolution. When Daniel O'Connell became a teetotaller at the hands of the Irish people in the autumn of 1840, it was less an act of political opportunism (although it certainly was that) and more an acknowledgement of the nature of his political influence and a tribute to the newfound centrality of the moral meaning of Temperance to Irish identity. An appreciation of this fact not only reveals how willing O'Connell was, in the right circumstances, to cast off narrow political calculations, but also provides a greater appreciation of the terms in which he understood his own relationship to the Irish people. Repeal represented a break with the political process, and was itself the product of an emergent Irish politics, a politics that had much more to do with Irish than English sensibilities. If the juncture of Temperance and Repeal produced a set of demands that were impossible to accommodate within the context of contemporary British politics, that only demonstrates the degree to which Irish politics were becoming increasingly incompatible with England's.[170]

The connections between Repeal and Temperance, therefore, were much deeper and more complicated than has generally been recognised. On their most obvious level, they were made manifest by the enthusiastic participation of so many Irish men and women in both movements. The effectiveness of Repeal's overtures to millions of Irish teetotallers as such, moreover, was not surprising given the nature of the Temperance movement's own tactics and rhetoric. Enthusiasm for Temperance was stoked by meetings, dinners and, particularly, the parading of Mathew as 'leader', and nurtured in Temperance reading rooms, all rituals that were closely associated with O'Connell and contemporary political behaviour. O'Connell and other Repealers, inspired by the strength of these popular gatherings, had very little work to do to redirect these enthusiasms towards Repeal, particularly after Mathew cautiously retired from the field for a time in 1843. If Mathew and a number of his associates were not Repealers, they nevertheless grounded the CTAS's rhetorical appeal to the masses in powerful collective notions about Ireland's exalted past, degraded present, and potential for a regenerated future. This ground, so well-prepared by generations who had lamented Ireland's bondage, had already produced a rich sentimental harvest for more recent Irish patriots, particularly poets such as Thomas Moore; but no man was better prepared to reap that harvest than Daniel O'Connell.

By becoming for a time the nation's 'first teetotaller' O'Connell, aided and abetted by a willing Liberal press and by many of Mathew's most influential supporters, was uniquely positioned to convince many teetotallers that their moral transformation was best understood as the advent to a still-more significant political moment, one that in fact never came. The Temperance movement never recovered the initiative it had ceded so completely in 1843. This was certainly the result of Repeal preempting its financial consolidation. Even more importantly, however, O'Connell and his supporters had been so successful in entangling the two causes that the CTAS was unable to recover its autonomy after the collapse of the Repeal movement.

CHAPTER EIGHT

Temperance in Decline, 1843–1856

The retreat of the CTAS was an uneven phenomena, and the Temperance movement remained strong in a few areas into the 1850s.[1] This fact has contributed to differences of opinion among historians about the timing and the causes of its decline.[2] The failure of the crusade was ultimately bound up in its relationship to Ireland's dominant political and religious power systems. The Temperance movement, despite its enormous popularity and the support of many in the Catholic Church, was regarded with caution, concern, dismay and even hatred by too many influential churchmen. The Church, therefore, refused to endorse the crusade and, by withholding its vital support, did much to prevent the CTAS from consolidating its accomplishments. Just as importantly, the patriotic dimension of Temperance's appeal had been forged into a political instrument by Daniel O'Connell over the first years of the 1840s, and was used thereafter in service of his bid for the Repeal of the Act of Union. Political upheaval completely halted Temperance's momentum early in 1843, and after that year a very serious decline promptly set in. After Mathew's serious indebtedness was not relieved in 1843 and subsequently became public knowledge over the course of 1844, the CTAS's ability to promote Temperance effectively ended. Most of that organisation's overwhelming popular influence, based as it was on the powerful but also ephemeral quality of moral authority, vanished over the course of 1844–46. During that time, backsliding on a large scale became common in many parts of the country. Before the effects of the famine were ever felt, Temperance was no longer a serious social force in most of Ireland. The death-throes of so enormous an organisation were surprisingly brief, while the awful calamity of the Famine provided a brutal and effective *coup de grâce* for the movement. Finally, when the Irish bishops and Roman authorities successfully blocked Mathew's bid to become the Bishop of Cork in 1847, even Mathew's personal ascendancy as the movement's leader was compromised.

TEMPERANCE IN CRISIS: FINANCES, 1843–1844

In December 1843, Father Mathew, addressing a Cork Temperance gathering, confessed to having a 'heart eaten up by care and solicitude of every kind'.[3] It had, indeed, been a difficult year for Mathew and the CTAS. The request for indulgences for his teetotallers made late in 1842 had met with studied silence from Rome. Only five of the Irish bishops had affixed their signatures to the Mathew testimonial appeal, while O'Connell's political posturing and Repeal rent had done a great deal to ensure that the desperately needed contributions to that fund amounted to little more than a trickle. The Repeal movement, meanwhile, had divided Mathew and his more principled supporters from those who were anxious for political change.

Temperance gatherings were little noticed during the Repeal Year, and most societies appear to have followed Mathew's example of eschewing popular demonstrations and pageantry amidst the nearly revolutionary upheaval. In part because Repeal had reinforced temperate social norms, backsliding had been contained, but as large-scale Repeal meetings came to an end and Daniel O'Connell languished in luxurious confinement in Richmond prison, the CTAS's future became more precarious. As 1844 began, Mathew's profound depression, though exacerbated by family troubles, was really rooted in the evident stagnation of his movement.[4]

Mathew's finances, never in a healthy state, were by early 1844 in fact in actual crisis, culminating in Mathew's public arrest for debt in August 1844, necessitating the awkward transformation of his triumphal testimonial appeal into an urgent relief fund. Mathew's fiscal crisis had preceded his involvement in the Temperance movement; his church in Cork was thousands of pounds in debt and remained unfinished.[5] The Temperance crusade, however, involved Mathew in expenditures of a different order of magnitude, and the movement's very success ensured mushrooming expenses that quickly consumed the resources available to the society. 'The agents in great public movements', Mathew pointed out to one correspondent, 'cannot proceed without money', and the CTAS's expenses were many.[6] Mathew employed up to three secretaries, at the cost of some £200 per year, to cope with his extensive correspondence, to arrange for the printing and distribution of a variety of Temperance literature, to prepare the busy itinerary of visits, to enrol members in Cork while he was travelling, and to distribute cards and medals via parish priests and society presidents all over the country.[7] In addition to the printing and postage costs for all the above, which John Francis Maguire estimated averaged

£8–10 per week between 1839 and 1843, or some £2,000 for the period, the CTAS dispensed literally millions of Temperance medals and at least as many cards.[8] Assuming, conservatively, that some three million medals were distributed, they alone would have cost Father Mathew over £42,000. Additionally, hundreds of silver and a few gold Temperance medals were also required, mostly for the clergy low and high. Maguire reported, for instance, that Mathew's visit to Maynooth in June of 1840 alone had cost the society over £230 in silver medals.[9] Mathew's liberal distribution of charity in every town he visited ensured further considerable expense. Between 1839 and 1843, Mathew conducted some 300 missions, and assuming (very conservatively) that he distributed only £25 at each, he dispensed at least £7,500.[10] The actual figure was probably closer to £10,000. 'He was too liberal in his donations for charitable and other purposes connected with the temperance movement', admitted James McKenna, the CTAS's exasperated secretary, in 1844. 'I often remonstrated with him but in vain.'[11]

Additionally, Mathew was the particular patron of many of Ireland's Temperance bands and a well-known 'soft touch', because he had great difficulty refusing requests for assistance.[12] As he later explained, once the movement was underway 'applications for pecuniary support poured in from all sides, and, unhappily for me, I have not learned to say no, and whilst a shilling remained, I never closed my ears and hands against the cries of the unfortunate'.[13] This improvidence was more than simply a consequence of the Capuchin's compassion.[14] In part, Mathew later admitted, his liberality had stemmed from his anxiety 'to rebut the calumny of being influenced by pecuniary motives', a charge most vigorously raised against him by Archbishop John MacHale of Tuam and Bishop William Higgins of Ardagh.[15] Mathew also realised the money-making propensities that so many associated with his crusade were responsible for much of its appeal among those clerics he relied upon for invitations. 'The success of my mission, morally speaking', he insisted to James Haughton, 'demanded in each locality the utmost I could afford.'[16] In 1844, James McKenna noted that Mathew's response to his demands for increased frugality during his visits was that 'the cause could not progress without this mode of action'.[17]

If Mathew had received anything like the revenue from the sale of medals that was due to him, all might have been well. According to the theory worked out by James McKenna and reluctantly agreed to by Mathew, in the early days of the crusade as the debts mounted, new members were to pay a shilling each to Mathew or to the president of their local society in exchange for their card and medal. This plan was often ignored in practice, as Mathew turned no one away and often gave money to postulants who arrived in Cork penniless, having spent their own on a 'farewell to whiskey'. Once enrolments began to take place in massive numbers outside Cork, the system completely broke down. Here the failure of the presidents of local societies, most of them clergymen, to collect the money due was very widespread and very costly. William Delany, one of the movement's secretaries, complained to Mathew of being forced to settle one obligation of £130 'for a person who has been imposing on you, and for medals not one of which ever passed through my hands, but which you have given to a set of unprincipled priests, who impulsively and without conscience fatten themselves on your labours'.[18] To one correspondent, Mathew confessed that 'it would have been better for me if I had never dispensed either cards or medals – from my position as a clergyman I could not enforce payment from my agents, and I was obliged to pay the manufacturers'.[19] To another, he observed, 'Little do they know of the true state of things who have charged me with making wealth by the sale of medals – If I had been paid for all that were distributed, it would not compensate the pecuniary losses of my family by teetotalism. As for myself I never wished for money but I am anxious to pay my debts, and to be able to continue my efforts to promote the glorious cause – The sale of medals and cards at present would not defray the expenses of my secretary, James McKenna'.[20]

Mathew returned a small donation sent to him by Richard Barry, a curate at Newtownbarry in the diocese of Ferns.[21] News of Mathew's financial difficulties had reached Barry, and he wrote to Mathew confessing that he had given some 20 medals away to the poor of his parish, and had neglected to forward their cost to Cork. Touched by the gesture, Mathew nevertheless observed that 'if you had given one thousand gratis instead of twenty, it was my wish to have the poor supplied in that way'. 'You little know me', Mathew gently chided, 'if you consider me exact in pecuniary arrangements. It pains me to have received so much money from you on a former occasion', Mathew added, bitterly concluding, 'if others had paid me, even half of what they received, I would be able to pay the manufacturers and defray my travelling expenses which is all I ever wished for.' The idea that Father Mathew was wealthy and that the movement was turning a profit, and Mathew's own liberality in distributing cards and medals gratis to those who pleaded poverty, doubtless contributed to the careless attitude of so many of his lieutenants during the crusade's crucial early years, when most of the debt was incurred.

By 1844, Mathew's debts were in the neighbourhood of £7,000.[22] In the preceding years, he had alternated between using the existence of his debts as evidence that he was not profiting by the Temperance movement, and obscuring the degree of his difficulties.[23] During his first visit to Dublin, for example, in April 1840, Mathew defended his sale of medals by explaining that giving them away in the early days of the movement had left him 'embarrassed and in debt'.[24] At a New Year's Day meeting in Cork in 1841, Mathew had ridiculed those who claimed that 'Father Mathew wishes to make money'.[25] There was not enough made from medal sales in Cork to cover the salaries of his secretaries, a 'considerably affected' Mathew insisted, while he was £1,500 poorer because of the crusade and £1,100 in debt at that time to 'Birmingham medal manufactures'. A letter to the editor of the *Freeman's Journal*, published the following 2 February, called attention to Father Mathew's debts and proposed a national subscription to relieve them.[26] In a public letter to his friend Maurice Lenihan, however, published a few weeks later, Mathew 'implored' him 'to prevent a public subscription for me. It is not necessary, and would prove injurious to the temperance cause'.[27]

Some 22 months later, Peter Purcell, in a public letter dated 4 November 1842, proposed a new campaign:

> I have, in conjunction with other gentlemen who entertain the same opinions as myself on this interesting question, thought it most desirable to ascertain the feelings and views of influential people connected with Ireland, as to the propriety and expediency of affording to the country an opportunity of testifying to the merits of the Reverend Mr Mathew … responses indicated such a latent but wide spread enthusiasm to exist on this subject – only waiting for a vent to burst forth – as to leave me without grounds for hesitation in bringing the subject before the country, to be dealt with in a manner commensurate with its importance and utility.[28]

'It would, of course', Purcell added, 'be highly presumptuous of me to express my opinion as to what the testimonial should be, and I have, therefore, never done so; for it will be more agreeable and satisfactory to have that subject discussed when a committee is formed.' But, Purcell assured potentially nervous contributors, 'it will be obvious that no sectarian object can be contemplated – no religious prejudice of any creed or any class invaded – no political sentiment involved or compromised, by erecting one great national testimony of regard to a man who, by raising the people from vice and intemperance to habits of sobriety and industry, has elevated the character of the country, promoted its tranquillity, and laid the foundation for its future prosperity'. 'I can, however, venture to believe', Purcell concluded optimistically, 'I am not too sanguine in supposing that large, ample, and most abundant resources will be forthcoming.'

Since he had derailed a similar proposal some two years earlier, Mathew's financial situation had considerably worsened. Additionally, the dignified style of this new testimonial was much more to his liking. There was no mention of debts, and the proposed mode of proceeding, by way of a public meeting and a host of aristocratic subscribers, was also ideal from his point of view. The indications were that Mathew keenly hoped to use the funds the testimonial might raise to extinguish his debts and finance future missions without having to make any embarrassing revelations. Although he did not participate in any of its public activities, it is quite clear from the attention this (and subsequent) appeals received in his correspondence that Mathew staked all on its successful outcome.

Unfortunately for Mathew, the campaign, which began with such promise at a glittering banquet in Dublin in January 1843, was a disaster. The lack of dates in Father Mathew's correspondence makes it very difficult to sort out all the details, but the broad parameters of the failure are clear enough, and have indeed been carefully examined in earlier works. The committee in Dublin, headed in effect by James Haughton, raised the ire of Father Mathew, initially by contemplating a monument or some use of the funds in lieu of simply supplying Mathew with money to use as he saw fit.[29] As Mathew later explained to an English contributor, 'the Dublin Testimonial Committee' did not 'originally contemplate to afford me pecuniary assistance; but had in view the erection of a monument'.[30] 'In Mr James Haughton I possess unbounded confidence', Mathew added, 'but he is only one and the advocates of a monument might bias his opinion.' 'You do not clearly see how matters are conducted here', Mathew added sadly, 'and do not apprehend the consequences, that appear so manifest to me. We are a divided people, and even on the subject of temperance cannot unite.' Mathew was, in fact, deeply suspicious of the Dublin committee. To another ally he insisted that 'I wish to be free. It would be more in unison with my wishes to be left to struggle unaided with my difficulties than to place the generous subscriptions of a sympathising public at the disposal of a committee'.[31] Mathew was worried that *'my sincere friends may withdraw from it as disquiet has often occurred on such fractious bodies'*. 'Differences of opinion may arise', he noted, 'and the benevolent intentions of my benefactors may be forfeited. The money extended for my relief and the promotion of temperance may be wasted or misapplied.' To yet another confidant, he admitted, 'I am no advocate for, as far as it is called, an enduring monument', but longed for the day when, 'with funds at my command', he 'would be able, with God's assistance, to administer the pledge to every one of the rising generation in Ireland'.[32]

Over the course of 1843, Mathew appears to have been aggravated by the reluctance of the committee to forward a portion of the money already raised to finance his trip to England.[33] The fund-raising itself went very slowly, hindered as much by Mathew's unwillingness to discuss the state of his finances, or how he might apply the money raised, as it was by the lack of urgency on the part of the committee. Mathew received, for instance, a note from W.W. Simpson, a land agent for the wealthy and influential Marquis of Downshire, in February 1843, which contained a direct request from the Marquis for an accounting of the way in which 'the large sum raised by the sale of medals has been applied? Certainly not for Father Mathew's individual benefit; but has no part of it been applied to secular or political purposes?'[34] Mathew waited over six months to reply, and when he did so only curtly 'assure[d] the most noble the Marquis of Downshire, I have not appropriated the produce of the medals to sectarian or political purposes'.[35]

Matters came to an unpleasant head shortly after Mathew's public arrest while administering the pledge at Chapelizod on 18 August 1844 for his delinquency in paying medal manufacturers. Early in October, an English Unitarian Minister, Thomas Hincks, received permission from Mathew to publish the extent of his embarrassment.[36] The wrangling with Haughton intensified as the Dublin Committee decided to assist Mathew immediately, but only in return for an explicit accounting of expenditures and the right to control the dispersal of funds. Haughton duly sent enquiries to Mathew in Cork, explaining in October 1844, to James Webb, a mutual friend, that 'it was the unanimous opinion [of the Testimonial Committee] that some such enquiries must be made and answered before the committee can come before the public and with clean hands recommend the testimonial money in the way that *they all wish it may be applied*'.[37] In a letter written the following day, Webb warned Richard Dowden, a Cork Temperance advocate and a confidant of Mathew's, that Haughton was 'of the opinion that he cannot get over asking for a reply to the letter he wrote for the committee. He thinks that nothing can be done in an expanded way or on a large or effectual scale without an explanation of the way in which the debts were contracted'.[38] 'Indeed', he noted, in an attempt to cushion the blow, 'I think it is plain that people won't know how much to give', adding that 'Mr James Haughton says it will not only be necessary to pay the debts, but to set Father Mathew on his legs so that he can go on independently and without encumbrances – and that some assurances should be given that no such system of expenditures shall be countenanced in future as shall bring on another catastrophe like the present – in the event of the present being got over.'

Mathew was outraged and deeply wounded by the proposed 'interference'. In a letter he sent to Richard Allen in Dublin on 29 October, he indicated he was willing to provide an accounting of his 'pressing debts' (which he estimated to be about £7,000) but nothing further.[39] 'The Mathew Testimonial Committee', he insisted, 'has not placed itself in a position to entitle it to demand from me any details. There are circumstances of a private nature connected with my embarrassments that I could not publish.' 'To put myself into the hands of a committee', he resolved, 'who could control my mission, and treat me as a hireling, is what I do not intend.' To his friend Charles Gavan Duffy, Mathew was even less restrained in his references to Haughton and the committee. He would not, he insisted, deal with 'a self-appointed committee' and 'unfold to them my most private affairs[,] allow them to arrange with my creditors, and receive from them whatever pittance they may deem sufficient to supply my daily wants – To this I will never submit – I would rather take a staff in my hand, and walk to the temperance meetings, and depend for support on the affection of my poor teetotallers'.[40] To John Spratt, Mathew complained of Haughton's unwillingness to furnish small sums to satisfy the pressing claims of creditors and his demands for an accounting of the movement's expenditures. 'It does not show a kind disposition towards me', Mathew pointed out, 'because I presumed to differ from his opinion, to attribute to me motives, and threaten me with influencing against me the Noblemen and others who had espoused my cause.' Haughton, Mathew concluded, 'ought rather have humility enough to doubt his own judgement, and acquiesce in the opinion of him, who was most interested', and 'should not have displayed so much eagerness to take possession of what a generous confiding public intended for me'.[41]

Mathew reacted, not only by complaining, but also by authorising his friends in England to raise money independently. Meanwhile, he formed an alternative committee in Cork, under the control of men he could trust, including current and former mayors William Fagan and Thomas Lyons, as well as John Francis Maguire.[42] In his address marking the establishment of the Cork organisations, Maguire condemned the Dublin committee for allowing Mathew to be arrested for debt, and promised to place any funds raised at his disposal:

> The Cork Committee are in possession of Mr Mathew's entire confidence, and are actuated only by two grand motives – a wish to remove

> Father Mathew from his present difficulties, and an earnest desire to advance and render permanent the Temperance reform. To effect the first object, in the best manner, they wish that all persons who are anxious to subscribe to the present fund, SHOULD FORWARD THEIR SUBSCRIPTIONS DIRECT TO CORK ... Every sum received ... shall be acknowledged in the public prints, and, if received by one or another of the treasurers, immediately handed over to Father Mathew, who, the Committee rightly think, is the ONLY party who should have the disposal of the funds for an object so peculiar and so delicate. Then, as to the surplus, the very large surplus – which they confidently hope may remain after discharging all the pecuniary obligations of Father Mathew, they are also of the opinion that, as no man is so well acquainted with the working of the temperance movement, as its successful leader, *he alone* should be entrusted with the funds placed at his disposal by the gratitude as well as the wisdom of the nation.[43]

His correspondence indicates that Mathew urged many to bypass the Dublin Committee in this way.[44]

All these fund-raising efforts produced very disappointing results. The *Nation* had anticipated a return from the Mathew Testimonial of somewhere between £9,000 and £16,000, insisting that 'at all events, they cannot possibly fall short of it'.[45] A letter from Mathew to a supporter indicated that he expected at least this much from the various appeals.[46] Although the Mathew Testimonial had no difficulties in attracting prominent subscribers, many of them failed actually to send any money.[47] The Testimonial wound up producing a mere £968 after expenses, and by mid-1845 only £8,300 had been raised from both appeals combined, much of it from England.[48] Subsequent, supplementary appeals were even less successful, and there were more urgent calls for charity in Ireland after 1845.[49]

The Mathew appeals failed for a number of reasons. Obviously dissension and disorganisation played some part, but probably the most significant reason was the failure of either committee to organise anything like a popular, broad-based fund-raising drive, such as the Repeal rent campaign or the annual O'Connell tribute, which raised £48,000 and £20,000 respectively in 1843.[50] The tone of the fund-raising efforts on Mathew's behalf was by comparison quite elevated, marked by aristocratic chairmen, 'collectors' from the landed gentry, and elaborate banquets. While it is true that the Dublin Committee, some five months after the campaign had been announced, finally urged the masses to contribute ('the shillings of the poor would, in the aggregate, mount to much more than the pounds of he rich'), little or nothing of a practical nature appears to have been done to organise the appointment of wardens or collectors on the parish level.[51] Mathew himself vacillated between an unwillingness to appear before the poor as a supplicant, and a bitter sense that the Irish people had abandoned him in his hour of need. On the one hand, Mathew observed to Richard Webb sometime shortly after the establishment of the Cork committee that 'there have been too many calls upon the teetotallers, and I do not intend to add to the number', adding that 'my appeal is to the empire at large'. On the other hand, other letters indicate that he expected the rank-and-file teetotallers of Ireland to provide for his relief, and was disappointed by their failure to do so. 'I am justified in saying the teetotallers of Ireland have not upheld me', Mathew complained at one point to James Haughton, 'they have not contributed for my relief half of what I expended for their happiness.'[52]

While Mathew's stubborn unwillingness to appeal directly to the people or to detail his financial particulars certainly played their parts in the failure of the relief efforts, and incompetence or at least a certain lack of imagination can be laid at the feet of many of the organisers, the principal reasons for their failure have already been laid out in previous chapters. There were two non-governmental organisations in Ireland that engaged in successful fund-raising among the Irish people during this period – the Catholic Church, and O'Connell's political machine. The Irish bishops for their part refused to endorse the Mathew testimonial and the Church's efforts on Mathew's behalf were limited to a few kind words and the active cooperation of a handful of priests and bishops. Once the movement fell on hard times, the weak support that Mathew had among so many of the rank-and-file clergy, particularly those drawn to the movement primarily by its money-making potential, quickly melted away.

O'Connell's relationship to the fund-raising campaign was more complex, but ultimately no more helpful. O'Connell had endorsed the testimonial, opening its inaugural meeting with a long speech, and when Mathew's bankruptcy became public knowledge he had written a public letter demanding that Mathew's financial security be ensured. It is clear, however, that Mathew regarded O'Connell's influence with a baleful eye, and strongly suspected him and his allies of seeking to gain greater control of the movement by means of his influence over the Dublin Testimonial Committee. 'Do not commit me to their keeping', Mathew begged John Spratt at one point, referring to O'Connell and his allies' involvement in the Mathew Testimonial.[53] The fact that James Haughton was a close ally of O'Connell's was another difficulty, as his and O'Connell's support for Temperance undercut the testimonial's appeal to upper-class (and generally Tory) supporters in England and Ireland. Additionally, there are strong indications (see

Chapter 7) that O'Connell withheld the kind of organisational and practical assistance that might actually have produced a successful popular Mathew appeal. In this way, O'Connell's influence worked against the appeals, to such a degree that Mathew held O'Connell particularly responsible for their failure.[54]

The Mathew appeals then, while they eventually produced enough money to settle Mathew's most pressing debts, failed to place the movement on a sound financial footing. His inability to shower charity on local communities reduced the incentive for the majority of priests who were not Temperance enthusiasts to invite Mathew to the very parishes that were most in need of his presence. After 1843, Mathew increasingly found himself preaching to a dwindling congregation. Moreover, the financial cloud over his head, and Mathew's resultant intense embarrassment, appeared to have greatly diminished the air of triumph and celebration that was so much a part of early Temperance gatherings. Mathew spent much more of his time in Cork. As the advertisement for one appeal for funds for Mathew described his situation after 1843, Mathew was 'compelled to labour with means grievously restricted, aided by contributions small, occasional and uncertain', while 'resources have frequently failed when most needed'.[55] The CTAS, unable to patronise histories, ballad collections and Temperance bands, print propaganda for the movement, employ secretaries, or distribute medals and cards on any grand scale, had for all intents and purposes ceased to exist. All of this occurred at precisely the moment that public opinion was most distracted by the Repeal campaign. After mid-1843, Temperance in Ireland was upheld mainly by the efforts of scattered and disorganised individual local societies.

TEMPERANCE IN RETREAT: BACKSLIDING, 1844–1846

Not surprisingly, the result of this state of affairs was widespread desertion from the Temperance standard. This desertion, much like Temperance's early growth, was a local phenomenon, in the sense that it appears to have happened very rapidly in some areas, and very slowly in others, influenced basically by the behaviour of local leaders and the willingness of a critical mass of teetotallers to abandon communal insistence on public sobriety. James Maher, the parish priest of Carlow in the diocese of Kildare and Leighlin, had observed this pattern as early as April 1842, noting in a letter to his nephew Paul Cullen in Rome that among his own parishioners the pledge 'has not been broken by one in every hundred', but in a few other areas 'it is said there has been a great falling off'.[56] The local character of Temperance's decline is most apparent, perhaps, from an examination of magistrates' diaries that survive from this period. These sources make it quite clear that while behaviour remained orderly in some areas, there was a widespread increase in public drunkenness and its attendant problems in many parts of Ireland between 1843 and 1845. The experience of Edward Hill, a stipendiary magistrate based in Longford, was typical of many others. Through 1841 and 1842, Hill had taken repeated note of the remarkable quiet that prevailed at public gatherings. He began to notice an increase in public drunkenness and 'rioting' by mid-1843.[57] In June 1843, Hill observed, of the Longford fair, that 'towards evening the people became very riotous and there was more fighting than I have seen for several years.' The following Christmas was very disturbed, and Hill often remarked on problems over the course of 1844. There was 'intoxication at Edgeworthstown market' on 10 March, for example, and the Longford fair in June was marked by 'a great deal of drunkenness and rioting and during the night there were 38 men arrested'. The Longford market and the Ballyleague fair the following August were rife with 'riot and assault', and indeed the Longford market for the rest of the year was notable for 'intoxication and being extremely violent'. In October, Hill concluded, on the basis of these problems and a sudden rise in applications for publican licences, that 'teetotalism is on the decline'.[58]

The decline that many in authority could not ignore did not go unnoticed by Temperance's supporters. In April 1844, for example, a 'Clare Catholic' complained about the clergy in his area, noting, 'Alas!' that 'some of them seem lately to have become luke-warm' in Mathew's service, 'seldom or never speaking to their flocks on the subject, and the natural consequence has been that numbers have deserted the Mathew fold, and been betrayed to return to their former evil practice of intemperance'.[59] When Patrick Fogarty, the parish priest of Lismore in the diocese of Waterford contributed to the Cork Mathew fund in October 1844, he reported, 'I regret exceedingly to observe in many parts of Ireland a very great defection from the Banners of Total Abstinence'.[60] 'A timely remedy', he suggested, 'should be applied to an evil so deeply to be deplored. Nothing can arrest its progress but the more frequent visits of the Apostle of Temperance to those places.' John Francis Maguire agreed with Fogarty, insisting in his address inaugurating the Mathew appeal that 'all men, who know anything of the working of the cause, know it for a fact', during Mathew's visit to England, 'though during his absence many able men were banded together as guardians of the flock' 'still, with all their exertion, their zeal, their labour, their eloquence, their influence and their example, the cause was going back in Cork (cries of "hear, hear")'.[61] Mathew's subsequent inability to tour was even more ominous to Maguire. 'If then, it be so in this city', he wondered, 'with so many rooms and so many influential friends, what must Father Mathew's absence from the country districts occasion?'

In Cork city, early in 1845, meanwhile, the *Constitution* reported a notable increase in public drunkenness, and determined that 'the temperance movement is not looked on, by the lower orders, at least in this city, in the favourable light it had been in former years'.[62] Around June of 1845, Mathew admitted to the Knight of Kerry that there were 'very numerous instances of pledge-breaking' in that part of the country.[63] According to Father Mathew, matters were no better in Clonmel, although he was pleased to discover, in March 1845, that his old school friend Charles Bianconi had been elected mayor. Recently, Mathew complained, 'our glorious cause' had been 'unworthy of the support of the authorities of your town'; now, 'Temperance will flourish in Clonmel – I flatter myself that my hopes will be fully realised and that a stop will be put to the rise of Intemperance in that portion of my much loved Tipperary'.[64] By 1846, the problem of unrepentant and unpunished backsliding was so serious that Mathew, despite his ongoing financial difficulties, sponsored *The Temperance Catechism*, the work of one of his brother priests, which was occasioned by the author's sense that men were 'too easily induced to relapse into old and ruinous habits', while 'the evil contagion of bad example so rapidly scatters itself, that an incessant warfare against the growth of vice is necessary'.[65]

Among the first casualties of the retreat of Temperance were the public demonstrations that had once been such graphic demonstrations of the movement's strength. In 1844, many parades were cancelled because of political tensions; those that were held in succeeding years were often displays of weakness. On Saint Patrick's Day, 1845, in Limerick, for example, the bands and societies marched, but an unheard-of 20 persons were taken up for drunkenness, that same day, while local papers noted ominously that the total for Dublin had been 85.[66] At Nenagh, Co. Tipperary a few months later, a small procession was jeered at and attacked by 'pledge-breakers and habitual drunkards'.[67] At Birr the same year, 'Temperance bands' engaged in a drunken brawl, and broke many of their instruments.[68] The *Dublin Evening Mail* described Saint Patrick's Day demonstrations in 1845 in Dublin with contempt.

> The last dregs of the cup of Teetotalism have been this day run off the public streets. Nothing more ridiculous can be imagined than the

> procession, as it was called, of the ragged remnant of this silly fanaticism. The very bands have forgotten the few tunes they were once supposed to play – and the instrument and the uniforms were in a deplorable state of disrepair … Why Father Spratt chose to make this parade, except to exhibit the inanity and exhaustion of the movement, it were hard to tell.[69]

The *Mail* was hardly a friend to Temperance, but no rebuttal of their description of the event seems to have appeared in the Liberal papers. By the following year, the situation had worsened. One Dublin paper quoted the *Cork Constitution*'s account of the Saint Patrick's Day Temperance parade there as 'a very wretched affair, being principally composed of boys and girls from several monks' schools'.[70] After noting continued increases in public drunkenness in Cork, the Dublin editor conceded that 'we suspect, if the truth were known, the case would be found to be pretty much the same nearer home'. There had been no Temperance parade in Dublin on Saint Patrick's Day, 1846 at all, and the editor went on to wonder 'can it be there has been a desertion from the ranks here also? We very much apprehend that such has been the fact, and if so we are sorry for it'. It was difficult to escape the conclusion that Father Mathew had 'undertaken a task altogether beyond his power to accomplish. It is no easy matter, as the Reverend gentleman must have ere this time discovered, to eradicate a vice so inveterate among the lower orders of the Irish as that of drunkenness'. John Spratt's prompt response, insisting that there would be a parade 'soon enough' and denying that Temperance had 'failed altogether', was far from convincing.[71]

TEMPERANCE OUT OF FAVOUR: THE PRESS, 1843–1845

Evidence describing the state of the Temperance movement from 1844 is very thin largely because the subject faded from the pages of the Irish press over the course of 1843. This fact is obvious to any researcher attempting to follow Father Mathew's movements, let alone find accounts of the meetings, parades, funerals and other public demonstrations that were the lifeblood of the crusade. How remarkable that decline was is evident in the table below, which reports the number and kinds of Temperance stories which appeared in four pro-Temperance Irish newspapers during the same six-week period (1 March to 15 April) from 1840 to 1845.[72]

As the table indicates, there was over a 75 per cent decline (from 88 to 21) in the total number of Temperance stories in these Irish papers

TABLE 8.1: Items relating to Temperance in four Irish newspapers, 1840–1845

YEAR	Issues from 1/3 to 15/4	Editorials	Temperance Events	Letters to the Editor	Other	Total Temperance Stories	Combined Total Stories
1840	**19**/13/13/13	**13**/7/4/1	**3**/16/9/13	**3**/2/0/5	**3**/3/2/6	**22**/28/15/25	88
1841	**20**/13/13/13	**3**/3/2/1	**7**/9/3/4	**2**/0/0/1	**0**/0/1/1	**12**/12/6/7	37
1842	**20**/13/13/13	**3**/3/2/0	**5**/11/1/3	**4**/2/2/1	**0**/0/1/2	**12**/16/6/6	40
1843	**20**/13/13/14	**5**/1/1/1	**9**/6/1/8	**5**/1/0/0	**1**/0/0/0	**20**/8/2/9	39
1844	**20**/13/13/12	**1**/1/0/0	**7**/4/1/1	**0**/0/0/0	**2**/0/0/1	**10**/5/1/2	18
1845	**20**/13/13/13	**0**/1/0/1	**6**/3/2/2	**1**/1/1/0	**2**/0/0/1	**9**/5/3/4	21

KEY: **Figures in Bold** are for the *Southern Reporter.*
Underlined Figures are for the *Limerick Reporter.*
Italicised Figures are for the *Nenagh Guardian.*
Standard Figures are for the *Tipperary Free Press.*

between 1840 and 1845 during this same six-week time frame. The decline appears to have occurred in two stages – after the initial excitement about Temperance wore off after 1840, the number of articles dropped dramatically from 88 to 37. For three years, this figure held fairly constant, but after 1843, it plummeted again. Just as important as this quantitative decline, a qualitative change in press coverage was also discernible. In the early years of the crusade, editorials on Temperance were common, and accounts of meetings and parades were often detailed. These four papers contained 42 editorials on the subject of Temperance during the three years of 1840–42; but only 12 were printed in the three years that followed, with only four of these appearing after 1843. Accounts of meetings and demonstrations, meanwhile, became progressively more perfunctory over the same time period.

This declining interest in the Temperance movement on the part of the press both reflected and contributed to the erosion of enthusiasm for the cause. Mathew, who had carefully courted the press in the movement's early days, was deeply troubled by the trend, and ascribed it to political distractions. 'The Repeal press', he complained, in an undated letter written sometime after 1843 to an English friend, John Russell, 'is hostile or at least indifferent to the progress of temperance.'[73] 'The Liberal papers', he informed the same correspondent in another letter, 'are in such terror of Mr O'Connell that is difficult to induce them to publish anything in favour of temperance.'[74] Late in 1843 or early in 1844, he made much the same criticism to James Haughton.[75] 'The repeal or national papers do not advocate temperance', he insisted, adding that '*the* Nation *never supplies its pages with a single paragraph in favour of our sacred cause.*' On another occasion he admitted to Haughton that he was 'much cast down and dispirited', in part because 'our meetings do not appear in the Cork papers; I am disgusted with their apathy, I have ceased to importune the editors to gain publicity for our proceedings'.[76] 'Teetotalism, like every other virtue, tho' praised, is looked coldly upon', Mathew sadly observed in 1845 to Michael Meehan, a curate in the parish of Kilrush, 'lest people's minds should be diverted from politics. The public press and public patriots have thrown temperance to the dogs – this is a painful subject, and I am afraid to dwell upon it, though my heart is full.'[77]

The evidence indicates that there was much truth in Mathew's complaints. Temperance coverage in the Irish press, at least as measured by these same four papers, was eclipsed by articles on Repeal after 1840, as the table below indicates:

TABLE 8.2: Items relating to repeal in four Irish newspapers, 1840–1845

YEAR	Issues from 1/3 to 15/4	Editorials	Repeal Events	Letters to the Editor	Other	Total Repeal Stories	Combined Total Stories
1840	**19**/13/*13*/13	**5**/1/*2*/0	**2**/2/*0*/1	**3**/2/*2*/0	**1**/0/*0*/6	**11**/5/*4*/7	27
1841	**20**/13/*13*/13	**2**/11/*1*/3	**9**/10/*0*/12	**0**/3/*1*/0	**0**/1/*1*/3	**11**/25/*3*/18	57
1842	**20**/13/*13*/13	**1**/7/*2*/1	**6**/8/*1*/5	**0**/0/*0*/0	**0**/0/*0*/0	**7**/15/*3*/6	31
1843	**20**/13/*13*/14	**6**/19/*9*/8	**26**/36/*3*/25	**4**/4/*2*/3	**0**/2/*0*/1	**36**/51/*14*/36	137
1844	**20**/13/*13*/13	**22**/16/*7*/9	**23**/25/*7*/25	**1**/0/*3*/2	**4**/2/*3*/1	**50**/43/*20*/37	150
1845	**20**/13/*13*/13	**3**/9/*4*/5	**10**/18/*6*/15	**0**/0/*0*/0	**0**/0/*0*/1	**13**/27/*10*/21	71

KEY: **Figures in Bold** are for the *Southern Reporter.*
Underlined Figures are for the *Limerick Reporter.*
Italicised Figures are for the *Nenagh Guardian.*
Standard Figures are for the *Tipperary Free Press.*

As the tables demonstrate, both years of precipitous decline in press coverage of Temperance (1841 and 1844) were marked by increases in the same papers' attention to the Repeal cause.

THE IRISH AND DRINK, 1843–1852

There was not only a great deal of anecdotal evidence of rapidly declining enthusiasm and increased pledge-breaking in many parts of Ireland after 1843, even while the Irish press was accused by Mathew of abandoning the crusade, but the government statistics related to alcohol consumption reinforce the impression that the movement was in decline. The most important indications of rising consumption are provided by the alcohol duty figures for 1842–52.

TABLE 8.3: Proof-gallons[78] of spirit charged with duty in Ireland, 1842–1852, with population and per-capita consumption figures[79]

YEAR	GALLONS	POPULATION	PER CAPITA CONSUMPTION
1842	5,290,650	*8,206,700*	*0.64*
1843	5,546,483	*8,238,375*	*0.67*
1844	6,451,137	*8,269,850*	*0.78*
1845	7,605,196	*8,301,425*	*0.92*
1846	7,952,076	*8,333,000*	*0.95*
1847	6,037,383	*7,976,877*	*0.76*
1848	7,072,933	*7,620,754*	*0.93*
1849	6,973,333	*7,262,631*	*0.96*
1850	7,408,086	*6,908,608*	*1.07*
1851	7,550,518	*6,552,385*	*1.15*
1852	8,208,256	*6,500,000*	*1.26*

The table demonstrates the rise in per capita consumption that occurred after 1842, which increased by nearly 33 per cent between 1843 and 1846, from 0.67 to 0.95 proof-gallons. Figures for 1847–49 represent consumption during famine years, but it is significant to note that the rise from 1843–46 still held steady after a decline in 1847. After the famine, the steady upward trend continued, and if per capita consumption remained below the estimated figure of 1.52 recorded in 1838, it exceeded the rate that had prevailed in the early 1830s, and matched the 1.22 figure attained in 1836. Once again, this figure must be qualified by the fact that a significant percentage of Irish spirit production was illegal, and that legal production figures varied in relation to fluctuations in duty figures. Still, arrests for illicit distillation, an admittedly inexact measure of the prevalence of illegal production, increased even more dramatically than legal production, as the next table indicates.

As Table 8.4 reveals, nearly twice as many were arrested for illicit distillation in 1844 as in 1843, and the 1843 total more than doubled the figure for 1842, the nadir of arrest figures for the 1830s and 1840s. While much of the dramatic rise that occurred in 1843 must have been a response to the dramatic duty increase of March 1843 (from 2s 4d to 3s 8d), the duty decrease of August 1843 (from 3s 8d to 2s 8d) did not bring arrest figures for the middle 1840s back down to anything like the low figures that prevailed in the early years of the decade. Only the onset of famine reduced illicit distillation, which also recovered strongly in the later 1840s and early 1850s. What these statistics, coupled with the anecdotal evidence presented earlier, demonstrate is that the communal consensus that was the essential achievement of the CTAS during

TABLE 8.4: Detections and arrests for illicit distillation in Ireland, 1842–1852, with duty figures[80]

YEAR	NUMBER OF DETECTIONS/ ARRESTS	DUTY PER GALLONS ON IRISH SPIRIT FOR HOME CONSUMPTION
1842	881	2s 8d; from 3/11: 3s 8d
1843	1,895	From 8/1: 2s 8d
1844	3,456	2s 8d
1845	2,574	2s 8d
1846	2,178	2s 8d
1847	1,370	2s 8d
1848	946	2s 8d
1849	2,385	2s 8d
1850	2,654	2s 8d
1851	3,545	2s 8d
1852	3,466	2s 8d

1839–41 broke down over the course of the middle 1840s. By the time the famine arrived in force in 1846–47, Temperance was already in full retreat across most of Ireland.

TEMPERANCE FINALLY ECLIPSED: FAMINE AND EPISCOPAL REJECTION, 1846–1848

The awful advent of the potato famine accelerated Temperance's decline in a number of ways. First and foremost, of course, it ravaged with particular ferocity the same poor who had disproportionately embraced teetotalism. Government relief efforts in poorer areas, inadequate as they may have been, may have had the practical effect of keeping per capita alcohol consumption levels during the famine years surprisingly high. Cash payments to labourers unused to having an income, no matter how small, sometimes resulted in the purchase of alcohol in addition to, or in lieu of, food, and Mathew complained of the close connections between overseers, paymasters and the shebeens that sprang up around public works projects in a letter to Charles Trevelyan on 20 November 1846.[81]

Despite occasional indications of concern about backsliding, Mathew maintained a dogged, unrealistic optimism about his cause through the famine years, placing particular emphasis on the 'rising generation's' role in promoting Temperance. In February 1848 he conceded to the president of an emigrant CTAS branch in Sydney, Australia, that 'we have fallen, it is true on hard times, yet taking Ireland as a whole not one in one hundred has been found base enough to violate his solemn pledge'. 'It will cheer their human hearts', he hoped, of the exiled tee-totallers, 'to hear that our sacred society is still pursuing its forward progress, and has come forth from our later tribulations purified like gold from the furnace. The whole of the rising generation has been enrolled under our spotless banner.'[82]

Mathew also admitted, however, that his own ability to promote Temperance had been severely impaired owing to his extensive involvement in relief efforts. Not only was Mathew actively involved in lobbying the government for increased assistance for Ireland's starving poor, he served on Cork's relief committee and organised a soup kitchen outside the friary in Cove Street.[83] His efforts involved him in further debt that he could ill afford, and whatever recovery his finances had made since 1844 was sacrificed in the process. Furthermore, although Mathew toured on behalf of Temperance through much of 1846, by the end of the year 'every hour' of his time was taken up 'with the care of the perishing poor'.[84] In May 1847, he informed a correspondent that 'the awful state of this city, did not permit me to be absent for a single day, during the last six months', while later in that year he told John Furlong, a curate at New Ross in the diocese of Ferns, that 'the horrors of the famine and latterly of pestilence, have so thickened upon us that I cannot reconcile it with my feelings to leave Cork'.[85] 'As soon as the Lord will be mercifully pleased to grant an alleviation of our suffering', he promised, 'I shall with pleasure renew my exertions in the sacred cause of temperance.' The sufferings of the Irish people, however, were to continue for some time, and Mathew had even more personal difficulties to contend with in the meantime.

In the spring and summer of 1847, the last major opportunity to reinvigorate the failing Temperance movement was also lost. When the Bishop of Cork, John Murphy, died unexpectedly on 1 April, the great question over the next several months in the Irish Church was who would be his successor. As was customary, the senior clergy of Cork met immediately after the obsequies on 5 April and elected Thomas Barry, the parish priest of Bantry, Vicar Capitular to govern the diocese until a new bishop should be appointed. The procedure governing the appointment of bishops in Ireland, in effect since the promulgation of the rescript from Propaganda of 1 June 1829, provided a four-step process, in which the parish priests of the diocese commended three names, or *terns*, to Propaganda, and the bishops of the province then convened and reported to Propaganda on the worthiness of the three candidates on the *terna*. On receiving both the commendation of the clergy and the report of the bishops, the authorities of Propaganda drew up a *Ristretto con Sommario*, or a brief of the case with relevant documents, for the consideration of the cardinals of Propaganda, who would then make their recommendation to the Pope for his authoritative approval.

The parish priests of Cork, therefore, convened immediately after the memorial mass, or 'Month's Mind', for their late bishop on 5 May, with the Archbishop of the province of Cashel, Michael Slattery, presiding. Of the 27 votes cast that day, Father Mathew received 12 votes, as *dignissimus*, or most worthy, while William Delany, the parish priest of Bandon, received 11 as *dignior*, or more worthy, and Thomas Barry, the Vicar Capitular, received two, as *dignus*, or worthy.[86] There were apparently two single votes for other candidates not named to the *terna*. The next day, 6 May, the Bishops of the province of Cashel met in Cork under the presidency of their metropolitan to report to Propaganda on the worthiness of the three candidates. The bishops of Waterford and Kilfenora were unable to attend because of illness. Of the five bishops who did attend, only one, John Ryan, the Bishop of Limerick, voted for Father Mathew, while the other bishops reported for William Delany.

Shortly after the meeting of the bishops, an address was presented to Father Mathew by a large number of the junior clergy, curates and chaplains, as well as a significant number of the regular clergy in Cork, extolling his many virtues, to which he replied. Both the address and the reply were published on 8 May in the *Southern Reporter* to the great consternation of those such as Thomas Barry, who considered such conduct to be a breech of the rescript.[87] Two days later on 10 May, Mathew wrote to Cullen in Rome soliciting his protection in the matter of his promotion for Cork. In this letter, Mathew particularly singled out the Bishop of Killaloe, Patrick Kennedy, who had 'from an infirmity of temper' been transformed from one of his 'warmest patrons' into a hostile critic.[88] 'If the result of the Right Reverend Dr Kennedy's hostility', Mathew explained, 'was only to prevent me from being nominated for the see of Cork, I would not suffer myself to be solicitous for the result. But it is a case of life and death for me and the temperance cause in Ireland.'[89] 'Relying on the deepest interest you have ever taken in me', Mathew concluded, 'I place my reputation with unbounded confidence in your hands.'

What Mathew apparently failed to understand, however, was that Cullen's commitment to him personally and to the CTAS had cooled considerably in recent years. Shortly after Cullen received Mathew's letter, he had occasion to write Archbishop MacHale about another episcopal appointment pending in his province, and in the course of his letter he must have expressed his misgivings about Mathew's candidacy for Cork. MacHale replied on 6 June in no uncertain terms.[90] 'You are perfectly right', he assured Cullen, 'about the other one from the South.' 'The matter', he advised, 'ought to be delayed and by making reference to the other Bishops, the real character of the man, with some heterodox preaching and teaching to boot, would be brought to light.' 'We want at present', he added in conclusion, 'men of a different calibre.'

In the meantime, Thomas Barry, the Vicar Capitular of Cork, wrote to his provincial, the Archbishop of Cashel, Michael Slattery, a long letter on 25 May, in which he expressed misgivings and indignation about the conduct of Mathew and his supporters in their efforts to compromise the procedure in Irish episcopal appointments. Barry explained that Mathew had not only approved the clerical address and had sent Dennis McLeod, his Capuchin confrère and the guardian of the Capuchin house in Cork to Rome to lobby for him, but another address extolling Mathew's virtues had been circulated for signatures among the laity. Barry then requested that Slattery report all this uncanonical behaviour to the authorities in Rome. Slattery immediately forwarded Barry's letter to Cardinal Franzoni, the Prefect of Propaganda, on 27 May, with a covering letter of his own deploring the conduct of Mathew and his friends, and begging the cardinal that the appointment to Cork be made without delay.[91]

By the time Slattery's letter and enclosure arrived in Rome, in fact, the customary *Ristretto con Sommario* had already been set in type for the consideration of the cardinals of Propaganda. It indicated every sign of being hurriedly put together by the authorities. The title page, for example, had for its subject the appointment of a Coadjutor to the Vicar Apostolic of the western district of Scotland, with the handwritten addition of 'and a bishop in Ireland' inserted. Both the *Ristretto* and the *Sommario* sections verged on the perfunctory, except that at the conclusion of the *Ristretto* the observation was made that 'it cannot have escaped the knowledge of your Eminences' that while the Holy See has not wished to interfere on the question of Temperance, the preferred candidate, Father Mathew, who has been its principle prop, would perhaps be someone to construe [this appointment] as a determination in favour of one side in that controversy'.[92] When the cardinals then met in the first week in June, they recommended Delany to the Pope for the see of Cork, for Cullen informed Slattery on 8 June, not only that the recommendation had been made, but also that the intrigues of Mathew's emissary had all been in vain. On 18 June, Cullen again wrote to Slattery assuring him that the Pope had confirmed Delany's appointment and that the requisite bulls for his consecration would soon be despatched.

Shortly after the Pope's authoritative approval of the appointment, Cullen wrote Mathew informing him of the decision. Mathew responded with a long, interesting and revealing letter that is worth quoting at some length because of the insights it allows into the character and personality of this complex man. 'Accept my heartfelt thanks', Mathew replied gratefully on 2 July, 'for your much prized letter, and for the unvarying kindness you have shown me, since I had the honour of your acquaintance.'[93] 'Now that the Very Reverend Dr Delany has been elected to the see of Cork', he explained, turning quickly to the business at hand, 'I am at liberty to express myself with freedom on this subject.'

> I never ambitioned as I mentioned in my former letter ecclesiastical dignities and I do not regret the decision at Rome. Yet I am not insensible to the consequences that are likely to result from my being set aside. The bishops of the province who supported the Very Reverend Dr Delany, have not been silent as to the motives that influenced them.
>
> Two of the Right Reverend prelates, the Bishop of Waterford and Kilfenora, were not in Cork at the election; yet their signatures were affixed to the postulation by the Archbishop, the Most Reverend Dr Slattery. His Grace says I am not as good a theologian as Dr Delany. I have no hesitation in asserting that I am, and I have also made Canon Law, my particular study. My knowledge of, and observance of ecclesiastical discipline, is well known. The clergy of this dioceses can bear witness of my labours as a missionary, though His Grace states my inexperience in this respect as one of his objections. He accuses me of imprudence in management of temporal affairs. I am not it is true a lover of money. I have shut up my gold and silver in the bowels of the poor. I was for a time indebted to the manufacturers of temperance medals. This debt was contracted in consequence of my overconfidence in the priests of Ireland, to whom I sent by their own direction large quantities of those medals, and too many of them made me no return. The generosity of the people of England enabled me to pay all my debts. His Grace also states that my nomination would not be pleasing to the great body of the clergy. The contrary is the fact. In speaking of me, His Grace has not enumerated my labours for three and thirty years for the glory of the great God, the exaltation of the holy Church, and the salvation of souls. His Grace Archbishop Slattery principally objected to my appointment on the grounds that it would be approval by the Holy See of the temperance movement in Ireland. But the setting of me aside by the Holy See is a public disapproval of my exertions in this sacred cause which the Lord has blessed with such wonderful fruits.
>
> I am crushed. I am annihilated by this decision. If I had been aware of the fact that five [sic] of the prelates of the province of Munster had

> signed, or were made to sign in favour of the Very Reverend Dr Delany I should have immediately resigned. Now I am degraded forever, having been *dignissimus* on the list, and set aside.

'If His Holiness', Mathew then proposed in conclusion, referring to the new Pope, Pius IX, 'does not actually condemn me and my labours, it would gratify me exceedingly, if, in the usual form, you would state to His Holiness my position, and the disapprobation heaped upon me by the late decision.' 'I would not presume', he finally assured Cullen, 'to intrude this long and tedious letter upon you, if I had not experienced your friendly protection in a former emergency, when storms of calumny burst over my devoted head. You then obtained for me from His Late Holiness, a mark of his approbation, and I hope you will be equally successful in the painful position in which I am at present placed.'

Two days later Mathew wrote Cullen what was, in effect, a postscript to this long letter.[94] 'Do not for a moment imagine', he reassured Cullen on 4 July, 'that the anxious and tedious letter I addressed to you on the 2nd, was dictated by disappointed ambition. My sole desire is to prevent the votes of the Archbishop and his suffragans, from causing a reaction in the public mind, by producing an impression amongst the people, that the Holy See disapproved of the temperance movement. His Holiness, who is loved and revered by the whole world, will not I confidently hope, permit such a catastrophe.' 'I cannot conceive how the Archbishop', Mathew then remonstrated again, referring to Slattery and the Bishops of Waterford and Kilfenora, 'could conscientiously affix the names of the Right Reverend Doctors Foran and French, who were absent to the postulation he forwarded to Rome. Neither of those prelates ever saw or heard of the Rev. Mr Delany, in whose favour their signatures were placed.' 'I am aware', Mathew further charged, 'that these Right Reverend prelates gave their proxy to the Most Reverend Dr Slattery. The doubt is, whether such a proceeding is right.' Mathew was, he concluded, 'confiding in your friendship to extricate me from the awful effects of the late decision'. Mathew's stock with Cullen, as the latter's correspondence with MacHale earlier that summer revealed, had fallen very low by this point. Mathew received no immediate mark of favour from the Pope, and no response from Cullen.

What indeed is to be made of this melancholy *mélange* of grievances, anxieties, self-justification, special pleading, misinformation and downright *naïveté* revealed in Mathew's letters to Cullen? Mathew's correspondence bears the mark of an ill-considered, ill-informed and frustrated desperation. The Capuchin's emotional reaction and the dramatic language he used to describe his circumstances certainly indicate just how concerned he really was about the state of Temperance in Ireland by mid-1847. There can be no doubt that Mathew read his rejection as the Church's final repudiation of his movement. Less than a week after he appealed to Cullen, Mathew insisted in a letter to Maurice Lenihan that 'the principle motive assigned by the Archbishop in his letter to Rome, for putting me aside was the unwillingness of the Prelates to pronounce in favour of the Temperance movement'.[95] By 23 August, he had determined, he explained to Cardinal Wiseman, that the decision constituted 'a death-blow' for the movement.[96] For Mathew this blow was all the more devastating because it was public, and because it was known to have come at the hands of the Irish bishops.

Slattery, as Mathew suspected, may have been instrumental in setting Mathew aside, but, as correspondence exchanged between Cullen and several bishops from all over Ireland over the course of the summer made clear, the decision to oppose the nomination reflected an episcopal consensus.[97] Time and time again, Mathew had demonstrated a willingness to place the interests of the CTAS ahead of all other considerations, and by 1847 few Irish bishops trusted his sense of proportion. His words and actions in connection with the Cork appointment confirmed their worst suspicions. John MacHale's comments have already been noted. Early in June, before the decision was known, John Cantwell of Meath, who professed to be 'a great admirer of [Mathew] as an apostle of temperance', thought that 'there are few priests in Ireland less fitted for the office in these times', while later that month William Higgins, claiming to speak for all the Tuam bishops, and those of Armagh as well, repeated longstanding concerns about Mathew's 'notorious latitudinarianism' that had 'scandalised even his most ardent former admirers', and insisted that 'his whole pledging career was based on a love of money'.[98] While the failure of Mathew's candidacy probably owed more to perceptions of his undue closeness to Protestants and English Catholics, as well as episcopal divisions over the Queen's Colleges, and attendant desire to avoid potential divisiveness on any other issue, than to any determination on the part of the hierarchy to condemn Temperance, it nevertheless punctuated the degree to which episcopal ranks had closed against the Apostle of Temperance.[99] By 1847, the decline of Mathew's movement and the awful calamity of the Great Famine had virtually extinguished the popular enthusiasm that had previously loomed so large in Mathew's careful treatment at the hands of the Irish bishops. Mathew put as brave a face on things as he could, but his rejection, coinciding as it did with yet another episode of personal financial difficulties and yet another year of crop failure and famine, must have devastated him.

THE END OF THE TEMPERANCE MOVEMENT, 1848–1856

Mathew never returned to sustained labour on behalf of Temperance in Ireland. In the wake of the Famine and his ecclesiastical disappointments, his health was then broken by a stroke in April 1848 which left him paralysed. After a partial recovery, his doctor still reported that 'his gait was every day more enfeebled, and intellectual labour became a struggle'.[100] Mathew left Ireland in July 1849 for a long-promised tour of America, hoping against hope that the Irish movement could struggle on while he found sufficient funds in the United States to revive the cause. In a letter to a friend in Philadelphia, he explained his fund-raising objectives, but warned that 'from illness, and excessive toil, my friends in the states will find in me, but a mere wreck of what I was, and I must throw myself on their kindness and forbearance whilst I shall be amongst them – I fear I will not be able to exert myself as I have hitherto, nor can it be expected that I will address public meetings'.[101] In fact Mathew spent his last active years in America, and despite ill-health, travelled through 25 states and administered the pledge to thousands, usually members of the Irish diaspora community, before his return to Ireland in November 1851, nearly two-and-a-half years after his departure. Mathew's hopes, however, of recovering his financial and physical health were disappointed. His American tour raised little if any money, and he returned to Ireland in very weakened health. A letter to an old friend, a Mrs Rathbone in Liverpool, written on 20 October 1851, immediate to his departure from America, told the sad story. 'I fear to return home', he informed her, 'so much is expected by my creditors. If I had foreseen my illness, I would not have incurred so much debt, which makes me miserable.' In a bitter and sombre tone, he added, 'I imprudently yielded to my feelings, to uphold the teetotallers and feed the hungry during the famine, and I unhappily incurred liabilities which can only be liquidated upon my death'.[102] Mathew was here alluding to the life insurance policy he had been obliged to purchase to reassure his creditors, the premium of which was paid by a government pension of £300 granted to him in 1847. In January 1852, two months after his return from America, at the age of 62, very pale and infirm, Father Mathew retired to his brother's residence at Rathcloheen, Co. Cork. Mathew, venturing only occasional letters to the Cork papers on the subject of Temperance, lived quietly until his death on 8 December 1856, when his creditors were finally satisfied.

In these immediate post-famine years, Temperance did not recover from the rapid and general decline it experienced after 1843. In that sense, Mathew's long absence and his ill-health after his return reflected the state of his movement. The Irish bishops were pleased to ignore the subject completely at the Synod of Thurles in 1850, an indication of how irrelevant the cause had become by that date. By the time John Forbes, a friend of Temperance, made a tour of Ireland in 1852, during which he made generally depressing observations in each town he visited about the often atrophied or non-existent state of local Temperance societies, the cause was but a shell of what it had been.[103] Mathew's movement left something of a legacy, of course, and Temperance lived on in some circles and even in a few communities for years after this date. The movement was also to rise, phoenix-like, in a very different form later in the century under the Jesuit James Cullen and his Pioneers, but Mathew's Mighty Moral Movement, as such, had collapsed between 1843 and 1846.[104] Never again would Temperance as a social movement wield independent power in Irish society and politics.

Conclusion

The CTAS was a popular movement in every sense of the word. Father Mathew was carefully recruited by local Temperance advocates in Cork in April 1838, who were determined from the beginning to launch a national crusade to convert the entire Irish people to the 'doctrine of total abstinence'. The CTAS's advocates appealed to the people's patriotism, and urged a total national reformation in drinking habits as the best way to regenerate the whole Irish nation. Temperance was a means to an end, not an end in itself. As a local organisation, the CTAS developed an aggressive, forceful and distinctive approach to spreading the gospel of Temperance, and adopted procedures and practices designed to encourage and assist in the conversion of large numbers of people. In and around Cork city, unprecedented numbers, including hard drinkers among the poor, embraced the movement, especially in the summer and autumn of 1839. By the time Father Mathew visited Limerick and Waterford respectively in November and December, enthusiasm for the Temperance cause was already widespread in the southwest of Ireland.

Mathew's missions to Limerick and Waterford represented a crucial breakthrough in the development of the CTAS as a popular movement. Unprecedented as spectacles of enthusiasm and conversion, those two meetings brought Mathew into the forefront of the crusade and inaugurated a period of systematic missionary Temperance expansion that continued without pause for the next three years. As a regional mass movement, Temperance caught the imagination of supporters, observers and critics all over the United Kingdom. Inspired by the movement's patriotic rhetorical appeal, the example of so many reformed drunkards, and the spectacle of Temperance meetings, parades, tea parties and demonstrations, hundreds of thousands of Irish men, women, and children rushed to take the pledge.

In the spring and early summer of 1840, Father Mathew visited Dublin and Saint Patrick's College at Maynooth, using these missions as springboards to nationalising the CTAS's appeal and gaining acceptance of his mission among the Irish middle and upper classes and the Catholic clergy. Between 1840 and 1843, Mathew visited much of the country, and succeeded in reducing alcohol consumption by as much as 60 per cent. Even more remarkably, across most of Ireland a forceful Temperance ethic emerged and prevailed on public occasions of all sorts. By 1843, Temperance had become the dominant aspect of Irish public life.

This astonishing accomplishment was promoted and sustained by a powerful rhetorical consensus that was shared by the national and local leaders of the CTAS, most of their official and unofficial allies, and much of the populace who took the pledge in their millions. This rhetoric emphasised the providential, transformative, patriotic and communitarian aspects of the Temperance reformation, and promised, with both moral and political implications for the future of Ireland, nothing short of a revolution; a universal regeneration from a state of national degradation. This rhetorical vision was embraced in a variety of ways by ordinary Irish men and women, who viewed their local Temperance societies as a living part of this transformative process. Societies marched and demonstrated, held tea-parties, dances, dinners and even funerals, organised coffee houses and reading-rooms, subscribed to newspapers and formed bands. Members called each other to account, policed local fairs and patterns, disciplined pledge-breakers, drank cordials together, and intimidated those who refused to participate in the revolution – all with the conscious understanding of being part of a collective moral movement, and all in the service of this vision of a regenerated and transformed Ireland.

This revolution, however, for all its achievements, occupied a precarious position in Irish society. The Catholic Church to which probably 95 per cent of its adherents belonged was ambivalent about the CTAS, a serious problem for a movement whose local leaders were largely drawn from the clergy. The personal ambivalence of many priests and bishops, heightened by Father Mathew's place in the ecclesiastical power structure, the unorthodox nature of Temperance's theology, and the problem of ongoing divisions among the Irish bishops as a body on other issues prevented the Church from fully embracing the Temperance cause. Over time, the Church quietly and carefully withdrew its qualified support for both the CTAS and Father Mathew, though many priests and a few bishops still remained loyal.

The dissatisfaction that Mathew repeatedly expressed on the subject of clerical resistance to Temperance is very revealing, both in terms of his own understanding of the nature of the moral revolution he was leading, and in relation to the eventual disintegration of the crusade itself. Not only did Mathew signify that he was largely dependent on the bishops and his fellow Catholic priests to further the cause, but he was also disappointed by the level of support that he did receive, which was after all considerable. Clearly Mathew viewed his Temperance crusade as ultimately linked with the Church in the critical task of 'regenerating' Ireland. He expected nothing less than a total endorsement of the crusade by virtually all of Ireland's clergy. His sense of frustration at the failure of the clergy as a body to establish that all-important moral consensus in favour of total abstinence of which their people had given them a model was evident, and must be given its proper weight in any assessment of the CTAS's decline.

The political dimension of Temperance's appeal, meanwhile, made the movement a ripe target for co-option by Daniel O'Connell and his Repeal movement. In late 1839, O'Connell recognised in a temperate and reformed Ireland the moral mandate for political structures which promised a new relationship between England and Ireland. Temperance activists, institutions and enthusiasm provided the practical stuff out of which O'Connell's embryonic Repeal movement was formed. Mass Temperance meetings, themselves an escalated adaptation of O'Connellite Emancipation and Anti-tithe assemblies, provided inspiration for and a model of the 'Monster Meetings' of the Repeal Year of 1843, as O'Connell attempted to translate a moral transformation into a political programme. The conjunction of the two causes did serious damage to the CTAS, arresting its forward progress, discrediting its leader, demoralising its followers and crippling its finances.

The difficulties of Temperance after 1843–44 were especially manifest in Mathew's debts, the precipitous decline in popular interest in the proceedings of local societies, and widespread backsliding. While the retreat of the movement was more apparent in some locales than in others, and while Mathew and his more optimistic supporters still hoped for a revival, Temperance's decline after 1843 was every bit as dramatic as its earlier rise had been. By 1845, the Saint Patrick's Day Temperance parade in Ireland's capital city was an embarrassment to all concerned, and by 1846 it had to be cancelled to save what little face remained to the movement. The calamitous advent of the Great Famine in 1846–47 rendered any hope of the revival of the Temperance movement entirely moot, while Mathew's episcopal rejection for the see of Cork in 1847 and his rapidly deteriorating health merely accented the end of the cause.

IMPACT

Despite the collapse of the CTAS as a mass movement, the organisation's impact on Irish society was considerable. Father Mathew succeeded in fracturing the longstanding notion in Ireland that excessive drinking was in keeping with respectable behaviour. While the movement's short-term achievement of widespread total abstinence was unsustainable, and while spirit production figures for the late 1840s and early 1850s indicate that drinking made a strong comeback in Ireland, there is truth in John Francis Maguire's assertion that the crusade permanently 'improved the moral tone of society'.[1] This accomplishment was built upon by later more orthodox Irish Catholic Temperance reformers, who acknowledged their debt to Mathew and the spirit of collective action even when they regarded the CTAS in many ways as a false start in the campaign against drink.[2]

Furthermore, it is just as clear that, for many individuals, the crusade made the difference between life and death. Sober habits, and the meagre savings they allowed for, may have just barely provided for the emigration or subsistence of those relatively few members of the poorer classes who remained faithful to their pledge up until the Famine. John Francis Maguire's assertion, meanwhile, that 'numbers', many of whom no doubt would today be termed alcoholics, were 'rescued and redeemed' from 'misery and degradation' and 'remained faithful to the practice of total abstinence' for life is no doubt true, while Father Mathew himself always made it clear that he believed that 'the redemption of even one soul through temperance' was 'beyond the value of words'.[3] In that sense, the movement was, in its own terms, a success.

SIGNIFICANCE

The deeper historical significance of the crusade, however, lies in other areas. The demise of the Temperance movement, which resulted in large part from the anxious and cautious opposition of the Catholic Church, as well as Daniel O'Connell's merciless political opportunism, is illustrative of the predictable fate of the most extraordinary response to an evident social need in nineteenth century Ireland that was not rooted in existing religious or political power structures. The history of the CTAS provides a wonderful window into the sectarian and political tensions that so marked Ireland in the 1830s and 1840s, while the dynamics of the movement reveal a great deal about class and regional divisions, as well as the power of public opinion and the press in pre-Famine culture.

Seen in this light, the ultimate failure of the Temperance movement as an attempt at universal reform is most instructive. The movement's popular success was never consolidated. In the end, Father Mathew and the CTAS could attract but not lead, direct but not control, and inspire but not sustain, their millions of followers. The temptation is to ascribe a large portion of the blame for this failure to Mathew's flaws as a leader. The Apostle of Temperance was clearly uninterested in the kinds of compromise and cooperation that might have allowed him to establish a permanent place for the CTAS in Irish society. Although he possessed vision, energy, enthusiasm, optimism and charm aplenty, Mathew was also a stubborn moral reformer who lacked the patience, the tact, the humility and, perhaps, the worldly or political sophistication it would have taken to guarantee long-term success. Ironically, had he been less convinced of the righteousness of his cause in all its aspects, Mathew might have done more lasting good. He might have worked to tie his movement more closely to his Church, for example, or done more to defuse tensions surrounding the nature of the pledge by changing its wording or the method of its administration.

It would be unfair, however, to associate the decline of Temperance primarily with Father Mathew's evident shortcomings as a leader. His stubborn rejection of practically every effort to adjust a successful formula indicated that he understood (at least until the advent of Repeal) what many subsequent observers of the Temperance cause have not – that the movement had a life of its own, and that the CTAS's appeal was not primarily a function of his own charisma. Rather, the cause's viability depended on the integrity of its message, the powerful witness of transformed lives, and the overarching sense of a spiritual and national destiny that the CTAS constantly and consciously appealed to. Mathew could embody, embrace and articulate this message; he could be feted, addressed, honored and even loved for its sake; but he believed he was not in a position to change it.

Mathew's influence over the movement, therefore, while significant, was limited. It is quite clear from the few reflective statements he made on the subject that Mathew considered his hands to be tied when it came to shaping the nature of the movement he claimed to have 'found himself at the head of'. In 1842, for example, when Patrick Kenrick, the Bishop of Philadelphia, attempted to gain indulgences for a modified version of Mathew's Temperance societies among Irish immigrants, Mathew informed Tobias Kirby that he was 'overwhelmed with anguish'.[4] 'The results of the great temperance movement are allowed by all to be miraculous and to be the work of God', Mathew explained, 'and no one ought to interfere. Should the plan of Dr Kenrick be approved in Rome, there is an end to teetotalism.'

The Temperance movement's remarkable appeal was founded on the ambitious, visionary and idealistic character of its message of national regeneration. More moderate and limited calls to abandon drink had typically fallen on deaf ears. The CTAS's success bore witness to the determination of the bulk of the Irish Catholic people to regenerate themselves, and hence their nation, through sheer force of moral conviction, and to transcend the evils of poverty, degradation and foreign domination that they and so many others believed had come to define their condition as a community. As the Temperance movement seemed less and less likely to be able to fulfil its promises of total transformation, its hold over the people weakened. As the religious and political history of succeeding years amply demonstrates, however, this urge towards communal transformation in Ireland did not vanish with the collapse of the Temperance cause.

If the CTAS was so fundamentally concerned with self-definition and transforming the Irish sense of collective identity, the importance of the relationship between the Temperance crusade and the development of Irish Catholicism becomes apparent. It is worthwhile, therefore, to consider what the implications of the CTAS's remarkable accomplishments and equally remarkable demise might be for the study of the pre-Famine and post-Famine Catholic Church in Ireland. More particularly, it is vital to assess the proper relationship of the CTAS to the phenomena of the 'devotional revolution', that transformation of the Catholic Church in Ireland over the second half of the nineteenth-century from a disparate and disorganised body into an effective, disciplined and enormously influential institution. Much of the very useful and important debate about the devotional revolution that has taken place within Irish history over the past quarter-century has centred on changing mass attendance rates, the financing and constructing of church infrastructure, and changing numbers of clergy in relation to population.[5] The manifest achievement of Mathew's movement reminds historians not to neglect the powerful role the Irish people played in effecting social change.

The Temperance movement served, in effect, as John the Baptist to the devotional revolution's Christ. The fullest understanding of the devotional revolution requires the appreciation not only of demographic trends, the development of infrastructure, and high Church politics in Ireland and Rome, but also of the collective impact of the manifest enthusiasm and determination of literally millions of Irish men and women. The great success of the Temperance reformation on a popular level must be read in part as a dramatic demonstration of the inability of the pre-Famine Irish Church to meet the spiritual as well as the devotional needs of the Irish people. No sincere pastor who witnessed the Temperance crusade, whether or not he personally supported it, could have ignored the profound religious and moral implications of the success of such a remarkable and radical social movement. Understood in relation to other events of the 1840s, particularly the enormously successful parish mission movement that began in 1842, the extreme enthusiasm for Temperance suggests that the devotional revolution developed as that Church's response to the Irish people's own intense and amply demonstrated longing for spiritual and moral regeneration.

If the religious legacy of the Temperance crusade was bound up in the way that its mission overlapped with the Catholic Church's, its political significance was connected to the way it came to both express and shape popular conceptions of patriotism, even while it pointed towards the enormous importance of communal moral authority in an emergent Irish politics. It was in those senses that the Temperance cause as defined by the CTAS was explicitly political. Daniel O'Connell's striking success in co-opting the Temperance movement depended on his own instinctive appreciation of its true nature – and the deft substitution of an apparently unachievable political goal for a miraculously achieved moral one. An understanding of the development of the CTAS places the Repeal movement of the 1840s in its proper context. O'Connell's political campaign ultimately was not so much an attempt to 'agitate' in order to repeal the Act of Union as it was an ambitious effort to give political form to a moral revolution. For this reason, Repealers could not easily indulge in the practice of political compromise, or speak the language of British politics in order to attract liberal and radical English sympathisers. Repeal represented a radical break with the political process. It can only be understood as an outgrowth of the CTAS's success. If the juncture of Temperance and Repeal produced a set of demands that were impossible to accommodate within the context of contemporary British politics, that only demonstrates the degree to which Irish politics were becoming increasingly incompatible with those of England.

The CTAS's political dimension and its influence on the emerging Irish national consciousness cannot be dissociated from the cause's success as a popular movement. The bottom-up nature of the CTAS's spectacular growth, and the movement's explicit and repeated invocations of patriotism and wounded national pride as recruitment instruments, provide much food for thought. While pride of place in the history of the development of Irish nationalism is typically given to the connections between the Gaelic revival of the later nineteenth century and contemporaneous political developments, some scholars have acknowledged the importance of the pre-Famine period in the development of extra-political, cultural resistance to 'anglicisation', and the early 1840s are recognised as important years for the emergence of popular Irish nationalism.[6] The impact of the Young Ireland movement, via the *Nation* newspaper established in October 1842, was supposed to have built, or begun to have built, both a cultural and a political programme for nationalism out of the popular patriotism and the post-Emancipation political achievements of Daniel O'Connell.

If Irish historiography rightly recognises the importance of the early and middle 1840s as a crucial time for the development and dissemination of nationalist thought in Ireland, it has generally taken popular enthusiasm for those ideas for granted. The traditional understanding of this period is considerably clouded when the nature and popularity of this grass-roots Temperance movement, which both O'Connell and many of the Young Irelanders were seriously involved with, is appreciated. It is therefore of particular significance that the Temperance movement's most dramatic growth occurred while the journalist Charles Gavan Duffy laboured in provincial obscurity, Thomas Davis was a relatively unknown Dublin barrister, and even the great Daniel O'Connell was frustrated and discouraged by his inability to inspire the masses to action. No one who lived through these few years of triumphant Temperance could have ever forgotten them. Many of the important figures in Irish political life for the next several decades, including Duffy and Davis, as well as John Francis Maguire, John O'Connell, William Smith O'Brien and Justin McCarthy, to name but a few, were enthusiastic supporters of the CTAS. These facts suggest a dialogue between political elites and popular patriotic imagination rather than the mere dominance of either a top-down or a bottom-up account of the development of Irish nationalism.[7] The CTAS's success owed much more to the actions of the Irish people in their millions than it did to the manipulations or exhortations of any set of any definable set of 'elites', the vast majority of whom, whatever their ultimate relationship to the CTAS, were utterly confounded by the speed and enthusiasm that marked the movement's expansion.

When the Temperance cause collapsed in the mid-1840s, it left behind not so much a new standard of moral social behaviour, as a new benchmark for the potential of collective action in Ireland. The subsequent history of overt nationalism in Irish political and cultural life, and even the subsequent development of Catholicism in the country, owed much to the intoxicating vision of corporate, communal, patriotic and moral transformation provided, however briefly, by the lingering tangible success of the Temperance cause. The Temperance movement, therefore, has rightful claim to a significant place in the historical understanding of pre- and post-Famine Ireland. If the CTAS itself may be said to have failed, the model of popular involvement it so dramatically provided, and the potential influence of public opinion in its moral dimension that it demonstrated so forcefully, has remained a dominant feature of Irish public life down to the present day.

On a deeper level, the history of the CTAS suggests the beginnings of an explanation for the origins and persistence of this moral dimension in the Irish national imagination.[8] The Temperance cause's accomplishments are incontrovertible evidence of a widespread popular hunger – a nearly universal collective anxiety – for a counter-story to the already (by 1840) well-developed myth of Ireland's degeneration into a degraded colonial slave-state. This myth was clearly widely felt on the personal, as well as the political level. Temperance rhetoric comfortably moved back and forth between Ireland's national degradation and the personal degradation of the individual Irish drunkard, and made much of a supposedly universal perception of outsiders, particularly of the English, that the Irish were a fallen and drunken race. Temperance rhetoric was made of the same stuff, and served as an expression of the same very real collective sentiments that came to define the emerging nationalist project in Ireland, and made it, at its core, such a deeply moral undertaking in the eyes of its proponents. In that sense, the Repeal and Temperance movements were rooted in precisely the same dynamic in the development of Irish nationalism and Irish identity. Both thrived on the parallel sense of personal degradation, and the humiliating condition of Ireland as a disparaged national entity. The relationship between degradation and regeneration was at the centre of the Temperance cause, and also lived at the centre of the nationalist project in Ireland, before and long after the 1840s.

POSTSCRIPT

The introduction to this book indicated that a close study of the CTAS should be linked to broader debates about the nature of national identity, and might be expected to shed some light on both the contested 'colonial' status of Ireland, and the peculiar problems of the evolution of national identity in colonial circumstances. It may of course be, as Eric Hobsbawm has somewhat dismissively suggested, that the evolution of nationalism in its Irish context was 'anomalous'.[9] It is certainly possible that Irish nationalism is particularly parochial – *sui generis*, however interesting it may be to a few narrow specialists.[10] The peculiarity of Irish national development, involved as it may have been with geographical, linguistic and cultural circumstances, at bottom derived from the tensions produced by Ireland's historical status, by the beginning of the nineteenth century, as a colonial 'halfway house'. Ireland was, by then, Britain's oldest colony with a long history of oppression and rebellion, but was at the same time ever more closely integrated into British economic, political, social and imperial structures. In Ireland, the resultant mixture of identification and resentment complicated the development of nationalism, but also rendered it especially interesting for comparative purposes. In particular, it is likely that a more widely appreciated understanding of the development of Irish nationalism might bring a broad range of scholars closer to bridging the wide gulf that currently exists between accounts of nationalism that make sense in nineteenth century Europe, and other understandings of that powerful force that are rooted in colonial circumstances. It is incumbent upon historians of Ireland, who appreciate that nation's peculiar relationship to Britain and the British Empire, to Europe and to the Atlantic world, to explore and explain the 'anomaly' of Irish national development, for the sake of creating an Irish history that can be better understood and appreciated from without as well as from within.

Notes

INTRODUCTION

1. Lawrence J. McCaffrey's *Daniel O'Connell and the Repeal Year* (Knoxville, KY: University of Kentucky Press, 1966), pp. 21–3, provides a thoughful exception.
2. George Cornell Bretherton, 'The Irish Temperance Movement, 1833–1847' (PhD Dissertation, Columbia University, 1978); 'Against the Flowing Tide' in Susanna Barrows and Robin Room (eds), *Drinking: Behavior and Belief in Modern History* (Berkeley: University of California Press, 1991), pp. 147–62.
3. John Quinn, 'Father Mathew's Temperance Crusade in Ireland, 1838–1856' (PhD Dissertation, Notre Dame University, 1992); Quinn, 'The "Vagabond Friar": Father Mathew's Difficulties with the Irish Bishops, 1840–1856', *Catholic Historical Review* 8 (October 1992), pp. 542–56.
4. Theobald Mathew's father, James, was steward of the Mathew family estate at Thomastown in Tipperary, where Theobald was born in 1790. The Mathews were landed gentry of Welsh origin, and had come to Ireland in the seventeenth century, married well, and converted to Protestantism. The family fortunes reached their height in 1797 when Francis Mathew was made an Earl. James Mathew was part of a cadet branch and was probably a Catholic (Theobald's mother, Anne Whyte, certainly was), and young Theobald was the favourite of the heiress of the Mathew estate, Lady Elizabeth Mathew. It was she who paid for Theobald's education. (Elizabeth Malcolm, *Ireland Sober, Ireland Free: Drink and Temperance in 19th Century Ireland* [Syracuse: Syracuse University Press, 1986], pp. 101–4; Colm Kerrigan, *Father Mathew and the Irish Temperance Movement, 1838–1849* [Cork: University Press, 1992], pp. 38–9.)
5. Mathew was ordained a Capuchin priest in 1814, and served briefly in Kilkenny before being assigned to Cork the same year. In Cork, prior to 1838, Mathew was best known as the founder of a charitable organisation known as the Josephians, who offered practical assistance to the poor, and as the founder of St Joseph's Cemetery which provided for the interment of poor Catholics in Cork.
6. See, for example, David Vincent, *Bread, Knowledge and Freedom: A Study of Nineteenth-Century Working Class Autobiography* (Cambridge: Methuen & Co., 1981), esp. pp. 170–1 and 183, as well as Brian Harrison, *Drink and the Victorians* (London: Faber and Faber, 1971), for pre-Mathewite Temperance in Britain and its emphasis on self-improvement. See also Lillian Shiman, *Crusade Against Drink in Victorian England* (London: Macmillan, 1988), pp. 29–33.
7. See, for example, Mathew's speech in Dublin reported in the *Freeman's Journal*, 30 September 1840, or his comments at a Temperance banquet in Limerick, *Cork Examiner*, 18 October 1841.
8. See Joseph Gusfield, 'Benevolent Repression: Popular Culture, Social Structure, and the Control of Drinking' in Susanna Barrows and Robin Room (eds), *Drinking Behavior and Belief in Modern History* for a summary of scholarship on 'public order' concerns and the Weberian rationalisation of leisure as it bears on alcohol/temperance issues, esp. pp. 403–13. In addition to Foucault generally, especially in *The Birth of the Clinic* (New York: Pantheon Books, 1973), see Harry Gene Levine, 'The Discovery of Addiction: Changing Conceptions of Habitual Drunkenness in America', *Journal of Studies on Alcohol* 39 (1978),

pp. 143–74 for seminal work on temperance as a harbinger of increasing social control. See also Elizabeth Malcolm, 'The Rise of the Pub: A Study in the Disciplining of Popular Culture', in J.S. Donnelly and Kerby A. Miller (eds), *Irish Popular Culture 1650–1850* (Dublin: Irish Academic Press, 1998).

9. The precise nature of Ireland's relationship to Britain, and her status as a 'colony' is of course fiercely contested. For some interesting recent views of the subject, see S.J. Connolly, 'Eighteenth Century Ireland – Colony or Ancien Regime?' in *The Making of Modern Irish History* (London: Routledge, 1996), pp. 15–33; Crawford Young, *The African Colonial State in Comparative Perspective* (New Haven, CT: Yale University Press, 1994), pp. 46–8; Declan Kiberd, *Inventing Ireland: The Literature of the Modern Nation* (Cambridge, MA: Harvard University Press, 1995), pp. 1–8. Stephen Howe's *Ireland and Empire* (Oxford: Oxford University Press, 2000) provides the best overview of the historiographical debate.

CHAPTER 1

1. See Colm Kerrigan, *Father Mathew and the Irish Temperance Movement, 1838–1849* (Cork: University Press, 1992), pp. 64–5; 132–52, 175–6, 182. Kerrigan denies that Temperance had 'any kind of formulated ideology'; George Cornell Bretherton, 'The Irish Temperance Movement, 1833–1847' (PhD Dissertation, Columbia University, 1978) also emphasises the necessity of Catholic clerical leadership in general, pp. 214–16, 229–30, 257; Elizabeth Malcolm, *Ireland Sober, Ireland Free: Drink and Temperance in 19th Century Ireland* (Syracuse: Syracuse University Press, 1986), pp. 106–7, 121–2, also points out the materialistic appeal of the Temperance message; John Quinn, 'Father Mathew's Temperance Crusade in Ireland, 1838–1856' (PhD Dissertation, Notre Dame University, 1992), pp. 2–3, 134–5.
2. See Bretherton, 'The Irish Temperance Movement', generally for an exhaustive and informative look at Temperance in Ireland before 1839. See also Malcolm, *Ireland Sober*, for a more digested version.
3 See Richard Stivers, *A Hair of the Dog: Irish Drinking and American Stereotype* (Philadelphia: University Park Press, 1982), pp. 179–80.
4. Thomas Newenham, *A Statistical and Historical Inquiry into the Progress and Magnitude of the Population of Ireland* (London: 1805), pp. 232–3.
5. Mathew to Tobias Kirby, 11 February 1842, Kirby Correspondence, Irish College, Rome. (From Emmet Larkin's transcription of the Correspondence, University of Chicago. Hereafter, K.)
6. Susanna Barrows and Robin Room (eds), *Drinking: Behavior and Belief in Modern History* (Berkeley: University of California Press, 1991), p. 7.
7. See John Dunlop, *The Philosophy of Artificial and Compulsory Drinking Usage in Great Britain and Ireland* (London: Houlston and Stoneman, 1839). See also Brian Harrison, *Drink and the Victorians* (London: 1971), pp. 17, 94–5; Norman Longmate, *The Waterdrinkers: A History of Temperance* (London: Hamish Hamilton, 1968), p. 15; Stivers, *A Hair of the Dog*, pp. 15–33; Elizabeth Malcolm, *Ireland Sober*, pp. 49–50.
8. The scholarship on Temperance is vast. In addition to Harrison, Malcolm and Longmate, see Lillian Shiman for a fine appreciation of the movement in Britain (*Crusade Against Drink in Victorian England* [London: Macmillan, 1988]); James S. Roberts, *Drink, Temperance, and the Working Class in Nineteenth-Century Germany* (Boston: Allen and Unwin, 1984), pp. 19–21. See also Joel Bernard, 'From Fasting to Abstinence: The Origins of the American Temperance Movement', in Barrows and Room (eds), *Drinking*, p. 337. Of course, attempts to control drinking and alcohol use did not begin with the efforts of nineteenth century advocates of voluntary temperance associations.
9. For connections between Temperance and Evangelicalism, see Longmate, *The Waterdrinkers*, Harrison, *Drink and the Victorians*, pp. 93–4, and James David Hunter, *Evangelicalism: The Coming Generation* (Chicago: University of Chicago Press, 1987), p. 119.
10. This is something of a contrast with English and Scottish temperance of the same period, which was also strongest in cities, particularly among dissenting working men – see Harrison, *Drink and the Victorians*. 'Total Abstainers' were more successful than 'Moderation Men' in England; in Ireland their progress was more limited. See Longmate,

The Waterdrinkers, pp. 53–63 and Malcolm, *Ireland Sober*, p. 99.
11. Malcolm, *Ireland Sober*, pp. 56–100.
12. There were a few outspoken advocates of Temperance among the priesthood, notably Henry Young in Dublin, John Foley in Yougal, Co. Cork, and Patrick Fahy in Galway. Among the bishops, only James Doyle, bishop of Kildare and Leighlin, supported early efforts. See Bretherton, *The Irish Temperance Movement*, p. 211 and Malcolm, *Ireland Sober*, pp. 68–9.
13. Doyle to G.W. Carr of the Hibernian Temperance Society, 29 December 1829, cited in Malcolm, *Ireland Sober*, p. 84.
14. John Francis Maguire, *Father Mathew: A Biography* (London: Longman, Roberts and Green, 1863), p. 66.
15. *Cork Examiner* (*CE*), 28 August 1844. Mathew and Martin were both guardians of Cork's workhouse.
16. First-hand accounts of the CTAS's early days are in McKenna's manuscript history of the Temperance crusade, located in the Capuchin Archives in Church Street, Dublin (McKenna MSS) and the *Cork Examiner* of 12 September and 13 September 1890 (The Mathew Centennial). This issue included an interview with O'Connell, still living at that time. There are problems with both these sources. McKenna's is the unabashedly propagandistic work of a man who must be regarded as a colourful enthusiast, if not a fanatic (see Maguire, *Father Mathew*, p. 113, who knew him well); while O'Connell's is the retrospective account of a man more than half century after the historic events described.
17. Maguire, *Father Mathew*, p. 75.
18. Ibid., pp. 73–5. See also Bretherton, *The Irish Temperance Movement*, for information on Lyons.
19. Theobald Mathew to Richard Dowden, 9 March 1838, Day Papers #47 Class D. (CAI).
20. John F. Maguire, *The Doctrine of Total Abstinence Justified* (Cork: William Morten, 1838), p. 1.
21. For an interesting appreciation of the Cork middle class during this period, see John O'Brien, 'The Catholic Middle Classes in Pre-Famine Cork' (O'Donnell Lecture) (Cork: National University of Ireland, 1979).
22. See Kerrigan, *Father Mathew*, pp. 34–5; also Malcolm, *Ireland Sober*, pp. 90–5; the most comprehensive treatment of pre-Mathewite Temperance in Ireland is still George Bretherton's 'The Irish Temperance Movement, 1833–1847', esp. chapters IV and V for the trend towards Catholicisation.
23. M to Richard Dowden, 9 March 1838, Day Papers #47 Class D. (CAC). This was probably a reference to John Brown, a curate in the Bishop of Cork's mensal parish.
24. *Cork Standard* (*CS*), 11 April 1838. Perhaps the other two priests referred to were the other Capuchins in Cork, who did in fact assist Father Mathew in subsequent months.
25. Malcolm, *Ireland Sober*, p. 106.
26. See John O'Connell's interview in the *CE*.
27. Mathew to Kirby, 11 February 1842, Kirby Correspondence (hereafter K).
28. Mathew to Kirby, 25 February 1842 (K).
29. *Freeman's Journal* (*FJ*), 5 January 1841.
30. Maguire, *Father Mathew*, pp. 108–9. Maguire quotes the entire speech, but his biography is by no means always accurate. No other copy survives, but Maguire was working from various sources no longer extant. As he doubtless attended the meeting, he may have been quoting from memory. The speech he quotes is clearly a thoughtful and carefully considered piece, and makes mention of local activists who were by no means prominent in the crusade's later years. Some of the turns of phrase, additionally, recur in later speeches and correspondence of Mathew. The occasion would have been considered to be a very important one by Maguire, Martin, McKenna and other activists, so it is not surprising that the speech would have been preserved in some form. The text is probably authentic.
31. McKenna MSS, pp. 95–6.
32. Maguire, *Father Mathew*, p. 107.
33. Ibid., p. 112.
34. *CS*, 20 April 1838. *Irish Catholic Directory* for 1841 identifies Reardon. See *Philanthropist*

and National Temperance Advertiser (*PNTA*), 5 May 1838, for details of third meeting. Mathew is not mentioned.
35. *CS*, 11 June 1838.
36. *Southern Reporter* (*SR*), 26 January 1839; *Dublin Weekly Herald* (*DWH*), 30 March 1839.
37. *CE*, 12 September and 13 September 1890.
38. For example, McKenna's visit to Dunmanway, *CS*, 17 August 1838.
39. The *Cork Standard* of 9 March 1838, urged that a subscription fund be established to bring Hocking to Cork. When he arrived three months later, he was introduced and feted by leading members of Mathew's society. For Smith's meeting, see *PNTA*, 27 October 1838; for information on Smith see Malcolm, *Ireland Sober*, pp. 94–5.
40. See, for example, *DWH*, 3 August 1839.
41. McKenna MSS, p. 53.
42. Maguire, *Father Mathew*, p. 311.
43. Malcolm, *Ireland Sober*, p. 110.
44. Maguire, *Father Mathew*, p. 113.
45. See, for example, *CE*, 1 July 1842.
46. *CS*, 11 July 1838.
47. *CS*, 23 July 1838.
48. *CS*, 17 August 1838. The account of the second meeting is McKenna's own, printed in *PNTA*, 27 October 1838.
49. *CS*, 23 January 1839.
50. *SR*, 26 January 1839. The *Southern Reporter* noted that many more who were denied tickets remained outside for the duration of the meeting.
51. *DWH*, 23 March 1839.
52. *CS*, 11 July 1838.
53. *PNTA*, 8 September 1838 (letter dated 31 August 1838).
54. *PNTA*, 27 October 1838 (letter dated 19 October 1838).
55. *SR*, 26 January 1839. The *Cork Standard* also carried an account of the meeting. Significantly, this was the *Reporter*'s first substantial notice of Mathew's society.
56. *DWH*, 30 March 1839 (letter dated 11 March 1839).
57. *DWH*, 4 May 1839.
58. Maguire, *The Doctrine*.
59. Ibid., p. vi.
60. Ibid., p. 74.
61. Ibid., pp. 75–6.
62. *DWH*, 10 August 1839.
63. *PNTA*, 8 September 1838 (letter dated 31 August 1838).
64. Maguire, *The Doctrine*, p. 74.
65. This was according to a letter from McKenna to the *PNTA*, dated 19 October 1838 (*PNTA*, 27 October 1838). McKenna made the same claim in a letter to the *Dublin Weekly Herald*, 1 December 1838. This is the last reference I can find to Murphy's society; it was, of course, in McKenna's interest that Murphy be seen to be a supporter of the cause. It may have simply become absorbed by Mathew's organisation. Murphy is usually portrayed as being uninterested in Temperance work, in part because his family were prominent distillers, but his actual relationship to the cause (and to Mathew) may have been more complicated.
66. *DWH*, 30 March 1839 (letter dated 11 March 1839). McKenna claimed to have copies of the reports of each committee.
67. *DWH*, 11 May 1839.
68. Longmate, *The Waterdrinkers*, pp. 46–7.
69. Maguire, p. 312.
70. Ibid., p. 312. The quote is from a speech delivered by Mathew in London, August 1843.
71. 'By this sign shall you conquer.' The story of Constantine's conversion to Christianity was, of course, well known, and the selection of this quote is intriguing. A popular and well-known Flora Hastings poem, 'The Cross of Constantine', was occasionally reprinted in the Irish press during the 1830s and 1840s. (See, for example, *Tipperary Free Press*, 27 July 1839.)
72. Neesan MSS, p. 150. It is unclear from any extant source when medals and cards were

introduced, but they all were in place within a year or so. Medals were certainly in widespread use throughout the Cork societies by early 1839; a handbill advertising a meeting in January 1839 urges members to wear them, and McKenna's poem read at the meeting refers to the medal (Day Papers, CAC.) The *Tipperary Free Press* (*TFP*) noted on 16 November 1839 that medals were at first 'worn only by a few' because 'the poorer members ... had no means of purchasing them', although 'recently' they became 'necessary bonds and fitting tokens of the pledge'. A few days earlier the same paper discussed medals and cards as standard tokens of having pledged (*TFP*, 13 November 1839).

73. Maguire, *Father Mathew*, p. 114.
74. Ibid.
75. Maguire's pamphlet would not have been available until late September 1838.
76. *TFP*, 13 November 1839.
77. *Dublin Evening Press (DEP)*, 6 November 1839.
78. For example, John Francis Maguire's pamphlet gives the CTAS membership as 5,000 in mid-September 1838. Maguire quotes a correspondent of Mathew who claimed his card dated 19 July 1839 was number 14,449 (Maguire, *Father Mathew*, pp. 302–3).
79. McKenna MSS, p. 421.
80. *PNTA*, 5 May 1838.
81. Patrick Rogers, 'A Century After', *Capuchin Annual*, 1939, p. 176. Maguire mentions the presence of many 'veterans' of the cause, and 'several of the personal followers of Father Mathew' at the small first meeting (Maguire, p. 108).
82. *PNTA*, 5 May 1838.
83. Maguire, *Father Mathew*, pp. 111–12. Maguire claims the site was made available to Father Mathew by a Mrs O'Connor, 'one of his sincerest friends and most devoted followers'.
84. *CS*, 17 August 1838. Other commentators have not hesitated to point out instances of pressure from the upper orders to induce servants and employees to take the pledge. There has been less attention paid to examples of the reverse. Many foremen were publicans, and urban workers were typically paid in the pub their foreman owned or had an interest in, who in turn expected a degree of custom. The tension caused by an individual or a group of workers taking the pledge would have been considerable.
85. *PNTA*, 8 September 1838. (Statement made at a Cork meeting on 31 August.)
86. *SR*, 26 January 1839. This report was certainly guarded in tone, although it was not hostile. The *Southern Reporter*, like other mainstream liberal papers, was hesitant to endorse the movement, in part because of the extensive influence of the drink trade. Another factor was no doubt the sectarian nature of the Irish press; the rival *Cork Standard*, a Tory/Protestant paper, was described prior to Mathew's accession to the cause as 'a true friend' to the total abstinence movement, which was reason enough for the *Reporter* to oppose it (*CS*, 7 April 1838).
87. *DWH*, 4 May 1839.
88. Once again, there were in fact many teetotal societies already in Munster. The *Irish Temperance and Literary Gazette* listed 127 active societies in Ireland on the eve of Mathew's assumption of his mission, but most of these local societies would have been Protestant in both membership and leadership (*ITLG*, 3 March 1838).
89. Malcolm, *Ireland Sober*, pp. 114–15.
90. Ibid.
91. Kerrigan, *Father Mathew*, p. 55. He points out that although 'superstition' was a powerful argument against the crusade in the Tory press from the movement's earliest successes in 1839, none of these sources linked the failure of the potato crop to the growth of the movement.
92. See 'William Wilde's Table of Irish Famines', ed. E. Margaret Crawford in *Famine: The Irish Experience, 900–1900*, ed. E. Margaret Crawford (Edinburgh: John Donald Publishers Ltd., 1989), pp. 22–3. Food prices at Waterford, for example, were only very slightly affected – see Peter Solar, 'The Great Famine was no Ordinary Subsistence Crisis', in Crawford, *Famine*, p. 121.
93. David Thomson and Moyra McGusty (eds), *The Irish Journals of Elizabeth Smith* (Oxford: Clarendon Press, 1980), pp. 16, 20. In 1840, Paddy was fired for his fondness for drink, and rehired by Elizabeth Smith only when 'his temperance medal and the entreaties of himself and his friends ... softened my heart after some weeks of obduracy, for I was

very angry with him'.

94. See, for example, *SR*, 19 November 1839.
95. John Dunlop, *The Philosophy of Artificial and Compulsory Drinking Usage in Great Britain and Ireland* (London: Houlston and Stoneman, 1839), p. 133.
96. See, for example, *Cork Total Abstainer*, 5 March 1841 (three men discharged after 15 years' service for taking the pledge; complaints about foremen involved in pubs).
97. *FJ*, 26 September 1840.
98. *Tait's Edinburgh Magazine*, April 1840.
99. John Foley, a charismatic curate at Youghal in the diocese of Cloyne and Ross near Waterford, for example, established a remarkably successful Temperance society independent of the CTAS about the same time. Foley's society kept pace with Father Mathew's in terms of membership for most of the period covered by this chapter, but proved incapable of further expansion, probably because it had a more elaborate and personalised initiation process and made no use of cards or medals. The fact that Foley's society was also more directly connected with particular religious practices and the Irish language was no barrier to expansion around Youghal, may have contributed to the preference of urbanites and the powerful Dublin press for Mathew's version of Temperance. See *Waterford Chronicle*, 10 October 1839, 5 November 1839, 21 December 1839, 28 December 1839, 28 January 1840; *CS*, 13 November 1839, 15 November 1839, 15 January 1840; for an account of John O'Connell of the CTAS's early days and Mathew's thoughts on Foley, *CE*, 13 September 1890.

CHAPTER 2

1. *Nenagh Guardian* (*NG*), 17 August 1839; *Tipperary Free Press* (*TFP*), 28 September 1839.
2. *Southern Reporter* (*SR*), 8 June 1839.
3. [Rev. J. Quin], 'Temperance Movement in Ireland', *Dublin Review*, May 1840, p. 467.
4. John Francis Maguire, *Father Mathew: A Biography* (London: Longman, Roberts and Green, 1863), p. 128.
5. Ibid., pp. 121, 128.
6. Ibid., p. 129.
7. *Galway Patriot* (*GP*), 14 August 1839. See also *DEP*, 12 October 1839 for a similar description of a CTAS branch in Gort.
8. *Temperance Confidential Reports, 1840*, Circular of D. McGregor, Constabulary Inspector General, and the Lord Lieutenant, National Archives, OPMA 131/10 (hereafter, *CR*).
9. See the *CR*, reports of Croker, Plummer, Kitson, Wright, Creagh, Burke, Thate, Cummins, etc.
10. *Tait's Edinburgh Magazine*, 1 April 1840.
11. *TFP*, 13 November 1839.
12. *DEP*, 24 September 1839 (reprinted from the *Waterford Chronicle* (*WC*)); *SR*, 21 September 1839. See also *DEP*, 8 October 1839; *TFP*, 23 November, 25 November, 27 November 1839; *DWH* 30 November 1839.
13. *TFP*, 25 October 1839.
14. *TFP*, 6 November 1839.
15. *DWH*, 26 October 1839, 23 November 1839.
16. *TFP*, 2 October 1839.
17. See, for example, *NG*, 15 June 1839; *Cork Standard* (*CS*), 21 June 1839; *SR*, 21 September 1839, and 16 November 1839; *TFP*, 2 October 1839, *Limerick Reporter* (*LR*) (reprinted in TFP, 16 November 1839); *DEP*, 24 September 1839 and 19 October 1839; *GP*, 14 August 1839.
18. *DEP*, 24 September 1839 and 19 October 1839.
19. *SR*, 21 September 1839. John Francis Maguire's pamphlet, published a year earlier, had acknowledged that about 150 out of 5,000 pledged at that time were known to have broken it (John Francis Maguire, *The Doctrine of Total Abstinence Justified* (Cork: William Morten, 1838), p. 76).
20. *TFP*, 2 October 1839.
21. *SR*, 5 October 1839.

22. *SR*, 31 October 1839.
23. Mathew to the Secretary of the Belfast Total Abstinence Society, 26 November 1839, cited in Father Augustine, *Footprints of Father Mathew, O.F.M. Cap., the Apostle of Temperance* (Dublin: Browne and Nolan Ltd., 1947), p. 109.
24. Ibid., p. 119.
25. *Limerick Standard* (*LS*), 26 November 1839.
26. Augustine, *Footprints of Father Mathew*, p. 119.
27. George Cornell Bretherton, 'The Irish Temperance Movement, 1833–1847' (PhD Dissertation, Columbia University), pp. 209–10.
28. The *ITLG* remarked on the establishment of the coffeehouse, 21 April 1838.
29. *LS*, 12 July 1839.
30. Augustine, *Footprints of Father Mathew*, p. 110.
31. *LS*, 19 July 1839.
32. The *DEP* reprinted it on 8 October from the *WC* of some days earlier. See also *SR*, 5 October 1839. A copy of a handbill, entitled 'Important Letter from the Mayor of Limerick to the Rev. Theobald Mathew', Dublin: Irish Temperance Union, 1839, is in the Day papers held by the Cork Archives Council.
33. *SR*, 5 October 1839.
34. *DEP*, 8 October 1839.
35. The *DEP* of 31 October 1839 reprinted a notice of the planned visit from the *LS*.
36. Father Mathew to Rev. John Nolan, 22 November 1839, printed in *CS*, 27 November 1839.
37. Father Mathew to Rev. James Raleigh, printed in *LR*, 26 November 1839.
38. *CS*, 2 December 1839.
39. *LC*, 30 November 1839.
40. *LR*, 3 December 1839.
41. Ibid.
42. Elizabeth Malcolm, *Ireland Sober, Ireland Free: Drink and Temperance in 19th Century Ireland* (Syracuse: Syracuse University Press, 1986), p. 116.
43. Press reports varied as to the number who pledged; 150,000 was the most common figure cited.
44. Most recently by Colm Kerrigan, *Father Mathew and the Irish Temperance Movement, 1838–1849* (Cork: University Press, 1992), pp. 58–9.
45. Gary Owens has made some useful observations on the vagaries of crowd size estimates in the pre-Famine period, 'Nationalism Without Words: Symbolism and Ritual Behaviour in the Repeal "Monster Meetings" of 1843–45', in James S. Donnelly, Jr. and Kerby A. Miller (eds), *Irish Popular Culture, 1650–1850* (Dublin: Irish Academic Press, 1997), pp. 243–69. Even allowing for typical exaggerations, the size of the Limerick meeting was of a new order of magnitude.
46. *LS*, 3 December 1839.
47. Mathew to an unnamed correspondent ('My dear Sir'), 8 December 1839, Quaker Archives Port. 8a, item 21a Dublin (from Pimm Family Collection).
48. Father Mathew to Rev. John Falvey (PP, Glanmire, Co. Cork), n.d., Father Mathew Correspondence, Capuchin Archives, Dublin, A 177.
49. A committee was formed to ensure that the dangerous scenes at Limerick were not repeated – see Kerrigan, *Father Mathew*, p. 60.
50. *WC*, 12 December 1839.
51. Kerrigan, *Father Mathew*, p. 60; Malcolm, *Ireland Sober*, p. 117.
52. Foran informed late arrivals in Waterford on 12 December that they could take the pledge from Mathew at Wexford. *WC* 12 December 1839.
53. Augustine, *Footprints of Father Mathew*, p. 126.
54. *CS*, 23 December 1839.
55. The map is drawn from contemporary newspaper accounts, supplemented by the careful observations of Father Augustine. The estimate is approximate because Mathew's progress was frequently arrested by enthusiastic crowds and unscheduled stops during his tourings were the rule rather than the exception. Thousands were often pledged and Mathew was sometimes delayed for a day or more. The newspapers did not always note these stops.
56. Augustine, *Footprints of Father Mathew*, p. 149.
57. *WC*, 19 March 1840.

58. A banner carried by James McKenna at the CTAS's Easter procession in Cork on 18 April claimed 'two million members' for the society. *SR*, 25 April 1840.
59. *WC*, 7 January 1840.
60. *SR*, 9 January 1840; *TFP*, 14 December 1839.
61. See, for example, 'A New Christmas Ballad, About Father Mathew and the Temperance Societies', printed in *CS*, 4 January 1840. The same song appeared in a variety of newspapers throughout Ireland, and the Irish Temperance Union had 10,000 copies printed.
62. *CS*, 2 December 1839, *WC*, 21 December 1839, *DWH*, 7 December 1839.
63. *WC*, 28 December 1839 (letter dated 26 December).
64. *WC*, 14 January 1840.
65. *SR*, 28 January 1840.
66. Quoted in *LS*, 6 December 1840.
67. *LS*, 24 December 1839.
68. *The Times*, 2 January 1840.
69. See the Constabulary Reports, March 1840, NLI. This aspect of the Reports is examined more closely in Chapter 7.
70. *Nenagh Guardian* (*NG*), July 1839; see also the *Limerick Standard* (*LS*)'s warning about Mathew and his 'superstitious followers', 19 July 1839.
71. Quoted in *LS*, 10 December 1839. See also the *Waterford Mail*'s complaints about 'miracle mongering' quoted in *LS*, 6 December1839.
72. *LS*, 10 December 1839.
73. *LS*, 6 December 1839.
74. *Mayo Constitution (MC)*, 28 July 1840.
75. See, for example, Kerrigan, *Father Mathew*, pp. 132–52; Malcolm, *Ireland Sober*, pp. 121–2; George Cornell Bretherton, 'Against the Flowing Tide: Whiskey and Temperance in the Making of Modern Ireland' in Susanna Barrows and Alan O'Day (eds), *Drinking: Behavior and Belief in Modern History* (Berkeley: University of California Press, 1991), p. 158.
76. Malcolm, *Ireland Sober*, pp. 121–2; see also S.J. Connolly, *Priests and People in Pre-famine Ireland* (New York: St Martin's Press, 1982), p. 117. Mathew does not conform to the typical profile of such priests provided by Connolly. He was not an outsider except in the sense that he was a regular priest and that he strongly advocated temperance, although his early career, with his dismissal from Maynooth and removal from Kilkenny, may have been sufficiently scandalous to have produced some outsider status. How well known these incidents were by 1838 is not clear; Mathew himself never mentioned them and indeed appears to have endeavoured to conceal them. Mathew carried himself, all accounts agree, like a gentleman or an aristocrat, albeit a kindly one. Certainly within Cork he was a respected and popular figure who appears to have been quite well integrated into the city's religious structures.
77. Kerrigan, *Father Mathew*, p. 55.
78. A stock story in the Irish press from 1840 on was the 'Awful Consequences of Breaking the Pledge', which related, without comment, accounts making the rounds of the locality about the often deadly misfortunes of pledge breakers.
79. See, for example, Mathew's speech in Dublin where he asserted that 'millions' never got them at all, citing as evidence his recent visit to Booterstown, where 7,000 pledged and 'only 300' took cards and medals: *Dublin Journal of Temperance, Science, and Literature*, 2 July 1842. See also John O'Neill, *A Defense of the Roman Catholic Temperance Society Dedicated to the Very Rev'd Theobald Mathew*, 1840 (Halliday Collection, Royal Irish Academy) for an exchange (originally appearing in the *Connaught Journal*) on the subject of temperance medals and superstition.
80. *CR*, Circular of D. McGregor, Constabulary Inspector General, and the Lord Lieutenant, National Archives, OPMA 131/10.
81. *SR*, 29 November 1839.
82. *Waterford Chronicle* (*WC*), 21 December 1839.
83. Rev. James Bermingham, *A Memoir of the Very Rev. Theobald Mathew, with an Account of the Rise and Progress of Temperance in Ireland* (Dublin: Milliken and Son, 1840), p. 19.
84. *CR*.
85. *FJ*, 24 September 1840.

86. *Cork Total Abstainer* (*CTA*), 20 February 1841.
87. *LR*, 29 May 1840. Kenyon is perhaps best remembered as the 'Patriot Priest' of the 1848 rebellion.
88. The *Dublin Evening Mail* reported that a handbill circulated in March 1840 made much of miracle cures attributed to Mathew. The article made it clear that the handbill was not sponsored by Mathew. See Kerrigan, *Father Mathew*, p. 146.
89. Augustine, *Footprints of Father Mathew*, pp. 120–1.
90. *CS*, 18 December 1839.
91. Maguire, *Father Mathew*, p. 122.
92. *WC*, 10 December 1840.
93. By late 1840, Dungarvan was renowned for the size and strength of its teetotal society, particularly among the fishermen. See *WC*, 17 September 1840; *FJ*, 18 January 1841 and 20 May 1841. Fishermen in other places were also very forward in the movement, see, for example, the *Connaught Journal* on the fishermen of Galway and St John's, 23 June 1840.
94. *TFP*, 18 December 1839.
95. *CR*; see in particular reports from John Morgan (Corrofin, Co. Clare); Portumna, Co. Galway; William Heard (Tulla, Co. Clare); George Hill (Enniscorthy, Co. Wexford: 'any person who continues to drink, is hooted at when met, and in two instances, where I had a drunken man, in custody, the mob wanted me to give him up, so that they might "*duck*" him at the pump'); Louis Anderson (Cahir, Co. Tipperary).
96. Bermingham, *A Memoir*, p. 32.
97. *CS*, 16 November 1839 (letter dated 6 November 1839).
98. Ibid., p. 69.
99. Letter of J.A. Besim to W. Jones, 16 March 1840, from *CR*.
100. From *SR*, 2 December 1839.
101. Mathew told *Tait's Edinburgh Magazine* in February 1840 that he never expected to attract more than 500 followers.

CHAPTER 3

1. *Waterford Chronicle* (*WC*), 19 March 1840.
2. Ibid.
3. *Connaught Journal* (*CJ*), 19 March 1840.
4. James Haughton to 'Bible Christian', 10 February 1840, reprinted in Samuel Haughton, *A Memoir of James Haughton* (Dublin: E. Ponsonby, 1877), p. 293, Appendix.
5. *Constabulary Reports*, *CR*, NLI, Return of George Wright, Waterford City.
6. Colm Kerrigan, *Father Mathew and the Irish Temperance Movement 1838–1849* (Cork: University Press, 1992), p. 65; Elizabeth Malcolm, *Ireland Sober, Ireland Free: Drink and Temperance in 19th Century Ireland* (Syracuse: Syracuse University Press, 1986), p. 133. There were, of course, areas where Protestants did take the pledge in numbers, particularly at some of Mathew's later missions in Ulster.
7. *WC*, 11 February 1840.
8. *CR*, NLI, Return of George Wright, Waterford City.
9. See *CR* of Croker in Ennis, Binoon in Portumna, Co. Galway, Malony in Mountmellick, Queen's County, and Smith in Rathkeale, Co. Limerick.
10. See *CR* of Carpenter in Dingle, Slattery in Cappoquin, Co. Waterford, and Croker in Clonmel.
11. Fitzgerald was echoed by others, including Fletcher in Listowel, Co. Kerry, and Warburton at Ballinasloe, Co. Galway.
12. The CTAS's own propaganda will be the subject of Chapter 4.
13. The National Library of Ireland has several collections of these Cork ballads/poems, which were essentially humorous character sketches of notable young locals who assembled for day-trips to Skillig. The intended audience was probably Cork's well-to-do classes.
14. 'The Cosey Hall Mercury', from the Madden Ballad Collection, NLI, v.34–5 #97.
15. Dublin was, of course, the centre for much of the pre-Mathewite Temperance movement

in Ireland. The Irish Temperance Union, established in 1839, drew much of its strength from Dublin's Quaker and Unitarian communities. Most of Ireland's Temperance publications came out of Dublin, not to mention the movement's only newspaper, the *Dublin Weekly Herald*. Priests, notably Henry Young, Andrew O'Connell, William Yore and John Spratt, the Carmelite, led active Temperance societies in Dublin for some time prior to Mathew's crusade (see Malcolm, *Ireland Sober*, pp. 84–5, 93–5).

16. Mathew made the remark in Dublin when he returned there in September, 1840. *FJ*, 29 September 1840.
17. *DEP*, 25 January 1840.
18. *FJ*, 27 March 1840.
19. *FJ*, 28 March 1840.
20. *FJ*, 30 March 1840.
21. Ibid.
22. The *Freeman's Journal*, which counted some 50,000 and indicated that police sources were in close accord with this figure, also admitted that many hundreds at least had been received into the society informally during the week. Additionally, Mathew gave the pledge to several thousand persons on Sunday who were omitted from this accounting. See *FJ* of 4 April 1840 and 6 April 1840.
23. This was certainly the case on Wednesday, Thursday, Friday and Saturday, when the papers make specific mention of many who did not get the chance to pledge. On both Wednesday and Thursday, Mathew was forced to administer the pledge to several hundreds who would not leave until he did so.
24. *FJ*, 6 April 1840.
25. *FJ*, 4 April 1840.
26. See *FJ*, 4 April 1840, 6 April 1840.
27. 55,000 pledged in two days on 28 and 29 September 1840, according to the *Freeman* of 30 September.
28. *FJ*, 2 April 1840.
29. The dangers were revealed quite clearly during Mathew's second visit to Dublin later in 1840. Despite the presence of over 100 police, including 18 on horseback, and the additional assistance of a company of stewards from local Temperance societies armed with white wands, who discharged their duties 'most usefully and properly, save too great a propensity, in our opinion, to use those wands or sticks upon the heads of the poor people, who were, perhaps, too anxious to press forward towards the platform', order could not at times be preserved, and on one occasion as a batch was being admitted to Beresford Square 'a tremendous rush took place among the crowd outside, and the efforts of the police to keep back the people were altogether useless'. *FJ*, 29 September 1840.
30. On Wednesday, for example, Mathew pledged 19 batches over the course of approximately six hours, or only one batch roughly every 20 minutes. Batch size varied between 300 and 1,200, and averaged something over 520 postulants each. The police, many of them mounted, carefully controlled the number of people allowed into the open area in front of the Custom House steps. See *FJ*, 2 April 1840.
31. Anon., *An Accurate Report of the Proceedings of the Very Rev. Theobald Mathew in Dublin in the Cause of Temperance When Eighty Thousand Persons Took the Pledge with the Sermon Preached by him in the Church of the Conception, Marlborough Street* (Dublin: Richard Grace, 1840).
32. *FJ*, 31 March 1840.
33. *Irish Catholic Directory* (*ICD*), 1841.
34. *FJ*, 1 April 1840
35. Ibid.
36. *FJ*, 2 April 1840.
37. *FJ*, 6 April 1840.
38. *WC*, 9 April 1840.
39. *FJ*, 2 April 1840.
40. Ibid.
41. *Southern Reporter*, 25 April 1840.
42. *FJ*, 13 June 1840; *WC*, 18 June 1840.
43. The tour was announced early in May; see the *Freeman*'s notice of the planned tour and

their account of a Grand Tea Party in Leeds on 11 June at which Father Mathew was to have been the guest of honour. *FJ*, 5 May 1840, 16 June 1840.

44. *FJ*, 13 June 1840.
45. Ibid. The details of ticket prices and an elaborate order of arrangements can be found in the *FJ*, 10 June 1840. Just how highly Mathew valued this first visit may be judged from a letter to Laurence Renehan, Maynooth's president after 1845, and vice-president during this 1840 visit. Although undated, the letter is addressed to Renehan in his capacity as president, and probably refers to a visit to Maynooth that took place in 1846. In it, Mathew agrees to rearrange his schedule and accept an invitation to come to Maynooth, noting, 'This I would not do were it not for the great object you propose, an object whose successful accomplishment will cause immense benefit for the Church.' Mathew reveals his taste for the dramatic in his refusal to dine at the college the night before as 'it would not provoke a good effect to have me in the college until the *moment* of my introduction to the young gentlemen whose conversion to teetotallism you are seeking'. FMC A 174.
46. The 'Tribute' appeared in the *FJ* on 27 June 1840 and the *Waterford Chronicle* on 18 August 1840. A letter to Father Mathew from a W. O'Connor in Ballyporeen, Co. Tipperary, dated 29 July 1840, thanks the CTAS for sending a copy of the 'Tribute' and hopes that it will be 'taken and digested, through Ireland, with the most beneficial effect'. W. O'Connor to Mathew, 29 July 1840, FMC A295.
47. Father Augustine, *Footprints of Father Mathew, O.F.M. Cap., the Apostle of Temperance* (Dublin: Browne and Nolan Ltd., 1947), p. 269.
48. Tracing Mathew's movements is no easy task. The newspapers provide the best information, but they are very erratic, particularly after 1840, or, when reprinting material from provincial papers, in including accurate dates. Temperance news, in particular in later years, was prone to being published as space allowed, often days or weeks after it was received. Additionally, Mathew frequently changed his itinerary, staying extra days or taking advantage of last-minute invitations that might advance his cause. For this reason, although the papers occasionally published his upcoming visits, it can often be difficult to verify that meetings took place as scheduled. Furthermore, longer visits to large towns in particular typically produced flying visits to surrounding villages that often went unnoticed and unreported. Father Augustine, alone among Mathew's biographers, made a good effort to trace his movements, although not in any systematic way, or with the use of maps. My dates are based on his, but are supplemented by my own educated guesses and often-frustrated efforts to pin down the elusive Capuchin. Some inaccuracies, unfortunately, are probably still present.
49. Particularly long missions (more than three days) have been counted twice for the purposes of this map.
50. Kevin Whelan, 'The Regional Impact of Irish Catholicism 1700–1850', in *Common Ground: Essays on the Historical Geography of Ireland* (Cork: University Press, 1988), pp. 264–7 notes that the 'richer Catholic farming areas of the 'Wexford/Waterford/Tipperary/Kilkenny/Cork area', along with the 'Wexford-Limerick axis' of towns, was the locus of increasing 'formal Catholicism', the O'Connell annuity in the 1830s, and the Temperance movement. Leonard Hochberg and David Miller, inspired by ideas contained in Michael Hechter's *Internal Colonialism: The Celtic Fringe in British National Development, 1536–1966* (Berkeley: University of California Press, 1975), have developed a working network of regions and macro-regions in pre-Famine Ireland along the lines of G.W. Skinner's work on China and Carol Smith's on Latin America. The 'culture hearth' they describe in the southeast is characterised by larger farms and less dependence on Ireland's administrative centre, Dublin. It is also, as they note, citing Whelan, the cradle of Emmet Larkin's 'The Devotional Revolution in Ireland, 1850–75' (AHR 77 [1972], pp. 625–52). Much of their work has been presented at conferences but remains unpublished (Leonard Hochberg and David Miller, *Internal Colonialism in Geographic Perspective: The Case of Pre-famine Ireland* [unpublished paper], p. 36) but see Leonard J. Hochberg and David J. Miller, 'Constructing a Central-Place Hierarchy from a Commercial Directory', *Historical Methods*, 25 (1992), pp. 80–94.
51. Gary Owens's thought-provoking '"A Moral Insurrection": Faction Fighters, Public Demonstrations, and the O'Connellite Campaign' (unpublished paper, 1996)

demonstrates that most of the 'pacification' meetings described took place in Limerick and Tipperary.

52. Emmet Larkin, 'Church, State, and Nation in Modern Ireland', *AHR* Vol. LXXX, No. 5 (December 1975). Gary Owens notes the activity of the class described by Whelan in the pacification campaign; their role in bolstering Temperance, as noted above, was no less significant: Owens, 'Nationalism without Words: Symbolism and Ritual Behaviour in the Repeal "Monster Meetings" of 1843–45', in James S. Donnelly, Jr. and Kerby A. Miller (eds), *Irish Popular Culture, 1650–1850* (Dublin: Irish Acadmic Press, 1997), p. 25, citing Kevin Whelan in *The Tree of Liberty: Radicalism, Catholicism, and the Construction of Irish Identity, 1760–1830* (Cork: Cork University Press, 1996), p. 54. See also Whelan, 'Regional Impact', especially pp. 262–3.
53. *Nation*, 3 December 1842.
54. Malcolm, *Ireland Sober*, p. 126.
55. *Limerick Reporter*, 25 August 1843.
56. Children were given the pledge, a practice which inflated the ranks of the temperate with large numbers who never drank, although this was more characteristic of Temperance after 1843. Still, pledging was generally reserved for school-age children, and no accounts of early Temperance meetings, not even critical ones, made mention of large numbers of very young postulants.
57. *Parliamentary Papers*, H.C. 1852–53 (547) XCIX.
58. Per capita English spirit consumption was less than Irish, at 0.53 proof-gallons in 1831, but this was offset by much greater proportional beer-drinking (0.94 barrels per capita, compared to 0.10 in Ireland). English and Scottish spirit consumption is from George B. Wilson, *Alcohol and the Nation* (London: Nicholson and Watson, 1940), p. 337, Table 3. Population figures for both countries are from Chris Cook and John Stevenson, *The Longman Handbook of Modern British History, 1714–1980* (London: Longman, 1983).
59. See Wilson, *Alcohol and the Nation*, p. 369. See also Kerrigan, *Father Mathew*, p. 25 and Malcolm, *Ireland Sober*, p. 99. The best examination of illicit distillation in Ireland in this period is found in K.H. Connell's 'Illicit Distillation' in K.H. Connell (ed.), *Irish Peasant Society* (Oxford: Oxford University Press, 1968).
60. K.H. Connell, 'Illicit Distillation'. The revenue police were increasingly professional, numerous and vigilant after being reorganised in 1836. Kerrigan, *Father Mathew*, p. 25.
61. Wilson, *Alcohol and the Nation*, p. 369, Appendix F, Table 14.
62. Ibid., pp. 390–403, Appendix F, Tables 24 and 25.
63. Norman Longmate, *The Waterdrinkers: A History of Temperance* (London: Hamish Hamilton, 1968), p. 115.
64. Quoted in Emmet Larkin, 'The Roman Catholic Clergy in Nineteenth Century Ireland', p. 11.
65. Quoted in John Barclay Shiel, *Dr Shiel's Historical Account of the Temperance Movement in Ireland* (Dublin: Samuel J. Machen, 1843), p. 9.
66. Mr and Mrs S.C. Hall, *Ireland: Its Scenery and Character*, vol. 1 (London: Virtue and Co., 1842), p. 37.
67. Ibid., p. 46.
68. Ibid., pp. 37–8.
69. *CR*, NLO, Return of George Wright, Waterford City.
70. Three other constables did not answer the question.
71. CSO Miscellaneous Books, Stipendiary Magistrates' Diaries.
72. CSO Misc. Books, Stip. Mag. Diary #2.
73. Ibid.
74. Ibid., #6.
75. Ibid., #22.
76. Ibid., #26.
77. Ibid., #23.
78. Longmate, *The Waterdrinkers*, pp. 114–15.
79. Backsliding was of course a problem in some places, particularly in towns such as Cork and Dublin. Many of Mathew's second and third visits were responses to private reports of backsliding.
80. Several of the *CR* and the Magistrate's Diaries note that whiskey tents had now

disappeared and were replaced by tents selling food and tea.

81. See *CR*, NLO, Return of George Wright, Waterford City.
82. *FJ*, 18 December 1840. Address of the Boyle Total Abstinence Association to Father Mathew, 20 September 1840, cited in *Cork Standard*, 28 September 1840.
83. Shiel, *Dr Shiel's Historical Account*, pp. 13–14.
84. *WC*, 23 January 1841.
85. Haughton to Garrison, 26 September 1842, from Haughton, *A Memoir of James Haughton*, p. 294.
86. *Nation* (*N*), 3 December 1842.
87. McKenna MSS, Address of the Erris TAS.
88. McKenna MSS, p. 78.

CHAPTER 4

1. See Brian Harrison, *Drink and the Victorians* (London: Butler and Tanner, 1971), pp. 120–22; See also Norman Longmate, *The Waterdrinkers: A History of Temperance* (London: Hamish Hamilton, 1968), pp. 63, 69–70.
2. Ibid.
3. For more on Martin, see William Logan, *Early Heroes of the Temperance Reformation* (Glasgow: 1873).
4. Father Augustine, *Footprints of Father Mathew, O.F.M. Cap., the Apostle of Temperance* (Dublin: Browne and Nolan Ltd., 1947), p. 101.
5. Ibid., p. 102.
6. Probably the best account of the political education of the rising Catholic middle class can be found in Oliver MacDonagh's two volume life of Daniel O'Connell. For a general overview of the developing Irish Catholic middle class, see R.F. Foster, *Modern Ireland, 1600–1972* (London: Penguin Press, 1988), pp. 96–9.
7. See, for example, John Francis Maguire, *An Address Delivered to the Members of the Cork Literary Association at the Closing of Their First Session* (Cork: 1845), p. 20; *Haliday Pamphlets*, v. 1939. RIA.
8. McKenna MSS, p. 51. It is unclear how much of this mostly undated essay material was composed in the earliest days of the movement and how much was retrospectively written during 1843–44 when the *CTA*'s financial woes cost McKenna his job. Mostly the latter, one suspects, but some portions at least appear, from internal evidence, to have been written (or based on notes written) in the days before Father Mathew travelled outside Cork, that is, between April 1838 and December 1839. McKenna was collecting material all along (not surprising for a secretary), particularly addresses from local societies and press clippings, but also including his own observations and notes.
9. McKenna MSS, p. 115. The CTAS' membership began to grow exponentially after September 1839.
10. McKenna MSS, p. 87.
11. McKenna MSS, p. 88.
12. McKenna MSS, pp. 49–50.
13. McKenna MSS, p. 81.
14. Ibid.
15. McKenna MSS, p. 87.
16. McKenna MSS, p. 78.
17. McKenna MSS, p. 79.
18. McKenna MSS, p. 88.
19. McKenna MSS, pp. 49–50.
20. John Francis Maguire, *Father Mathew: A Biography* (London: Longman, Roberts and Green, 1863), p. 3.
21. Ibid., p. vi.
22. Ibid., pp. 5, 8.
23. *Cork Total Abstainer* (*CTA*), 20 February 1841.
24. *CTA*, 20 February 1841.
25. *CTA*, 27 February 1841.

26. *CTA*, 6 March 1841.
27. *CE*, 10 January 1842
28. Newspaper circulation figures in Ireland did not exceed 3,000 during this period, for even the most popular papers, and average circulation (in 1830) was about 550. However, newspapers typically passed through many hands, and the availability of papers (in pubs, coffee houses, and, of course, temperance reading rooms) often allowed even the illiterate some access to the news they contained. See Brian Inglis, *The Freedom of the Press in Ireland* (London: Faber & Faber, 1954), p. 191 and Appendix C.
29. Maguire, *Father Mathew*, pp. 168–9.
30. Mathew to Kirby, 5 May 1842 (K).
31. *Waterford Chronicle*, 1 February 1840.
32. *FJ*, 17 August 1840.
33. *FJ*, 6 April 1840.
34. *FJ*, 17 August 1840
35. *FJ*, 30 September 1840.
36. *WC*, 16 June 1840.
37. *CTA*, 27 February 1841.
38. Mathew to Ferrian (24 March 1842), FMC A 803. (This letter, like so many others in the Mathew correspondence, is undated, but since 1842 is the only year in the early 1840s that Saint Patrick's Day fell on a Thursday, it is possible to assign a date.)
39. *WC*, 16 June 1840.
40. Augustine, *Footprints of Father Mathew*, p. 240.
41. *FJ*, 17 November 1840.
42. *FJ*, 13 April 1841.
43. Mathew to W.W. Simpson, 22 October 1841, quoted in John Barclay Shiel, *Dr Shiel's Historical Account of the Temperance Movement in Ireland* (Dublin: Samuel J. Machen, 1843), p. 6.
44. *FJ*, 31 March 1840.
45. *WC*, 12 May 1840.
46. *WC*, 16 June 1840.
47. *FJ*, 6 April 1840; Mathew to Dr Lees, 14 October 1844 FMC A 407, Mathew to ?, 10 February 1848, FMC A 814; Mathew to Webb, n.d., FMC A 1904. See also *FJ*, 6 April 1840, for an example of the use of this term in a platform speech.
48. *WC*, 16 June 1840.
49. *FJ*, 17 August 1840.
50. The Liberal press repeatedly pointed out the decline in revenue, either by simply reporting without comment the decreasing returns, or by cheering, as the 9 April 1840 *Waterford Chronicle* did, Mathew's decision to offer the pledge at Beresford Place in Dublin, 'the locale of the Customs House ... the situation, therefore, answers the further purpose of an open insult to the revenue of the kingdom'.
51. Mathew later denied making these controversial remarks, and maintained that his attack on publicans had been misunderstood as a criticism of the governance of Ireland. *FJ*, 31 August 1840.
52. Maguire, *Father Mathew*, p. 221.
53. *FJ*, 18 October 1841.
54. *FJ*, 1 January 1841.
55. *FJ*, 17 November1840.
56. *WC*, 9 April 1840.
57. *FJ*, 24 October 1840.
58. *WC*, 25 August 1840.
59. Text of the pledge is in Augustine, *Footprints of Father Mathew*, p. 116.
60. Mathew referred correspondents to this work (and another, Donegal physician John Shiel's *Dr Shiel's Historical Account of the Temperance Movement in Ireland, Compiled from Authentic Documents and Published Under the Patronage and with the Approbation of the Apostle of Temperance, the Very Reverend Theobald Mathew*, which appeared in 1843), rather than continually explain the rise of the Temperance cause (see, for example, Mathew to Dr J. Leer, 14 October 1844 [FMC A 403]). Shiel's work seems to have been less concerned with inspiring teetotallers, or recruiting new ones, than with assuring increasingly concerned

politically conservative allies of Father Mathew (most of them English) that Mathew and his cause had no connection whatsoever with the then rapidly rising tide of Repeal. This task was given a new urgency because of the grim financial situation faced by Mathew and his cause, and his need to raise money among his English sympathisers.

61. See, for example, Father Mathew to Rev. T. O'Sullivan, 5 November 1846 (FMC A 39). Mathew approved of O'Sullivan's speech and was forwarding copies to the papers. Mathew certainly printed up and distributed 30,000 copies of Charles Gavan Duffy's speech in favour of temperance, in October 1841. See Charles Gavan Duffy, *My Life in Two Hemispheres* (London: T.F. Unwin, 1903), p. 55.
62. The mayor of Limerick, for example, thanked Father Mathew for forwarding a Temperance pamphlet to him prior to Mathew's first visit to Limerick. *Important Letter of the Mayor of Limerick to the Rev. Theobald Mathew* (Dublin: Irish Temperance Union, 1839), Day Papers, CAC, Cork, Ireland.
63. W. O'Connor to Mathew, FMC A 295.
64. *FJ*, 27 June 1840. The article, 'A Tribute to Father Mathew', is dated 21 June 1840. It was reprinted in the press as well; see *WC*, ? August 1840. Both John Francis Maguire and Father Augustine use parts of this piece, without revealing its source. Maguire in particular was probably working from the printed and circulated version of the article.
65. *WC*, 17 May 1840, contains advertising for, and a review of, the work.
66. *SR*, 6 June 1840 (letter dated 8 May 1840).
67. Rev. James Bermingham, *A Memoir of the Very Rev. Theobald Mathew* (Dublin: Milliken and Son, 1840), p. 19.
68. Ibid., p. 16.
69. Ibid., p. 30.
70. Ibid., p. 38.
71. Ibid., p. 6.
72. Ibid., p. 30.
73. Ibid., p. 19.
74. See, for example, *WC*, 16 May 1840, where it was claimed that demand was 'intense' for the pamphlet, which was widely advertised as 'available at all booksellers'.
75. *WC*, 15 May 1840.
76. William MacNamara Downes, *Temperance Melodies for the Teetotallers of Ireland* (Cork: S.M. Thompson, 1843). Mathew's letter is dated 10 August 1842.
77. *FJ*, 15 August 1840.
78. *WC*, 12 December 1839. Advertisements for 'cheap music for temperance bands – native music for Ireland' were regular features in the *Nation*, see 15 October 1842.
79. *CS*, 6 November 1839.
80. *WC*, 7 January 1840.
81. *SR*, 24 March 1840.
82. Maguire, *Father Mathew*, p. 287.
83. *FJ*, 18 October 1841.
84. *N*, 15 October 1842.
85. *TFP*, 2 October 1839.
86. *SR*, 23 November 1839.
87. *SR*, 9 January 1840. See also the editorial of 28 January 1840.
88. *FJ*, 16 March 1841.
89. Relatively few of these survive, except in published collections (contemporary or otherwise) and in the case of those few which made their way into the press of the day.
90. James Martin, *The Wounded Soldier: A Tale of Waterloo with Other Poems on Temperance* (Kells: T.K. Henderson, 1841), RIA Haliday #1808. Martin's preface is dated 25 January 1841. Martin's claims about his readership can be found in *The Truth Teller, or, Poems on Various Subjects* (Kells: T.K. Henderson, 1842), RIA Haliday #1840.
91. Philip Connell, *The Medal and Glass* (Kells: T.K. Henderson, 1841), RIA Haliday 1813.
92. See, for example, *CS*, 3 January 1840.
93. *CTA*, 20 February 1841.
94. *CTA*, 6 March 1841.
95. *WC*, 8 September 1840.
96. Some 100 of these were preserved by James McKenna as an appendix to his unpublished

MSS, while a number of others were reprinted in full or in part by local newspapers.

97. There was nothing novel in this custom; Daniel O'Connell, popular clergymen, and indeed any public figure were likely to receive such addresses on important occasions.
98. Unless otherwise noted, all addresses cited are from McKenna MSS. Most of these addresses are not dated.
99. See also the addresses from Killeary, Lydden, Mitchelstown and Innismouth, Co. Cork.

CHAPTER 5

1. Most commentators on the crusade have assumed that this aspect of the movement is a significant indicator of Father Mathew's personal charisma, a charisma that they argue was intimately connected with, in addition to Father Mathew's own public persona, the powerful role of the priest in pre-Famine Ireland. See, for example, Elizabeth Malcolm, *Ireland Sober Ireland Free: Drink and Temperance in 19th Century Ireland* (Syracuse: Syracuse University Press, 1986), pp. 107, 121–2; George Cornell Bretherton, 'The Irish Temperance Movement, 1833–1847' (PhD Dissertation, Columbia University, 1978), p. 216; Quinn notes S.J. Connolly's work on the status of priests in popular religion and claims that much of Mathew's appeal derived from that status. John Quinn, 'Father Mathew's Temperance Crusade in Ireland, 1838–1856' (PhD Dissertation, Notre Dame, 1992), pp. 45, 108. Anthropologist Lawrence Taylor's recent work underscores this argument (see, for example, 'The Priest and the Agent'). Still, it would not do to ignore other potentially appealing aspects of pledging in public, including a widespread sense that the meaning of the act was intimately bound up with the larger community. This is all the more important if we accept that pledging was, as Malcolm suggests, at least in part an 'emotional' act.
2. The *Waterford Chronicle*, 21 January 1840, for instance, reprinted from the *Kilkenny Journal* details of the preparation for an early meeting at Kilkenny. With only two days notice before Father Mathew's arrival, Father J.P. O'Reilly had notices printed in the local paper and 'a few handbills posted through the city ... the intelligence, however, spread throughout the city and the suburbs'. The German tourist J.G. Kohl, in Ireland in 1842, copied a handbill he picked up in Wexford announcing a visit by Father Mathew. J.G. Kohl, *Ireland* (New York: Harper and Brothers, 1844), pp. 56–7.
3. While on his tours, particularly in the early days of the crusade, Father Mathew occasionally administered the pledge in more or less impromptu fashion to crowds who gathered at crossroads, roadsides or whatever towns the horses were changed or watered. He was, as his biographers have noted, reluctant to miss any opportunity to gain converts, but he was also cautious about administering the pledge anywhere where local clergy had not specifically requested a visit.
4. See Emmet Larkin, 'Economic Growth, Capital Investment and the Roman Catholic Church in Nineteenth Century Ireland', in *The Historical Dimensions of Irish Catholicism* (New York: Arno Press, 1976). See also Desmond Keenan, *The Catholic Church in Nineteenth Century Ireland* (Totowa, NJ: Gill and Macmillan, 1983), pp. 114–29.
5. *FJ*, 29 September 1840.
6. Except in cases of extremely bad weather. At Kells, during a driving rain on 18 January 1841, for example, Mathew apologised for administering the pledge inside the chapel. *FJ*, 27 January 1841.
7. *Galway Patriot* (*GP*), 3 October 1838. That article also reported large demonstrations in Balrothery, Co. Dublin, and Ballykine, Co. Mayo. As always, the crowd size estimates cannot be relied upon. They tend to be optimistic estimates, often deliberately inflated for political purposes. The anti-tithe agitation had recurred a number of times during the 1830s, and was in full swing during the summer of 1838. See, for example, the *Dublin Evening Press*, 7 June 1838, which reports on an anti-tithe meeting at Kilmacthomas, County Waterford, and estimates the crowd to have been 20–40,000. Another meeting at Iverk, Co. Kilkenny that same summer is supposed to have attracted 50,000. (*DEP*, 14 July 1838).
8. *FJ*, 3 April 1841.
9. *WC*, 12 December 1839.

10. Lyons to Mathew, 5 August 1840, FMCA 194 (Father Mathew visited Castlebar from 26 to 28 July).
11. *FJ*, 6 June 1842.
12. *FJ*, 15 January 1842. The local society still assembled outside his lodging, banners flying and bands playing, after discovering his arrival.
13. *FJ*, 22 March 1842.
14. *WC*, 11 February 1840.
15. *FJ*, 9 January 1842.
16. *FJ*, 26 September 1840.
17. *FJ*, 23 September 1840.
18. Kohl, *Ireland*, p. 27.
19. See, for example, the *Waterford Chronicle*'s account of a city dinner party at the town hall, 7 January 1840.
20. *Alexis de Tocqueville's Journey in Ireland*, trans. and ed. by Emmet Larkin (Washington: Catholic University of America Press, 1990), p. 6.
21. *FJ*, 1 July 1840.
22. *WC*, 7 January 1840.
23. *FJ*, 15 January 1841.
24. *WC*, 25 February 1840.
25. *CE*, 2 September 1841.
26. *FJ*, 18 December 1840.
27. *FJ*, 29 September 1840.
28. *FJ*, 4 December 1840.
29. *FJ*, 26 March 1840; *Nation*, 25 March 1843; *Nation*, 22 October 1842.
30. More on this in Chapter 7. Father Augustine, *Footprints of Father Mathew, O.F.M. Cap., the Apostle of Temperance* (Dublin: Browne and Nolan Ltd., 1947), p. 204.
31. *FJ*, 18 October 1841.
32. There is an increasing volume of scholarship on the general subject of women and the Temperance movement; see, for example, Janet Chafetz and Anthony Dworkin, *Female Revolt: The Rise of Women's Movements in World and Historical Perspective* (Totowa: Rowman and Littlefield, 1986); Janet Giele, *Two Paths to Women's Equality: Temperance, Suffrage, and the Origins of Modern Feminism* (New York: Twayne, 1995); and Suzanne Stuggenborg, *Gender, Family, and Social Movements* (London: Pine Forge Press, 1998).
33. Women were sometimes urged to convert because drunken women were a common and particular mark of Irish degradation, and drunkenness among wives and mothers was even more socially reprehensible than among men; on other occasions they were reassured that their virtue was unquestioned but the particular power of their moral example was needed by the CTAS because of the influence of mothers over sons and of young women over young men.
34. Reports of M. Cashman (Galway) and H. Blake (Kildysart).
35. Quoted in *Limerick Standard* (*LS*), 10 December 1839.
36. *LS*, 20 December 1839.
37. *WC*, 12 December 1839.
38. *WC*, 1 September 1840.
39. Augustine, *Footprints of Father Mathew*, p. 145; *FJ*, 19 November 1840.
40. This provides an interesting counterpoint to the trend detected in contemporary French nationalism by Joan Landes in *Women and the Public Sphere In the Age of the French Revolution* (Ithaca: 1988).
41. See, for example, accounts of dinners and tea parties in the *Galway Vindicator*, 10 July 1841; *SR*, 14 November 1840; *CE*, 6 September 1841.
42. See, for example, parade descriptions in the *FJ*, 16 June 1840; 26 November 1840; 17 March 1841; 21 April 1841; 15 October 1841; or the *DEP*, 19 March 1839.
43. There were some interesting exceptions to this generalisation. There are a few isolated examples of separate women's societies, although it is not clear that these were not simply auxiliary branches of men's societies. A women's total abstinence society in Waterford, formed just before Mathew's visit, was mentioned in the press (*TFP*, 20 November 1839). The Clogheen TAS had a women's society headed by the local Catholic curate. Women presided at the meetings, proposed toasts and made speeches (*WC*, 15

September 1840). There was at least one meeting in Dublin of the Women's National Temperance Society, where two women spoke 'for the first time', *PNTA*, 7 July 1838 (the society was not affiliated with Mathew's).

44. *TFP*, 13 November 1839. The 1841 census noted the relatively high literacy rate of more than 40 per cent in Ireland.
45. *Cork Standard*, 2 December 1839.
46. *N*, 17 December 1842.
47. Report of T. Carpenter (Dingle).
48. R.J.L. to Father Mathew, n.d., FMCA 2128.
49. John Francis Maguire, *Father Mathew: A Biography* (London: Longman, Roberts and Green, 1863), pp. 296–305.
50. Many of the constabulary reports mention that pubs were now selling only coffee; see the *CR* of P. Morgan, Brudenell Plummer, G. Rich, and Thomas Carpenter.
51. *FJ*, 27 August 1840.
52. *FJ*, 2 July 1840.
53. *FJ*, 26 November 1840.
54. *FJ*, 17 March 1841.
55. See, for example, *FJ*, 28 July 1841 (the Seagoe band was attacked on its way to Belfast), *N*, 5 November 1842 (a Dungannon demonstration was assaulted); *N*, 31 December 1842 (the Monaghan band was attacked).
56. *Two Letters of W.T. Hamilton* (13 March 1840, 14 March 1840), National Archives, OP 1840/2.
57. See, for example, Stipendiary Magistrate's Diary, Diary of G. Fitzgerald for 1840. National Archives; CSO Misc. Books, #40.
58. *CR*, reply of SI Mark O'Malley Burke, Kenmare, Co. Kerry, 19 March 1840. See also reply of A.B. Hill, Dunmore, Co. Kilkenny, 30 March 1840 and reply of Nicholas (illeg.), Arthurstown, Co. Wexford, 23 March 1840.
59. *CR*, reply of William Kelly, Thomastown, Co. Kilkenny, 22 April 1840.
60. *WC*, 11 July 1840.
61. FMC A 1038 (Private). Another undated letter (to the Rev. J. McNamara, PP of Kinsale), relates the postponement of another Easter procession in Cork 'from prudential interest' because Daniel O'Connell planned to attend.
62. *WC*, 11 July 1840.
63. Ibid.
64. *FJ*, 15 July 1840.
65. Letter of J.A. Besim to W. Jones, 16 March 1840, from *CR* of W. Jones.
66. *WC*, 28 May 1840.
67. *DEP*, 8 October 1839; *WC*, 23 July 1840; *FJ*, 17 March 1840; *WC*, 2 January 1840.
68. *DEP*, 9 October 1839.
69. Nicholas Foran of Waterford was one bishop who ordered his clergy to refuse the sacraments to those who violated the pledge until they made 'public atonement' (*FJ*, 1 August 1841). See also *CR*, reply of John Morgan, Corrofin, Co. Clare (n.d.): priests 'refuse the rites of the church to such as will not join'.
70. *WC*, 27 August 1840.
71. Not to be confused with a related contemporary and historiographical debate about the connection between the Temperance movement and a general decline in crime in Ireland. As Kerrigan has explained, although Temperance probably played some part in accelerating a decline already occurring in the crime rate, the variables involved in both record-keeping and the changing nature of policing in this period are too numerous to make any particular claims (Colm Kerrigan, *Father Mathew and the Irish Temperance Movement, 1838–1849* [Cork: University Press, 1992], pp. 86–106).
72. See generally *Stipendiary Magistrate's Diaries*, CSO Misc. Books, National Archives.
73. *Stipendiary Magistrate's Diaries*, CSO Misc. Books, #22 (Diary of Neale Browne).
74. See Samuel Clark and James Donnelly (eds), *Irish Peasants: Violence and Political Unrest 1780–1914* (Madison: University of Wisconsin Press, 1983).
75. *CS*, 3 February 1840.
76. *FJ*, 7 August 1840, 4 September 1840.
77. *WC*, 7 July 1840.
78. Ibid.

79. *N*, 24 December 1842.
80. *WC*, 3 November 1840.
81. *SR*, 20 March 1840.
82. *FJ*, 12 September 1840.
83. One recipe for cordials included 2 pounds of ginger, 8 pounds of brown sugar, 1 ounce of Cayenne pepper, 2 ounces of coriander seed, 3 quarts of water, ¼ ounce of lemon oil, 1 ounce of cinnamon, 1 quart spirits of wine, and 4 gallons of whiskey (*WC*, 14 July 1840).
84. *FJ*, 26 August 1841.
85. *N*, 22 October 1842.
86. *FJ*, 30 May 1842 (letter dated 28 May 1842).
87. *FJ*, 14 October 1840 (letter dated 12 October, and signed 'a teetotaller'). A publican, Patrick Reilly, responded to this letter a few days later, and insisted that his cordials were alcohol-free (*FJ*, 18 October 1840).
88. *CR*.
89. *Kilkenny Journal*, 13 June 1840.
90. 'Rules of the St Mary's Temperance and Mortality Society' (Limerick: C. O'Brian, 1839) (Kitson Constab Rept.).
91. *TFP*, 24 February 1841.
92. *The Miner, A Poem Founded on Facts Connected with the Present State of the Temperance Cause in Bonmahon, County of Waterford (By the Author of 'Nothing Else')* (Waterford: John Killilea, 1841).
93. Ibid., pp. iv, 23.
94. *FJ*, 23 April 1840.
95. *SR*, 17 December 1839.
96. *Nenagh Guardian*, 4 April 1840.
97. *FJ*, 4 March 1842.
98. *KJ*, 3 June 1840.
99. Ibid.
100. *N*, 3 December 1842.
101. *Cork Examiner*, 18 October 1841.

CHAPTER 6

1. In a very few instances, local societies were organised by trade associations.
2. Mathew to Haughton (n.d.), FMC A 1088.
3. Desmond Keenan, *The Catholic Church in Nineteenth Century Ireland* (Totowa, NJ: Gill and Macmillan, 1983), pp. 60–4.
4. William Thackeray, *The Irish Sketch Book* (Boston: James Osgood, 1871), p. 318.
5. J.G. Kohl, *Travels in Ireland* (New York: Harper and Brothers, 1844).
6. See *FJ*, 29 September 1840, for Father Mathew's account of his own clerical education, which is limited to an appreciation of his mentor Father Celestine Corcoran, the Dublin Capuchin who supervised his preparation for holy orders, and who was a 'a rigid disciplinarian'.
7. Elizabeth Malcolm, *Ireland Sober, Ireland Free: Drink and Temperance in 19th Century Ireland* (Syracuse: Syracuse University Press, 1986), p. 104.
8. John Francis Maguire, *Father Mathew: A Biography* (London: Longman, Roberts and Green, 1863), p. 10. Numbers of regular clergy come from Donal Kerr, *Peel, Priests and Politics* (Oxford: Clarendon Press, 1982), p. 186. The overall total (for 1840) of priests in Ireland can be found in Emmet Larkin, 'The Roman Catholic Clergy in 19th Century Ireland', and the number of Capuchins in Ireland in the *Irish Catholic Directory* for 1840.
9. Keenan, *The Catholic Church in Nineteenth-Century Ireland*, pp. 143–4.
10. Rev. Patrick Rogers, *Father Theobald Mathew* (Dublin: Browne and Nolan Ltd., 1945), pp. 13–14.
11. Maguire, *Father Mathew*, pp. 21–2. By all accounts, Mathew was exonerated of the charges.
12. There are good accounts of the controversy in Father Augustine, *Footprints of Father Mathew, O.F.M. Cap., the Apostle of Temperance* (Dublin: Browne and Nolan Ltd., 1947), pp. 80–2 and Malcolm, *Ireland Sober*, pp. 105–6.

13. See *CTA*, 22 May 1841; Malcolm, *Ireland Sober*, p. 105. For church costs, see Keenan, *The Catholic Church*, pp. 120–2. The accusation that Mathew was using money from the crusade to fund his church was noticed, for example, in *Fraser's Magazine*, January 1840.
14. See, for example, *Connaught Journal*, 15 August 1840.
15. *FJ*, 17 August 1840.
16. *Dublin Weekly Herald*, 11 April 1840.
17. Maguire, *Father Mathew*, p. 56.
18. Mathew to Blake (n.d.), FMC A 983.
19. Mathew to Simpson, 22 October 1841, quoted in John Barclay Shiel, *Dr Shield's Historical Account of the Temperance Movement in Ireland* (Dublin: Samuel J. Machen, 1843), p. 6. Simpson was a land agent in the employ of the Marquis of Lansdowne.
20. *WC*, 1 February 1840.
21. See Keenan, *The Catholic Church*, pp. 171–3 for a brief discussion of the 'Second Reformation' in pre-Famine Ireland. Father Tom Maguire, whose enormously popular debates with the Rev. T.M. Gregg and other Protestants packed lecture halls and sold thousands of newspapers and pamphlets, was but one of the active 'controversialists' during the 1830s and 1840s.
22. See, for example, Mathew's apology at Kells on 18 January 1841, for administering the pledge inside a chapel during a severe storm: *FJ*, 27 January 1841.
23. *FJ*, 29 September 1840.
24. Mathew to Simpson, 22 October 1841, in Shiel, *Dr Shiel's Historical Account*, p. 6.
25. Mathew to *Cork Constitution*, 27 April 1843, reprinted in *FJ*, 3 May 1843.
26. Mathew to Bullen (n.d.), FMC A 34.
27. Mathew to Haughton (n.d.), FMC A 1622.
28. *FJ*, 24 Septembr 1840.
29. See Mathew's response to the above letter, also in the *FJ*, 24 September 1840.
30. Mathew to Clarke, [May/June 1843] (n.d.), FMC A 1593. (This letter is one of 21 still extant written about the same time to Maynooth students who had decided to renounce the pledge formally. Mathew mentions in one letter that his brother, who died in April 1843, had passed away about a month before he was writing. The letters, therefore, appear to have been written in the middle of 1843.)
31. Journal of John O'Sullivan, PP of Kenmare. Entry of 11 October 1843. Kerry Diocesan Archives.
32. *WC*, 18 January 1840.
33. *WC*, 7 May 1840.
34. *FJ*, 29 September 1840.
35. See, for example, *Connaught Journal*, 17 December 1840.
36. Joseph Prost, 'Memoirs' (unpublished MSS, copy held by Emmet Larkin at the University of Chicago).
37. Archbishop John Hughes of New York had attended Mathew's first Maynooth mission in June 1840, and had been so impressed he spent several days travelling with the Capuchin.
38. Prost MSS, pp. 74–8. In his introduction to this section of his memoirs, Prost claims he has nine objections, but he omits a fifth and sixth. I have taken the liberty of re-numbering the objections here.
39. In September 1846 Patrick Dorrian, later the Bishop of Down and Connor but at the time a curate in Belfast, wrote a letter opposing temperance in the *Northern Whig*, in response to a visit to Belfast by the Dublin Carmelite and Temperance activist John Spratt. Dorrian expressed his confidence in 'the proper use of the sacraments as a means of reclaiming the most abandoned sinners', including drunkards. Ambrose Macauley, *Patrick Dorrian, Bishop of Down and Connor, 1865–1885* (Dublin: Irish Academic Press, 1987), p. 58.
40. *WC*, 1 February 1840.
41. Mathew to Kirby, 5 May 1842 (K).
42. See, for example,. Rev. T. E. Gill, *Sermon on Saint Patrick's Day* (Dublin: T. O'Gorman, 1841); J. Venedy, *Ireland and the Irish During the Repeal Year, 1843* (Dublin: James Duffy, 1844), p. 106. See also speech of Nicholas Foran, *WC*, 7 January 1840, and James Maher to Paul Cullen, 25 August 1843. Archives of the Dublin Archdiocese (hereafter, ADA), 32/1 Dr Murray 1843–44. Daniel O'Connell was particularly prone to making this claim; see *FJ*,

16 April 1840.

43. *WC*, 23 June 1840, *FJ*, 1 August 1841.
44. *FJ*, 21 September 1840.
45. 'Rules of Saint Mary's Temperance and Mortality Society, Established July 28, 1839, Limerick' (Limerick: C. O'Brian, 1839), copied in the constabulary report of Wilson Kitson, Ennistymon (*CR*).
46. Dowling to Mathew, 31 July 1840, quoted in Malcolm, 'The Catholic Church and the Irish Temperance Movement 1838–1901', *Irish Historical Studies*, XXIII, 89 (May 1982), p. 2.
47. *Tablet*, 29 July 1843; 26 August 1843; 2 September 1843.
48. *Tablet*, 2 September 1843.
49. Mathew to Kirby, 11 February 1842 (K).
50. *FJ*, 20 February 1843; 22 March 1843.
51. Romans 14: 2–3; 13–17; 20–21. (New American Bible)
52. Mathew to Kirby, 11 February 1842 (K).
53. Ibid.
54. *Tablet*, 16 September 1843. Lucas also claimed to have been besieged by letters from priests, in and out of Ireland, praising him for calling Mathew's crusade to task for its intolerance and fanaticism.
55. Macauley, *Patrick Dorrian*, p. 58. Dorrian's remarks appeared in the *Northern Whig*.
56. Prost MSS, p. 77.
57. *FJ*, 29 September 1840. Kinsella never denied refusing to bless the medals, but he did specifically deny parts of these comments. Mathew insisted (in public) that they were 'lies'.
58. Dowling to Mathew, 31 July 1840, quoted in Malcolm, 'The Catholic Church …', p. 2.
59. O'Sullivan Journal, 13 October 1843, Kerry Diocesan Archives.
60. *FJ*, 24 September 1840.
61. *FJ*, 18 November 1840.
62. *Tablet*, 16 September 1843.
63. *WC*, 9 May 1840.
64. *FJ*, 22 May 1841.
65. Slattery Papers (NLI), P 6001-1842/24.
66. *Tablet*, 23 September 1843.
67. *FJ*, 1 August 1841.
68. *FJ*, 10 March 1843. See O'Sullivan Journal, 13 October 1843, Kerry Diocesan Archives. According to O'Sullivan, when this practice became known, he was 'brought before the authorities in Rome, and was it not for the explanation the Bishop was able to give of my motives and my character, I would have been cited'.
69. *Tablet*, 2 September 1843; 16 September 1843.
70. Franzoni to Slattery, 22 September 1842, Slattery Papers, MSS P6001, Letter #24, NLI; Franzoni to Murray, 22 September 1842, Murray Papers, Dublin Archdiocesan Archives.
71. Augustine, *Footprints of Father Mathew*, p. 324.
72. Ibid., pp. 328–33. The Mathew correspondence contains 22 replies from Mathew to students, all probably written about the same time in May/June 1843. FMC A 1578–1599.
73. Mathew to Cloney (n.d.), FMC A 1592.
74. Mathew to Rev. Barry (n.d.), FMC A 1591.
75. Mathew to Rev. O'Neill (n.d.), FMC A 1596
76. The 1842–43 crisis was not the end of Mathew's relationship with Maynooth. He visited the college more than once in subsequent years, and administered the pledge there again. Still, the divisions persisted and he never enjoyed a triumph there as nearly complete as his first visit in 1840. In writing, for example, to accept the invitation of Laurence Renehan to administer the pledge at the college, probably in 1844, Mathew alluded to ongoing divisions over Temperance: 'I know you too well, my dear Dr Renehan, to attribute your silence [on the question of temperance] to opposition, and I am not at all unaware of the obstacles you have to contend with.' FMC A 174.
77. Mathew to Kirby, 5 May 1842 (K).
78. *Alexis de Tocqueville's Journey in Ireland*, ed. Emmet Larkin (Washington: Catholic University of America Press, 1990), p. 48.
79. *WC*, 28 December 1839.

80. Malcolm, *Ireland Sober*, p. 123; Augustine, *Footprints of Father Mathew*, p. 186.
81. My own research has provided the names of over 200 priests who either took the pledge, or participated in temperance meetings, dinners or processions between 1839 and 1843.
82. *WC*, 10 September 1840.
83. *SR*, 9 January 1840.
84. *Cork Standard*, 3 January 1840. Other priests who administered the pledge and distributed Mathew's medals in advance of Mathew's visit to their area included Jeremiah O'Leary, the parish priest of Castle Island and Michael Devine, the parish priest of Dingle, both in the diocese of Kerry (*FJ*, 31 December 1840 and 1 August 1841); Richard Gibbons, the parish priest of Eglish at Castlebar in the archdiocese of Tuam (*FJ*, 28 July 1840); Patrick O'Reilly, a vicar general of the diocese of Kilmore and the parish priest of Urney and Annaliffe near Cavan, and John Mathew of the same diocese (*FJ*, 30 July 1840 and 26 December 1840).
85. *Cork Examiner*, 9 March 1842.
86. Mathew to Kirby, 5 May 1842 (K).
87. Mathew to Kirby, 20 September 1840 (K).
88. Mathew to Cullen, 20 September 1841 (C).
89. Mathew to Kirby, 25 February 1842 (K).
90. Mathew to Kirby, 20 September 1842 (K).
91. See Emmet Larkin, 'The Roman Catholic Clergy in Nineteenth Century Ireland' (unpublished lecture), pp. 10–11; S.J. Connolly, *Priests and People in Pre-Famine Ireland* (New York: St Martin's Press, 1982), pp. 66–7.
92. Mathew to Kirby, 20 September 1842 (K).
93. Journal of John O'Sullivan, 13 October 1843 entry, Kerry Diocesan Archives.
94. *FJ*, 29 September 1840.
95. See Emmet Larkin, 'The Roman Catholic Clergy in Nineteenth Century Ireland'; S.J. Connolly, *Priests and People in Pre-Famine Ireland.*
96. Mathew to Kirby, 20 September 1842.
97. George Cornell Bretherton, 'The Irish Temperance Movement, 1873–1847' (PhD Dissertation, Columbia University, 1978), p. 235; Rogers, *Father Theobald Mathew*, pp. 52–3.
98. O'Connor to Mathew, 10 March 1840, FMC A 300.
99. See, for example, Eugene O'Reilly (PP of Navan and Vicar General in the Diocese of Meath) to Mathew, 9 August 1840, FMC, 'Father Mathew's Letters' file.
100. Kenyon to Mathew, 10 July 1840, quoted in Father Augustine, *Footprints of Father Mathew*, p. 157.
101. *Limerick Reporter*, 29 May 1840.
102. Augustine, *Footprints of Father Mathew*, p. 251.
103. Journal of John O'Sullivan, 13 October 1843, Kerry Diocesan Archives.
104. Haughton published his letter in spite of Mathew's advice, in the *Freeman's Journal*, 6 April 1844. This contributed to the growing estrangement between the two men.
105. Mathew to Haughton (n.d.), FMC A 184.
106. Mathew to Murphy (n.d.), FMC A 1129.
107. Mathew to Kirby, 15 September 1842 (K).
108. Bretherton, 'The Irish Temperance Movement', pp. 233, 240. Coen issued a pastoral letter in April 1838 urging his priests to 'forward the blessed revolution'.
109. Mathew stayed with Keating in April, 1840 when he visited his diocese, and also met with the bishop the following month: *WC*, 9 April 1840, *FJ*, 23 April 1840. Mathew later claimed Keating not only as a strong supporter, but also as a teetotaller: *FJ*, 1 January 1841. James Browne supported branches of the CTAS at least by the summer of 1840, and travelled with Father Mathew when he visited Cavan in June 1841: *FJ*, 3 July 1840; 5 June 1841. He was also the patron of the Cootehill branch of the CTAS. Michael Blake was a strong advocate of temperance, and joined Father Mathew at a church dedication/temperance mission in Lurgan in 1841. He brought 14 of his priests to an earlier mission, and spoke at length in praise of Father Mathew at a grand tea party in Newry the same year: *FJ*, 29 July 1841; 29 September 1841; *Newry Examiner*, 2 October 1841. John Cantwell attended an early temperance mission in July 1840, and personally escorted Mathew on a subsequent visit to Navan: *FJ*, 14 July 1840; 22 March 1842.

110. Colm Kerrigan, *Father Mathew and the Irish Temperance Movement, 1839–1849* (Cork: University Press, 1992), p. 156. McGettigan apparently did not remain a teetotaller for long.
111. For examples of Foran leading Temperance meetings, see *WC*, 17 January 1840; 17 March 1840; 9 May 1840; 23 June 1840 or *FJ*, 29 October 1840; 25 August 1841.
112. *FJ*, 1 October 1840; 1 August 1841.
113. *FJ*, 6 August 1841.
114. *WC*, 17 March 1840.
115. *FJ*, 14 October 1842.
116. For Murray's letter, see Murray to Mathew, 11 July 1840, FMC 'Letters to'. The letter was not published, but the fact that the visit was at Murray's invitation was, see *FJ*, 29 September 1840.
117. *FJ*, 16 November 1840.
118. Murray to Cullen, 21 September 1841 (C).
119. *Tipperary Free Press*, 29 January 1840.
120. *CS*, 17 June 1840; *FJ*, 1 August 1841, 4 September 1841.
121. *Nation*, 25 February 1843. The others were Edward Kernan of Clogher, William Kinsella of Ossory, Francis Healy of Kildare and Leighlin, and George Browne of Galway. For Egan's private remarks on Temperance, see the Journal of John O'Sullivan, 13 October 1843, Diocesan Archives, Kerry.
122. For a copy of the invitation, see Kinsella to Mathew, 2 April 1842, McKenna MSS, p. 613.
123. Mathew visited Drogheda on 8 May 1842.
124. Denvir, for one, was supposed to have had 'misgivings about the emotionalism, excitement and extent of the pledge'. Ambrose Macauley, *Patrick Dorrian, Bishop of Down and Connor, 1865–1885* (Dublin: Irish Academic Press, 1987), p. 57.
125. *FJ*, 31 May 1841. Bretherton, 'The Irish Temperance Movement', p. 241; Archbishop Ullathorne, *From Cabin Boy to Archbishop* (London: Burns Oates, 1941).
126. *FJ*, 16 May 1841.
127. *WC*, 17 March 1840.
128. Mathew to Haughton, FMC A 171 (n.d.); FMC A 1622 (n.d.).
129. For observations on MacHale's difficult but interesting personality, see Emmet Larkin, 'The Quarrel Among the Roman Catholic Hierarchy Over the National System of Education in Ireland, 1838–1841' (Cambridge: MIT Press, 1965), pp. 122, 142. Paul Cullen wrote in 1854 that 'MacHale loves to find himself in opposition'; Cullen's impression was shared by many others. Donal Kerr, *Peel, Priests and Politics* (Oxford: Clarendon Press, 1982), pp. 23–4.
130. Burke to Mathew, 23 March 1840, McKenna MSS, p. 613.
131. *Mayo Constitution*, 25 August 1840. The *Constitution*, which reported the refusal, was a Tory, anti-temperance paper, and no friend of the archbishop. In promoting the belief that the break with MacHale was occasioned by Mathew's refusing to help finance the archbishop's alternative to the national education system, the *Constitution* may simply have been trying to exploit the most serious and public faultline in pre-Famine Catholicism. Still, Mathew's visit to Balla *was* cancelled, and MacHale's opposition to Mathew was widely commented on in succeeding months. It does seem clear that MacHale demanded to control the revenue Mathew's movement might generate in his diocese. The story of the revenue's proposed use for the archbishop's schools was so well-known that Mathew took pains to deny it explicitly in a public letter the following year; see *Kerry Examiner*, 20 April 1841.
132. Burke to Mathew, 4 September 1840, FMC A 31.
133. In that year, the diocesan clergy had placed the popular Burke first on the required *terna* of three candidates to fill the vacant archbishopric of Tuam, but MacHale, second on the *terna*, was preferred by Rome for the mitre, a decision that set the stage for a number of public clashes between the two men. Even a sympathetic historian of the archdiocese acknowledged the bitterness of the dispute. After his appointment, MacHale attempted to assume control of Burke's parish at Westport, one of the richest in the diocese, and transfer Burke to a remote part of Tuam. Burke resisted, and, with the help of Rome, was successful. 'Probably Dr MacHale's contest with Dean Burke about the Westport parish, and his defeat at the Dean's hands, embittered him a little. Whatever the reason, it is

certain that he was embittered, and wrote of the Dean with great asperity.' Rt. Rev. Msgr. Dalton, *The History of the Archdiocese of Tuam* (vol. II) (Dublin: Phoenix Pub. Co. Ltd, 1928), p. 8.
134. Shane McGuire, 'A Profile of Bernard Burke (1789–1861)', *Cathair Na Mart*, Vol. 7, No. 1 (Westport: Historical Society, 1987), p. 65.
135. *FJ*, 14 July 1840
136. *MC*, 25 August 1840. The Constitution's report to this effect was not contradicted.
137. See Burke's letter to Mathew; see also the 'Letter of a Galway Teetotaller' complaining about MacHale's dispensing with the pledge and issuing cards and medals independently of Mathew, *Connaught Journal*, 17 December 1840. See also Bretherton, 'The Irish Temperance Movement', p. 245.
138. Augustine, *Footprints of Father Mathew*, p. 204.
139. Ibid., p. 207.
140. *Dublin Weekly Herald*, 19 June 1841.
141. Augustine, *Footprints of Father Mathew*, pp. 207–8. Burke was not in attendance when the resolution was passed.
142. Mathew to O'Connell, 5 July 1841, in *FJ*, 7 July 1841.
143. O'Connell's resolution was published in the *ICD* for 1842, with approving commentary. Mathew's response, although mentioned, was not reprinted.
144. *FJ*, 9 July 1841.
145. *FJ*, 20 July 1841.
146. Mathew to Cullen, 12 September 1841 (C).
147. A milder version of this condemnation appears to have been delivered in English at Tuam about the same time. Quinn, 'Father Mathew's Temperance Crusade in Ireland', p. 166.
148. Mathew to Cullen, 21 September 1841 (C).
149. *FJ*, 25 May 1840. See *ICD*, 1841, 273, for a solicitation for donations and description of the 'Grecian' church, which was to be 'the most extensive, and the most elegant, Catholic Church of modern times'.
150. *FJ*, 12 August 1840.
151. Davys to Mathew, 12 August 1840, FMC A 44.
152. Ibid.
153. J. Burke to Mathew, 4 September 1840, FMC A 31. Mathew's informant was a priest in the diocese of Tuam, undoubtedly Joseph Burke, a curate at Ballinarobe.
154. *WC*, 13 August, 27 August 1840.
155. *WC*, 13 August 1840.
156. *WC*, 27 August 1840.
157. Burke to Mathew, 4 September 1840, FMC A 31. Much later, Higgins accused Mathew, in a letter to Paul Cullen, of 'notorious latitudinarianism' and specifically mentioned that Mathew 'preached from the Protestant version of the Scriptures, and despite of remonstrance placed a corrupt text on his medals'. Higgins to Cullen, 30 June 1847. From Emmet Larkin's transcribed copies of the Cullen Correspondence in the Irish College, Rome (C).
158. Burke to Mathew, 4 September 1840, FMC A 31.
159. *FJ*, 12 September 1840.
160. *FJ*, 3 April 1841.
161. Higgins to Cullen, 30 June 1847 (C).
162. W. O'Connor to Mathew, 29 July 1840, FMC A 295. Mathew's correspondent, a layman, appears to have been connected with the Ballporeen branch of the CTAS in the diocese of Waterford and Lismore.
163. O'Connell's response appeared in the press as well; see Augustine, *Footprints of Father Mathew*, p. 207.
164. Mathew to Kirby, 5 May 1842. (K).
165. *Tablet*, 30 September 1843.
166. Mathew to Haughton (n.d.), FMC A 1622.
167. *Tablet*, 30 September 1843.
168. John Ennis to Daniel Murray, 30 May 1840, Calendar of Murray Correspondence, File 31/8.

169. *FJ*, 29 August 1840, *Connaught Journal*, 3 September 1840. Cullen attended temperance meetings at Freshford in Tipperary and Athy in Kildare.
170. Mathew to Kirby, 6 October 1841 (K).
171. Mathew to Cullen, 12 December 1840. Cited in Augustine, *Footprints of Father Mathew*, p. 202.
172. Augustine, *Footprints of Father Mathew*, p. 203.
173. *FJ*, 3 September 1841, Cullen to Mathew, 10 October 1841, cited in Augustine, *Footprints of Father Mathew*, p. 202.
174. Mathew to Cullen, 20 September 1841.
175. *CE*, 1 September 1841; *FJ*, 3 September 1841.
176. Mathew to Rev. Hanlon, 27 August 1846, FMC A 96.
177. Mathew to Cullen, 20 September 1841 (C).
178. Cullen to Mathew, 10 October 1841, cited in Augustine, *Footprints of Father Mathew*, p. 210.
179. *FJ*, 15 June 1840.
180. Augustine, *Footprints of Father Mathew*, p. 203. See *FJ*, 16 March 1841 for an example of informal reports of Gregory XVI's enthusiasm for Mathew's cause.
181. The report was reprinted in the *CE*, 8 October 1841, and the *FJ*, 7 October 1841.
182. Mathew to Kirby, 6 October 1841 (K).
183. *Belfast Vindicator*, 31 January 1842; *FJ* 4 February 1842.
184. Mathew to Kirby, 11 February 1842 (K).
185. *CE*, 18 February 1842.
186. Mathew to Kirby, 18 February 1842 (K).
187. *CE*, 27 April 1842, *FJ* 30 September 1842.
188. Mathew to Kirby, 5 May 1842 (K).
189. I suspect similar letters were sent to Crolly and MacHale, although MacHale's papers have been lost and the Armagh diocesan archives, at the time of writing, were not granting access to researchers. Copies of the Franzoni letter exist in the Diocesan Archives in Dublin (Franzoni to Murray, 22 September 1842, Calendar of Murray Papers in DDA, 31/9) and in the microfilmed Slattery Papers in the National Library (the originals are at Thurles), Franzoni to Slattery, 22 September 1842, Slattery Papers, NLI 6001 1842/24.
190. Murray to Franzoni, 14 October 1842, Murray Papers, DDA, File 31/9; Slattery to Franzoni, 6 October 1842, Slattery Papers, NLI 6001 184/24.
191. Slattery's opinion on the nature of the pledge was also reflected in the document from his papers discussed earlier, the printed circular on the Temperance movement that was apparently distributed to all diocesan clergy sometime during 1842, designed to assure 'uniformity of opinion' among his priests on the subject. Temperance Circular, Slattery Papers, NLI P 6001 1842/24.
192. Mathew to Kirby, 15 September 1842 (K).
193. Mathew to Kirby, 28 September 1842 (K).
194. Mathew to Cullen, 30 October 1845 (C).
195. Mathew to Cullen, 27 December 1845 (C).
196. Mathew to John Murphy, O.F.M. Cap. (n.d.), FMC 'Father Mathew's Letters' folder.
197. Mathew to Kirby, 5 May 1842 (K).
198. Mathew to ? (n.d.; fragment) FMC A 651. The '+' in the emotional last sentence is Mathew's; it is a mark he did not normally use to stand for 'and'. Perhaps he meant to emphasise the sacred character of the 'blood Guiltiness' of his opponents.

CHAPTER 7

1. Lawrence J. McCaffrey's *Daniel O'Connell and the Repeal Year* (Knoxville, KY: University of Kentucky Press, 1966), pp. 21–3, gives a thought-provoking appraisal of the connections between the two causes. General histories often ignore or downplay the moral underpinning of the Repeal movement; see, for example, K. Theodore Hoppen, *Ireland Since 1800: Conflict and Conformity* (London: Longman, 1989), p. 79; even otherwise excellent examinations of O'Connellism such as Oliver MacDonagh's *The Emancipist* (New York: St Martin's Press, 1989), p. 185, fail to give the subject the attention it deserves.

2. Some of this complexity is acknowledged in recent studies of Father Mathew and his movement. Colm Kerrigan devotes a chapter to the subject, and indicates that it would have been impossible for the Temperance and Repeal movements to remain completely separate (Colm Kerrigan, *Father Mathew and the Irish Temperance Movement, 1838–1849* (Cork: University Press, 1992), pp. 107, 113). Kerrigan, however, does not provide any systematic evaluation of the nature of their connection. Elizabeth Malcolm, in her study of Temperance and politics in nineteenth century Ireland, also notes the strong links between the movements, and provides an excellent starting point from which to consider the nature and consequences for both movements, in greater detail (Elizabeth Malcolm, *Ireland Sober, Ireland Free: Drink and Temperance in 19th Century Ireland* (Syracuse: Syracuse University Press, 1986), pp. 128–33). Although the unpublished dissertations of George Bretherton and John Quinn both acknowledge the existence of Repeal-Temperance connections, they do not support Malcolm in her assertion that the movements formed a strong 'alliance'. (Malcolm, *Ireland Sober*, p. 132.) Bretherton in particular denies that there was a 'natural' affinity between the two causes, of which Temperance was the stronger, and portrays Mathew as an anti-O'Connellite enamoured by Ireland's English connection (George Cornell Bretherton, 'The Irish Temperance Movement, 1833–1847' (PhD Dissertation, Columbia University), pp. 275–84.) Quinn views Temperance as an increasingly important auxiliary to Repeal after 1843 in a number of practical ways, and acknowledges that Mathew resisted O'Connell's efforts to link the causes. While he notes that the connection presented problems for Mathew, and agrees with Malcolm that it drove some Protestants away from the cause, he does not attribute the decline of Temperance to the Repeal movement (John Quinn, 'Father Mathew's Temperance Crusade in Ireland, 1838–1856' (PhD Dissertation, Notre Dame, 1992), pp. 171–94). Other published biographies of Mathew provide a great deal of practical information on the Temperance/Repeal connection, particularly Father Augustine and John Francis Maguire. Frank Mathew, Father Mathew's nephew, also provides an impressionistic but very thought-provoking look at the emotional connection between the two movements (Frank J. Mathew, *Father Mathew: His Life and Times* (London: Cassell and Co. Ltd, 1890).
3. See Rionach Ui Ogain, *The Immortal Dan: Daniel O'Connell in Folk Tradition* (Dublin: Geography Publications, 1995), for a fascinating overview of Daniel O'Connell and popular memory.
4. R.D. Webb to J.A. Collins, 2 April 1842, Webb Family Correspondence, TCD, BPL MS A.1.2 v.12(2) AS letters to G, #41.
5. The brewery later failed, a failure that the elder O'Connell often attributed to the Temperance campaign. Patrick Lynch and John Vaizey claim in *Guinness's Brewery in the Irish Economy, 1759–1876* (Cambridge: Cambridge University Press, 1960), p. 91, that the brewery was so poorly managed and the beer so indifferent that it would have failed even 'had Father Mathew been a brewer's advocate'.
6. 'O'Connell's Porter', anon., Madden Ballad Collection #566, NLI.
7. *Hansard's Parliamentary Debates*, series 3, vol. 24, 1834, p. 967.
8. Malcolm, *Ireland Sober*, p. 130.
9. *DEP*, 16 August 1838.
10. *SR*, 7 August 1838.
11. See *CS*, 10 August 1838; *SR*, 7 August 1838. The newspapers make no mention of who the cause's supporters were, although men such as Joseph Hayes, Thomas Lyons and perhaps even John Francis Maguire were the most likely advocates.
12. See, for example, *TFP*, 11 August 1838; *Waterford Mirror*, 11 August 1838, See also *DEP* editorials, 9 August 1838 and 11 August 1838.
13. The *Dublin Evening Post*'s supportive editorials noted that the plan was an attempt to imitate the American Colonies' successful response to Parliamentary tyranny, as did the *Southern Reporter*. The *Waterford Mirror* observed that the movement was 'Pro-repeal' (11 August 1838).
14. *CS*, 24 August 1838.
15. *CS*, 24 August 1838; *SR*, 28 August 1838.
16. The *Southern Reporter* endorsed the Precursor Society on 30 August 1838; the *Dublin Evening Post* also became a supporter of the movement and did not mention non-

consumption after mid-August, when O'Connell's opposition became apparent.

17. *DEP*, 5 March 1839 (letter dated 1 March 1839).
18. Charles Chenevix, *The Great Dan* (London: Triad Grafton, 1984), pp. 258–60.
19. O'Connell to Fitzpatrick, 25 August 1839, Maurice R. O'Connell (ed.), *The Correspondence of Daniel O'Connell* (Dublin: Irish University Press, 1977), v. VI, #2658, p. 278.
20. *DEP*, 3 September 1839.
21. *DEP*, 3 October 1839.
22. *SR*, 3 October 1839.
23. *SR*, 22 October 1839.
24. *SR*, 7 December 1839. James Haughton had 10,000 copies of this speech printed up in broadsheet form and distributed across Ireland. Father Augustine, *Footprints of Father Mathew, O.F.M. Cap., the Apostle of Temperance* (Dublin: Browne and Nolan Ltd., 1947), p. 107.
25. *WC*, 24 December 1839.
26. Dower to O'Connell, 30 December 1839, *OCC* IV.
27. See, for example, Mathew's final speech in Dublin before leaving for the Parlimentary session, *WC*, 14 January 1840.
28. *Dublin Weekly Herald*, 28 March 1840.
29. *Connaught Journal*, 19 March 1840. The crowd was 80,000 'on the lowest calculation'.
30. Augustine, *Footprints of Father Mathew*, p. 175.
31. John Francis Maguire, *Father Mathew: A Biography* (London: Longman, Roberts and Green, 1863), p. 150.
32. See, for example, *CR*, Report of P. Morgan, Roscrea, Co. Tipperary; Report of John Barron, Ennistymon, Co. Clare; Report of George Hill, Enniscorthy, Co. Wexford; Report of J. J. Thate, Charleville, Co. Cork.
33. *CR*, Report of B. Clinch, Kilcummin, Co. Galway; Report of Louis Anderson, Cahir, Co. Tipperary; Report of Mark O'Malley Burke, Kenmare, Co. Kerry.
34. *CR* (illegible) Macroom, County Cork; Report of John Croker, Clonmel, Co. Tipperary; Report of W. Coffey, Dromore, Co. Galway; Report of (illeg.) Thompson, Kilkenny, County Kilkenny.
35. *CR*, Report of W. Lewis, County Galway.
36. *Limerick Standard*, 24 December 1839.
37. *London Times* (*LT*), 2 January 1840.
38. *WC*, 14 January 1840.
39. *SR*, 9 January 1840.
40. *WC*, 14 January 1840 (letter dated 11 January 1840)
41. *WC*, 19 March 1840. See also *Connaught Journal* (*CJ*) 19 March 1840.
42. *SR*, 24 March 1840.
43. *Kilkenny Journal*, 21 March 1840.
44. *FJ*, 31 March 1840.
45. *FJ*, 2 April 1840; *DWH*, 11 April 1840.
46. *The Times* was joined in its criticisms of processions by the *Dublin Evening Mail*.
47. *FJ*, 6 April 1840.
48. *SR*, 7 April 1840.
49. *SR*, 18 April 1840.
50. *FJ*, 18 April 1840. Ullathorne gives a wonderful description of Maguire's character, including his penchant for plunging red-hot pokers into glasses of whiskey before embarking on public-house political discussions with O'Connell or his associates. Archbishop Ullathorne, *From Cabin Boy to Archbishop* (London: Burns Oates, 1941). Ullathorne's work is an autobiographical recollection, but in 1838 the *Cork Standard* had delivered a satire of Maguire teaching the Pope how to make whiskey punch: '"Put 'n the sperits first", says his riv'rence, "and then put in the sugar, and remember, every dhrop of wather you put in after that spoils the punch".' *CS*, 4 May 1838.
51. *TFP*, 11 April 1840.
52. The *SR* printed the ballad on 18 April 1840. See also 'A Tri-part Ode to Father Mathew', which also lampoons Tory anti-temperance, *SR*, 9 April 1840.
53. *WC*, 11 April 1840.
54. *FJ*, 7 April 1840.
55. *FJ*, 13 April 1840.

56. *WC*, 14 April 1840.
57. *FJ*, 16 April 1840.
58. Widespread opposition to 'militaristic' temperance processions among Protestants and political conservatives in Ireland is noted in many of the Constabulary Reports, and was, by early 1840, a standard component of practically all Tory critiques of the crusade. Mathew realised that these demonstrations made his movement politically suspect, but was by and large unable to prevent them, even in Cork where his influence was greatest. See, for example, Mathew to Rev. J. MacNamara, V.G. (n.d.), FMC A 619 (cancelling a Cork Easter parade would 'avoid great risk'); Mathew to Rev. John Spratt (n.d.), FMC A 1038 ('I do not believe our society would lose a single member by its [Dublin's Easter Temperance procession] being postponed or wholly omitted this year, and in my opinion a great risk would be avoided.')
59. Rev. James Bermingham, *A Memoir of the Very Rev. Theobald Mathew, with an Account of the Rise and Progress of Temperance in Ireland* (Dublin: Milliken and Son, 1840), p. 6.
60. Mathew to Bermingham, 28 May 1840, published in *SR*, 6 June 1840.
61. Oliver MacDonagh, *The Emancipist* (New York: St Martin's Press, 1989), p. 187.
62. *FJ*, 10 June 1840.
63. *FJ*, 7 July 1840.
64. *FJ*, 16 July 1840.
65. *FJ*, 22 July 1840. The strategy was discussed in an open letter to the Irish people from O'Connell, 21 July 1840.
66. *WC*, 1 August 1840.
67. *FJ*, 6 August, 8 August, 17 August 1840.
68. MacDonagh, *The Emancipist*, p. 188.
69. *FJ*, 28 July 1840.
70. *WC*, 15 August 1840.
71. *FJ*, 31 August 1840.
72. See Joseph Hayes to Daniel O'Connell, 14 August 1840, *OCC* VI, #2735, pp. 352–3, for a succinct, and deeply pessimistic account of the progress and prospects of Repeal.
73. *FJ*, 10 September 1840.
74. *WC*, 26 September 1840.
75. *FJ*, 8 October 1840.
76. *SR*, 6 October 1840.
77. *FJ*, 9 October 1840.
78. *FJ*, 13 October, 14 October, 15 October, 16 October, 20 October, 21 October 1840; *WC*, 5 November 1840.
79. *FJ*, 30 September 1840.
80. Maguire, *Father Mathew*, pp. 148–9.
81. See, for example Mathew's speech at Swords in November (*FJ*, 17 November 1840); as well as his letters to Edward Bullen and John Butler (FMC A 206; 245.)
82. *SR*, 19 November 1840. O'Connell's letter accepting the invitation, dated the 14th, had appeared in the *Southern Reporter* of the 17th. In it the Liberator had argued that while 'it is true that, as teetotallers merely, we have no distinctive politics; but it is equally true that we do not abandon our politics by becoming teetotallers. On the contrary, whatever were the political sentiments of a man before he took the pledge – especially if they were Liberal – they become the more fixed, the more steady, and the more available for useful and patriotic purposes, by reason of his sobriety'.
83. The letter, dated 24 January 1841, was reprinted in the *FJ* on 1 February 1841.
84. Mathew to Edward Bullen (n.d.), FMC A 33.
85. Mathew to William West (n.d.), FMC A 1742.
86. Mathew to Dr John Shiel (n.d), FMC A 1041.
87. O'Connell met the Vintners Association at the Theatre Royal in Abbey Street on 3 July, where he insisted that his support of temperance, which had cost him 'at least 500 honest votes in this city' was not a reflection of the esteem in which he held his listeners, *FJ*, 5 July 1841. On the hustings several days later he again apologised for the effects of temperance on 'one of the very best classes of our fellow citizens', *FJ* 6 July 1841. An anti-O'Connell pamphlet by an 'Insolvent Vintner' was an important piece of election propaganda, and despite editorials and letters to the editor urging those involved in the

liquor trade to support O'Connell, he did not poll well among his old allies, *FJ*, 8 July 1841.

88. See MacDonagh, *The Emancipist*, pp. 192, 235.
89. *FJ*, 26 July 1841.
90. MacDonagh, *The Emancipist*, p. 219.
91. *Cork Examiner* (*CE*), 28 March 1842.
92. *CE*, 28 March 1842. O'Connell had been elected Lord Mayor of Dublin the previous October.
93. Maguire, *Father Mathew*, p. 151.
94. Malcolm, *Ireland Sober*, p. 151; *CE*, 28 March 1842.
95. *FJ*, 30 March 1842.
96. Mathew to Richard Allen, 7 April 1842, Dublin: Quaker Archives, Allen Album 14. The letter was published in the *Cork Examiner* on 13 April, and the *Dublin Journal of Temperance, Science, and Literature*, 14 May 1842. See also Mathew's comments in Dublin in June, *CE*, 1 July 1842.
97. *CE*, 4 May 1842.
98. *FJ*, 17 May 1842.
99. O'Connell to Mathew, 3 July 1842, FMC 'Letter From Daniel O'Connell' folder.
100. *Tralee Examiner*, 19 July 1842.
101. At Waterford, the corporation were 'Repealers almost to a man' and the people were well-organised, *Nation*, 19 November 1842 (*N*). John O'Connell praised Limerick for its 'perfect state of organisation', which he insisted was the best in Ireland, *N*, 24 December 1842.
102. In an undated letter to Thomas O'Connell, Mathew explained that in Cork 'the Repeal Committee in this city is composed of Teetotallers, Mr Thomas Lyons at their head, but the question has never even been alluded to in any of our rooms – they have repeal rooms for repeal purposes'. FMC 'Letters to C' Folder.
103. O'Connell's dispute with Mathew over the Westport Branch of the CTAS has already been noticed (Chapter 6), and Mathew's correspondence mentions other disagreements. Spratt and Mathew later quarrelled over Spratt's unauthorised visit to Belfast and Spratt's role in the Mathew Testimonial.
104. *N*, 29 October 1842.
105. Mathew to Murphy (n.d.), FMC 'Father Mathew's Letters' Folder. Private.
106. Ibid.
107. Ibid. Haughton's Repeal sympathies certainly annoyed Mathew; see Mathew to Haughton (n.d.), FMC A 184.
108. Mathew to 'My Dear Friend' (n.d.), FMC A 1130.
109. Mathew to Duff (n.d.), FMC A 1716, Private.
110. Oliver MacDonagh claims that O'Connell was a teetotaller for 18 months, which means that O'Connell gave up the pledge shortly after his Easter meeting with Father Mathew, MacDonagh, *The Emancipist*, p. 1. O'Connell made very frequent references to his health in connection with teetotalling, and seemed surprised in 1840 when giving up alcohol improved his constitution. Perhaps a minor ailment or some perceived decline in vigour led him to adopt the very common doctor's 'health exception' to total abstinence.
111. *N*, 28 January 1843.
112. Augustine, *Footprints of Father Mathew*, p. 311.
113. MacDonagh, *The Emancipist*, pp. 219–27. For an excellent study of the rituals and practices that characterised Repeal meetings, see Gary Owens, 'Nationalism Without Words: Symbolism and Ritual Behaviour in the Repeal "Monster Meetings" of 1843–45', in James S. Donnelly, Jr. and Kirby A. Miller (eds), *Irish Popular Culture, 1650–1850* (Dublin: Irish Academic Press, 1997), pp. 243–69.
114. *N*, 6 May 1843.
115. *N*, 15 May 1843.
116. J. Venedy, *Ireland and the Irish During the Repeal Year of 1843* (trans. by W.B. McCabe) (Dublin: James Duffy, 1844), 34.
117. Ibid., p. 27.
118. Ibid., p. 59.
119. *FJ*, 21 March 1843.

120. Particularly *Father Mathew* and *On Visiting the Botanic Gardens. The Spirit of the Nation* (Dublin: 1843), p. 3, RIA Haliday 1865.
121. Reprinted in Marie Fitzgibbon and Michael Mulcahey, *The Voice of the People: Songs and History of Ireland* (Dublin: O'Brian Press, 1982), p. 88.
122. J.Kearney, *Mr J. Kearney's Original Comic Songs* (Dublin: 1844), p. 2.
123. John Lennon, 'The United Voices of Tara and Clonfert' (Dublin: O'Brian, 1843); RIA Haliday 1870.
124. John Lennon, *The Irish Repealer's Mountain Harp of the Triumphant Year of 1843* (Dublin: O'Brian, 1843).
125. James Healy, *The Irish Minstrel, or a Collection of Repeal Melodies, Under the Patronage of the Repeal Wardens of Dublin* (Dublin: Bernard Madden, 1843), p. 21. Similar associations occurred in popular songs before and after 1843, of course. A street ballad describing Father Mathew's visit to Glendalough in June, 1842 also praised 'our great Liberator,/ Brave Dan O'Connell, of worth and fame,/ That gained for us our emancipation,/ From base submission and servile chains', and concluded with the hope that the grand occasion would change the hearts of many in England. Reprinted in *The Healy Collection of Irish Street Ballads*, Vol. 4 (Cork: Mercier Press, 1969), p. 31. See also Catherine Luby, *Father Mathew; or Ireland as She Ought to Be, In Three Cantos* (Dublin: S.J. Machen, 1845).
126. *The Repealers,* an 1843 production, featured hypocritical characters including a 'drunken guager' who saw Ireland as a 'degraded, enslaved, insulted and persecuted nation (hear him) a nation of slaves'. Anon., *The Repealers* (Dublin: 1843), RIA Haliday 1870. In 1844, the *Dublin Evening Mail* printed an equally satirical *Bran-new Temperance Melody: To be said or Sung by all Loyal, National, Teetotal Repealers. Dublin Evening Mail* 6 March 1844.
127. Robert Young, *The Ulster Harmonist* (Derry: 1840), RIA Haliday 1785.
128. The letter was read at LNRA proceedings, *FJ*, 4 August 1841.
129. *FJ*, 10 August 1841.
130. *FJ*, 23 September 1840.
131. *FJ*, 23 September 1841.
132. *FJ*, 24 September 1841; 27 May 1842.
133. *FJ*, 14 September 1840.
134. Malcolm, *Ireland Sober*, p. 130.
135. *CTA*, 20 February 1841, and *CE*, 30 August 1841.
136. See Edward Kennedy, *The Inaugural Address to the Members of the Cork Temperance Institute* (Cork: George Nash, 1845). Justin McCarthy, the Irish parliamentarian, provides a fascinating description of Father Mathew and this institution in his autobiography, *The Story of an Irishman* (London: Chatto and Windus, 1904), pp. 31–43.
137. *FJ*, 27 March 1841.
138. *Circular addressed by order of the Irish government to the county inspectors of the constabulary force with the several answers received from these officers (1843); '...' to the stipendiary magistrates with '...'* (1843), Liverpool Record Office, Papers of the Earl of Derby, Box 34, cited in Kerrigan, *Father Mathew*, pp. 123–5. Not surprisingly, Limerick and Waterford were two areas cited as having particularly high degree of overlap.
139. As Gary Owens strongly suggests, these rituals, much more than O'Connell's speeches, were at the centre of Repeal gatherings. Owens, 'Nationalism without Words', p. 247.
140. At least for temperance meetings after the first few, which were more raucous affairs owing to the popularity of fond 'farewells to whiskey'.
141. Owens describes how 'symbol encrusted' Repeal cards were displayed in a variety of ways at meetings. Owens, 'Nationalism without Words', p. 253.
142. *FJ*, 12 October 1841. Not insignificantly, O'Connell praised Irwin as 'a man who had manifested so much common sense, and so much just discernment – who had evinced such a thorough understanding of their object, and of the means by which they sought to attain it ... Oh yes, Repealers and Teetotallers going hand and hand in such a good cause were such to carry it out effectually. He (Mr O'Connell) had fellow teetotallers joined with him in the common cause of their country. He did not, as a teetotaller, stand alone, and he was proud of it'.
143. *FJ*, 8 August 1840.
144. *FJ*, 23 February 1841.
145. *WC*, 19 March 1840, *FJ*, 8 October 1840.

146. See, for example, *FJ*, 24 August 1840; *SR*, 17 November 1840, for examples of O'Connell's comments on the subject.
147. Mathew to Haughton (n.d.) [early 1844], FMC A 184.
148. Mathew to Rev. Halligan (n.d.) [1844], FMC A 1227.
149. See Bretheton, 'The Irish Temperance Movement', p. 275.
150. Ibid., pp. 275–6.
151. *Nenagh Guardian*, 8 March 1843.
152. *Limerick Reporter*, 2 June 1843.
153. Augustine, *Footprints of Father Mathew*, pp. 284, 294. *Tablet*, 15 July 1843.
154. Augustine, *Footprints of Father Mathew*, p. 310.
155. Mathew to John Russell (n.d.), FMC A 123.
156. Laurence McCaffrey's *Repeal Year* contains a particularly effective description of the popular deflation of Repeal after Clontarf, Lawrence J. McCaffrey, *Daniel O'Connell and the Repeal Year* (Knoxville, KY: University of Kentucky Press, 1966), p. 207.
157. Mathew to Rev. Halligan (n.d.), FMC A 1227. The reference to O'Connell's liberation means this letter was composed before 4 September, 1844.
158. Mathew to F. B. Haly (n.d.), FMC A 1554 (Private). Haly was the editor of the pro-O'Connell *Pilot*.
159. Mathew to John Russell Esq. (n.d.), FMC A 123.
160. Mathew to Haly (n.d.), FMC A 825.
161. Mathew to Haly (n.d.), cited in Bretherton, 'The Irish Temperance Movement', p. 274.
162. Mathew to John Russell Esq. (n.d.), FMC A 123.
163. Mathew to John Russell, Esq. (n.d.), FMC A 124.
164. Mathew to [illeg.], [1844], FMC A 1164.
165. Mathew to Hansard, 20 October 1846, cited in Bretherton, 'The Irish Temperance Movement', p. 282.
166. Mathew to Thomas Cooke, Esq., 28 April 1846, FMC A 1847.
167. M. W. Chapman to R.D. Webb, 2 February 1842, TCD Webb Fam. Cor. (BPL MS A.1.2 v.12(2) ASL-G #30).
168. Mathew to [illeg.], [1844], FMC A 1164.
169. Mathew to John Russell (n.d.), FMC A 123.
170. It is interesting to note that contemporary social movements in England (Chartism in particular) were increasingly oriented towards Parliament; in Ireland Temperance/ Repeal activism sought to transcend and/or separate from the legislative process.

CHAPTER 8

1. John Forbes makes it quite clear that local leadership and the strength of local societies played a crucial part in keeping the movement active in a few places even as late as 1852. John Forbes, *Memorandums Made in Ireland in the Autumn of 1852* (London: Smith, Elder and Co., 1853).
2. Elizabeth Malcolm is ambivalent about the causes, but dates the beginning of a substantial weakening after 1842. She notes the important part played by the distraction of Repeal and the opposition of many in the Church to the movement, but places more emphasis on Mathew's increasing debts and the general disorganisation of the crusade; Elizabeth Malcolm, *Ireland Sober, Ireland Free: Drink and Temperance in 19th Century Ireland* (Syracuse: Syracuse University Press, 1986), p. 138. John Quinn locates the decline of the Temperance movement much later, chiefly attributing it to the famine, Mathew's declining health, and the increasingly sectarian nature of Irish society in the later 1840s and beyond; see John Quinn, 'Father Mathew's Temperance Crusade in Ireland, 1838–1856' (PhD Dissertation, Notre Dame, 1992), pp. 4, 223–70. Colm Kerrigan agrees with Quinn's later date for the decline's critical period, and also blames the famine, as well as Mathew's absence from Ireland during the Synod of Thurles in 1850. Colm Kerrigan, *Father Mathew and the Irish Temperance Movement 1838–1849* (Cork: University Press, 1992), pp. 170–80. Although George Bretherton acknowledges the negative effects of both the Repeal movement and the Famine, he maintains that the movement remained strong, particularly among the parish clergy, and only the rejection of Mathew's

episcopal nomination to the See of Cork in 1847 and his stroke in April 1848, prevented him from reinvigorating the cause in subsequent years. George Cornell Bretherton, 'The Irish Temperance Movement, 1833–1847' (PhD Dissertation, Columbia University), pp. 287, 295, 297. The account presented here differs from all of these in significant ways, although it is perhaps closest in spirit to Malcolm's.

3. John Francis Maguire, *Father Mathew: A Biography* (London: Longman, Roberts and Green, 1863), p. 188.
4. Father Mathew was profoundly affected by the death of his favourite brother Frank in May 1843.
5. See Chapter 6.
6. Mathew to James Haughton (n.d.), FMC A 1602.
7. Archbishop Ullathorne, *From Cabin Boy to Archbishop* (London: Burns Oates, 1941).
8. John Francis Maguire, *An Address Delivered by John Francis Maguire At a Public Meeting Held in Cork, on the 11th of November, 1844, for the Purpose of Taking Measures to Free Father Mathew from his Pecuniary Embarrassments* (Cork: 1844), p. 16.
9. Ibid.
10. Mathew certainly gave away much more at earlier missions, but as he began to grow more concerned about his finances he tried to limit these donations, with only moderate success.
11. McKenna to the *Tablet*, 5 November 1844, draft, but marked 'not sent', quoted in Kerrigan, *Father Mathew*, p. 79.
12. For Mathew's patronage of bands, see the Mathew correspondence generally, as well as reports of his missions – he often gave five or ten pounds directly to a band. See also Ullathorne, *From Cabin Boy to Archbishop*, pp. 193–4. Maguire claims that he often chided Mathew for his credulity in his dealings with the poor. Maguire, *Father Mathew*, p. 211.
13. Mathew to Richard Allen, 29 October 1844, Quaker Archives, Allen Album, 14a.
14. Mathew, it should be noted, was unexpectedly disappointed in the matter of a large inheritance from his cousin and godmother, Lady Elizabeth Mathew in 1841. See Kerrigan, *Father Mathew*, p. 79.
15. Mathew to Duff (private) (n.d.), FMC A 1758.
16. Mathew to Haughton (n.d.) FMC A 1521.
17. McKenna to the *Tablet* (unsent), 5 November 1844, quoted in Kerrigan, *Father Mathew*, p. 79.
18. Delany to Mathew, 25 July ??, FMC Letters (1) to (5) folder.
19. Mathew to Thomas [Olley?] (n.d.), FMC A 395. Olley appears to have been the agent of one of Mathew's medal suppliers.
20. Mathew to Rev. John Murphy (n.d.), FMC 'Father Mathew's Letters' folder.
21. Mathew to Rev. Barry (n.d.), FMC A 1495.
22. Quinn, 'Father Mathew's Temperance Crusade', p. 210. It is not clear if this figure represents his total indebtedness, or only 'pressing obligations', owed to people outside his large circle of family and friends.
23. See Mathew to Magill (n.d.), cited in Malcolm, *Ireland Sober*, p. 140 ('I concealed my difficulties from the world').
24. *FJ*, 2 April 1840.
25. *FJ*, 5 January 1841.
26. *FJ*, 2 February 1841.
27. *FJ*, 23 February 1841 (letter dated 17 February).
28. *N*, 12 November 1842 (letter dated 4 November).
29. The Duke of Leinster was the titular head of the committee, but as Mathew later reminded Richard Dowden, 'his grace the Duke of Leinster, did no good … except giving his own donation and the use of his name'. Mathew to Richard Dowden (private) (n.d.), FMC A 1104.
30. Mathew to Joseph Sturge [1845?], FMC A 782.
31. Mathew to John [Cloghen?], FMC A 1384.
32. Mathew to Richard Webb (n.d.), FMC A 1904.
33. Kerrigan, *Father Mathew*, p. 80. Father Augustine, *Footprints of Father Mathew, O.F.M. Cap., the Apostle of Temperance* (Dublin: Browne and Nolan Ltd., 1947), p. 366. £450 was eventually provided from the fund for the trip.
34. Simpson to Mathew, 22 February 1843, FMC 'Letters to Father Mathew'. Previous

chapters have noted how Mathew was alleged to have used some of the funds from medal sales in the construction of his own Church, and the presence of temperance bands, often funded by Mathew, at Repeal meetings has also been noted.

35. Mathew to Simpson, 25 July 1843, quoted in John Barclay Shiel, *Dr Shiel's Historical Account of The Temperance Movement in Ireland* (Dublin: Samuel J. Machen, 1843), p. 7.
36. See Augustine, *Footprints of Father Mathew*, pp. 366–8.
37. James Webb to Richard Dowden, 25 October 1844, Day Papers U140/C106, Cork Archive Council. Webb was writing to Dowden in Cork in an attempt 'chiefly to save James Haughton from any blame' from Mathew.
38. James Webb to Richard Dowden, 26 October 1844, DP U140/C107, CAC.
39. Mathew to Richard Allen, 29 October 1844, Quaker Archives, Allen Album. See also, Mathew to Haughton (n.d.) FMC A 1521, which is probably Mathew's formal reply to Haughton's October 1844 letter.
40. Mathew to Charles Gavan Duffy (private) (n.d.), FMC A 1758.
41. Mathew to Spratt (n.d.), FMC A 1889.
42. Quinn, 'Father Mathew's Temperance Crusade', pp. 210–12.
43. Maguire, 'An Address', p. 10.
44. See, for example, Mathew to Richard Webb (n.d.), FMC A 1904; Mathew to Joseph Sturge (n.d.), FMC A 782 ('It would gratify me more if my friends in England would correspond with myself or with the Committee in this city'). Mathew to Thomas Hincks (n.d.), FMC A 1477.
45. *N*, 31 December 1842.
46. Mathew to Rev. Philip Carpenter (n.d.), quoted in Augustine, *Footprints of Father Mathew*, p. 375.
47. Maguire, *Father Mathew*, p. 316. See also Mathew's letter to F.B. Haly, urging him to obtain a list 'of the nobility and gentry who signed the registration for the public meeting – distinguishing such as sent a donation'. Mathew to F.B. Haly (n.d.), FMC A 825.
48. Augustine, *Footprints of Father Mathew*, pp. 374–5.
49. See, for example, an appeal issued by a new Mathew relief committee in 1845, which sought to raise £7,000 and provide Mathew with an £800 annuity. *Mathew Annuity Fund*, [1845], Day Papers, Temp. U140D CAC; see also in the Day papers an account of the unsuccessful mission of Richard Dowden to England on Mathew's behalf in 1848, Day #156 Class D, CAC.
50. Augustine, *Footprints of Father Mathew*, p. 373.
51. The Committee's official request, dated 5 March 1843, appeared in the *Nation*, 25 March 1843.
52. Mathew to Haughton, FMC A 1602.
53. Mathew to Rev. John Spratt, private (n.d.), FMC A 934.
54. 'It was [O'Connell] who caused the failure of the Mathew Testimonial Subscription', Mathew to John Russell (n.d.), FMC A 123.
55. *Mathew Annuity Fund Appeal* (undated partial pamphlet), Day Papers, Temp. U 140D, CAC.
56. James Maher to Paul Cullen, 18 April 1842, Emmet Larkin's transcription of the Cullen Correspondence; originals held in the Irish College, Rome; hereafter C.
57. CSO Misc. Books Stip. Magis. Diary #31 (Edward Hill, Longford), SPO, Dublin.
58. See also the reports of Patrick Cheevers at Listowel, Co. Kerry (#16–17); G. Fitzgerald, Dungarvan, Co. Waterford (#42–5); William Cooke, Abbeyfeale, Limerick (#27); John Dropping, County Kildare (#20–1); W. Knavesborough, Mitchelstown, Co. Cork (#11); Illegible, Miltown Malbay, Co. Clare (#7–8). (Compare these reports with those of John Barron, the magistrate in the area before 1843); C.H. Tuckey, Carlow, Co. Carlow (#2–5).
59. *Limerick Chronicle*, 4 April 1844.
60. Rev. Fogarty to William Fagan, reproduced in McKenna MSS, pp. 973–4.
61. Maguire, 'An Address', pp. 19–20.
62. Reprinted in *Dublin Evening Mail*, 11 March 1845.
63. Mathew to Knight of Kerry [May/June, 1845], FMC A 1604. Mathew mentions a Sunday 22 June visit to Kerry – the 22nd fell on a Sunday in 1845.
64. Mathew to Charles Bianconi, 5 March 1845, FMC, from (5) to (1) Folder.
65. Rev. Mathew Scally, OCC, *The Temperance Catechism* (Dublin: W.J. Battersby, 1846), RIA Box 501, Tract 6. The dedicatory epistle from Father Mathew was dated 24 February 1846.
66. *LC*, 19 March 1845, 22 February 1845.

67. *Tipperary Vindicator*, 24 May 1845.
68. *Waterford Mirror*, 26 March 1845.
69. *Dublin Evening Mail*, 24 March 1845.
70. *Dublin Correspondent and Evening Packet* (*DCEP*), 16 April 1846.
71. *DCEP*, 18 April 1846.
72. This period was selected because it was the time of the year when Temperance societies scheduled their most significant public events – parades and dinners on Saint Patrick's Day and Easter.
73. Mathew to John Russell (n.d.), FMC A 123.
74. Mathew to John Russell (n.d.), FMC A 124.
75. Mathew to James Haughton (n.d.), FMC A 184. This was the letter in which Mathew warned Haughton not to criticise the Irish clergy for their lack of temperance enthusiasm (see Chapter 6) which dates it as being written prior to February 1844.
76. Mathew to James Haughton (n.d.), FMC A 1088.
77. Mathew to Rev. Michael Meehan [mid/late 1845], FMC 'Letters to C' file. The letter is, as usual, undated draft correspondence, but Mathew promises Meehan a visit for Sunday, 23 November. This date fell on a Sunday in 1845.
78. A proof-gallon is an alcohol constant; 57.1 per cent by volume of alcohol.
79. Alcohol and duty figures are from *Parliamentary Papers*, H.C. 1852–53 (547) XCIX. Population figures are from A. J. Fitzpatrick and W. E. Vaughn, *Irish Historical Abstract* (Dublin: RIC, 1978). Figures in italics are estimates. The rate of population decline between 1846 and 1851 is here assumed to have been constant.
80. From *Parliamentary Papers*, H.C. 1852–53 (547) XCIX.
81. Mathew to Trevelyan, 20 November 1846, quoted in Bretherton, 'The Irish Temperance Movement', p. 286.
82. Mathew to Rev. (illeg.), FMC A 814.
83. For Mathew's labours during the famine, see Augustine, *Footprints of Father Mathew*, pp. 392–426; Kerrigan, *Father Mathew*, pp. 170–72.
84. Mathew to ? [partial letter], 16 December 1846, FMC (Father Mathew's Letters).
85. Mathew to Mr Tristleton, 18 May 1847, FMC A 1279; Mathew to Rev. John Furlong, 27 ? 1847, quoted in Augustine, *Footprints of Father Mathew*, p. 426.
86. *Congregatio de Propaganda Fide, Acta*, 'Sulla Elezione del Vescovo di Cork in Irlanda', June 1847, v. 210.
87. See Barry's letter, and also Augustine, *Footprints of Father Mathew*, p. 428, for the text of Mathew's reply, which did note that his appointment depended on 'the decision of the Holy See'.
88. Mathew to Cullen, 10 May 1847, C.
89. It appears that Mathew's appointment *was* strenuously opposed by Patrick Kennedy, the Bishop of Killaloe. In one colourful letter to a friend Mathew described how Kennedy 'came to Cork breathing vengeance against me'. (Mathew to Lenihan, 8 July 1847, quoted in Bretherton, 'The Irish Temperance Movement', pp. 289–90.) John Ryan of Limerick also identified Kennedy as the principle opponent of the nomination (see Thomas Barry to Slattery, 25 May 1847, contained in Slattery to Franzoni, 25 May 1847, *Congregatio de Propaganda Fide, Scritture Rifirite Nei Congressi: Irlanda*, v. 29 pt. 1 [Newberry Library]). This may be a case of blaming the 'King's evil counselors', however. Slattery certainly opposed the nomination himself, as Mathew acknowledged, and all the bishops present except Ryan voted for Delany (Mathew to Lenihan, 8 July 1847). The reasons for Kennedy's opposition are unknown. He had strongly supported the CTAS in the early 1840s but soured on the movement in later years. He may have done so for any number of reasons, but given his particularly strident opposition to Mathew's episcopal nomination and the trouble he experienced over the years in his own Diocese with maverick priests, Mathew's open conflict with MacHale and Andrew O'Connell may have played an important part.
90. MacHale to Cullen, 6 June 1847, C.
91. Slattery to Franzoni, 25 May 1847, *Congregatio de Propaganda Fide, Scritture Rifirite Nei Congressi: Irlanda*, v. 29 pt. 1 (Newberry Library).
92. *Congregatio de Propaganda Fide, Acta*, 'Sulla Elezione del Vescovo di Cork in Irlanda', June 1847, v. 210.

93. Mathew to Cullen, 2 July 1847, C.
94. Mathew to Cullen, 4 July 1847, C.
95. Mathew to Maurice Lenihan, 8 July 1847, quoted in Bretherton, 'The Irish Temperance Movement', p. 290.
96. Mathew to Wiseman, 23 August 1847, quoted in Bretherton, 'The Irish Temperance Movement', p. 290. This letter was part of an ill-considered and unsuccessful attempt to enlist the English College in Rome in his campaign for a mark of Papal approval.
97. The *Acta* of the Sacred Congregation noted that Mathew's nomination had been refused 'only in part' because of his Temperance activity.
98. Cantwell to Cullen, 8 June 1847, C; Higgins to Cullen, 30 June 1847, C.
99. Mathew was a supporter of the controversial Queen's Colleges; see, for example, Mathew to Penefeather, FMC A 933.
100. Augustine, *Footprints of Father Mathew*, p. 480.
101. Mathew to Colonel Sherburne, 7 April 1849, Mathew Correspondence, NLI, MSS 5055 #15.
102. Mathew to Mrs Rathbone, 20 October 1851, quoted in Augustine, *Footprints of Father Mathew*, p. 517.
103. See Forbes, *Memorandums made in Ireland*, passim.
104. See Diarmaid Ferriter, *A Nation of Extremes: The Pioneers in Twentieth-Century Ireland* (Dublin: Irish Academic Press, 1999), as well as Lambert McKenna, *Life and Work of Rev. James Aloysius Cullen* (London: Longman's, Green and Co., 1924).

CONCLUSION

1. Frank J. Mathew, *Father Mathew: His Life and Times* (London: Cassell & Co., Ltd., 1890), p. 221. John Francis Maguire, *Father Mathew: A Biography* (London: Longman, Roberts, and Green, 1863), p. 245.
2. For later Catholic Temperance in Ireland, see Elizabeth Malcolm, *Ireland Sober, Ireland Free: Drink and Temperance in 19th Century Ireland* (Syracuse: Syracuse Univrsity Press, 1986), pp. 306–21.
3. Maguire, *Father Mathew*, p. 545; Father Augustine, *Footprints of Father Mathew, O.F.M. Cap., the Apostle of Temperance* (Dublin: Browne and Nolan Ltd., 1947), p. 561.
4. Mathew to Kirby, 5 May 1842 (K).
5. See Emmet Larkin, *The Historical Dimensions of Irish Catholicism* (Washington: Arno Press, 1984); David W. Miller, 'Irish Catholicism and the Great Famine', *Journal of Social History*, September, 1975; Eugene Hynes, 'The Great Hunger and Irish Catholicism', *Societas*, Spring 1978; and S.J. Connolly, *Priests and People in Pre-Famine Ireland* (New York: St Martin's Press, 1982). See also S.J. Connolly, *Religion and Society in Nineteenth Century Ireland* (Dundalk: Dundalgen Press, 1985), pp. 42–60; there is an excellent overview of the devotional revolution in *Piety and Power in Ireland: Essays in Honour of Emmet Larkin*, ed. by Stewart Brown and David W. Miller (Notre Dame: 2000).
6. See, for example, F.S.L. Lyons, *Culture and Anarchy in Ireland (1890-1939)* (Oxford: Oxford University Press, 1979); John Hutchinson, *The Dynamics of Cultural Nationalism: The Gaelic Revival and the Creation of the Irish Nation State* (London: Allen and Unwin, 1987). D.G. Boyce's excellent *Nationalism in Ireland* (London: Routledge, 1982), esp. Chs. 5–6, recognises the importance of the 1830s and 1840s for the evolution of Irish nationalism but interestingly enough does not mention the Temperance movement.
7. On a related point, see Anthony D. Smith's observation in *Nations and Nationalism in a Global Era* (London: Polity Press, 1995), pp. 80-81, that the dynamic of nationalism must 'pivot' on the 'complex relationship' between elite 'aims and activities' and 'mass sentiments and memories'.
8. Here I am deeply indebted to aspects of Partha Chatterjee's interrogation of Benedict Anderson's *Imagined Communities*. (Benedict Anderson, *Imagined Communities* (New York: Verso, 1991). Chatterjee argues for the existence of a dynamic within colonial national imagination that creates its own domain of cultural sovereignty 'before it begins its political battle with the Imperial power'. This 'inner' domain is essentially a moral one, characterised by cultural, spiritual, educational and domestic concerns which are

widely understood to comprehend 'the "essential" marks of cultural identity'. Partha Chatterjee, *The Nation and Its Fragments* (Princeton: Princeton University Press, 1993), Ch. 1.

9. E.J. Hobsbawm, *Nations and Nationalism Since 1780* (Cambridge: Cambridge University Press, 1990), p. 37.
10. John Hutchinson's recent essay on Irish nationalism is rightly critical of insular approaches to the subject ('Irish Nationalism', in D. George Boyce and Alan O'Day (eds), *The Making of Modern Irish History* (London: Routledge, 1996), pp. 100–17. This history of the CTAS endeavours to participate in the movement of contemporary scholarship on nationalism away from what Ronald Suny has categorised as 'sterile definitions and typologies' and 'towards historically grounded elaborations of the actual making of nationalities and nations'. (Ronald Suny, *The Revenge of the Past: Nationalism, Revolution, and the Collapse of the Soviet Union* [Stanford: Stanford University Press, 1993], pp. 5–6). This shift in emphasis, it seems to me, is grounded in the conviction that *all* nationalisms are to some degree anomolous. The recognition of this fact does not necessarily lead to a rejection of comparative study of nationalism, but it does mandate significant historical effort.

Bibliography

A. ARCHIVES CONSULTED

Capuchin Archives (Dublin)
- Mathew Correspondence
- James McKenna, *A History of the Temperance Reformation in Ireland, England, and Scotland*

Cork Archives Institute (Cork)
- Day Papers

Diocesan Archives
- Dublin Archdiocesan Archives (ADA), Dr Murray's Papers
- Cashel Archdiocesan Archives, Slattery Papers (held in microfilm form by NLI)
- Kerry Diocesan Archives, Journal of John O'Sullivan, Parish Priest of Kenmare

Friend's Library (Dublin)
- Pimm Family Collection
- Webb Papers

Prof. Emmet Larkin's Transcriptions of the Cullen Correspondence and the Kirby Correspondence from the Irish College, Rome (K). Also the Journal of Joseph Prost (Chicago).

National Library of Ireland (NLI) (Dublin)
- Madden Ballad Collection
- Theobald Mathew Correspondence

Father Neesan's Private Collection of Mathew Materials and Writings (Cork)

Royal Irish Academy (RIA) (Dublin)
- Haliday Pamphlets

National Archives (Dublin)
- CSO Miscellaneous Books, Stipendiary Magistrates' Diaries
- *Temperance Confidential Reports, 1840* (*CR*)

Trinity College (Dublin)
- Webb Family Correspondence

B. OFFICIAL DOCUMENTS

Acta, Congregatio de Propaganda Fide

Congregatio de Propaganda Fide, Scritture Rifirite Nei Congressi: Irlanda, v. 29.

First Report of The Commissioners of Public Instruction, Ireland (London: HMSO, 1835).

Hansard Parliamentary Debates.

Spirits Distilled and Charged with Duty in Ireland, 1800–1852), H.C. 1852–53 (547) XCIX.

C. CONTEMPORARY PAMPHLETS/BOOKS

Alexis de Tocqueville's Journey in Ireland, trans. and ed. by Emmet Larkin (Washington: Catholic University of America Press, 1990).

Anon., *An Accurate Report of the Proceedings of the Very Rev. Theobald Mathew in Dublin in the Cause of Temperance When Eighty Thousand Persons Took the Pledge with the Sermon Preached by him in the Church of the Conception, Marlborough Street* (Dublin: Richard Grace, 1840).

Anon., *The Repealers* (Dublin: William Curry, 1843).

Bermingham, Rev. James, *A Memoir of the Very Rev. Theobald Mathew, with an Account of the Rise and Progress of Temperance in Ireland* (Dublin: Milliken and Son, 1840).

Connell, Philip, *The Medal and Glass* (Kells: T.K. Henderson, 1841).

Downes, William MacNamara, *Temperance Melodies for the Teetotallers of Ireland* (Cork: S.M. Thompson, 1843).

Dunlop, John, *The Philosophy of Artificial and Compulsory Drinking Usage in Great Britain and Ireland* (London: Houlston and Stoneman, 1839).

Forbes, John, *Memorandums Made in Ireland in the Autumn of 1852* (London: Smith, Elder and Co., 1853).

Gill, Rev. T.E., *Sermon on Saint Patrick's Day* (Dublin: T. O'Gorman, 1841).

Hall, Mr and Mrs S.C., *Ireland: Its Scenery and Character* (3 vols) (London: Virtue and Co., 1841–43).

The Healy Collection of Irish Street Ballads, Vol. 4 (Cork: Mercier Press, 1969).

The Irish Minstrel, or a Collection of Repeal Melodies, Under the Patronage of the Repeal Wardens of Dublin (Dublin: Bernard Madden, 1843).

Kearney, J., *Mr J. Kearney's Original Comic sons* (Dublin: 1844).

Kennedy, Edward, *The Inaugural Address to the Members of the Cork Temperance Institute* (Cork: George Nash, 1845).

Kohl, J.G., *Ireland* (New York: Harper and Brothers, 1844).

Lennon, John, *The Irish Repealer's Mountain Harp of the Triumphant Year of 1843* (Dublin: O'Brian, 1843).

——, *The United Voices of Tara and Clonfert* (Dublin: O'Brian, 1843).

Luby, Catharine, *Father Mathew; or Ireland as She Ought to Be, In Three Cantos* (Dublin: S.J. Machan, 1845).

Maguire, John Francis, *The Doctrine of Total Abstinence Justified* (Cork: William Morten, 1838).

——, *An Address Delivered by John Francis Maguire At a Public Meeting Held in Cork, on the 11th of November, 1844, for the Purpose of Taking Measures to Free Father Mathew from his Pecuniary Embarrassments* (Cork: 1844).

——, *An Address Delivered to the Members of the Cork Literary Association at the Closing of Their First Session* (Cork: 1845).

Martin, James, *The Wounded Soldier; A Tale of Waterloo with Other Poems on Temperance* (Kells: T.K. Henderson, 1841).

——, *The Truth Teller, or, Poems on Various Subjects* (Kells: T.K. Henderson, 1842).

The Miner, A Poem Founded on Facts Connected with the Present State of the Temperance Cause in Bonmahon, County of Waterford (By the Author or 'Nothing Else' (Waterford: John Killilea, 1841).

Newenham, Thomas, *A Statistical and Historical Inquiry into the Progress and Magnitude of the Population of Ireland* (London: 1805).

O'Neill, John, *A Defense of the Roman Catholic Temperance Society Dedicated to the Very Rev'd Theobald Mathew* (Halliday Collection, Royal Irish Academy, 1840).

Scally, Rev. Mathew, *The Temperance Catechism* (Dublin: W.J. Battersby, 1846).

Shiel, John Barclay, *Dr Shiel's Historical Account of the Temperance Movement in Ireland* (Dublin: Samuel J. Machen, 1843).

The Spirit of the Nation (Dublin: James Duffy, 1843).

Thackeray, William M., *The Irish Sketch Book* (Boston: James Osgood, 1871).

Thomson, David and Moyra McGusty (eds), *The Irish Journals of Elizabeth Smith* (Oxford: Clarendon Press, 1980).

Venedy, J., *Ireland and the Irish During the Repeal Year, 1843* (Dublin: James Duffy, 1844).

Young, Robert, *The Ulster Harmonist* (Derry: Sentinel Office, 1840).

D. NEWSPAPERS/PERIODICALS

Connaught Journal (*CJ*)
Cork Examiner (*CE*)
Cork Standard (*CS*)
Cork Total Abstainer (*CTA*)
Dublin Correspondent and Evening Packet (*DCEP*)
Dublin Evening Mail
Dublin Evening Press (*DEP*)
Dublin Journal of Temperance, Science and Literature
Dublin Review
Dublin Weekly Herald (*DWH*)
Fraser's Magazine
Freeman's Journal (*FJ*)
Galway Patriot (*GP*)
Galway Vindicator
Irish Catholic Directory (*ICD*)
Irish Temperance and Literary Gazette (*ITLG*)
Kilkenny Journal
Limerick Chronicle
Limerick Reporter (*LR*)
Limerick Standard (*LS*)
London Times (*LT*)
Mayo Constitution (*MC*)
Nation (*N*)
Nenagh Guardian (*NG*)
Philanthropist and National Temperance Advertiser (*PNTA*)
Southern Reporter (*SR*)
Tablet
Tait's Edinburgh Magazine
Tipperary Free Press (*TFP*)
Tralee Examiner
Waterford Chronicle (*WC*)
Waterford Mirror

E. SECONDARY SOURCES, MEMOIRS, PUBLISHED CORRESPONDENCE

Anderson, Benedict, *Imagined Communities* (New York: Verso, 1991).

Augustine, Father, *Footprints of Father Mathew, O.F.M. Cap., the Apostle of Temperance* (Dublin: Browne and Nolan Ltd., 1947).

Barrett, James R., 'Why Paddy Drank: The Social Importance of Whiskey in Pre-Famine Ireland', *Journal of Popular Culture*, XI (1977).

Barrows, Susanna and Robin Room (eds), *Drinking: Behavior and Belief in Modern History* (Berkeley: University of California Press, 1991).

Boyce, D. George, *Nationalism in Ireland* (London: Routledge, 1982).

Boyce, D. George and Alan O'Day (eds), *The Making of Modern Irish History* (London: Routledge, 1996).

Bretherton, George Cornell, 'The Irish Temperance Movement, 1833–1847' (PhD Dissertation, Columbia University, 1978).

——, 'Against the Flowing Tide: Whiskey and Temperance in the Making of Modern Ireland', in Susanna Barrows and Alan O'Day (eds), *Drinking: Behavior and Belief in Modern History* (Berkeley: University of California Press, 1991).

Brown, Stewart and David W. Miller (eds), *Piety and Power in Ireland: Essays in Honour of Emmet Larkin* (Notre Dame: Notre Dame Press, 2000).

Cassidy, Tanya, 'Parodies of Paddy's Drinking: A Socio-historical Analysis of Cultural Stereotypes' (Paper presented at the American Sociological Association Annual Meeting, 1996).

Chafetz, Janet and Anthony Dworkin, *Female Revolt: The Rise of Women's Movements in World and Historical Perspective* (Totowa: Rowman and Littlefield, 1986).

Chatterjee, Partha, *The Nation and its Fragments: Colonial and Post-Colonial Histories* (Princeton, NJ: Princeton University Press, 1993).

Chenevix, Charles, *The Great Dan* (London: Triad Grafton, 1984).

Clark, Samuel and James S. Donnelly (eds), *Irish Peasants: Violence and Political Unrest 1780–1914* (Madison: University of Wisconsin Press, 1983).

Connell, K.H., *Irish Peasant Society* (Oxford: Oxford University Press, 1968).

Connolly, S.J., *Priests and People in Pre-Famine Ireland* (New York: St Martin's Press, 1982).

——, 'Eighteenth Century Ireland – Colony or Ancien Régime?' in D. George Boyce and Alan O'Day (eds), *The Making of Modern Irish History* (London: Routledge, 1996).

Cook, Chris and John Stevenson, *The Longman Handbook of Modern British History, 1714–1980* (London: Longman, 1983).

Corish, Patrick, *The Irish Catholic Experience* (Wilmington: Michael Glazier, 1985).

Crawford, E. Margaret, *Famine: The Irish Experience, 900–1900* (Edinburgh: John Donal Publishers Ltd., 1989).

Dalton, Rt. Rev. Msgr., *The History of the Archdiocese of Tuam* (Dublin: Phoenix Pub. Co. Ltd, 1928).

Davis, Richard, *The Young Ireland Movement* (Dublin: Gill and MacMillan, 1987).

Duffy, Charles Gavan, *My Life in Two Hemispheres* (London: T.F. Unwin, 1903).

Ferriter, Diarmaid, *A Nation of Extremes: The Pioneers in Twentieth-Century Ireland* (Dublin: Irish Academic Press, 1999).

Fitzgibbon, Marie and Michael Mulcahey, *The Voice of the People: Songs and History of Ireland* (Dublin: O'Brian Press, 1982).

Fitzpatrick, A.J. and W.E. Vaughn, *Irish Historical Abstract* (Dublin: RIC, 1978).

Foster, Roy, *Modern Ireland, 1600–1972* (London: Penguin Press, 1988).

Foucault, Michel, *The Birth of the Clinic* (New York: Pantheon Books, 1973).

Giele, Janet, *Two Paths to Women's Equality: Temperance, Suffrage and the Origins of Modern Feminism* (New York: Twayne, 1995).

Harrison, Brian, *Drink and the Victorians* (London: Butler and Tanner Ltd., 1971).

Haughton, Samuel, *A Memoir of James Haughton* (Dublin: E. Ponsonby, 1877).

Healy, James, *The Irish Minstrel, or a Collection of Repeal Melodies, Under the Patronage of the Repeal Wardens of Dublin* (Dublin: Bernard Madden, 1843).

Hechter, Michael, *Internal Colonialism: The Celtic Fringe in British National Development, 1536–1966* (Berkeley, CA: University of California Press, 1975).

Hobsbawm, Eric J., *Nations and Nationalism Since 1780* (Cambridge: Cambridge University Press, 1990).

Hochberg, Leonard J. and David J. Miller, 'Constructing a Central-Place Hierarchy from a Commercial Directory', *Historical Methods*, 252 (1992).

Hoppen, K. Theodore, *Ireland Since 1800: Conflict and Conformity* (London: Longman, 1989).

Howe, Stephen, *Ireland and Empire* (Oxford: Oxford University Press, 2000).

Hunter, James David, *Evangelicalism: The Coming Generation* (Chicago: University of Chicago Press, 1987).

Hutchinson, John, 'Irish Nationalism' in D. George Boyce and Alan O'Day (eds), *The Making of Modern Irish History* (London: Routledge, 1996).

Hynes, Eugene, 'The Great Hunger and Irish Catholicism', *Societas* (Spring 1978).

Inglis, Brian, *The Freedom of the Press in Ireland* (London: Faber & Faber, 1954).

Kearney, H.F., 'Father Mathew: Apostle of Modernization' in Art

Cosgrove and Donal McCartney (eds), *Studies in Irish History* (Dublin: University College Dublin, 1979).

Keenan, Desmond, *The Catholic Church in Nineteenth-Century Ireland* (Totowa, NJ: Gill and Macmillan, 1983).

Kerr, Donal, *Peel, Priests and Politics* (Oxford: Clarendon Press, 1982).

Kerrigan, Colm, *Father Mathew and the Irish Temperance Movement, 1838–1849* (Cork: University Press, 1992).

Kiberd, Declan, *Inventing Ireland: The Literature of the Modern Nation* (Cambridge, MA: Harvard University Press, 1995).

Larkin, Emmet, 'The Quarrel Among the Roman Catholic Hierarchy Over the National System of Education in Ireland, 1838–1841' (Cambridge: MIT Press, 1965).

——, 'The Devotional Revolution in Ireland, 1850–75', *AHR* Vol. LXXII (June 1972).

——, 'Church, State and Nation in Modern Ireland', *AHR* Vol. LXXX (December 1975).

——, 'Economic Growth, Capital Investment and the Roman Catholic Church in Nineteenth Century Ireland' in *The Historical Dimensions of Irish Catholicism* (New York: Arno Press, 1976).

——, *The Historical Dimensions of Irish Catholicism* (Washington: Arno Press, 1984).

——, 'Cardinal Paul Cullen' in Jeffrey von Arx (ed.), *Varieties of Ultramontanism* (Washington: Catholic University Press, 1998).

——, 'The Roman Catholic Clergy in Nineteenth Century Ireland' (unpublished lecture).

Levine, Harry Gene, 'The Discovery of Addiction: Changing Conceptions of Habitual Drunkenness in America', *Journal of Studies on Alcohol* 39 (1978).

Logan, William, *Early Heroes of the Temperance Reformation* (Glasgow: Scottish Temperance League, 1874).

Longmate, Norman, *The Waterdrinkers: A History of Temperance* (London: Hamish Hamilton, 1968).

Lynch, Patrick and John Vaizey, *Guinness's Brewery in the Irish Economy, 1759–1876* (Cambridge: Cambridge University Press, 1960).

Lyons, F.S.L., *Culture and Anarchy in Ireland (1890–1939)* (Oxford: Oxford University Press, 1979).

McCaffrey, Lawrence J., *Daniel O'Connell and the Repeal Year* (Knoxville, KY: University of Kentucky Press, 1966).

McCarthy, Justin, *The Story of an Irishman* (London: Chatto and Windus, 1904).

Macauley, Ambrose, *Patrick Dorrian, Bishop of Down and Connor, 1865–1885* (Dublin: Irish Academic Press, 1987).

MacDonagh, Oliver, *The Emancipist* (New York: St Martin's Press, 1989).

McGuire, Shane, 'A Profile of Bernard Burke (1789–1861)', *Cathair Na Mart*, Vol. 7, No. 1 (Westport: Historical Society, 1987).

McKenna, Lambert, *Life and Work of Rev. James Aloysius Cullen* (London: Longman's, Green and Co., 1924).

Maguire, John Francis, *Father Mathew: A Biography* (London: Longman, Roberts and Green, 1863).

Malcolm, Elizabeth, 'Temperance and Irish Nationalism', in F.S.L. Lyons and R.A.J. Hawkins (eds), *Ireland Under the Union: Varieties of Tension: Essays in Honour of T.W. Moody* (Oxford: Clarendon Press, 1980).

——, 'The Catholic Church and the Irish Temperance Movement 1838–1901', *Irish Historical Studies*, XXIII, 89 (May 1982).

——, 'Popular Recreation in Nineteenth Century Ireland', in Oliver Macdonagh *et al.* (eds), *Irish Culture and Nationalism, 1750–1950* (London: Macmillan, 1983).

——, *Ireland Sober, Ireland Free: Drink and Temperance in 19th Century Ireland* (Syracuse: Syracuse University Press, 1986).

——, 'The Rise of the Pub: A Study in the Disciplining of Popular Culture', in J.S. Donnelly and Kirby A. Miller (eds), *Irish Popular Culture 1650–1850* (Dublin: Irish Academic Press, 1998).

Mathew, Frank J., *Father Mathew: His Life and Times* (London: Cassell & Co. Ltd., 1890).

Miller, David W., 'Irish Catholicism and the Great Famine', *Journal of Social History* (September 1975).

Murphy, Ignatius, *The Diocese of Killaloe, 1800–1850* (Dublin: Four Courts Press, 1992).

O'Brien, John, 'The Catholic Middle Classes in Pre-Famine Cork' (O'Donnell Lecture) (Cork: 1979).

O'Connell, Maurice R. (ed.), *The Correspondence of Daniel O'Connell*, vols 5–7 (New York: Barnes & Noble, 1974).

Ogain, Rionach Ui, *The Immortal Dan: Daniel O'Connell in Folk Tradition* (Dublin: Geography Publications, 1995).

Owens, Gary, 'Nationalism Without Words: Symbolism and Ritual Behaviour in the Repeal "Monster Meetings" of 1843–45', in James S. Donnelly, Jr. and Kerby A. Miller (eds), *Irish Popular Culture, 1650–1850* (Dublin: Irish Academic Press, 1998).

Quinn, John, 'Temperance in Tipperary: Father Mathew and Archbishop Slattery, 1839–1854', *Tipperary Historical Journal*, No. 3 (1990).

——, 'The "Vagabond Friar": Father Mathew's Difficulties with the Irish Bishops, 1840–1856', *Catholic Historical Review* (October 1992).

——, 'Father Mathew's Temperance Crusade in Ireland, 1838–1856' (PhD Dissertation, Notre Dame, 1992).

——, 'Father Mathew's American Tour, 1849–51', *Eire/Ireland* vol. XXX (Spring, 1995).

Repcheck, Joseph. 'Father Mathew's Irish Temperance Campaign' (MA Thesis, University of Wisconsin, 1984).

Roberts, James S., *Drink, Temperance and the Working Class in Nineteenth-Century Germany* (Boston: Allen and Unwin, 1984).

Rogers, Rev. Patrick, 'A Century After', *Capuchin Annual*, 1939.

——, *Father Theobald Mathew* (Dublin: Browne and Nolan Ltd., 1945).

Shiman, Lillian, *Crusade Against Drink in Victorian England* (London: Macmillan, 1988).

Smith, Anthony D., *Nations and Nationalism in a Global Era* (London: Polity Press, 1985).

Stivers, Richard, *A Hair of the Dog: Irish Drinking and American Stereotype* (Philadelphia: University Park Press, 1982).

Stuggenborg, Suzanne, *Gender, Family, and Social Movements* (London: Pine Forge Press, 1998).

Suny, Ronald Grigor, *The Revenge of the Past: Nationalism, Revolution and the Collapse of the Soviet Union* (Stanford: 1993).

Taylor, Lawrence, *Occasions of Faith: An Anthropology of Irish Catholics* (Philadelphia: University of Philadelphia Press, 1995).

Tyrell, Ian, *Sobering Up: From Temperance to Prohibition in Antebellum America, 1800–1860* (Westport, CT: Greenwood Press, 1979).

Vincent, David, *Bread, Knowledge and Freedom: A Study of Nineteenth-Century Working Class Autobiography* (Cambridge: Methuen & Co., 1981).

Whelan, Kevin, 'The Regional Impact of Irish Catholicism 1700–1850', in *Common Ground: Essays on the Historical Geography of Ireland* (Cork: University Press, 1988).

——, *The Tree of Liberty: Radicalism, Catholicism and the Construction of Irish Identity, 1760–1830* (Cork: Cork University Press, 1996).

Wilson, George B., *Alcohol and the Nation* (London: Nicholson and Watson, 1940).

Ullathorne, Archbishop, *From Cabin Boy to Archbishop* (London: Burns Oates, 1941).

Young, Crawford, *The African Colonial State in Comparative Perspective* (New Haven, CT: Yale University Press, 1994).

Appendix

FATHER MATHEW'S TEMPERANCE MISSIONS

City/Town		Date
1839		
1)	Limerick, Co. Limerick	30/11–1/12
2)	Waterford, Co. Waterford	11–12/12
3)	Clonmel, Co. Waterford	17–18/12
1840		
4)	Kilkenny, Co. Kilkenny	16–18/1
5)	Abbeyleix, Queen's Co.	22/1
6)	Castlecomer, Co. Kilkenny	23/1
7)	Thurles, Co. Tipperary	24/1
8)	Cappoquin, Co. Waterford	26/1
9)	Tallow, Co. Waterford	29/1
10)	Lismore, Co. Waterford	30/1
11)	Cashel, Co. Tipperary	5–6/2
12)	Clonmel, Co. Waterford	7/2
13)	Tulla, Co. Clare	11/2
14)	Ennis, Co. Clare	12–13/2
15)	Gort, Co. Galway	15/2
16)	Rathdowney, Queen's Co.	23–24/2
17)	Birr, King's County	1–2/3
18)	Borrisokane, Co. Tipperary	3/3
19)	Nenagh, Co. Tipperary	4/3
20)	Galway, Co. Galway	12–14/3
21)	Loughrea, Co. Galway	15/3
22)	Rathmore, Co. Kerry	17/3
23)	Killimor, Co. Galway	20/3
24)	Roscrea, Co. Tipperary	21/3
25)	Dublin, Co. Dublin	28/3–4/4
26)	Enniscorthy, Co. Wexford	7–8/4
27)	Wexford, Co. Wexford	9/4
28)	New Ross, Co. Wexford	10/4
29)	Mitchelstown, Co. Cork	12/4

30)	Cashel, Co. Tipperary	26/4
31)	Limerick, Co. Limerick	4–6/5
32)	Newmarket-on-Fergus, Co. Clare	7/5
33)	Waterford, Co. Waterford	9–11/5
34)	Dungarvan, Co. Waterford	12/5
35)	Loughrea, Co. Galway	16–19/5
36)	Ahascaragh, Co. Galway	21/5
37)	Limerick, Co. Limerick	23–25/5
38)	Rathcormac, Co. Cork	31/5
39)	Tralee, Co. Kerry	2/6
40)	Killarney, Co. Kerry	5–6/6
41)	Maryborough, Queen's County	7–9/6
42)	Listowel, Co. Kerry	11–12/6
43)	Callan, Co. Kilkenny	13/6
44)	Maynooth, Co. Kildare	15–17/6
45)	Naas, Co. Kildare	18/6
46)	Rathkeale, Co. Limerick	19/6
47)	Limerick, Co. Limerick	23/6
48)	Galway, Co. Galway	24–25/6
49)	Westport, Co. Mayo	27–29/6
50)	Ballinarobe, Co. Mayo	30/6
51)	Westport, Co. Mayo	3/7
52)	Clonmel, Co. Waterford	5–6/7
53)	Navan, Co. Meath	11/7
54)	Duleek, Co. Meath	12/7
55)	Carrick-on-Suir, Co. Tipperary	14–16/7
56)	Portlaw, Co. Waterford	17/7
57)	Newport, Co. Mayo	22–25/7
58)	Castlebar, Co. Mayo	26–28/7
59)	Claremorris, Co. Mayo	29/7
60)	Balbriggan, Co. Dublin	2/8
61)	Naas, Co. Kildare	15–17/8
62)	Durrow, Queen's County	18/8
63)	Athy, Co. Kildare	23/8
64)	Freshford, Co. Kilkenny	25/8
65)	Clogheen, Co. Waterford	26/8
66)	Sandyford, Co. Dublin	30/8
67)	Athlone, Co. West Meath	6/9
68)	Banagher, King's County	8/9
69)	Portumna, Co. Galway	9/9
70)	Bruff, Co. Limerick	10/9
71)	Johnstown, Co. Kilkenny	13–15/9
72)	Boyle, Co. Roscommon	19–20/9
73)	Culloony, Co. Sligo	22–24/9
74)	Dublin, Co. Dublin	27–29/9
75)	Galway, Co. Galway	1–2/10

76)	Ahascaragh, Co. Galway	3–6/10
77)	Kiltamagh, Co. Mayo	7–9/10
78)	Sligo, Co. Sligo	10–13/10
79)	Strokestown, Co. Roscommon	14/10
80)	Roscommon, Co. Roscommon	15–16/10
81)	Gort, Co. Galway	19/10
82)	Limerick, Co. Limerick	21/10
83)	Carlow, Co. Carlow	25–28/10
84)	Castlerea, Co. Roscommon	29–30/10
85)	Ballina, Co. Mayo	1/11
86)	Ballybag, Co. Tipperary	5/11
87)	Cahir, Co. Tipperary	11/11
88)	Dublin, Co. Dublin	14–17/11
89)	Kinlough, Co. Leitrim	19/11
90)	Roscommon, Co. Roscommon	21/11
91)	Cavan, Co. Cavan	25–26/11
92)	Kilrush, Co. Clare	29/11–1/12
93)	Ferns, Co. Wexford	3/12
94)	Wexford, Co. Wexford	5–6/12
95)	New Ross, Co. Wexford	7/12
96)	Waterford, Co. Waterford	8/12
97)	Tulla, Co. Clare	13/12
98)	Newcastle West, Co. Limerick	15–16/12
99)	Abbeyfeale, Co. Limerick	17–18/12
100)	Dingle, Co. Kerry	19–21/12
101)	Kinsale, Co. Cork	27/12
1841		
102)	Limerick, Co. Limerick	2–4/1
103)	Cashel, Co. Tipperary	10–11/1
104)	Thurles, Co. Tipperary	12–13/1
105)	Kells, Co. Meath	16–18/1
106)	Ballyshannon, Co. Donegal	20–22/1
107)	Kilkee, Co. Clare	23–24/1
108)	Waterford, Co. Waterford	27/1
109)	Kilmacow, Co. Waterford	28–29/1
110)	Newtownbarry, Co. Wexford	31/1–1/2
111)	Ballyragget, Co. Kilkenny	3–4/2
112)	Dunlavin, Co. Wicklow	5/2
113)	Castledermot, Co. Kildare	6/2
114)	Stradbally, Queen's County	7/2
115)	Mountmellick, Queen's County	8/2
116)	Templemore, Co. Tipperary	10/2
117)	Mallow, Co. Cork	14/2
118)	Dunmanway, Co. Cork	21/2
119)	Bantry, Co. Cork	29/2–2/3

120)	Kenmare, Co. Kerry	2/3
121)	Caherciveen, Co. Kerry	4/3
122)	Iveragh, Co. Kerry	6–7/3
123)	Carrickmacross, Co. Monaghan	13–14/3
124)	Monaghan, Co. Monaghan	16–17/3
125)	Clogher, Co. Tyrone	18/3
126)	Castlepollard, Co. Westmeath	19/3
127)	Turbetstown, Co. Meath	21/3
128)	Trim, Co. Meath	25/3
129)	Kilbeggan, Co. Westmeath	28–29/3
130)	Killarney, Co. Kerry	13–20/4
131)	Milltown, Co. Kerry	18/4
132)	Castletown, Co. Louth	1/5
133)	Kinnegard, Co. West Meath	2/5
134)	Clonaslee, Queen's County	5/5
135)	Naas, Co. Kildare	6–7/5
136)	Maynooth, Co. Kildare	13–14/5
137)	Toomyvara, Co. Tipperary	16/5
138)	Templemore, Co. Tipperary	17/5
139)	Roscrea, Co. Tipperary	18–19/5
140)	Birr, King's County	20/5
141)	Castleblaney, Co. Monaghan	23/5
142)	Dourmott, Co. Monaghan	25/5
143)	Ballyjamesduff, Co. Cavan	30–31/5
144)	Bailieborough, Co. Cavan	1/6
145)	Shercock, Co. Monaghan	2/6
146)	Cootehill, Co. Cavan	4–5/6
147)	Larah, Co. Wicklow	6–7/6
148)	Cavan, Co. Cavan	8–9/6
149)	Dromahair, Co. Leitrim	10/6
150)	Letterkenny, Co. Donegal	13–16/6
151)	Banbridge, Co. Down	19–22/6
152)	Birmingham, England	28/6
153)	Kilenaule, Co. Tipperary	18–19/7
154)	Cashel, Co. Tipperary	23–24/7
155)	Seagoe, Co. Armagh	25–26/7
156)	Carrigaline, Co. Cork	1–2/8
157)	Newry, Co. Down	14/8
158)	Warrenpoint, Co. Down	15/8
159)	Newry, Co. Down	17–19/8
160)	Slane, Co. Meath	21/8
161)	Kanturk, Co. Cork	29–30/8
162)	Belmullet, Co. Mayo	4–7/9
163)	Erris, Co. Mayo	11–12/9
164)	Ballaghhadereen, Co. Roscommon	16/9
165)	Lurgan, Co. Armagh	25–28/9

166)	Thomastown, Co. Kilkenny	3/10
167)	Ballinasloe, Co. Galway	7/10
168)	Newtownsanders, Co. Kerry	10/10
169)	Tralee, Co. Kerry	11/10
170)	Tulla, Co. Clare	12/10
171)	Limerick, Co. Limerick	13–16/10
172)	Tullamore, King's County	17–18/10
173)	Dublin, Co. Dublin	21–22/10
174)	Altymass, Co. Mayo	24/10
175)	Foxford, Co. Mayo	26/10
176)	Loughglinn, Co. Roscommon	27/10
177)	Mountrath, Queen's County	31/10
178)	Kilkeedy, Co. Limerick	4/11
179)	Wicklow, Co. Wicklow	7/11
180)	Barrow, Co. Kerry	10/11
181)	Castletown Roche, Co. Cork	14/11
182)	Monaghan, Co. Monaghan	20/11
183)	Rockcorry, Co. Monaghan	21/11
184)	Clones, Co. Monaghan	28–29/11
185)	Crussakeele, Co. Meath	5–6/12
186)	Kells, Co. Meath	7–8/12
187)	Ballinacargy, Co. West Meath	12/12
188)	Milltownpass, Co. West Meath	18–21/12

1842

189)	Maryborough, Queen's County	2/1
190)	Limerick, Co. Limerick	7/1
191)	Loughrea, Co. Galway	9/1
192)	Galway, Co. Galway	10–12/1
193)	Elphin, Co. Roscommon	15–16/1
194)	Boyle, Co. Roscommon	18/1
195)	Waterford, Co. Waterford	23/1
196)	Kill, Co. Waterford	25/1
197)	Moira, Co. Down	30/1–4/2
198)	Cooraclare, Co. Clare	13/2
199)	Kilrush, Co. Clare	14–15/2
200)	Callaghansmills, Co. Clare	27/2
201)	Convoy, Co. Donegal	6/3
202)	Letterkenny, Co. Donegal	7–8/3
203)	Stranorlar, Co. Donegal	9–10/3
204)	Donegal, Co. Donegal	11–13/3
205)	Navan, Co. Meath	17–18/3
206)	Rathvilley, Co. Carlow	10–12/4
207)	Mulingar, Co. Westmeath	17/4
208)	Kilmacthomas, Co. Waterford	21–22/4
209)	Dungarvan, Co. Waterford	23–25/4

210)	Arklow, Co. Wicklow	28/4
211)	Blarney, Co. Cork	1/5
212)	Drogheda, Co. Louth	8–9/5
213)	Cappamore, Co. Limerick	15/5
214)	Kilfenora, Co. Clare	22–23/5
215)	Ennis, Co. Clare	24/5
216)	Corrofin, Co. Clare	25/5
217)	Ennistimon, Co. Clare	26/5
218)	Lisdoonvarna, Co. Clare	27/5
219)	Miltown Malbay, Co. Clare	29/5
220)	Thomastown, Co. Kilkenny	30/5
221)	Glendalough, Co. Wicklow	3–4/6
222)	Lucan, Co. Dublin	5–6/6
223)	Bansha, Co. Tipperary	12/6
224)	Durrow, Queen's County	19/6
225)	Nenagh, Co. Tipperary	20–21/6
226)	Blackrock, Co. Dublin	24/6
227)	Dublin, Co. Dublin	26–27/6
228)	Enfield, Co. Meath	29/6
229)	Moroe, Co. Limerick	3/7
230)	Bantry, Co. Cork	9–12/7
231)	Killarney, Co. Kerry	14/7
232)	Tralee, Co. Kerry	15–16/7
233)	Kilgarvan, Co. Kerry	17–18/7
234)	Castletown Bere, Co. Kerry	23–25/7
235)	Dublin, Co. Dublin	31/7
236)	Templeport, Co. Cavan	1–2/8
237)	Ennistimon, Co. Clare	21–22/8
238)	Limerick, Co. Limerick	23/8
239)	Borisoleigh, Co. Tipperary	28–29/8
240)	Carlow, Co. Carlow	3/9
241)	Kilkenny, Co. Kilkenny	5/9
242)	Moycullen, Co. Galway	11/9
243)	Barna, Co. Galway	12/9
244)	Shangarry, Co. Cork	18/9
245)	Ardmore, Co. Waterford	26–27/9
246)	Kilrush, Co. Clare	30/9–1/10
247)	Carrigaholt, Co. Clare	2–3/10
248)	Charleville, Co. Limerick	5–6/10
249)	Bree, Co. Wexford	9/10
250)	Enniscorthy, Co. Wexford	10/10
251)	New Ross, Co. Wexford	11–12/10
252)	Wexford, Co. Wexford	12/10
253)	Emyvale, Co. Monaghan	15–17/10
254)	Monaghan, Co. Monaghan	18/10
255)	Athy, Co. Kildare	20–21/10

256)	Paulstown, Co. Kilkenny	22–23/10
257)	Crossdoney, Co. Cavan	28/10
258)	Kilmore, Co. Wexford	1/11
259)	Ballybonedon ?, Co. Leitrim	6/11
260)	Kildysart, Co. Clare	12–15/11
261)	Killimore, Co. Roscommon	27/11
262)	Limerick, Co. Limerick	31/11
263)	Ballina, Co. Mayo	4/12
264)	Passage West, Co. Cork	8/12
265)	Newinn, Co. Tipperary	18/12
266)	Cork, Co. Cork	19/12

1843

267)	Douglas, Co. Cork	1/1
268)	Waterford, Co. Waterford	6–7/1
269)	Callan, Co. Kilkenny	8/1
270)	Tipperary, Co. Tipperary	10–12/1
271)	Gortnahoe, Co. Tipperary	13–15/1
272)	Limerick, Co. Limerick	4/3
273)	Emly, Co. Tipperary	5/3
274)	Mullinahone, Co. Tipperary	6/3
275)	Enniskillen, Co. Fermanagh	11–12/3
276)	Wheathill, Co. Fermanagh	13–14/3
277)	Clones, Co. Monaghan	15/3
278)	Rosslea, Co. Fermanagh	17/3
279)	Tyllholland, Co. Monaghan	18/3
280)	Dublin, Co. Dublin	21/3
281)	Skibereen, Co. Cork	25/3
282)	Rosscarbery, Co. Cork	26/3
283)	Drumcolliher, Co. Limerick	2/4
284)	Limerick, Co. Limerick	6/4
285)	Tracton, Co. Cork	9–10/4
286)	Timoleague, Co. Cork	22–23/4
287)	Gorey, Co. Wexford	1/5
288)	Kinsealy, Co. Dublin	3/6
289)	Dublin, Co. Dublin	5–6/6
290)	Passage West, Co. Cork	22/6

MAP A
Temperance Missions by County, 1839–1840

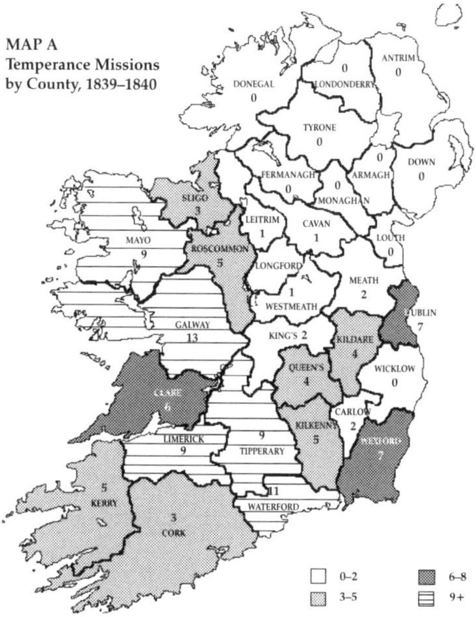

MAP B
Temperance Missions by County, 1841

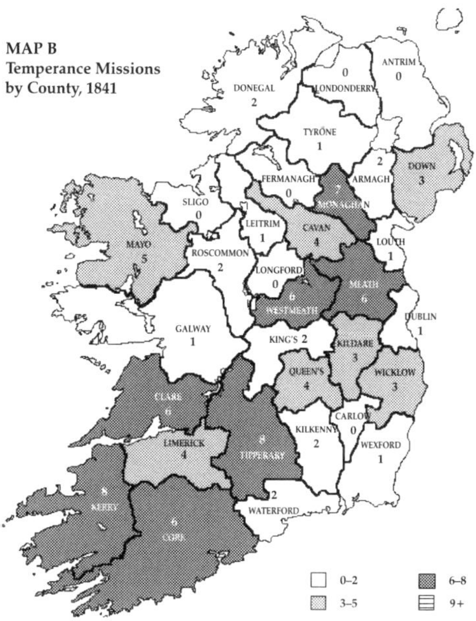

MAP C
Temperance Missions by County, 1842

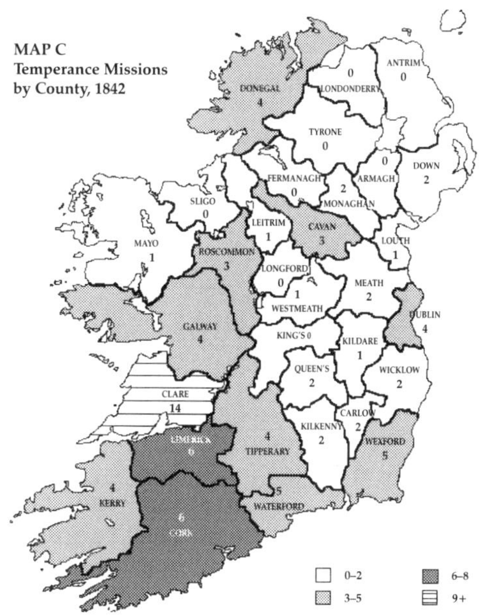

MAP D
Temperance Missions by County, to June 1843

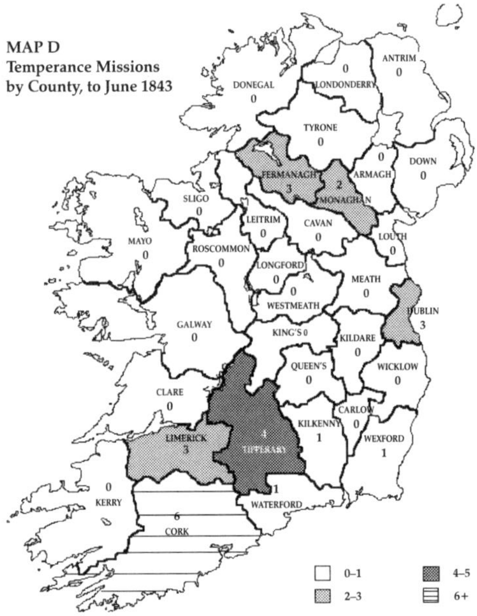

MAP E
Temperance Missions by County, 1839–1843

Index